DISPARITIES
IN SCHOOL
READINESS

DISPARITIES IN SCHOOL READINESS

How Families Contribute to Transitions into School

EDITED BY ALAN BOOTH • ANN C. CROUTER

Lawrence Erlbaum Associates
Taylor & Francis Group

New York   London

Lawrence Erlbaum Associates
Taylor & Francis Group
270 Madison Avenue
New York, NY 10016

Lawrence Erlbaum Associates
Taylor & Francis Group
2 Park Square
Milton Park, Abingdon
Oxon OX14 4RN

© 2008 by Taylor & Francis Group, LLC
Lawrence Erlbaum Associates is an imprint of Taylor & Francis Group, an Informa business

Printed in the United States of America on acid-free paper
10 9 8 7 6 5 4 3 2 1

International Standard Book Number-13: 978-0-8058-5981-2 (Softcover) 978-0-8058-6435-9 (Hardcover)

Library of Congress Cataloging-in-Publication Data

Disparities in school readiness : how families contribute to transitions into school / editors Alan Booth and Ann C. Crouter.
    p. cm. -- (The Penn State University family issues symposia series)
    Includes bibliographical references and index.
    ISBN-13: 978-0-8058-5981-2 (alk. paper)
    1. Readiness for school--United States. 2. Child development--United States. I. Booth, Alan, 1935- II. Crouter, Ann C.

LB1132.D57 2007
372.21'8--dc22
        2007014909

Visit the Taylor & Francis Web site at
http://www.taylorandfrancis.com

and the LEA Web site at
http://www.erlbaum.com

THE PENN STATE UNIVERSITY FAMILY ISSUES SYMPOSIA SERIES

Series Editors
Alan Booth and Ann C. Crouter
Pennsylvania State University

Booth/Dunn: Stepfamilies: Who Benefits? Who Does Not?

Booth/Dunn: Family-School Links: How Do They Affect Educational Outcomes?

Booth/Crouter/Landale: Immigration and the Family: Research and Policy on U.S. Immigrants

Booth/Crouter: Men in Families: When Do They Get Involved? What Difference Does It Make?

Booth/Crouter: Does It Take a Village? Community Effects on Children, Adolescents, and Families

Booth/Crouter/Clements: Couples in Conflict

Booth/Crouter: Just Living Together: Implications of Cohabitation on Families, Children and Social Policy

Crouter/Booth: Children's Influence on Family Dynamics: The Neglected Side of Family Relationships

Crouter/Booth: Work-Family Challenges for Low-Income Parents and Their Children

Booth/Crouter: The New Population Problem: Why Families in Developed Countries are Shrinking and What It Means

Booth/Crouter: Romance and Sex in Adolescence and Emerging Adulthood: Risks and Opportunities

Booth/Crouter: Disparities in School Readiness: How Families Contribute to Transitions into School

Contents

Preface

Dramatic changes have occurred in the thinking of educators, researchers, and policy makers about the transition into school and the many factors that influence school readiness. Once focused on discrete skills, such as identifying letters and numbers, school readiness research now recognizes the critical importance of early developmental experiences that foster the social-emotional regulation skills and executive brain function that support and interface with specific language and cognitive capabilities to promote school engagement and capacity to learn in school.

Significant disparities exist at school entry in those core regulatory and learning capacities that support successful transition and engagement in school. Poverty is an especially invidious source of disparity. Parental functioning, including maternal depression and social isolation, increases risk for child learning delays and school transition difficulties. The contributions to this volume illuminate the roots of the striking disparities in children's acquisition of the many interrelated competencies (e.g., executive function, language skills, and social skills) that culminate in school readiness, with an emphasis on the roles families play in exacerbating or minimizing those disparities.

This volume is arranged according to the conference sessions, which focused on specific subthemes within the area of school readiness. The 2005 conference had four subthemes: inequalities in children's school readiness at school entry; effects of family processes on early brain development and academic skills acquisition; parental conceptualization and organization of non-familial experiences for children; and effects of child risk characteristics and family processes on the development of children's behavioral context. As is being found more and often in current research and examinations of research themes, each panel's topic required interdisciplinary examination, and so the authors of the papers presented both at the conference and in this volume emphasize interdisciplinary studies and perspectives on issues in school readiness.

In the first section of the volume, Penn State sociologists George Farkas and Jacob Hibel paint a broad portrait of school readiness at the entry to school using data on cognitive performance and social behavior from a national sample of American kindergarten children who participated in the Early Childhood Longitudinal Survey—Kindergarten Cohort (ECLS-K). They identify groups that are particularly disadvantaged at this important transition and explore some of the reasons for their condition. Taking other perspectives on this issue are developmental psychologist Michael López, Director of the National Center for Latino Child & Family Research, along with his co-author Sandra Barrueco; an expert on Head Start, sociologist Jane McLeod of Indiana University; and a team of co-authors that includes Erica Odom, Nadya Pancsofar, and Kirsten Kainz, scholars from the College of Education at the University of North Carolina, Chapel Hill, and is led by Lynne Vernon-Feagans, a psycholinguist.

In the second section of the volume, Susan Landry, a developmental psychologist in the Department of Pediatrics at the University of Texas Health Science Center, Houston, and Karen Smith, a clinical psychologist at the University of Texas Medical Branch, Galveston, move to a more process-oriented level of analysis. Their chapter outlines what we know about the specific family processes that scaffold the acquisition of literacy, numeracy, language, and cognitive skills and integrates Landry's own intervention research findings with those of others in the field. Their comments stimulate discussion among authors from other disciplines, including Clancy Blair, a developmental scholar at Penn State, Guang Guo, a sociologist at the University of North Carolina, Chapel Hill along with graduate student Jonathan Daw, and Kyle Snow, program director, Early Childhood Education for RTI (Research Triangle Institute International).

Sociologists Annette Lareau of the University of Maryland and Elliot Weininger of the State University of New York, Brockport make adept use of qualitative methods and set the stage for the third section of the volume. They examine how children's non-familial experiences unfold in advantaged and less advantaged family contexts and the roles that extracurricular activities may play in shaping children's school-related competencies. Although the focus here is on children's activities outside the family, Lareau and Weininger's in-depth interviews with parents reveal that mothers and fathers play an important role in creating—or constraining—these opportunities. Bringing their own expertise to bear on this part of the picture of school readiness are developmental psychologist Diane Hughes, New York University, demographer Sandy Hofferth, the University of Maryland, and developmental researcher Joseph Mahoney, Yale University, along with developmental psychologist Jacquelynne Eccles, the University of Michigan.

The fourth section focuses on the development of children's behavioral control, a crucial ingredient in school readiness. Susan Campbell, Chair of Clinical and Developmental Programs at the University of Pittsburgh, and Camilla von Stauffenberg, a doctoral candidate in the same program, outline this complex set of issues using empirical examples from the National Institute of Child Health and Human Development (NICHD) Study of Early Child Care (SECC). Their compelling longitudinal data address the ways in which child risk characteristics and family processes combine to undermine the development of children's behavioral control in ways that jeopardize their ability to adapt well to school. Hirokazu Yoshikawa, a developmental scholar in Harvard University's School of Education, Ray DeV. Peters, a developmental psychologist at Queens University in Ontario, Canada, along with Diana Ridgeway, a cognitive scientist at Carleton University in Ottawa, Canada, and Karen Bierman, a child clinical psychologist at Penn State, along with graduate students Robert Nix and Kerry Makin-Byrd, round out the fourth section by considering some of the program and policy implications of the emerging picture of school readiness.

The final chapter is an integrative commentary by Becky Sanford DeRousie and Rachel Durham, graduate students at Penn State in Human Development and Family Studies and Sociology, respectively. This interdisciplinary team deftly summarizes the themes woven throughout the volume and suggests next steps for research.

The research and perspectives described in these chapters should appeal to a broad range of audiences, from developmental and education al psychologists, to program implementation and development practitioners, to federal and state policy makers concerned with issues of school readiness, to family and early childhood experts. The list goes on and on—there is something in this volume for everyone studying, working with, and parenting children, who are concerned with school readiness.

Acknowledgments

The editors are grateful to the many organizations at Penn State that sponsored the 2005 Symposium on Family Issues and this resulting volume, including the Population Research Institute, the Children, Youth, and Families Consortium, the Prevention Research Center, the Center for Human Development and Family Research in Diverse Contexts, the Center for Work and Family Research, and the Departments of Human Development and Family Studies, Labor and Industrial Relations, Psychology, and Sociology, and the Women's Studies Program. The editors also gratefully acknowledge essential core financial support in the form of a five-year grant from the National Institute of Child Health and Human Development (NICHD), as well as ongoing, substantive guidance and advice from Christine Bachrach of NICHD and Lynne Casper, formerly of NICHD and now at the University of Southern California. We also are grateful for the support and commitment of Lawrence Erlbaum Associates in publishing the volumes in this series. The ongoing support of all of these partners has enabled us to attract excellent scholars from a range of backgrounds and disciplines—the sort of group on whom the quality and integrity of the series depends.

A lively, interdisciplinary team of scholars from across the Penn State community meets with us annually to generate symposia topics and plans and is available throughout the year for brainstorming and problem solving. We appreciate their enthusiasm, intellectual support, and creative ideas. In preparing for the symposium and this volume, we relied heavily on the school readiness expertise of our Penn State colleagues Karen Bierman, Clancy Blair, George Farkas, Mark Greenberg, Scott Gest and Adele Miccio and are grateful for their wise counsel. We also sincerely thank David Baker, Scott Gest, Leif Jensen, and Celene Domitrovich for presiding over symposium sessions.

The many details that go into planning a symposium and producing a volume cannot be over-estimated. In this regard, we are especially grateful for the assistance of our administrative staff, including Tara Murray, Kim Zimmerman, and Sherry Yocum. Finally, we could not have accomplished this work without the incredible organizational skills, hard work, and commitment of Carolyn Scott and Barbara King. Their attention to the many details that go into organizing a good conference and edited book series made it possible for us to focus on the ideas.

—Ann C. Crouter
—Alan Booth

I

Inequalities In Children's School Readiness at School Entry

1

BEING UNREADY FOR SCHOOL: FACTORS AFFECTING RISK AND RESILIENCE

George Farkas
Jacob Hibel
Pennsylvania State University

Inequality in school readiness is a subject whose time has come. There are several reasons for this. Most important has been the finding that cognitive inequality across social class and race/ethnic groups first appears early in the preschool period, and accounts for a significant share of the adult inequality experienced by these groups. Our understanding in this area has been facilitated by the availability and analysis of new data, and has in turn stimulated further data collection and analyses that have confirmed and expanded our knowledge. Finally, this research has stimulated public policy and program innovation, so that interventions serving preschool-aged children and their families are under intense scrutiny and development.

From a theoretical perspective, sociologists and psychologists have converged on relatively similar descriptions of the forces determining variation in children's school readiness. The prime mover is variation in the resources possessed, and the stresses experienced, by parents and their children. These include the biological, health-related, social, psychological, and economic characteristics and conditions that occur for children, their parents, and their environments. These in turn explain how parenting habits and activities vary across families, and produce differences in children's school readiness. In particular, families that suffer economic, social, and/or psychological hardship, and have few parental or publicly provided resources to cope with these, tend to experience higher rates of school unreadiness than do more advantaged families.

The goal of this chapter is to provide an empirical summary of the basic facts in this research area. Thus, our analyses are organized around the following research questions:

(1) How do individual and family background characteristics, such as parental education, race/ethnicity, family structure, and other variables affect child birth weight, parenting activities and resources, and federal program participation during the preschool years?

(2) How do these individual and family background characteristics affect being unready for school along cognitive and behavioral dimensions?

(3) To what extent are the effects of family background characteristics on school unreadiness mediated by (explained by) the effects of these

3

characteristics on child birth weight, parenting activities and resources, and program participation?

(4) In sum, which children are at greatest risk of school unreadiness, and what are the magnitudes of these risks?

To answer these questions, we analyze a relatively new data source—the Early Childhood Longitudinal Survey, Kindergarten Cohort (ECLS-K)—containing measures of the cognitive and behavioral performance of a representative national sample of children who entered kindergarten in 1998. We do so using a statistical technique—multilevel modeling—that accounts for the sampling structure used in data collection. Our predictor variables are family, student, and program-participation characteristics. These are used in two stages of analysis.

First, the most exogenous variables (those that cause outcomes of interest to us, but are not themselves caused by variables in our model), such as student gender and race/ethnicity, family structure, parental age, education and income, and geographical location, are used to predict child and family outcomes and actions during the preschool period. These outcomes and actions include the child's birth weight, age at school entrance, and a myriad of program participation and parenting characteristics that may affect the child's school readiness. These include participation in WIC, Food Stamps, AFDC/TANF, and Head Start. They also include (a) the student's participation in organized arts and crafts, performing arts, sports activities, and educational trips, (b) parental involvement in the student's school, and (c) the presence of a home computer and the number of books available for the child in the home.

Second, we run regressions to predict cognitive and behavioral outcomes when students enter kindergarten (for an examination of how these two types of variables combine to determine stratification outcomes, see Farkas [1996, 2003, forthcoming]). In measuring these dependent variables, we have made an important change from the work of previous analysts of the ECLS-K data. Rather than predict the full range of variation in these outcomes, we have focused on the student's risk of being unready for school, defined as falling into the bottom twenty percent of cognitive and behavioral performance. This way of defining the dependent variable more sharply targets those children at greatest risk of subsequent school failure. (We chose the 20% cutoff as a reasonable marker of students who are likely to be performing low enough that their teachers may question their ability to function successfully in the regular classroom. Nationally, approximately 10% of students receive special education services.)

Each of these (multilevel logistic) regressions is run in two stages. The first uses as predictors only the most exogenous student and family characteristics— gender, race/ethnicity, parental education, and so on. This shows the total effect of each of these variables on the outcome in question. The second adds the variables measuring child and family outcomes and actions during the preschool period—such as the child's birth weight, program participation, parenting, and family resource variables—as predictors to the equation. This regression shows both the effects of these variables on the outcome in question, and the extent to which these mediating variables help explain the relationship between the exogenous variables and the outcome.

Finally, we use these estimated equations to calculate predicted values showing how youths' probability of being unready on each of the outcomes increases when an increasing number of risk factors are present at the family or individual level. The chapter concludes with a summary of findings and a discussion of issues for future research.

A caution must be noted—answering our research questions in a "causal" way will be difficult. This is because a large number of parental and child characteristics, resources, and activities are important to school readiness; they are correlated with one another, and even the comprehensive data we will be using lack measures of some of them. For example, we are seeking to separate the readiness effects of the following variables: parental education, the number of children's books in the home, whether there is a computer in the home, organized sports activities the child was engaged in, organized arts activities the child was engaged in, educational trips the child was taken on, parental involvement in the child's school, and participation in compensatory programs such as Food Stamps and Head Start. Yet despite this rich set of parenting variables, two important variables are not available on our data set—the vocabulary knowledge and usage of parents, and their employment of these in shaping their children's knowledge and use of language. However, these parental variables are both correlated with the variables we will be using and also have their own effect on child cognitive outcomes (Durham & Farkas, 2004; Farkas & Beron, 2004; Hart & Risley, 1995, 1999; Landry & Smith, this volume; Whitehurst & Lonigan, 2002). As a result, if we find that, say, the number of children's books in the household is associated with higher school readiness, we will still not know whether this is because reading these books to the child directly increases readiness, or whether it is simply that parents who buy such books are the same parents whose own language skills are particularly strong, a key readiness strength that they pass on to their children through everyday verbal interaction.

This "omitted variable bias" problem is ubiquitous in non-experimental social science. But it is more than usually important in a study such as ours, which seeks to investigate the effects of a variety of parenting variables while omitting such important and correlated variables as parental language knowledge and use. A consequence is that our results are accurate as a description of those characteristics of families and children where school unreadiness is high. But they are less accurate as a test of the relative strength of the different factors that may be *causing* this unreadiness. In this paper we consider our statistical results to be descriptive, while tentatively looking for those causal mechanisms that seem best supported by the pattern of our results, as well as by logic and prior research.

Prior Research

The study of social class and race/ethnicity effects on the cognitive development of preschool children, as well as programmatic efforts to ameliorate these, date back to the 1960s and 1970s, when Labov (1972), Bernstein (1977), and Heath (1983) researched sociolinguistic differences across class and race, and Head Start began large-scale efforts to increase school readiness among disadvantaged preschoolers (Zigler & Valentine, 1979). Since these beginnings, research has grown in many directions. Perhaps the over-riding theme in this work has been family risk factors, and the ways that multiple risk factors within the same family greatly increase the readiness problems experienced by children. An important, but less-examined research topic focuses on factors that provide resilience and assist children to succeed despite the presence of risk factors.

Student-level risk factors include low birth weight, speech/language impairment, and other health or developmental disabilities (Currie, 2005; Reichman, 2005). Family risk factors include a single-parent household, a teenage mother, a mother who dropped out of high school, a family living in poverty, and a non-English speaking home (Brooks-Gunn & Markman, 2005; Duncan & Magnuson, 2005). These family factors affect the development of children via their effect on the parenting activities, actions, and resources that are used in child-raising. In particular, low vocabulary usage, family distress and disorder, and harsh and ineffective parenting are often found in low-income households, also leading to a correlation with race/ethnicity (Brooks-Gunn & Markman, 2005; Duncan, Brooks-Gunn, & Klebanov, 1994; Duncan & Magnuson, 2005; McLoyd, 1990, 1998). In related work, reading researchers have found that the best preschool predictors of first grade reading success are oral vocabulary knowledge, phonemic awareness (the ability to hear and manipulate the separate sounds in spoken English), and letter-sound knowledge (Whitehurst & Lonigan, 2002). Most important is good cognitive skill instruction in the context of a warm and responsive parenting style (Landry & Smith, this volume). Since research has shown that more extensive cognitive skill instruction is likely to be provided in higher SES and white households than in lower SES and minority households (Beron & Farkas, 2004; Farkas & Beron, 2004; Phillips et al., 1998), the connection between family background and school readiness is reinforced. In addition to this linguistic mechanism for the transmission of school success from parent to child, Lareau's (2003, this volume) ethnographic work has drawn attention to social class differences in the organized activities that parents arrange for their children. She finds that higher SES parents schedule their children for a variety of arts, sports, and other activities, whereas lower SES parents allow their children to "develop naturally," with less adult involvement. At present, we do not know whether parental language use or organized activities exert the larger effect on school readiness.

Federal intervention programs such as the Special Supplemental Nutrition Program for Women, Infants, and Children (WIC), the Food Stamp Program, Welfare or Job Search support, and Head Start can support resilience despite the presence of family risk factors. However, since these programs enroll those children most at risk, their positive effects are applied to such children, and are often unable to overcome these risks (for a wide-ranging review, see Brooks-Gunn, 2003). Further, Head Start has been criticized for having no organized instructional curriculum and doing too little to increase the cognitive preparation of children, for example, by teaching the letters (Whitehurst & Massetti, 2004). However, other researchers have found positive effects of Head Start (Magnuson & Waldfogel, 2005). Importantly, a recent, random-assignment study of Head Start has found positive effects on increasing the number of times the parent read to the child, and increasing the child's ability at letter-word identification, letter naming, vocabulary, and color naming (U.S. Department of Health and Human Services, 2005). Unfortunately, these effects are relatively modest in magnitude—on the order of .1–.2 of a standard deviation—and some are present for 3-year-olds, but not for 4-year-olds. When this is combined with the finding of no effects on oral comprehension and phonological awareness or on early mathematics skills, and one also considers the fade-out typically observed for such early intervention effects as children age, it is clear that we must find a way to increase the magnitude of positive Head Start effects.

Where behavioral readiness for school is concerned, a similar research literature has developed since the 1960s. As reviewed by Loeber (1990), Hinshaw (1992), Yoshikawa (1994), Campbell (1995, this volume), and Farrington (1996), these studies, typically undertaken by developmental psychologists, psychopathologists, or criminologists find that the same set of risk factors, including low parental education, single parenthood, teenage parenthood, and poverty, tend to be associated with higher levels of behavior problems among children. Also, behavior disorders in parents, often associated with these family risk factors, have further negative effects on behavioral outcomes for their children. As with cognition, the causal mechanisms are believed to flow from parent background characteristics, through parenting actions, activities, and resources, to child outcomes first observed in the preschool years. In particular, physical discipline, rather than reasoning and guilt, appears to be more common in lower SES and African American households, leading to less advantageous child behavior outcomes (Bradley, Corwyn, McAdoo, & Coll, 2001; McLeod & Nonnemaker, 2000; McLoyd & Smith, 2002), although this issue is controversial (for arguments and evidence that physical discipline is less damaging to African American than to white children, see Deater-Deckard, Dodge, & Sorbring, 2005).

Further, large-scale programs, such as Head Start, appear to have been less than fully successful in ameliorating these problems. In fact, a large national study recently reported that the longer students have been in Head Start, the greater the behavior problems they manifest (NICHD Early Childcare Research Network, 2003).

The recent random-assignment study of Head Start (U.S. Department of Health and Human Services, 2005) did find modest positive effects (about .1 of a standard deviation) in teaching parents to reduce their use of physical discipline (spanking), but these occurred only for 3-year-olds and not for 4-year-olds. There were no effects in getting parents to increase their use of timeout as an alternative. There were significant, modest effects in reducing hyperactive behavior problems among 3-year-olds, but none among 4-year-olds. There were also no effects on reducing aggressive or withdrawn behavior problems, and no effects in increasing social skills, social competencies, or approaches to learning. The latter finding is particularly bothersome since the Approaches to Learning behaviors have been shown to be the key variable involved in increasing cognitive performance, net of prior cognitive performance (Tach & Farkas, forthcoming). When the small sizes of these behavior effects for 3-year-olds are considered, and the lack of effects for 4-year-olds, plus the typical fadeout of effects as children age are also taken into account, it is clear that Head Start must do much better if it is to adequately prepare disadvantaged students to be behaviorally ready for school. This is particularly important since teachers judge behavioral unreadiness to be *the* largest problem they encounter in the early school years, and such unreadiness has been shown to have persistent effects on subsequent school achievement (Hamre & Pianta, 2001; McLeod & Kaiser, 2004; Rimm-Kaufman, Pianta, & Cox, 2000).

Data, Measurement, and Methods

We analyze ECLS-K data for kindergarten in fall 1998. The ECLS-K is a nationally representative, multi-stage cluster sample of elementary schools, classes within these schools, and students within these classes (U.S. Department of Education, 2000). We use multi-level regression models so that our standard errors are adjusted for data grouping, and we use the logistic specification since our dependent variables are dichotomous (Raudenbush & Bryk, 2002).

The principal dependent variables are reading, mathematics, and general knowledge test scores, as well as teacher judgments of the student's learning-related behaviors (referred to in the ECLS-K study as Approaches to Learning). The tests are scored using Item Response Theory (IRT). The behavior measure is constructed from the teacher's responses to items asking about the child's attentiveness, task persistence, eagerness to learn, learning independence, flexibility, and organization. In other studies, I and my colleagues have found that this behavior variable significantly predicts later test score performance, even after controlling prior performance (Bodovski & Farkas, 2004; Tach & Farkas, forthcoming). Further, when several different teacher-judged behaviors are included in the model, it is the only one that has a significant relationship with test scores.

We use these variables to measure a student's risk of being unready for school by creating a dummy variable that is coded one if the student's score falls into the bottom 20% of all students. These are the key dependent variables for our analyses. Independent and mediating variables include student and family characteristics, federal program participation, and parenting activities and resources. Appendix 1 contains a description of the measurement of these variables in detail. Most of these are self-explanatory. However, the parenting activities require some explanation. Arts & Crafts is coded 1 if the child participated in organized arts or crafts lessons in 1998, 0 otherwise. Sports/Clubs is coded from 0 to 3 according to whether the child took part in any of the following in 1998: attended sporting events, participated in organized athletic events, or participated in organized clubs. Performing Arts is coded 1 if the child participated in organized performances, or received dance, music, or drama lessons in 1998, 0 otherwise. The Educational Trips variable is coded from 0 to 4 according to whether the child went on a trip to a museum, zoo, library, or concert in 1998. Parental Involvement is coded from 0 to 6 according to whether a parent participated in the following in 1998: school open house, PTA meeting, parent advisory group, fundraising activity, school event, or volunteering at school. Beyond directly benefiting children, these activities may serve as proxy measures for other, unmeasured parental activities or characteristics that have more powerful effects on child development. Nevertheless, it will be interesting to see which, if any, of these activities significantly affect child outcomes, when all the other variables are controlled.

Descriptive Statistics

Table 1.1 shows means and standard deviations for the variables. Twelve percent of mothers were high school dropouts, and 29% were high school graduates. Thirty three percent had some college, and 25% were college graduates or higher. Information is missing on the education of 18% of fathers; the distribution of values for the remainder is similar to that for mothers. Eighteen percent of families are living in poverty. The average family income is approximately $55,000. Thirteen percent of mothers are immigrants, and 11% of homes are non-English-speaking. Sixty percent of the children are white, non-Hispanic, 13% are African-American, 17% are Hispanic, 5% are Asian, and 5% belong to other ethnicities (this category includes Native Americans). Sixty-nine percent of children are being raised in two-parent families, and 20% in single-mother families. The rest are divided among a variety of family types. The average number of siblings is 1.4. Forty-one percent of the children are being raised in urban areas, 39% in the suburbs, and 21% in rural areas. Where children are concerned, the South is the most populous region, followed in order by the Midwest, West, and Northeast.

Table 1.1
Descriptive Statistics (N = 16,135)

	Mean	S.D.	Min.	Max.
Low Reading	.20	.40	0	1
Low Math	.20	.40	0	1
Low General Knowledge	.20	.40	0	1
Low Behavior	.22	.41	0	1
Low Reading and Behavior	.08	.28	0	1
Mom No HS	.12	.32	0	1
Mom HS Grad	.29	.46	0	1
Mom Some College	.33	.47	0	1
Mom College Grad	.25	.43	0	1
Dad's Ed. Missing	.18	.39	0	1
Dad No HS	.09	.29	0	1
Dad HS Grad	.25	.43	0	1
Dad Some College	.22	.41	0	1
Dad College Grad	.25	.43	0	1
Family in Poverty	.18	.39	0	1
Family Income	54,679.85	56,339.26	0	1,000,000
Mom Immigrant	.13	.33	0	1
Non-English Home	.11	.32	0	1
White	.60	.49	0	1
Black	.13	.34	0	1
Hispanic	.17	.37	0	1
Asian	.05	.21	0	1
Other Ethnicity	.05	.22	0	1
Male	.51	.50	0	1
Teen Mom	.26	.44	0	1
Two Parent Family	.69	.46	0	1
Single Mom	.20	.40	0	1
Single Dad	.01	.11	0	1
Step Mom	.01	.07	0	1
Step Dad	.07	.26	0	1
Adopted	.01	.09	0	1
Other Family Type	.01	.11	0	1
Number of Siblings	1.44	1.14	0	11
Urban	.41	.49	0	1
Suburban	.39	.49	0	1
Rural	.21	.40	0	1
Northeast	.19	.39	0	1
Midwest	.26	.44	0	1
South	.32	.47	0	1
West	.23	.42	0	1
Birth Weight	6.94	1.34	1	13
Age at K Entry	68.44	4.35	45.77	83.97
Number of Books	76.20	58.89	0	200
Has Home Computer	0.57	0.49	0	1
Arts & Crafts	0.14	0.35	0	1
Sports/Clubs	1.06	0.90	0	3
Performing Arts	0.29	0.45	0	1
Educational Trips	1.66	1.18	0	4
Parental Involvement	3.74	1.55	0	6
WIC During Pregnancy	.437	.4869	0	1
WIC During Infancy	.3864	.4960	0	1
AFDC/TANF	.1075	.3097	0	1
Food Stamps	.1782	.3826	0	1
Head Start	.1563	.3631	0	1

The average birth weight of these children was 6.9 pounds. Their average age when surveyed in the fall of kindergarten was 68.4 months. The average number of books available for each child was 76.2. Fifty-seven percent of these children were being raised in a household with a home computer. Fourteen percent had been scheduled for organized arts or craft activities, and 29% had attended performing arts activities. The average child scored 1.06 out of a maximum of three possible organized sports and club activities, 1.66 out of a possible 4 educational trips, and the parents averaged 3.74 out of a possible 6 school involvement activities. Where program participation is concerned, 44% of mothers were involved in WIC during pregnancy, and 39%were involved during infancy. Eleven percent of mothers participated in AFCD/TANF and 17.8% in Food Stamps, and 15.6% of the children participated in Head Start.

Determinants of Birth Weight and Program Participation

Table 1.2 shows the results of the regression models predicting the child's birth weight and family participation in each of the federal programs. Participation in WIC during pregnancy was higher for less educated mothers and fathers, ethnic minorities, and teenage mothers. It was also higher for family types other than two-parent, rural, and southern families.

As with other federal assistance programs, WIC tends to recruit the most disadvantaged families and children, so that its overall effect involves results from opposing forces of disadvantage and program effect (Devaney, 1998). Thus, when we estimate this effect on outcomes such as the child's birth weight, we may fail to find an overall positive effect. Indeed, this is what we see in the birth weight regression (column 2 of Table 1.2), where the effect of WIC during pregnancy is not statistically significant. Other results in this column show significant negative effects of a high school dropout father, poverty, ethnic minority status, teenage motherhood, stepparents, adoption, and other family types, and urban and southern residence on birth weight.

The third column of this table shows the regression predicting participation in WIC during infancy. The results generally resemble those for WIC during pregnancy.

The fourth column shows results for Food Stamp participation. Many of the effects resemble those for WIC participation, but are somewhat larger in magnitude. As with WIC, participation is particularly strong when the mother is a high school dropout. There are also particularly strong effects of the family being in poverty, being African American, and being a single mother.

The fifth column shows the determinants of AFDC/TANF participation. These are particularly strong when the mother dropped out of high school, the family is in poverty, among African Americans and Asians, and among single mothers and fathers. Participation in this program is particularly low in the South.

Table 1.2
Multilevel Regression Models Predicting Program Participation and Birth Weight[1]

	WIC During Pregnancy	Birth Weight (Pounds)	WIC During Infancy	Food Stamps	AFDC/TANF	Head Start
Intercept	-1.76***	7.01***	-1.44***	-3.35***	-4.06***	-3.13***
Mom No HS	1.29***	-0.03	1.36***	1.63***	1.21***	0.67***
Mom HS Grad	0.87***	-0.05	0.86***	1.18***	0.80***	0.73***
Mom Some College	0.72***	-0.01	0.71***	0.98***	0.70***	0.65***
Dad No HS	1.23***	-0.11*	1.28***	0.51**	0.68**	0.56***
Dad HS Grad	0.77***	-0.06	0.81***	0.45**	0.59**	0.56***
Dad Some College	0.55***	-0.03	0.56***	0.17	0.26	0.17
Dad's Ed Missing	0.38*	-0.04	0.38*	0.50*	0.39	0.25
Family in Poverty	0.03	-0.09**	0.03	0.97***	0.79***	0.12
Family Income	-0.00003***	-0.00000	-0.00003***	-0.00004***	-0.00003***	-0.00003***
Mom Immigrant	-0.07	0.02	-0.05	-0.47***	-0.31**	0.01
Non-English Home	0.143	0.03	0.29**	-0.23	-0.34*	0.21
Black	1.08***	-0.44***	1.23***	0.74***	0.69***	1.58***
Hispanic	0.50***	-0.14**	0.53***	0.17	0.25*	0.64***
Asian	0.48**	-0.43***	0.29*	0.51**	0.91***	1.01***
Other Ethnicity	0.61***	-0.07	0.72***	0.43**	0.43***	0.87***
Male	0.11**	0.27***	0.07	-0.06	0.10	-0.03
Teen Mom	0.70***	-0.07*	0.68***	0.40***	0.49***	0.37**
Single Mom	0.83***	-0.10	0.96***	1.20***	1.59***	0.55**
Single Dad	1.21***	-0.05	1.04***	1.18***	1.37***	1.59***
Step Mom	0.67*	-0.32*	0.30	-0.24	0.05	0.52
Step Dad	0.97***	-0.19***	1.17***	0.94***	1.27***	0.60***
Adopted	-18.18	-0.67***	0.14	-0.39	0.56	0.93**
Other Family Type	0.60**	-0.71***	1.35***	0.80***	2.18***	0.82***
Number of Siblings	0.04	0.06***	0.07**	0.25***	0.15***	0.08**
Urban	0.07	-0.07*	0.09	0.36***	0.17	-0.01
Rural	0.41***	0.02	0.52***	0.42***	0.04	0.61***
Midwest	-0.01	0.03	-0.03	-0.38**	-0.33**	0.07
South	0.17*	-0.07*	0.11	-0.18	-0.77***	-0.13
West	-0.09	0.05	-0.16	-0.11	0.15	0.20
WIC During Pregnancy		-0.03				

*** p < 0.001 ** p < 0.01 * p < 0.05
[1] Models predicting program participation (binary outcomes) employ a multilevel logistic regression framework. The birth weight model employs multilevel linear regression.

The final column shows the determinants of Head Start participation. This program is of particular interest for our study, since more than any other large-scale program, Head Start's goal is to increase the school readiness of disadvantaged children. As with the other programs, participation is higher among less well-educated mothers and fathers, although somewhat surprisingly this higher probability is relatively constant among all mothers with less than a college education. Once again somewhat surprisingly, we find no significant effect of poverty on Head Start participation (although it is negatively affected by overall family income, with a magnitude similar to that of the other programs). Ethnic minorities are much more likely than whites to use Head Start, with the strongest effect for African Americans. There is also elevated program participation among children of teenage and single mothers, as well as those from rural families.

Determinants of Parenting Activities and Resources

Table 1.3 shows the results for parenting activities and resources. Previous studies have hypothesized that one or another of these is important in creating social class and race/ethnicity differences in school readiness, but none has included them all in a quantitative study to estimate their relative magnitudes of effect on being unready for school.

Examining the first five columns of this table, it is useful to read across the rows to see which variables have similar patterns of effect on these parental activities. In all cases the mother's education is strongly and regularly associated with these parenting activities. As others have reported (see, for example, Lareau, 2003, this volume), better-educated parents are much more likely to be involved in and to schedule these activities for their children. Reading across the rows, we see that this is true for the education of both mother and father and for all of these activities. We also find that poverty decreases these activities, most strongly for parental school involvement, followed by sports/clubs and educational trips. Arts and crafts and performing arts activities are not significantly affected by poverty (at least within the ability of these survey items to accurately capture such activities). We also find that total family income is significantly and positively associated with all of these activities. Clearly, these parenting activities are strongly linked to parental social class.

When the mother is an immigrant and the home is non-English speaking, participation in these activities decreases. They are also less likely to occur among ethnic minority families, with the strongest effects observed for decreased parental school involvement among blacks and Asians, and decreased participation in sports and clubs among Asians. Not surprisingly, boys are very much less likely than girls to be scheduled for performing arts activities. Family structures other than the two-parent type show lower involvement with these activities, as does having a teenage mother. Not surprisingly, because of the access issue, rural families are less likely to undertake educational trips.

Table 1.3

Multilevel Regression Estimates of Parental Activities, Resources, and Child Age at K Entry[1]

	Participates in Arts & Crafts	Participates Performing Arts	Participates in Sports/ Clubs	Educational Trips	Parental School Involvement	Age at K Entry (Months)	Number of Books in Home	Has Home Computer
Intercept	-1.05 ***	0.50 ***	1.38 ***	2.04 ***	4.38 ***	67.14 ***	113.11***	1.43 ***
Mom No HS	-0.84 ***	-1.03 ***	-0.35 ***	-0.50 ***	-0.71 ***	0.19	-26.09 ***	-0.99 ***
Mom HS Grad	-0.65 ***	-0.71 ***	-0.22 ***	-0.32 ***	-0.40 ***	0.20	-18.05 ***	-0.68 ***
Mom Some College	-0.33 ***	-0.31 ***	-0.09 ***	-0.16 ***	-0.12 ***	0.06	-9.02*	-0.34 ***
Dad No HS	-0.29 *	-1.01 ***	-0.35 ***	-0.35 ***	-0.49 ***	-0.12	-18.99 ***	-1.15 ***
Dad HS Grad	-0.23 **	-0.56 ***	-0.19 ***	-0.24 ***	-0.32 ***	-0.21	-13.37 ***	-0.76 ***
Dad Some College	-0.13	-0.32 ***	-0.13 ***	-0.16 ***	-0.14 ***	-0.11	-6.90***	-0.34 ***
Dad's Ed Missing	-0.41 *	-0.55 ***	-0.10 *	-0.27 ***	-0.29 ***	-0.29	-7.36 *	-0.72 ***
Family in Poverty	-0.04	-0.12	-0.19 ***	-0.16 ***	-0.39 ***	0.11	-7.21 ***	-0.45 ***
Family Income	0.000001 ***	0.000002 ***	0.000001 ***	0.000001 ***	0.000001 ***	-0.000000	0.00006 ***	0.00001 ***
Mom Immigrant	-0.19	-0.31 ***	-0.16 ***	0.04	-0.11 **	-0.31 *	-9.72 ***	-0.02
Non-English Home	-0.48 ***	-0.19 *	-0.17 ***	-0.12 **	-0.46 ***	-0.07	-24.34 ***	-0.55 ***
Black	-0.15	0.30 ***	-0.19 ***	0.11 **	-0.37 ***	-0.78 ***	-38.58 ***	-0.55 ***
Hispanic	-0.21 *	-0.16 *	-0.10 ***	0.02	-0.09 *	-0.38 **	-22.08 ***	-0.43 ***
Asian	-0.11	0.02	-0.46 ***	0.09	-0.57 ***	-0.55 **	-30.10 ***	-0.09
Other Ethnicity	0.19	0.11	-0.12 ***	-0.05	-0.23 ***	-0.48 **	-18.44 ***	-0.34 ***
Male	-0.33 ***	-1.58 ***	0.10 ***	-0.06 **	-0.05 *	0.62 ***	-3.23 ***	-0.02
Teen Mom	-0.12	-0.22 ***	-0.02	-0.00	-0.22 ***	0.15	-4.39 ***	-0.15 **
Single Mom	0.14	-0.03	-0.13 ***	0.09	-0.33 ***	0.28	-6.55 **	-0.37 **
Single Dad	-0.67 **	-0.48 *	-0.23 ***	0.14	-0.66 ***	0.45	-25.50 ***	-0.88 ***
Step Mom	-0.16	-0.12	-0.18	-0.06	-0.51 **	0.53	-12.98 *	-0.26
Step Dad	-0.34 **	-0.33 **	-0.10 ***	-0.04	-0.32 ***	0.15	-8.35 ***	-0.41 ***
Adopted	-0.12	0.29	-0.13	-0.13	0.13	-0.11	9.09 *	-0.10
Other Family Type	0.00	0.02	-0.25 ***	-0.12	-0.30 **	1.58 ***	-7.14	-0.44 *
Number of Siblings	-0.03	-0.07 ***	0.02 ***	-0.02 *	0.01	0.18 ***	2.36 ***	0.05 *
Urban	0.05	0.06	-0.04	-0.00	-0.02	0.27 *	-0.15	-0.03
Rural	-0.29 **	-0.11	-0.06 *	-0.27 ***	-0.17 **	0.50 **	-1.45	-0.24 ***
Midwest	0.01	0.01	0.05	0.09 *	0.23 ***	1.62 ***	-3.10 *	-0.16 *
South	-0.18 *	0.23 **	0.01	0.06	0.21 **	0.98 ***	-5.00 **	-0.17 *
West	0.13	0.22 **	-0.01	0.17 ***	0.30 ***	-0.34	1.00	-0.05

*** p < 0.001 ** p < 0.01 * p < 0.05

[1] Models with binary dependent variables (Arts & Crafts, Performing Arts, Has Home Computer) employ a multilevel logistic regression framework. All other models in Table 1.3 employ multilevel linear regression.

The final three outcomes in Table 1.3 measure, respectively, the student's age at kindergarten entry, the number of books available for the child, and whether or not the family has a home computer. The first of these indicates whether the parents have taken advantage of the opportunity sometimes available to children whose birthday falls near the cutoff for kindergarten entry to delay the child's entry, so that they are more mature when school begins. Prior research has shown that, at least for boys, this can be a useful strategy (Riordan, 2002). The other two variables provide an indication of the learning-related resources available to the child in the home, and may also indicate the parents' intensity of focus on education generally, and education of the child, specifically.

Where the child's age is concerned, immigrant and ethnic minority children are younger than non-immigrant and white children, suggesting that if any parents are strategizing in this way, it is the latter groups. Boys are also significantly older than girls, supporting the likelihood that at least some deliberate strategizing is occurring. Regional effects are likely due to regional differences in typical beginning dates for the fall term.

The number of children's books in the home may be one of the more accurate measure of parental interest in providing instruction to the child, particularly after controlling the (relatively large) effects of parental income. This is because these materials are focused on learning, and, since parents have little knowledge about quantity norms for such books, bias due to "socially desirable" answering patterns may be reduced. We find that the number of books is positively associated with parental education and negatively associated with family poverty. Immigrant and non-English speaking homes own fewer books. So do ethnic minority households, and these effects are relatively large, particularly for African-Americans and Asians. Families other than two parent families have fewer children's books, with a particularly large negative effect for single-father households.

As with children's books and scheduled activities, the presence of a home computer is strongly associated with parental social class. In particular, there are large differentials in such ownership according to the mother's educational level. Also striking, however, are the somewhat larger differentials according to the father's education. Due to the "home office effect," computer ownership appears to fall more into the father's domain than most other educational resources.

Not surprisingly, home computer ownership increases with family income and is lower among the poor. It is unrelated to immigrant status, but significantly less likely in non-English-speaking homes. It is particularly less likely in African American and Hispanic families. It is also less likely among teenage mothers and where the household is other than two-parent. It is less likely in rural areas, and most likely in the Northeast.

Determinants of Being Unready for School

Table 1.4 shows the results of regressions predicting cognitive and behavioral unreadiness for school. Cognitive unreadiness is defined as falling into the bottom 20% of all students on tests of reading, mathematics, or general knowledge. Behavioral unreadiness is defined as falling into the bottom 20% of all students on the teacher's judgment of what the ECLS-K calls Approaches to Learning, a scale composed of items concerning attentiveness, task persistence, eagerness to learn, learning independence, flexibility, and organization. (We regard this variable as the best measure of learning-related behaviors since, when the behaviors measured on the ECLS-K are entered together as predictors of test scores, net of prior test scores, this is the only one with a significant effect. Also, unlike the measure of externalizing behaviors, the black-white difference in scores on Approaches to Learning is independent of the teacher's race.) Finally, we also show regressions predicting a variable coded one for students who were both unready in reading and also in behavior, zero otherwise. These are specified as logistic regressions, since the dependent variables are dichotomous.

Each dependent variable is predicted in two stages. First, we predict unreadiness using the student and family background characteristics. Second, we add the potentially mediating birth weight, student age, program participation, and parenting activities and resources variables to the equation. These provide estimates of the total effects of student and family background characteristics on unreadiness, of those mediating variables that have the strongest effects on unreadiness, and of the extent to which these explain the individual and family background effects.

Both the mother's and the father's educational level are strongly predictive of reading readiness, with large and regular gradients as one moves across the educational categories. Net of these, the family being in poverty and total family income are also significantly associated with unreadiness. Clearly, the student's reading readiness is strongly affected by parental social class background.

The children of immigrants are more likely to be unready in reading, and children from a non-English-speaking home have a very much increased chance of falling into this category (this effect would be even higher except for the fact that children who failed to demonstrate a basic level of English language proficiency were excluded from testing). Hispanics show a strongly elevated risk of reading unreadiness; so too do African Americans, although the effect is weaker. Consistent with previous research, males have a significantly higher risk of reading unreadiness than females. We also find that having a teenage mother, a single mother, or a single father significantly increases the risk of reading unreadiness. In addition, a larger number of siblings increase the risk. Finally, the risk is higher in rural areas and in the West.

Table 1.4

Multilevel Logistic Regression Models of School Readiness

Model	Low Readiness: Reading		Low Readiness: Math		Low Readiness: General Knowledge	
	1	2	1	2	1	2
Intercept	-3.50***	4.31	-2.90***	6.52***	-3.39***	7.19***
Mom No HS	1.12***	0.92***	1.07***	0.84***	0.80***	0.46***
Mom HS Grad	0.69***	0.56***	0.71***	0.56***	0.46***	0.24*
Mom Some College	0.38***	0.31**	0.32***	0.24**	0.21*	0.11
Dad No HS	0.74***	0.53***	0.59***	0.34**	0.56***	0.23
Dad HS Grad	0.53***	0.37**	0.50***	0.33**	0.42***	0.18
Dad Some College	0.30**	0.21*	0.27**	0.19	0.19*	0.07
Dad's Ed Missing	-0.26	0.11	0.19	0.03	0.22	0.02
Family in Poverty	0.35***	0.25**	0.27***	0.13	0.35***	0.20*
Family Income	-0.00001***	-0.000004***	-0.00001***	-0.00001***	-0.00001***	-0.000004***
Mom Immigrant	0.29**	0.23*	-0.08	-0.16	0.48***	0.39***
Non-English Home	1.29***	1.27***	0.71***	0.60***	1.56***	1.45***
Black	0.22**	-0.14	0.58†††	0.17	1.36***	0.97***
Hispanic	0.66***	0.53***	0.51***	0.33	0.96***	0.76***
Asian	0.08	-0.24	0.67***	0.36**	0.90***	0.55***
Other Ethnicity	0.39**	-0.21	0.52***	0.31**	0.78***	0.56***
Male	0.39***	0.44***	0.22***	0.27***	0.01	0.04
Teen Mom	0.23***	0.18**	0.21***	0.14*	0.24***	0.18**
Single Mom	0.31*	0.19	0.31*	0.17	0.25	0.09
Single Dad	0.60**	0.44*	0.60**	0.39	0.45*	0.22
Step Mom	0.35	0.31	0.41	0.35	0.07	-0.04
Step Dad	0.14	0.00	0.17	0.02	0.13	-0.03
Adopted	0.44	0.48	0.38	0.39	0.53	0.53
Other Family Type	0.38*	0.32	0.34	0.25	0.18	0.09
Number of Siblings	0.16***	0.20 ***	0.14 ***	0.17 ***	0.13 ***	0.16 ***
Urban	0.09	0.08	-0.05	-0.06	0.12	0.10
Rural	0.24**	0.22*	0.17*	0.15*	0.17	0.12
Midwest	0.12	0.32**	-0.06	0.16	0.01	0.27*
South	0.15	0.27**	-0.03	0.11	0.19	0.35**
West	0.39***	0.43***	0.13	0.12	0.30**	0.33**
Birth Weight		-0.08***		-0.11***		-0.10***
Age at K Entry		-0.10***		-0.12***		-0.13***
Number of Books		-0.004***		-0.003***		-0.01***
Has Home Computer		-0.23***		-0.21***		-0.35***
Arts & Crafts		-0.03		-0.05		-0.18
Sports/Clubs		-0.09*		-0.11**		-0.12**
Performing Arts		-0.24**		-0.17*		-0.20**
Educational Trips		-0.01		-0.02		-0.02
Parental Involvement		-0.07***		-0.08***		-0.10***
WIC During Pregnancy		0.15		0.17		0.08
WIC During Infancy		0.08		0.10		0.17
AFDC/TANF		0.19*		0.23**		0.12
Food Stamps		0.13		0.15		0.18*
Head Start		-0.00		0.05		0.02

Table 1.4 cont.

Model	Low Readiness: Classroom Behavior		Low Readiness: Reading and Behavior	
	1	2	1	2
Intercept	-2.56***	3.19***	-4.60***	3.11***
Mom No HS	0.43***	0.23*	0.97***	0.70***
Mom HS Grad	0.13	-0.00	0.57***	0.40*
Mom Some College	0.08	0.02	0.42**	0.34*
Dad No HS	0.50***	0.32**	0.71***	0.50**
Dad HS Grad	0.40***	0.28**	0.58**	0.43**
Dad Some College	0.23**	0.18*	0.26	0.20
Dad's Ed Missing	0.29*	0.19	0.33	0.19
Family in Poverty	0.24*	0.09	0.23*	0.07
Family Income	-0.000001*	-0.00000	-0.00001***	-0.00001**
Mom Immigrant	-0.11	-0.16	-0.16	-0.22
Non-English Home	0.03	-0.06	0.46***	0.36**
Black	0.36***	0.11	0.40***	0.06
Hispanic	0.08	-0.04	0.55***	0.39**
Asian	-0.13	-0.34*	0.16	-0.15
Other Ethnicity	0.04	-0.11***	0.46**	0.27
Male	0.82***	0.88***	0.69***	0.74***
Teen Mom	0.19**	0.12***	0.30***	0.25**
Single Mom	0.38**	0.29*	0.40**	0.27
Single Dad	0.65**	0.49**	0.84**	0.66*
Step Mom	0.40	0.33	0.32	0.27
Step Dad	0.46***	0.35***	0.28**	0.17
Adopted	0.72**	0.76***	0.80*	0.86*
Other Family Type	0.49**	0.45*	0.58*	0.53*
Number of Siblings	-0.02	-0.00	0.08**	0.10**
Urban	-0.01	-0.01**	0.07	0.05
Rural	0.07	0.03	0.24*	0.20
Midwest	0.09	0.23**	0.19	0.40**
South	0.12	0.19*	0.31*	0.45**
West	0.19*	0.21*	0.43**	0.44**
Birth Weight		-0.05**		-0.07**
Age at K Entry		-0.07***		-0.10***
Number of Books		-0.00		-0.003**
Has Home Computer		-0.17**		-0.21*
Arts & Crafts		-0.08		-0.11
Sports/Clubs		-0.08**		-0.10*
Performing Arts		-0.04		-0.10
Educational Trips		-0.01		-0.02
Parental Involvement		-0.07***		-0.07**
WIC During Pregnancy		0.12		0.13
WIC During Infancy		-0.02		-0.04
AFDC/TANF		0.10		0.18
Food Stamps		0.08		0.19
Head Start		0.17**		0.07

*** $p < 0.001$ ** $p < 0.01$ * $p < 0.05$

The second column of these calculations adds the possible mediating mechanisms to the model. Many of these have significant effects, in expected directions, on reading readiness. Higher birth weight and older age decrease the risk of unreadiness. So does having more books and a home computer. Among parenting activities, sports/clubs, performing arts, and parental involvement in school all significantly reduce unreadiness. By contrast, arts and crafts activities and educational trips have no significant effect on unreadiness. This suggests that, net of controls, the first three types of activities are either effective themselves, or are correlated with effective parenting activities, while the latter two are not.

Unfortunately, none of the federal programs significantly decreases reading unreadiness. Indeed, participation in one—AFDC/TANF—is associated with increasing unreadiness. Of course, as noted above, this is likely due to the fact that these programs tend to recruit those families and children who are most disadvantaged.

With all of these mediating variables in the model, some of the background effects are reduced in magnitude (that is, their effects are partially explained by the mediators). The largest reductions occur for the parental education, poverty, Hispanic, other ethnicity, and single-parent variables. Clearly the mediating variables *do* tap dimensions that account for some of the differences in readiness across these households.

The third column of this table repeats the regression against background characteristics, but this time predicting low readiness in mathematics (basic elements of numbers, shapes, and so on). Many of the patterns are similar to those for reading readiness, but there are significant differences. In particular, having an immigrant mother is no longer significant, and the effect of a non-English speaking home is greatly reduced. Both of these are expected, given the importance of oral English language in reading preparation. We also find that African Americans and Asians show a larger effect on unreadiness for mathematics than for reading. For African Americans, this is consistent with previous findings (Fryer & Levitt, 2004). For Asians, it is a new finding, and is likely explained by our focus, for the first time, on predicting the probability of the child's falling at the low end of readiness. That is, by comparison with whites, Asians are more heterogeneous, with a greater percentage of students at both the lower and upper tails of the readiness distribution. Males show a smaller effect on mathematics than on reading unreadiness. Thus the fact that males tend to do better in mathematics than in reading is evident even in the preschool period.

The fourth column of this table adds the mediating variables to the regression. Without exception, these have effects similar to the ones they had for predicting reading unreadiness. In particular, among the parenting variables, sports/clubs, performing arts, and parental involvement in school once again exert statistically significant effects in decreasing school unreadiness, and these findings strengthen the inference that these variables tap parenting practices that make a significant difference for children. In addition, the effects of arts and crafts activities and educational trips once again fail to achieve statistical significance, suggesting that, net of controls, these variables *do not* tap practices that make a difference in children's cognitive readiness. As with reading, we also find that none of the program participation variables shows a significant effect in decreasing unreadiness, although AFDC/TANF is associated with significantly increased unreadiness.

The fifth column of Table 1.4 shows results for the effects of background characteristics on unreadiness as measured by the general knowledge (social studies and science) test. These effects are generally similar to those for reading and mathematics, with, once again, some notable differences. These include larger effects on unreadiness among children from a non-English speaking home, and among African Americans, Hispanics, and Asians. The African American effect has been reported before (Fryer & Levitt, 2004), but the others have not.

The sixth column of this table adds the mediating variables to the equation predicting unreadiness in general knowledge. Once again, their pattern of effects and non-effects is similar to that for reading and mathematics. One difference is that the home computer effect is larger for general knowledge. This is plausible, since the presence of a home computer suggests that parents are employed in a knowledge-related occupation or industry, and/or that they have a personal interest in information acquisition and usage.

With these variables controlled in the equation, a number of the background characteristics effects are at least partially explained. The decrease in these effects is particularly large for mother's and father's education, as well as for African Americans and Asians. Clearly, children's risk of low general knowledge when school begins is strongly affected by their parents' own store of information, and the actions they take in transmitting it to their children.

The next two columns of Table 1.4 show the results for predicting behavioral unreadiness for school—falling into the bottom 20% of students on teacher-judged learning-related behaviors such as paying attention and completing tasks. Parental education matters once again, but the effects are smaller, and, at least for mothers, significant effects are confined to the children of high school dropouts. Thus, to the extent that parental education measures social class background, this variable has a smaller effect on behavioral unreadiness than it does on cognitive unreadiness. Poverty also increases behavioral unreadiness, but neither immigrant status nor speaking a language other than English at home show significant effects. Among ethnic groups, only African Americans have an elevated risk of behavioral unreadiness. (As shown by Downey and Pribesh [2004] and by Tach and Farkas [forthcoming], these teacher judgments of the student's Approaches to Learning are independent of the teacher's race.) As has been reported previously (Riordan, 2002), males have a much higher rate of behavioral unreadiness than females. This higher rate is also observed for children from families other than two-parent.

The next column shows the results after adding the mediating variables. Higher birth weight and older age both significantly reduce behavioral unreadiness, findings that are consistent with psychopathologists' results showing biological and developmental effects on at least some behavior problems. The number of books in the household has no significant effect on behavior, but having a home computer is associated with lower behavior problems. Perhaps the latter variable serves as an indicator of more intellectually focused parents, employing more successful child-raising strategies.

As before, children scheduled for sports/clubs and parents with greater school involvement are associated with significantly reduced risks of school unreadiness. Consistent with our previous results, arts and crafts activities and educational trips have no effect on unreadiness. One difference from previous findings is that where behavior is concerned, performing arts activities also have no effect on school readiness.

With one exception, the program participation variables are unrelated to behavioral unreadiness. This exception is Head Start, which is associated with an increase in unreadiness. This is consistent with some recent findings (NICHD Child Care Network, 2003), and continues to be an issue in efforts to improve Head Start. It appears to be contradicted by the small positive effects in reducing hyperactive behavior among 3-year-olds reported in the recent random-assignment study of Head Start (U.S. Department of Health and Human Services, 2005), but this study found no effects on hyperactivity among 4-year-olds, and no effects on other behaviors among either age group. It is possible that once the children in the random-assignment study reach the 5-year-old age mark of the ECLS-K children, their behaviors will more closely resemble those we are observing in Table 1.4. In any event, there is little evidence for a significant *positive* effect of Head Start on 5-year-olds.

Controlling these mediating variables reduces the effect sizes of several of the background variables. This is true for parental education, poverty status, family income, African Americans, teenage mothers, and family types other than two-parent. Thus, parenting appears to play a role in the learning-related behaviors of children from these families.

The final analyses in this table predict a variable that combines cognitive and behavioral unreadiness. It is coded "1" if the child is in the bottom 20% on both reading and Approaches to Learning. By creating this variable, we have identified those children who are at greatest risk of school failure, since their cognitive and behavioral preparations are both near the bottom of the distribution. The probability of either outcome by itself is 20%, so if these outcomes were independent, the probability of both occurring would be .2 times .2, or .04. However, as seen in Table 1.1, the mean of this variable is actually .08. This is the result of the variables being correlated. Thus, 8% of children in the sample are at very high risk of later school failure.

The first of these columns shows the total effects of the background characteristics on the probability of falling into this group. This risk is strongly related to the parents' education, particularly when the mother, father, or both are high school dropouts. It increases when the family is in poverty, and decreases with family income. It increases in non-English-speaking homes, and among African Americans, Hispanics, and other ethnic minority families. It is substantially higher for males than for females. It is also higher for the children of teenage mothers, and for children raised in non-two-parent households. Siblings raise this risk, as does rural residence. The risk is higher in the South and the West than in the Northeast.

The final column adds the mediating variables to this equation. We find that higher birth weight, age, and number of books in the home all reduce the risk of combined reading and behavioral unreadiness, as does the presence of a home computer. Sports/clubs and parental involvement in school are also associated with reduced unreadiness, whereas arts and crafts activities, performing arts activities, and educational trips have no significant effect. None of the program participation variables are significantly associated with unreadiness.

With these variables controlled, a number of background effects are reduced in magnitude. As before, these include parental education and poverty. They also include non-English home, black, Hispanic, and other ethnicity. Particularly interesting is that the African American effect is completely explained by the mediating variables. Substantial portions of the family structure effects are also explained by these variables. Clearly, parenting plays a significant role in both cognitive and behavioral school readiness, and such parenting varies significantly across the dimensions of social class, race/ethnicity, and family structure.

The magnitudes of these effects are most easily comprehended by looking at how predicted probabilities of unreadiness change as one moves across the values of the independent variables. For a student with any one risk factor, the probability of being unready for school on any of the dimensions increases, but modestly. More important is how the probability of unreadiness increases dramatically when the number of risk factors for a given student cumulates. This is illustrated in Table 1.5, where we begin by calculating the probability of unreadiness for the base category of students having no risk factors. Among these students, the mother and father are both college graduates, the family is not in poverty and has the sample average income, the mother is not an immigrant, English is spoken in the home, the student is a white female, the mother was not a teenage mom, there are two biological parents in the home, there are the average number of siblings, and the family lives in a suburb in the Northeast. For this base student, the predicted probability of reading unreadiness is .03, of mathematics unreadiness, .04, and of behavioral unreadiness, .07.

Table 1.5

Predicted Probabilities of Reading, Mathematics, and Behavioral Unreadiness; Risk Factors Combined Cumulatively

	Reading	Math	Behavior
Base	0.03	0.04	0.07
Mom Dropout	0.08	0.12	0.10
+ Dad Dropout	0.15	0.19	0.15
+ Poverty	0.24	0.30	0.19
+ Male	0.32	0.35	0.35
+ Teen Mom	0.38	0.40	0.40
+ Single Mom	0.45	0.47	0.49
+ Black	0.51	0.62	0.58
or			
+ Hispanic	0.61	0.60	0.51
+ Immigrant	0.68	0.58	0.48
+ Non-English Home	0.89	0.74	0.49

Now, we sequentially add risk factors to the equation. We see that each additional factor increases the probability of unreadiness for all outcomes. By the time the seventh factor is added to the equation, the probability of unreadiness on each of the outcomes is above .5. This strongly supports the standard research finding in this area—it is the children with multiple risk factors who constitute the sub-populations at greatest risk.

Finally, we ask about the possibility of interaction effects—that is, do the effects of some variables depend upon the values of others? In particular, from a "risk and resilience" point of view, are the negative effects of a risk factor such as family poverty significantly ameliorated when the family involves children in a higher number of performing arts activities, have a home computer or a relatively large number of children's books in the home, or when the child is older when schooling begins?

We tested for these effects by adding interaction terms between family poverty and each of these variables in the equations to predict low readiness in reading, mathematics, general knowledge, classroom behavior, and combined reading and behavior problems.

We found that none of the interactions were significant for either low reading or combined low reading and behavior problems. However, higher numbers of books did appear to foster resilience for mathematics and general knowledge, and a home computer or performing arts activities fostered resilience in the behavior domain. We consider these results to be mixed. They suggest some, but limited, possibilities for parenting variables to ameliorate the effects of poverty.

Discussion

We have used ECLS-K data to estimate the effects of student and family background characteristics, as well as mediating variables including parenting activities and resources and federal program participation, on school unreadiness when kindergarten begins. We found that a great many family and individual characteristics affect school unreadiness. Particularly strong and widespread effects on cognitive unreadiness occur when the mother or father did not complete high school and when English is not spoken at home. Generally weaker, but still highly significant effects are observed for other categories of parental education, family poverty and income generally, immigrant status, race/ethnicity, gender, family structure, and number of siblings. Similar effects were found for behavioral unreadiness, although these are generally smaller than those for cognitive unreadiness. For behavioral unreadiness, the strongest determinants are being male, being raised by a single father, and being adopted.

A number of the mediating variables also show significant effects on unreadiness, although their magnitudes are generally smaller than those for the exogenous individual and family characteristics. Higher birth weight, older age, more children's books, and a computer in the home are associated with greater readiness. So too are participation in organized sports and clubs and performing arts activities, as well as parental involvement in the child's school. Interestingly, however, neither arts and crafts activities nor educational trips are found to have significant effects on readiness. Perhaps most disappointing, federal programs— WIC, AFDC, Food Stamps, and Head Start—show little positive effects on readiness. Further, the effect of Head Start participation in increasing behavioral unreadiness may be a concern, since it is consistent with other research in this area (NICHD Early Childcare Research Network, 2003). Even if, as reported by the random-assignment study (U.S. Department of Health and Human Resources, 2005), Head Start effects on behavior are positive, but are small in magnitude and occur only for 3-year-olds, there is still a need for improvement.

When the mediating variables are added to the equations, a number of the individual and family characteristics are partially explained. This is particularly the case for the parental education, income, race/ethnicity, and family structure variables, whose effects are partially explained by the child's birth weight, the number of books and the presence of a computer in the home, the child's participation in sports/clubs and performing arts activities, and parental involvement in the child's school. These findings suggest that, as reported by previous researchers, these effects operate at least partially via the differential parenting resources and activities of the different groups of parents.

Finally, we showed that it is the existence of multiple risk factors that most powerfully increases unreadiness. When multiple risks are present, the student's predicted probability of unreadiness begins to increase toward 50% and above. There are some, but limited, possibilities for parenting behaviors to moderate the negative effects of family poverty.

What are the large-scale implications of these findings, and where is further research needed? First, the failure of federal programs (particularly Head Start) to show positive effects on readiness is disappointing. Much work is needed in this area. (For one promising effort, see the discussion of Early Head Start by Love et al. [2001]. For one analysis of the reasons that Head Start fails to show better effects on readiness, see Whitehurst and Massetti [2004].) The random assignment study of Head Start (U.S. Department of Health and Human Services, 2005) is an excellent initiative since it measures both parenting behaviors and child outcomes. The early results from this study suggest that greater efforts on the part of Head Start program managers and operators will be needed if we are to achieve the larger effects necessary to substantially increase the cognitive and behavioral readiness of disadvantaged youth.

Second, our findings about the positive effects of some, but not all, parenting activities, are suggestive, but require further investigation. We need more detailed data to separate those parenting activities that have true effects on readiness from those that are merely correlated with other, unmeasured variables that may be causing the effects. In particular, it would be desirable to separate the effects of organized activities such as those measured on the ECLS-K, from parental oral language transmission which may exert more powerful effects on readiness (Durham et al., 2004; Farkas & Beron, 2004; Hart & Risley, 1995). Much work is now underway in the study of school readiness, as is evidenced by the other chapters in this volume. We have come a long way in our understanding, but we still have a long way to go if basic inequalities are to be reduced.

References

Bernstein, B. (1977). *Class, codes, and control*. London: Routledge and Kegan.

Beron, K., & Farkas, G. (2004). Oral language and reading success: A structural equation modeling approach. *Structural Equation Modeling, 11*, 110–131.

Bodovski, K., & Farkas, G. (2004). *Behavior problems and student engagement as determinants of kindergarten learning*. Paper presented at the Annual Meetings of the American Sociological Association, August, San Francisco, CA.

Bradley, R., Corwyn, R., McAdoo, H. P., and Coll, C. G. (2001). The home environments of children in the United States. Part II: Relations with behavioral development through age thirteen. *Child Development, 72*, 1868–1886.

Brooks-Gunn, J. (2003). Do you believe in magic? What we can expect from early childhood intervention programs. *Social Policy Report, 17*, 3–14.

Brooks-Gunn, J., & Markman, L. (2005). The contribution of parenting to ethnic and racial gaps in school readiness. *The Future of Children, 15*, 139–168.

Campbell, S. (1995). Behavior problems in preschool children: A review of recent research. *Journal of Child Psychology and Psychiatry, 36*, 113–149.

Currie, J. (2005). Health disparities and gaps in school readiness. *The Future of Children, 15*, 117–138.

Deater-Deckard, K., Dodge, K. A., & Sorbring, E. (2005). Cultural differences in the effects of physical punishment. In M. Rutter & M. Tienda (Eds.), *Ethnicity and causal mechanisms*. Cambridge, UK: Cambridge University Press.

Devaney, B. (1998). The special supplemental nutrition program for women, infants, and children. In J. Crane (Ed.), *Social programs that work* (pp. 184–200). New York: Russell Sage Foundation Press.

Downey, D., & Pribesh, S. (2004). When race matters: Student/teacher racial matching and teachers' evaluations of students' behavior. *Sociology of Education, 77*, 267–282.

Duncan, G., Brooks-Gunn, J. & Klebanov, P. (1994). Economic deprivation and early childhood development. *Child Development, 65*, 296–318.

Duncan, G., & Magnuson, K. (2005). Can family socioeconomic resources account for racial and ethnic test score gaps? *The Future of Children, 15*, 35–54.

Durham, R., et al. (2004). *Oral language skill: A mediating variable for the effect of social class background on elementary school performance*. Paper presented at the Annual Meetings of the American Sociological Association, Atlanta, GA.

Farkas, G. (2003). Cognitive skills and noncognitive traits and behaviors in stratification processes. *Annual Review of Sociology, 29*, 541–562.

Farkas, G. (Forthcoming). How educational inequality develops. To appear in D. Harris & A. Lin (Eds.), *The colors of poverty*. New York: Russell Sage Foundation Press.

Farkas, G., & Beron, K. (2004). The detailed age trajectory of oral vocabulary knowledge: Differences by class and race. *Social Science Research, 33*, 464–497.

Farrington, D. P. (1996). The explanation and prevention of youthful offending. In J. D. Hawkins (Ed.), *Delinquency and crime* (pp. 68–148). Cambridge: Cambridge University Press.

Fryer, R., & Levitt, S. (2004). Understanding the black-white test score gap in the first two years of school. *Review of Economics and Statistics, 86*, 447–464.

Hamre, B. R., & Pianta, R. (2001). Early teacher-child relationships and the trajectory of children's school outcomes through eighth grade. *Child Development, 72*, 625–688.

Hart, B. & Risley, T. (1995). *Meaningful differences in everyday experiences of young American children.* Baltimore: Paul Brookes.

Hart, B., & Risley, T. (1999). *The social world of children learning to talk.* Baltimore: Paul Brookes.

Heath, S. B. (1983). *Ways with words.* Cambridge: Cambridge University Press.

Hinshaw, S. (1992). Externalizing behavior problems and academic underachievement in childhood and adolescence: Causal relationship and underlying mechanisms. *Psychological Bulletin, 111*, 127–155.

Labov, W. (1972). *Language in the inner city: Studies in the Black English vernacular.* Philadelphia: University of Pennsylvania Press.

Lareau, A. (2003). *Unequal childhoods: Class, race, and family life.* Berkeley, CA: University of California Press.

Loeber, R. (1990). Development and risk factors of juvenile antisocial behavior and delinquency. *Clinical Psychology Review, 10*, 1–41.

Love, J. et al. (2001). *Building their futures: How early Head Start programs are enhancing the lives of infants and toddlers in low-income families.* Washington, DC: The Commissioner's Office of Research and Evaluation and the Head Start Bureau, Administration on Children, Youth, and Families.

Magnuson, K., & Waldfogel, J. (2005). Early childhood care and education: Effects on ethnic and racial gaps in school readiness. *The Future of Children, 15*, 169–196.

McLeod, J., & Kaiser, K. (2004). Childhood emotional and behavioral problems and educational attainment. *American Sociological Review, 69*, 636–658.

McLeod, J., & Nonnemaker, J. (2000). Poverty and child emotional and behavioral problems: Racial/ethnic differences in processes and effects. *Journal of Health and Social Behavior, 41*, 137–161.

McLoyd, V. (1998). Socioeconomic disadvantage and child development. *American Psychologist, 53*, 185–204.

McLoyd, V. (1990). The impact of economic hardship on black families and children: Psychological distress, parenting, and socioemotional development. *Child Development, 61*, 311–346.

McLoyd, V., & Smith, J. (2002). Physical discipline and behavior problems in African American, European American, and Hispanic children: Emotional support as a moderator. *Journal of Marriage and the Family, 64*, 40–53.

NICHD Early Childcare Research Network. (2003). Does amount of time spent in child care predict socioemotional adjustment during the transition to kindergarten? *Child Development, 74*, 976–1005.

Phillips, M., Brooks-Gunn, J., Duncan, G., Klebanov, P., & Crane, J. (1998). Family background, parenting practices, and the black-white test score gap. In C. Jencks & M. Phillips (Eds.), *The black-white test score gap* (pp. 103–148). Washington, DC: Brookings.

Raudenbush, S., & Bryk, A. (2002). *Hierarchical linear models: Applications and data analysis methods* (2nd ed.). Thousand Oaks, CA: Sage.

Reichman, N. (2005). Low birth weight and school readiness. *The Future of Children, 15*, 91–116.

Rimm-Kaufman, S., Pianta, R., & Cox, M. (2000). Teachers' judgments of problems in the transition to kindergarten. *Early Childhood Research Quarterly 15*, 147–166.

Riordan, C. (2002). *Male/female early achievement and development: Gender gaps among first time kindergarten children in the public schools.* Paper presented at the annual meeting of the American Educational Research Association, New Orleans, LA.

Tach, L., & Farkas, G. (Forthcoming). Learning-related behaviors, cognitive skills, and ability grouping when schooling begins. *Social Science Research.*

U.S. Department of Education, National Center for Education Statistics. (2000). *The kindergarten year.* NCES 2001-023R (K. Denton & L. M. Reaney). Washington, DC.

U.S. Department of Health and Human Services, Administration for Children and Families. (2005). *Head Start impact study: First year findings.* (M. Puma, S. Bell, R. Cook, C. Heid, & M. Lopez). Washington, DC.

Whitehurst, G., & Lonigan, C. (2002). Emergent literacy: Development from prereaders to readers. In S. Neuman & D. Dickinson (Eds.), *Handbook of early literacy research* (pp. 11–29). New York: The Guildford Press.

Whitehurst, G., & Massetti, G. (2004). How well does Head Start prepare children to learn to read? In E. Zigler & S. Styfco (Eds.), *The Head Start debates* (pp. 251–262). Baltimore, MD: Paul Brookes.

Yoshikawa, H. (1994). Prevention as cumulative protection: Effects of early family support and education on chronic delinquency and its risks. *Psychological Bulletin, 115*, 28–54.

Zigler, E., & Valentine, S. (1979). *Project Head Start: A legacy of the war on poverty.* New York: Macmillan.

Appendix 1.1
Measurement of ECLS-K Variables

Variable Name	Description
Low Reading	Child scored in the bottom 20% in reading in the fall of kindergarten
Low Math	Child scored in the bottom 20% in mathematics in the fall of kindergarten
Low General Knowledge	Child scored in the bottom 20% in general knowledge in the fall of kindergarten
Low Behavior	Child scored in the bottom 22% in teacher rating of classroom behavior (approaches to learning) in the fall of kindergarten
Low Reading and Behavior	Child scored in the bottom 20% in both reading and classroom behavior in the fall of kindergarten
Mom No HS	Child's mother did not graduate high school
Mom HS Grad	Child's mother received a high school diploma or the equivalent
Mom Some College	Child's mother attended some college, but did not receive a bachelor's degree
Mom College Grad	Child's mother received at least a bachelor's degree
Dad's Ed. Missing	Child's father's level of education was not reported
Dad No HS	Child's father did not graduate high school
Dad HS Grad	Child's father received a high school diploma or the equivalent
Dad Some College	Child's father attended some college, but did not receive a bachelor's degree
Dad College Grad	Child's father received at least a bachelor's degree
Family in Poverty	Child's household was below the poverty threshold in 1998
Family Income	Child's household income in 1998, in dollars
Mom Immigrant	Child's mother was born outside the United States
Non-English Home	The primary language in child's home is not English
White	Child's race/ethnicity is White, non-Hispanic
Black	Child's race/ethnicity is Black or African American, non-Hispanic
Hispanic	Child's race/ethnicity is Hispanic
Asian	Child's race/ethnicity is Asian
Other Ethnicity	Child's is of another or more than one race/ethnicity
Male	Child is male
Teen Mom	Child's mother first gave birth before the age of twenty
Two-Parent Family	Child lived with both biological parents in 1998
Single Mom	Child lived with biological mother only in 1998
Single Dad	Child lived with biological father only in 1998
Step Mom	Child lived with biological father and other mother (step-, adoptive, or foster) in 1998
Step Dad	Child lived with biological mother and other father (step-, adoptive, or foster) in 1998
Adopted	Child lived with two adoptive parents in 1998
Other Family Type	Child lived with other guardians in 1998
Number of Siblings	Total number of siblings with whom the child lived, including children of foster parent/guardian in 1998

Appendix 1.1 cont.

Variable Name	Description
Urban	Child lived in a central city 1998
Suburban	Child lived in an urban fringe area or large town in 1998
Rural	Child lived in a small town or rural area 1998
Northeast	Child lived in the Northeastern U.S. (CT, ME, MA, NH, RI, VT, NJ, NY, PA) in 1998
Midwest	Child lived in the Midwestern U.S. (IL, IN, MI, OH, WI, IA, KS, MN, MO, NE, ND, SD) in 1998
South	Child lived in the Southern U.S. (DE, DC, FL, GA, MD, NC, SC, VA, WV, AL, KY, MS, TN, AR, LA, OK, TX) in 1998
West	Child lived in the Western U.S. (AZ, CO, ID, MT, NV, NM, UT, WY, AK, CA, HA, OR, WA) in 1998
Birth Weight	Child's birth weight in pounds
Age at K Entry	Child's age at kindergarten entry in months
Number of Books	How many books child had in 1998
Has Home Computer	Child's family had a home computer in 1998
Arts & Crafts	Child took art lessons and/or craft lessons in 1998
Sports/Clubs	Number of following activities in which child took part in 1998: attended sporting events, participated in athletic events, participated in organized clubs
Performing Arts	Child participated in organized performances, and/or dance lessons, and/or music lessons, and/or drama lessons in 1998
Educational Trips	Number of following trips on which child went in 1998: museum, zoo, library, concert
Parental Involvement	Number of following activities in which child's parent participated in 1998: open house, PTA meeting, parent advisory group, fundraising, attend school event, volunteer at school
WIC During Pregnancy	Child's mother received WIC benefits during pregnancy
WIC During Infancy	Child received WIC benefits as an infant or child
AFDC/TANF	Child's family received AFDC/TANF in 1998
Food Stamps	Child's family received food stamps in 1998
Head Start	Child participated in the Head Start program

2

IN SEARCH OF MEANING: DISENTANGLING THE COMPLEX INFLUENCES ON CHILDREN'S SCHOOL READINESS

Michael L. López, Ph.D.
National Center for Latino Child & Family Research

Sandra Barrueco, Ph.D.
The Catholic University of America

Authors Farkas and Hibel, in their chapter, "Being unready for school: Factors affecting risk and resilience" (this volume), admirably take on an important and rather challenging topic—the examination of potential racial/ethnic disparities in children's school readiness. The resulting work raises a number of critically important conceptual, methodological, and statistical considerations for the field, especially with respect to navigating the complex interplay among sociodemographic characteristics, race/ethnicity, and culture.

Our comments regarding Farkas and Hibel's chapter are intended to serve as a point of departure for raising and discussing a number of considerations of relevance for the child development research community as a whole. The comments are organized into four broad clusters of related issues: (1) conceptual research design and sampling issues; (2) methods and measurement approaches; (3) data analytic strategies; and (4) interpretation of findings.

Conceptual Research Design and Sampling Issues

Two main conceptual research design and sampling issues are raised by the chapter: (a) How can researchers disentangle the relative influences of poverty versus racial, ethnic or cultural characteristics on children's school readiness, and (b) what approach should researchers use to examine the effects of federal poverty programs?

One of the most thought-provoking, conceptual questions raised in the chapter is the fundamental question about the primary influences on children's school readiness and the degree to which poverty and related sociodemographic characteristics may all but overshadow any actual racial, ethnic or cultural contributions. In other words, are the primary determinants of children's school readiness skills and abilities more a function of poverty and families' related sociodemographic characteristics (such as parental education), versus their racial, ethnic, and cultural background characteristics, or some combination of the different characteristics?

The literature documents the substantial, negative consequences of growing up in poverty on children's cognitive, academic and behavioral functioning, especially during the earliest years of life (e.g., Brooks-Gunn & Duncan, 1997; Duncan & Brooks-Gunn, 1997; Raver, 2004; Smith, Brooks-Gunn & Klebanov, 1997). Thus, when examining the unique influences of individual and family characteristics, such as race/ethnicity, parenting activities and resources, among other characteristics, it is critical to try to account for the substantial but distinct influence of the constellation of factors associated with poverty on children's developmental experiences and subsequent school readiness.

Another important consideration related to the powerful consequences of poverty is the degree of the disproportionate representation of different racial/ethnic subgroups across the full SES continuum, especially for those families living in poverty (and, as discussed later, those enrolled in federal poverty programs; Magnuson & Waldfogel, 2005). This discrepancy is illustrated in the following two statistics: (1) within the total population of children under the age of 5 years, white children compose 58% of the U.S. population, with Latinos composing 21.4%, or the second largest portion of the population of young children (U.S. Census Bureau, 2004a). In contrast, when looking at the population of children under the age of 5 years who are living in poverty in the U.S., the percentage of white children drops dramatically to 34%, whereas the percentage of Latinos rises to 33.9% and the percentage of non-Hispanic blacks also rises to 29.5% of the total population of young children (U.S. Census Bureau, 2004b) (see Figures 2.1 and 2.2).

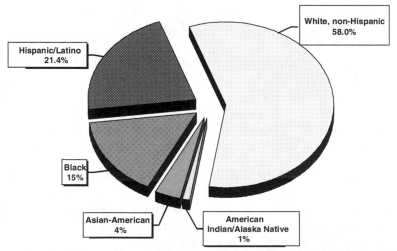

Source: Table 4: Annual estimates of the population by sex and age for the United States: April 1, 2000 to July 1, 2003. Population Division, U.S. Census Bureau.

Figure 2.1. National estimates of U.S. population by race/ethnicity—Children under 5 years—July 2003.

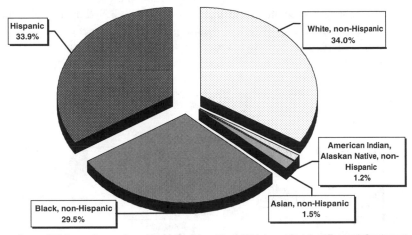

Source: Source: U.S. Census Bureau, Current Population Survey March 2004; Annual Social and Economic Supplement

Figure 2.2. National estimates of U.S. population by race/ethnicity–Children under 5 years in poverty—July 2003.

These striking differences clearly suggest a complicated interaction between race/ethnicity and poverty status, especially with respect to efforts to disentangle the unique contributions of each set of influences to children's school readiness. In response to such concerns, researchers have utilized a variety of approaches to try and account for the unique contributions of SES and related differences in children's school readiness, across different racial/ethnic subgroups (e.g., Coley, 2002, Duncan & Magnuson; 2005, Fryer & Levitt, 2005; NCES, 2004).

In the 2004 NCES report, *From kindergarten through third grade; Children's beginning school experience*s, a family risk index was created as a way to examine the distinct influence of one or more of these risk factors on children's school readiness. A composite variable was created using the following variables: single-parent household, below federal poverty level, primary home language not English and maternal education less than a high school diploma or the equivalent. This family risk variable had a possible range from 0 to 4, representing the number of risk factors present for each child. When using this family risk factor, the initial unadjusted achievement gap in the 3rd grade, across racial/ethnic subgroups, was substantially reduced or eliminated across the domains of reading, mathematics and science (NCES, 2004). Although the approach may be considered to be a fairly basic or statistically unsophisticated approach to accounting for major differences in the sociodemographic characteristics of different racial/ethnic subgroups, it nevertheless helps to emphasize the importance or value of taking such issues into consideration.

In a related effort, Duncan and Magnuson (2005) utilized the findings from another study (Fryer & Levitt, 2004) that examined the ECLS-K data to graphically demonstrate the degree to which accounting for SES differences dramatically reduced the achievement gaps in reading and mathematics at the end of first grade across racial/ethnic groups, as evidenced in Figure 2.3.

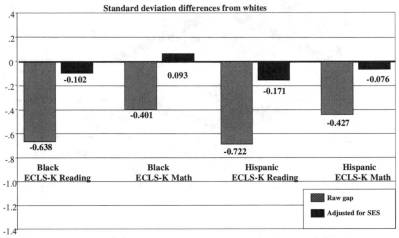

Source: Table adapted from Duncan & Magnuson (2005), Can family socioeconomic resources account for racial and ethnic test score gaps, Figures 3 & 4, p. 46.

Figure 2.3. Accounting for SES differences in test scores across racial/ethnic groups.

These various studies strongly support the argument that differences in socioeconomic characteristics account for a rather substantial proportion of the variance associated with observed differences in children's school readiness, across different racial/ethnic subgroups. Several of these researchers (Duncan & Magnuson, 2005; Phillips et al. 1998), as well as other researchers, have also asserted that many of the current approaches for measuring socioeconomic status variables may be too narrowly defined and do not capture a wide enough range of socioeconomic factors that include such things as the potential influences of neighborhoods, communities, and schools (e.g., Brooks-Gunn, Duncan & Aber, 1997; Lee & Loeb, 1995; Leventhal & Brooks-Gunn, 2000). Nevertheless, while additional refinements in the way in which socioeconomic characteristics are operationalized may prove fruitful, there also is evidence of a remaining difference that may represent very real differences due to other important factors, some unique to the specific racial, ethnic and cultural groups of interest. As some have argued (Brooks-Gunn & Markman, 2005; Phillips et al., 1998), a portion of these remaining differences may be related to the family background characteristics, parenting activities, and resources that are examined in the Farkas and Hibel chapter.

The second conceptual question raised by the Farkas and Hibel chapter is how to best examine program effects, particularly federal poverty programs that by definition are designed to target a very specific at-risk portion of the total population. Farkas and Hibel utilize the full, nationally representative ECLS-K sample to explore the possible mediating role of program participation in at-risk programs on children's school readiness across the country. However, only approximately 19% of the population of children in the ECLS-K sample live in poverty (Ritter, Moyi & Stewart, 2002) and thereby meet the eligibility requirements for some or all of the federal poverty programs, and roughly half of those actually receive services. It is both a conceptual *and* analytical challenge to suggest that participation in a program (even if 100% effective) by such a small proportion of students will result in a statistically significant increase in the whole population's school readiness. When examining the potential mediating role of federal poverty program participation on children's school readiness outcomes, it is likely best examined by using a more targeted sub-sample of children from lower income families, drawn from the larger ECLS-K sample. By doing so, one can better answer the primary question of interest, "does participation in a poverty-targeted program improve low-income children's outcomes", rather than a broad, unrealistic question, "does participation in a poverty-targeted program improve the outcomes of all children in the country"?

Methods & Measurement Approaches

In addition to the conceptual research design and sampling, or subsampling issues, a number of issues raised related to the methods and measures were used for the present study.

ECLS-K Data Set

The ECLS-K consists of a nationally representative sample of 22,782 children entering kindergarten in fall 1998. Given the nature of the ECLS-K sample, there are at least four distinct considerations or limitations in using such a sample to examine issues pertaining to children's school readiness prior to kindergarten:

1. A reliance on potentially biased retrospective parental data regarding such variables as Head Start or preschool enrollment, birth weight, among other earlier experiences or characteristics prior to school entry;
2. Limited access to data regarding children's actual skills and abilities in the year or years prior to kindergarten enrollment;
3. Issues associated with the low-income and poverty variables; and
4. The process of differentially screening out a substantial portion of the Latino children from Spanish-speaking homes for several of the key child assessment measures.

The potential bias in retrospective parental reporting of children's Head Start enrollment was carefully examined within the context of the ECLS-K study (NCES, 2001). In an early field test study there were clear indications that both parents and schools over reported actual Head Start participation (Taylor & Ingels, 1997). In response to these documented concerns, a Head Start Verification Study was built into the main ECLS-K study to address this issue. The Head Start Verification Study, which is described in the *Base Year Restricted-Use Head Start Data Files and Electronic Codebook* (NCES, 2001), essentially consisted of additional data collection activities that were undertaken to try and verify the accuracy of parent and school reports of Head Start participation. For the 3,520 children who were identified by either parent or school reports as having attended Head Start in the year prior to kindergarten, the additional verification efforts were able to confirm attendance only for approximately 53% of the children. Slightly over 22% of the children were verified not to have attended Head Start and for close to 25% attendance could not be confirmed, either due to the center not being located or due to the center not responding to the mailed verification materials.

The resulting ECLS-K data file contains several different Head Start participation variables, those that were derived directly from parent or school reports of Head Start attendance and an additional set of variables that are based on the different levels of verification. While the latter set of verified Head Start attendance variables are based on a convergence of several different sources of information, the resulting sample sizes associated with the different participation variables are limited to a range of anywhere from approximately 53% to 78% of the original sample of 3,520 children reported by parents or school as having attended Head Start. Thus, users of the data set must be cognizant of the strengths and weaknesses inherent in using any of the available Head Start attendance variables. It was not clear which Head Start variable was used in the present study.

The second concern about the ECLS-K data set relates to limited ability to accurately capture information on children's actual experiences, skills, and abilities in the year or years prior to kindergarten enrollment. While the reliance on some retrospective data may be unavoidable, it is important to recognize some of the potential limitations and sources of bias. The lack of available direct assessment data on children's actual school readiness skills and abilities prior to kindergarten and or information on the quality of their preschool experiences substantially limits the ability to draw inferences about the potential impact of any preschool experiences on children's school readiness at kindergarten entry. For example, there may be some systematic differences in children's cognitive and/or behavioral characteristics, above and beyond the influences of sociodemographic characteristics, which may differentially motivate certain parents to seek enrollment in particular types of preschool or early care programs. Without the availability of direct assessment data at the time of preschool entry or program quality data, it is impossible to estimate or conclude anything about the effects of preschool experiences on children's school readiness.

The third consideration raised by the use of the ECLS-K data set relates to several issues associated with the low-income and poverty variables utilized to examine Head Start effects. Ideally, a group of eligible children who did not participate in Head Start would be identified using the same standard of eligibility used to determine Head Start enrollment. However, the ECLS-K data set does not allow such a method for several reasons. First, the general guideline for Head Start eligibility is that family income should be at or below the 100% federal poverty threshold at the time of initial Head Start enrollment. However, in the ECLS-K study, household income information was not collected until the kindergarten year following Head Start attendance. Some families who had annual incomes below the federal poverty threshold during the previous year might be expected to have income above the threshold in the following year, just as other families might drop below the threshold (Brooks-Gunn & Duncan, 1997; Corcoran & Chaudry, 1997). Second, the household income variable used in the ECLS-K is different from the family income definition used to determine Head Start eligibility. The Head Start eligibility criterion includes only income from family members, whereas the ECLS-K definition includes income contributed by all household residents, including non-family members. Third, the Head Start eligibility guidelines allow up to 10% of the participants to be children from families with incomes above the federal poverty threshold. This small percentage of non-low-income families raises the average income level of the Head Start group, and makes it more difficult to use income as the sole determinant of similarity to the Head Start population.

Given the combination of concerns about the accuracy of parent and school reports of Head Start participation and the limitations in relying on retrospective data on income eligibility, it would not be surprising to find clear indications of potential selection biases when attempting to compare one or more of the possible Head Start participant groups and non-participants retrospectively from the ECLS-K sample. In other words, any of the groups of retrospectively reported Head Start participants when compared to low-income, non-participants are likely to be non-comparable on a number of important demographic characteristics of interest. As such, users of the ECLS-K data set must take such concerns into consideration when attempting to make any causal inferences based upon parent's and school's reports of children's experiences prior to kindergarten.

As an alternative, rather than trying to utilize a single low-income, non-Head Start group for making comparisons, it may be worth considering the use of several other income-to-needs ratio cutoffs. Besides the more stringent 100% federal poverty threshold, two other commonly used low-income thresholds may be useful. The 130% of the federal poverty level threshold is used as a national eligibility guideline for many programs, such as the USDA free lunch program, Food Stamps, and some parts of Medicaid.[1] The third option is to use a low-income level that

---

[1] For Medicaid eligibility guidelines, 130% and 133% of the poverty threshold both have been frequently used.

represents 185% of the federal poverty threshold and below, as this is the level used as the national eligibility guideline for a number of other federal poverty programs, such as the USDA reduced price lunch program and Women, Infants, and Children (WIC) program. The use of one or more of these low-income thresholds can help to alleviate some of the concerns about potential changes in income over time and the differences between the Head Start and ECLS-K definitions of family income. The broader low-income thresholds also would allow for a more complete examination of the influences of poverty on the school readiness of children of the "working poor", or those low-income families who may not be eligible for one or more of the federal poverty support programs.

The fourth area to consider when examining the ECLS-K data relates to the process used to differentially screen out a substantial portion of the Latino children from Spanish-speaking homes from receiving the administration of several of the key child assessment measures. As outlined in the *ECLS-K base year public-use Head Start data files and electronic codebook* (NCES, 2001), children from non-English-speaking homes were initially screened using a Spanish Oral Language Development Scale (OLDS) that was developed from three subtests of the pre-LAS 2000 (Duncan & DeAvila, 1998). The non-English-speaking children had to score above the empirically derived threshold score on the OLDS, indicating a minimal level of English oral proficiency, in order to be assessed with the English reading, general knowledge and mathematics direct assessments. However, those Spanish-speaking children scoring below the cutoff on the OLDS did receive versions of the mathematics and psychomotor direct assessments that had been translated into Spanish.

While this procedure ensured that results on assessments reflected children's abilities in these areas rather than their English proficiency, it is important to note the differential impact that this screening process had on the composition of the final sample, especially the sample of Latino children. Overall, of the 15 % of the total ECLS-K sample that was screened with the OLDS, about half of these children (7% of the total sample) did not receive the full administration of the direct child assessment battery (NCES, 2000). However, 80% of these children screened out of the full administration were Latino, representing almost a 30% reduction in the size of the Latino sample amongst the students who received the full battery of direct child assessments in the fall of kindergarten. Thus, users of the ECLS-K data set have to be cautious about the implications of such a substantial and differential reduction in the size of the sample of Latino children, especially when attempting to examine questions exploring potential racial/ethnic disparities in school readiness, as opposed to research questions which utilize the more complete set of parentally reported data and/or the mathematics assessment data.

Beyond the above-noted limitations inherent to the ECLS-K data set, there also were questions regarding the use of several of the ECLS-K measures. For example, the reliance primarily on fall kindergarten entry data limits the current examination to cross-sectional associations and less of a longitudinal examination of potential differences in the growth trajectories of children's school readiness skills and abilities, across the different racial/ethnic subgroups.

Another measurement issue raised in the chapter is related to the likely strong association between self-reported parental involvement and children's attendance of pre-kindergarten. Farkas and Hibel examine a variety of parental engagement variables, as well as the relationship between parent's report of their engagement with child academic achievement scores and behavioral ratings. The strong influence of parental engagement in developmental processes has been well established in the educational and psychological fields (e.g., Brody, Stoneman, & Flor, 1995; Grolnick & Slowiaczek, 1994; Pianta, Steinberg, & Rollins, 1995; Reynolds & Bezruczko, 1993) and it is an important factor to include in studies such as the present one, as Farkas and Hibel have done. Specifically, they focused on questions asked of parents regarding participation over the previous year in the following types of activities: arts and crafts, performing arts, sports/clubs, educational trips, and school involvement. In terms of predictors, they found that education, income, child gender, and dominant language consistently related to all of the parent engagement variables, while ethnicity related most consistently to sports/clubs and school activities. In terms of predicting child outcomes on academic measures and teacher ratings, school involvement was robust at the p<.001 level within this large sample. The authors also suggest that, "neither arts and crafts activities nor educational trips are found to have significant effects on readiness" (p. 24).

However, several limitations to the present study preclude it from being utilized to draw inferences about parental effects on kindergarteners' scholastic readiness. First, as the authors note in the last paragraph of their chapter, the relationships indicated by the parenting activities may actually reflect the influence of other unmeasured variables. In addition to the linguistic effect suggested by Farkas and Hibel, an important variable surprisingly missing from a study about school readiness was preschool or early childhood education (ECE) enrollment. Yet, ECE attendance is likely strongly related to, as well as confounded with, a number of the activities examined. For example, parents of kindergartners who had attended ECE likely had a greater opportunity to engage in the school-based activities comprising the parental involvement variable (e.g., attending open houses, PTA meetings, attending school events). Those parents whose children had not attended ECE (and/or who did not have older children) are likely to have scored lower on this scale measuring school involvement over the previous year since their child had not been in school. Further, ECE attendance has generally been linked with positive academic achievement scores (e.g., Barnett, 1995; Burchinal, 1999; Currie, 2001; Karoly et al., 1998). Without the inclusion of ECE attendance as a variable, it is difficult to surmise whether the positive relationship between the parental involvement variable and readiness outcome variables is due to parents' participation in school activities, children's attendance of an early childhood program, or a combination thereof. Along a similar vein, parents of ethnic minorities were found to engage less in school activities in the regression presented in Farkas and Hibel's Table 1.3. Since ethnic minorities are less likely to attend ECE than the white children (Magnuson & Waldfogel, 2005), it is possible that the lower parental report of engagement in school activities prior to kindergarten simply reflects lower levels of ECE participation.

The analytical approach undertaken also needs consideration when interpreting the results of the parenting variables. In attempting to examine the unique effects provided by each of the parenting activities, these variables were entered in the models concurrently, as reflected in Table 1.4. However, it is possible that the parenting variables were highly correlated with one another, as many of them usually are. The extent to which they are is unknown at this juncture since a correlation matrix is not presented in Farkas and Hilbel's chapter. In the event that the parent activity variables are highly correlated as suspected, it raises the possibility of multicollinearity. If a high degree of overlap exists between the parental activity variables and they are each entered into a regression equation, only the variable(s) with the strongest correlation with readiness will likely remain significant at the appropriate p-value for this sample size (here, parental school involvement). However, this result suggests neither (1) the non-significant variables (such as arts and crafts or educational trips) are not related to readiness, nor (2) the significant variables are the most influential types of parental activities that influence readiness. This is due to the fact that many factors affect the strength of correlations. These not only include the underlying "true" strength of the relationship, but prevalence rates, measurement error, and other unexamined confounds as well. For example, arts and craft activities had the lowest prevalence rate in the sample (Mean= 14%). At such a low prevalence, it has little likelihood to relate strongly to the nationwide mean and variation of readiness scores. It comes to no surprise that it was not found to be "uniquely" significant in the results (we discussed a similar perspective in the case of federal poverty programs). However, this does not suggest that engaging in arts and crafts may not play a significantly contributing factor to children's readiness if experienced by a greater percentage; it simply states that it did not uniquely affect the students in this national sample, given the prevalence, strength and uniqueness of relationship, reliability and validity of measurement, among other considerations.

Multicollinearity is potentially a difficulty for a number of other sets of variables in the models as well, such as education, income and poverty, immigrant and non-English speaking home. If a high correlation is found among conceptually related variables, then one could consider creating a latent variable, or a composite variable that effectively combines the strengths of each individual variable for examining each construct.

Data Analyses

In addition to the abovementioned suggestion to present a set of correlation matrices, it also would be beneficial for the readers of the Farkas-Hibel chapter to be able to examine any variations in sample size that may occur between analyses. One question that remains and that is critical for interpretation of the generalizability and robustness of the findings is whether the analyses were conducted only on participants with complete data sets or whether those with some missing data were excluded.

A final analytic consideration is the selection and composition of the variables themselves. For example, it is unfortunate that variables suggested as protective factors were not included in the analyses, including being white, having a college degree, being married, being from the North, etc. Doing so would provide a context for examining the relative risk of selected demographic variables. At present, the extent to which being of white descent is related to engaging in government poverty programs or low readiness on the measures is unknown. Given the significant representation of the white population in some poverty programs (e.g., USDA Food and Nutrition Service, 2003), it is certainly plausible that identifying as white significantly predicts some at-risk outcomes. We recommend that this and other hypothesized protective factors be included in future analyses in order to directly test the proposed protective and risk variables.

We wonder whether these variables were inadvertently excluded during the creation of the dichotomous variables. Based on Appendix 1.1, it appears that a case is scored a "1" on the black race variable, for example, if a "child's race/ethnicity is black, non-Hispanic". This suggests that they receive a "0" if they are not black. Thus, any analyses including black as a variable do not compare outcomes of blacks against those of whites; they compare blacks against the combination of all other ethnic groups. As such, none of the analyses directly compare ethnic minorities groups with the majority, white population, though this appeared to be the intent or interpretation of the authors at times.

A similar difficulty arises for the education variables, which may have even more detrimental effects for the interpretation of results. The effects for mothers who graduated from high school were compared to all other mothers, combining those who did not graduate from high school with those who had college diplomas. This appears to dilute the clarity with which we can examine educational effects. This weakness, combined with the multicollinearity difficulties that often arise when entering many related educational variables in an analysis, will likely need to be addressed in future analyses, possibly by creating a continuous educational variable.

Interpretation of the Findings

The final set of comments related to Farkas and Hibel is focused on the interpretation of the study findings.

In their chapter, the authors use teacher reports of behavioral adjustment from ECLS-K, but later compare the findings from these measures to the recent Head Start Impact Study findings based on parent's reports of children's behavior. Some caution should be used in making such comparisons between behavioral ratings from different types of informants, especially given the documented levels of disagreement in the literature between parent and teacher's reports of behavioral problems (Offord et al., 1996; Verhulst & Akkerhuis, 1989; Wolraich et al. 2004). As such, it may be useful to examine the set of more comparable findings from the Head Start Family and Child Experiences Survey (FACES).

Based upon the most recent findings from the FACES study, children in Head Start demonstrated both an increase in positive social skills and a reduction in hyperactive behavior from fall to spring, as reported by their teachers (ACF, 2003). Furthermore, by far the largest decreases in teacher-reported behaviors (shy, aggressive and hyperactive behaviors) occurred for those children who started off in the top quartile of negative behaviors at the time of entry into Head Start. Finally, higher teacher reported positive classroom behavior and lower problem behaviors during the Head Start year were associated with better performance on cognitive assessments at the end of the kindergarten year. In contrast to the interpretation suggested by Farkas and Hibel, these findings from the FACES study, along with the preliminary findings from the Head Start Impact Study, do suggest that Head Start is having a somewhat positive impact on improving children's positive social skills and reducing behavioral problems for the low-income children served by the program, which also appear related to subsequent improvements in their cognitive performance at the end of kindergarten.

The second concern about the context in which to interpret the current study findings has to do with the authors' interpretation of the magnitude of the preliminary findings from the Head Start Impact Study (ACF, 2005). It is important to note that these initial findings represent the overall, average impacts of Head Start and have not yet taken into account important variations in program quality, staff qualifications or program intensity (e.g., part-day vs. full-day), all factors that have been shown to further relate to differences in children's outcomes (e.g., Arnett, 1989; Elicker & Mathur, 1997; Howes, Phillips, & Whitebook, 1992; Howes, 1997; NICHD Early Child Care Research Network & Duncan, 2001; Vandell & Wolfe, 2000; Whitebook, Howes, & Phillips, 1989).

Furthermore, the Head Start Impact Study was designed to answer the question; does Head Start have a positive impact on the low-income children served? However, this question is quite different from the one that Farkas and Hibel (2005) seem most interested in examining: Can Head Start (or any similar intervention program) overcome the negative consequences of growing up in poverty? These are different questions and therefore require somewhat different strategies to answer each one, which then raises the question regarding whether the current study findings can or should be interpreted within the context of the Head Start Impact Study findings.

Regardless of whether or not the Head Start Impact Study findings provide a useful context for interpreting the current study findings, there also was a concern about how the Head Start Impact Study findings were portrayed. There certainly are differences in opinion about how to best interpret the relevance and pattern of small to moderate positive effects from early intervention studies (Aos et al., 2004; Glass, McGaw & Smith, 1981; McCartney & Rosenthal, 2000, Slavin, 1990; Wolf, 1986), such as those found across the cognitive, social-emotional, and health domains, as well as on parenting practices, favoring the children enrolled in Head Start. Farkas and Hibel refer to these findings as disappointing and suggest that the program has failed to show positive effects on children's school readiness. However, other researchers have tried to examine the Head Start Impact Study findings within the context of similar early childhood intervention studies. The Society for Research in Child Development (2005) presented this perspective in their detailed summary of the Head Start Impact Study findings:

> The positive effects of Head Start on children are comparable to or larger than those of other large-scale social programs. The effects of 9 months of Head Start on children's pre-reading and pre-writing skills are comparable to or larger than the effects of child care quality, welfare reform, wage-supplement programs, or reductions in classroom size on similar outcomes.[2] In addition, unlike these other social programs, Head Start improved children's health.[3] It is particularly impressive that Head

---

[2] "The National Head Start Impact Study results show that Head Start has small to moderate positive impacts on pre-reading, pre-writing for both 3- and 4-year-olds, at the end of the Head Start year. Positive effect sizes found to be statistically significant ranged from .10 to .24 for standardized assessments. In addition, Head Start had small positive impacts on vocabulary skills for 3-year-olds (effect sizes in the .10 to .12 range). *Child care quality:* In the most comprehensive national study of child care quality conducted to date, the NICHD Study of Early Child Care and Youth Development, researchers estimated that a 1-standard deviation increase in child care quality, sustained across 24 to 54 months of age, was associated with a small increase in the Bayley Mental Development Index (effect size .04 to .08) (NICHD Early Child Care Research Network & Duncan, 2003). *Welfare reform.* In a non-experimental analysis conducted in three U.S. cities following passage of the federal welfare reform legislation in 1996, Chase-Lansdale and colleagues found no evidence of effects of welfare reform on the cognitive or socio-emotional development of preschoolers (Chase-Lansdale, Moffitt, Lohman, Cherlin & Coley, et al., 2003). *Wage-supplement programs:* A recent set of experiments examined whether programs that provided incentives for low-income parents to work by providing wage supplements improved their children's school achievement. These programs reduced family poverty levels and increased income by between $1,500 and $2,000 a year, at follow-ups conducted 3 to 4 years after random assignment. They also increased the school achievement of young children in the first years of elementary school, with effect sizes ranging between .07 and .11 (Morris, Duncan, & Clark-Kauffman, in press). The Tennessee Study of Class Size randomly assigned kindergarteners to reductions in classroom size of about 35%, or a control condition of regular class size. After one year, the group assigned to smaller classes scored higher on two standardized reading tests (effect sizes of .21 and .23; Mosteller, 1995)" (SRCD, 2005).

[3] "Head Start's positive effect on overall health, for example, was six times larger than the average effect of schooling on health found across hundreds of studies in a recent meta-analytic review (Grott & van den Brink, 2005)" (SRCD, 2005).

Start produced these effects when many of the children in the study who were randomly assigned to the no-Head-Start group nevertheless were enrolled in child care centers.[4]

As highlighted by the SRCD (2005) summary, there is some reason to believe that the preliminary Head Start Impact Study findings may in fact be consistent with the findings from other comparable, early intervention research studies in the literature. SRCD (2005) identified additional key positive features from the overall Head Start Impact Study examining the effect of nine months of Head Start participation. For example, it noted that positive effects were evidenced in parenting practices and across children's cognitive, social, emotional, and development. Upon examining results indicating that Head Start had narrowed the gap by 45% in pre-reading skills between children in poverty and U.S. children as a whole, SRCD (2005) stated "few 9-month educational interventions have narrowed the gap between low-income children and U.S. children as a whole to this degree."[5] Reviews such as those provided by SRCD (2005) provide a comparative framework for examining program effects.

Summary

In conclusion, Farkas and Hibel should be commended for undertaking the ambitious challenge of exploring some of the factors associated with children being most at-risk for school failure. This certainly is an extremely important area for the field. However, as illustrated in this chapter, a number of questions, concerns, and considerations have been raised about the particular data set utilized to address these questions, as well as several of the methodological and data analytic strategies employed by the authors. It is our hope that these comments will help to stimulate the kind of collegial deliberations that may lead to a greater understanding of the many complexities of such undertakings, more advanced strategies for addressing these questions, as well the eventual advancement of the knowledge base to ensure children's school readiness.

---

[4] "Some (over 15%) even received Head Start. In addition, more than 10% of the group assigned to the Head Start group did not go on to utilize Head Start during the period of the current study. The report, using an appropriately conservative statistical approach (the "intent to treat" approach to experimental impact analysis), kept families in both of these groups in the analysis sample, analyzed within the groups to which they were randomly assigned. Because of these "crossovers," the reported positive effects may be underestimates" (SRCD, 2005).

[5] "See Johnson, Johnson, & Stanne (2000); Slavin & Madden (2001)".

References

Administration for Children and Families (ACF). (2005). *Head Start impact study: First year findings: Final report.* Washington, DC: Author.

Administration for Children, Youth and Families (ACF). (2003). *Head Start FACES 2000: A whole-child perspective on program performance, fourth progress report.* Washington, DC: Author.

Administration for Children and Families (ACF). (2001). *National evaluation of family support programs: Final report.* Washington, DC: Author.

Aos, S., Lieb, R., Mayfield, J., Miller, M., & Pennucci, A. (2004). *Benefits and costs of prevention and early intervention programs for youth.* Document #: 04-07-3901. CITY, STATE: Washington State Institute for Public Policy.

Arnett, J. (1989). Caregivers in day care centers: Does training matter? *Journal of Applied Developmental Psychology, 10,* 541–522.

Barnett, W. S. (1995). Long-term effects of early childhood programs on cognitive and school outcomes. *The Future of Children, 5,* 25–50.

Brody, G. H., Stoneman, Z., & Flor, D. (1995). Linking family processes and academic competence among rural African American youths. *Journal of Marriage and the Family, 47,* 567–579.

Brooks-Gunn, J., & Duncan, G.J. (1997). The effects of poverty on children. *The Future of Children, 7,* 55–71.

Brooks-Gunn, J., & Markman, L.B. (2005). The contributions of parenting to ethnic and racial gaps in school readiness. *The Future of Children, 15,* 139–168.

Brooks-Gunn, J., Duncan, G. J., & Aber, J. L. (Eds.). (1997). *Neighborhood poverty: Volume 1: Context and consequences for children.* New York: Russell Sage Foundation.

Burchinal, M. R. (1999). Child care experiences and developmental outcomes. *The Annals of the American Academy of Political and Social Science: The Silent Crisis in U.S. Child Care, 563,* 73–97.

Chase-Lansdale, P. L., Moffitt, R. A., Lohman, B. J., Cherlin, A. J., Coley, R. L., Pittman, L. D., et al. (2003). Mothers' transitions from welfare to work and the well-being of preschoolers and adolescents. *Science, 299*(5612), 1548.

Coley, R. J. (2002). *An uneven start: Indicators of inequality in school readiness.* Princeton, NJ: Educational Testing Service Policy Center. Available at: www.ets.org/research/dload/Unevenstart.pdf

Corcoran, M.E. & Chaudry, A. (1997). The dynamics of childhood poverty. *The Future of Children, 7,* 40–54.

Currie, J. (2001). Early childhood intervention programs: What do we know? *Journal of Economic Perspectives, 15,* 213–238.

Duncan, G. J. & Brooks-Gunn, J. (Eds.) (1997). *Consequences of growing up poor.* New York: Russell Sage.

Duncan, G. J. & Magnuson, K. (2005). Can family socioeconomic resources account for racial and ethnic test score gaps? *The Future of Children, 15,* 35–54.

Duncan, S. E., & DeAvila, E. A. 1998. *PreLAS 2000, A test of language development for four-, five-, and six-year olds, form C.* Monterey, CA: CTB-McGraw-Hill.

Elicker, J., & Mathur, S. (1997). What do they do all day? Comprehensive evaluation of a full school day kindergarten, *Early Childhood Research Quarterly, 12,* 459–480.

Fryer, R. & Levitt, S. D. (2004). Understanding the black-white test score gap in the first two years of school. *Review of Economics and Statistics*, *86*, 447–464.

Glass, G. V., McGaw, B., & Smith, M. L. (1981). *Meta-analysis in social research.* London: Sage.

Grolnick, W. S., & Slowiaczek, M. L. (1994). Parents' involvement in children's schooling: A multidimensional conceptualization and motivational model. *Child Development, 65,* 237–252.

Grott, W., & van den Brink, H. M. (2005). The health effects of education: A survey and meta-analysis. Working paper, University of Amsterdam: http://www1.fee.uva.nl/scholar/wp/wp50-04.pdf.

Howes, C. (1997) Children's experiences in center-based child care as a function of teacher background and adult-child ratio. *Merrill-Palmer Quarterly,* 43, 404–425.

Howes, C., Phillips, D., & Whitebook, M. (1992). Thresholds of quality: Implications for the social development of children in center-based child care. *Child Development, 63*, 449–460.

Johnson, D. W., Johnson, R. T., & Stanne, M. B. (2000). Cooperative learning methods: A meta-analysis. Retrieved July 2000 from the World Wide Web: http://www.clcrc.com/pages/cl-methods.html.

Karoly, L. A., Greenwood, P. W., Everingham, S. S., Hoube, J., Kilburn, M. R., Rydell, C. P., Sanders, M. & Chiesa, J. (1998). *Investing in our children: What we do and don't know about the costs and benefits of early childhood interventions.* Santa Monica, CA: RAND.

Lee, V., & Loeb, S. (1995). Where do Head Start attendees end up? One reason why preschool effects fade out. *Educational Evaluation and Policy Analysis*, *17*, 62–82.

Levanthal, T., & Brooks-Gunn, J. (2000). The neighborhoods they live in: The effects of neighborhood residence on child and adolescent outcomes. *Psychological Bulletin, 126*, 309–337.

Magnuson, K. A., & Waldfogel, J. (2005). Early childhood care and education: Effects on ethnic and racial gaps in school readiness. *The Future of Children, 15*, 169–196.

McCartney, K., & Rosenthal, R. (2000). Effect size, practical importance, and social policy for children. *Child Development, 71*, 173–180.

Morris, P., Duncan, G. J., & Clark-Kauffman, E. (2003). Child well-being in an era of welfare reform: The sensitivity of transitions in development to policy change. Unpublished manuscript, MDRC.

Mosteller, F. (1995). The Tennessee study of class size in the early school grades. *The Future of Children, 5*(2), 113–127.

National Center for Education Statistics. (NCES) (2000). *America's kindergartners* (NCES 2000-070). Washington, DC: National Center for Education Statistics.

National Center for Education Statistics. (NCES) (2000). *Early childhood longitudinal study, kindergarten class of 1998-99: Base year restricted-use Head Start data files and electronic codebook* (NCES 2000-097). Washington, DC: National Center for Education Statistics.

National Center for Education Statistics. (NCES) (2001). *Early childhood longitudinal study, kindergarten class of 1998-99: Base year public-use Head Start data files and electronic codebook* (NCES 2001–025). Washington, DC: National Center for Education Statistics.

National Center for Education Statistics. (NCES) (2004). *From kindergarten through third grade; children's beginning school experiences* (NCES 2004-007). Washington, DC: National Center for Education Statistics.

NICHD Early Child Care Research Network, & Duncan, G. (2003). Modeling the impacts of child care quality on children's preschool cognitive development. *Child Development*, *74(5)*, 1454–1475.

Offord, D. R., Boyle, M. H., Racine, Y., Szatmari, P., Fleming, J. E., Sanford, M. & Lipman, E. L. (1996). Integrating assessment data from multiple informants. *Journal of the American Academy of Child Adolescent Psychiatry*, *35*, 1078–1085.

Phillips, M., Brooks-Gunn, J., Duncan, G. J., Klebanov, P., & Crane, J. (1998). Family background, parenting practices, and the black-white test score gap. In C. Jencks & M. Phillips (Eds.), *The black-white test score gap* (pp. 103–145). Washington, DC: Brookings Institution.

Pianta, R. C., Steinberg, M. S., & Rollins, K. B. (1995). Teacher-child relationships and deflections in children's classroom adjustment. *Development and Psychopathology*, *7*, 295–312.

Raver, C. C., (2004). Placing emotional self-regulation in sociocultural and socioeconomic contexts. *Child Development*, *75*, 346–353.

Reynolds, A. J., & Bezruczko, N. (1993). School adjustment of children at risk through fourth grade. *Merrill-Palmer Quarterly*, *39*, 457–480.

Ritter, G., Moyi, P., & Stewart, T. (2002). *The impact of day care on school readiness: New information from Early Childhood Longitudinal Study (ECLS-K)*. Paper presented at the Annual Meeting of the Association of Educational Research (AERA). New Orleans, LA.

Slavin, R. E. (1990). *Cooperative learning: Theory, research, and practice*. Englewood Cliffs, NJ: Prentice Hall.

Slavin, R. E., & Madden, N. A. (2001). *Success for All: Research and Reform in Elementary Education*: Lawrence Erlbaum Assoc Inc.

Smith, J., Brooks-Gunn, J., & Klebanov, P. (1997). The consequences of living in poverty on young children's cognitive development. In G. J. Duncan & J. Brooks-Gunn (Eds.), *Consequences of growing up poor* (pp. 132–189). New York: Russell Sage.

Society for Research in Child Development. (2005). *Placing the first-year findings of the national Head Start impact study in context*. Washington, DC: Author. Available at: http://www.srcd.org/documents/policy/Impactstudy.pdf.

Taylor, J., & Ingels, S. J. (1997). *Early childhood longitudinal study – Head Start analysis report*. Chicago, IL: NORC.

U.S. Census Bureau. (March 2004a). Annual estimates of the population by sex, age and ethnicity for the United States; April 1, 2000 to July 1, 2003. Tables NC-EST2003-04-3, 5, 7, 12 & 13.

U.S. Census Bureau. (March 2004b). *Current Population Survey, annual social and economic supplement, detailed poverty tables*. Available at: http://pubdb3.census.gov/macro/032005/pov/toc.htm

USDA Food and Nutrition Service. (2003). *WIC program racial enrollment-April 2002*. Washington, DC: Author. Available at: http://www.fns.usda.gov/wic/racial-ethnicdata/2002piechart.htm

Vandell, D. L., & Wolfe, B. (2000). Child care quality: Does it matter and does it need to be improved? In K. Bogenschneider, B. Friese, K. Balling, & J. Mills (Eds.), *Early childhood care and education: What are states doing?* (pp. 1–11). Wisconsin Family Impact Seminar Briefing Report No. 17. Madison, WI: University of Wisconsin Center for Excellence in Family Studies.

Verhulst, F. C., & Akkerhuis, G. W. (1989). Agreement between parents' and teachers' ratings of behavioral/emotional problems of children aged 4–12. *Journal of Child Psychology and Psychiatry, 30*, 123–136.

Whitebook, M., Howes, C., & Phillips, D. (1989). *Who cares? Child care teachers and the quality of care in America-Final report of the National Child Care Staffing Study.* Oakland, CA: Child Care Employee Project.

Wolf, F. M. (1986). *Meta-analysis: Quantitative methods for research synthesis.* Newbury Park, CA: Sage.

Wolraich, M. L., Lambert, E. W., Bickman, L., Simmons, T., Doffing, M. A., & Worley, K. A. (2004). Assessing the impact of parent and teacher agreement on diagnosing ADHD. *Journal of Developmental and Behavioral Pediatrics, 25*, 41–47.

3
EXPLAINING THE GAP IN SCHOOL READINESS

Jane D. McLeod
Indiana University

The question of how and why early personal and social disadvantages shape the life course is a central defining concern of sociology. It is now evident, from research in many different substantive areas, that processes of stratification begin early, cross major life transitions, and involve a complex combination of personal and social attributes that work in concert to improve the life chances of some while diminishing those of others. Even those characteristics that we see as most personal and individual, such as personality, cognitive abilities, and behavioral predispositions, are shaped by our positions in important social hierarchies, and shape our future achievements in turn.

School readiness plays an important role in maintaining the existing stratification order. As many chapters in this volume attest, children who are not "ready" for school cognitively and behaviorally fare poorly in school settings. Farkas and Hibel take on the important task of tracing variations in school readiness back to their origins in social hierarchies, and estimating the contributions of family-related processes to explain those variations. To do so, they follow an approach that is consistent with the social structure and personality paradigm, one of several major theoretical traditions within sociological social psychology (Delamater, 2004). I should emphasize that the authors do not claim this approach, so I am imposing a framework that they may not accept but serves as a useful organizing device nevertheless.

The Social Structure and Personality Framework

The social structure and personality (SSP) paradigm is concerned with the relationship between macro-social systems or processes and individual feelings, attitudes, behaviors, and well-being. The SSP perspective conceives of the social world as a set of embedded circles, with the individual at the core surrounded by progressively larger and more complex social groupings, including dyads, small groups, communities, organizations and institutions, and the larger social system. In much the same way that one can peel away the layers of an onion to reveal the inner core, SSP researchers attempt to trace the processes through which components of the social system influence individuals and through which individuals affect social systems (House, 1981; McLeod & Lively, 2004) (Figure 3.1).

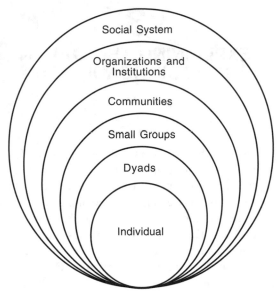

Figure 3.1. The social structure and personality framework.

SSP researchers distinguish their approach to macro-micro relations from other possible approaches by their adherence to three methodological and theoretical principles, first labeled and defined by House in 1981. These principles are the components, proximity, and psychological principles.

The Components Principle

This principle stipulates that researchers identify the specific components of the social system that are relevant to understanding the individual outcome of interest. Doing so requires a careful description of the social system as well as an adjudication of which components are most likely to affect proximal social environments and individual responses. In some cases, researchers identify one or more components a priori based on theoretical considerations; in others, they use the results of their analyses to determine which components are most important. In either case, they are oriented towards the most distal, exogenous variables that drive the causal processes of interest.

The Proximity Principle

This principle asserts that the effects of macro-social structures and processes are transmitted through contexts that impinge more directly on the individual—the formal organizations, small groups, and dyads in which macro-conditions derive material and symbolic reality. These contexts can be defined by domains of activity (e.g., work, family), by geographic location (e.g., neighborhoods), or by the structure of interpersonal relations as defined by social roles or social networks.

The Psychological Principle

The final principle directs our attention to the psychological mechanisms through which proximal structures and processes come to have relevance for individual outcomes. As an ideal, not always attained in practice, it demands a thorough understanding of individual psychology so as to permit the identification of specific mechanisms through which proximal experiences have their effects.

In sum, the SSP framework urges us to think carefully about relations across macro-, meso-, and micro-levels of social life. Although SSP studies rarely examine the linkages between every level with equal care, they are distinguished by their simultaneous consideration of multiple hierarchically organized features of the social environment (and I might add, therefore supported by recent developments in multilevel modeling; e.g., Bryk & Raudenbush, 1992).

Applying the Framework to Farkas and Hibel's Analysis

Inasmuch as Farkas and Hibel's research applies these principles, whether implicitly or explicitly, I would like to consider how they do so, what adhering to those principles teaches us, and what it leaves unexamined.

The Components Principle

The distal risk factors considered by Farkas and Hibel are individual-level markers of position in stratification hierarchies or, as labeled here, structured social disadvantage: parents' educational attainment, family income and poverty status, race/ethnicity, family structure, immigrant status, and primary language spoken at home. We could quibble over the details—about how we should understand the complex connections between socioeconomic position and family structure, about whether program participation, which enters the analysis in the next stage, is an indicator of disadvantage or a family resource—but I think it is reasonable to accept that these variables are intended simply to give some indication of where these families and children are located in hierarchies of relative advantage and disadvantage. Not surprisingly, the analyses show that almost all of these indicators are associated with almost all of the outcomes. There are some exceptions—and it may be worth thinking about how much those matter—but these exceptions are dwarfed by the general consistency in the results. Children who occupy disadvantaged social locations are also disadvantaged at the time of school entry cognitively and behaviorally.

The Proximity Principle

If those are the components of the macro-environment that matter, how do they become relevant to the day-to-day lives of children? Farkas and Hibel follow an approach to analyzing macro-micro relations that is consistent with that of most SSP researchers: using mediational models to estimate the relative contributions of meso-level experiences to explaining the effects of macro-conditions on individual outcomes. Models of this type aim to partition variance—to determine how much of the variation in the dependent variables is attributable to the mediators, and to determine how much of the effect of macro-conditions on individual-level outcomes can be explained by them.

In this case, the authors considered many individual and family experiences that may be implicated in cognitive and behavioral development: from birthweight to activities and resources to program participation. Their analysis demonstrates that some, but not all, of the effects of structured social disadvantage are explained by these family-related experiences. The effects of race/ethnicity and poverty are explained most consistently; results are a bit more mixed for the other predictors, but generally consistent with the claim that parenting activities and resources, in particular, explain some of the effects of the stratification indicators on school readiness.

The Psychological Principle

Moving to the final step, according to Farkas and Hibel, parenting actions and resources influence school readiness because they encourage the child's developing cognitive and interpersonal skills (or, when they are absent, act as stressors that inhibit development). Resources affect children's development through socialization processes or the facilitation of learning: children whose families have more resources—be they material or cultural—learn better control over their behaviors and develop more advanced cognitive skills than children whose families have fewer resources. They are taught to become the kind of student that teachers want in their classrooms.

With this final step in place, the model is complete in linking macro-level experiences to individual-level outcomes through parenting resources and actions. By applying the SSP framework to this specific problem, we can see the precision in our models encouraged by the framework. We can also see that the framework works well for its purpose in this case: as a means to identify gaps in school readiness and to determine how well they can be explained by family-related experiences.

Lingering Questions

Given all that the authors have accomplished here, we can ask two questions that encourage summary as well as action. What do we now know about the determinants of the gap in school readiness? And, what do we have left to learn? When considering these questions, I will make reference to more general questions that have been raised about the SSP approach, in particular, how we understand the processes that occur at the meso-level, how we conceptualize the causal "engine" for those processes, and the relative importance of material and symbolic processes in the creation and maintenance of social inequalities.

What we know from Farkas and Hibel's analysis is that everything matters, although perhaps not whether parents enroll their children in arts and crafts classes or take them on educational trips. That insight in and of itself is important because it alerts us to the complexity of the processes that foster school readiness. In effect, to close the gap, we have to intervene everywhere, an insight that drives multi-faceted intervention programs (Schorr, 2003). Yet, we can also ask: If we did intervene at all of these points, if we gave children more books and a home computer, if we got them involved in sports and performing arts activities, if we found a way for their parents to become more involved in their schools, would the gap in school readiness disappear? I do not know the answer to that question because I do not know much about all of the intervention research that has been conducted, but I suspect that it is "no." I have two reasons for thinking so.

First, as the authors openly acknowledge, the causal processes implied by their analyses are complex. Important variables may be missing from their models. Unmeasured features of parents' backgrounds and abilities, of the home environment, or of related domains of the child's life, may be associated with the features of those environments that were measured and may, in fact, be responsible for whatever mediation was observed here. The parenting resources and actions that appear to matter in these models may be proxies for other characteristics of parents—abilities, attitudes, and motivations—that influence their likelihood of providing those resources as well as their children's school readiness. More generally, we do not have a complete understanding of the determinants of parents' resources and actions in these circumstances. Some actions may reflect choices made within perceived constraints, others may be habitual, and still others may be motivated by imagined futures (see Emirbayer & Mische, 1998, for a theoretical discussion of these possibilities). Because we do not understand the origins of parents' resources and actions, we cannot estimate how much the resource or action itself makes a difference to school readiness. We know a lot about what *variables* make a difference, but not much about the underlying processes that they represent. (See Behrman, 2004, for a similar argument.)

Second, and related, it is possible that even if we were able to measure all relevant mediators and felt that we fully understood their internal causal relations, we still may not have identified the real causes of the gap in children's school readiness. My comments rely heavily on a parallel line of reasoning in health disparities research that has become very popular in recent years (Link & Phelan, 1995). It suggests that interventions at the proximal level, while effective for individuals, do not alter the distribution of outcomes across subgroups of the population, in part because the determinants of the population distribution of outcomes are different from the determinants of individual outcomes (Schwartz, 1994), but also because the real causes of subgroup disparities may be hidden in mediational analyses.

Here's how the reasoning unfolds in the case of health. There is a consistent association between socioeconomic status and health (see Robert & House, 2000; Williams & Collins, 1995, for reviews). Lower SES is associated with lower life expectancy, higher overall mortality, higher infant and perinatal mortality, and lower ratings of self-reported health (House & Williams, 2000; Ross & Wu, 1995; Sorlie, Backlund, & Keller, 1995). While this probably comes as little surprise, what is particularly interesting about the association is that it has persisted over the 20th century and, in fact, has grown stronger over time (Preston & Elo, 1995). This is true despite improvements in the living conditions of poor persons, more widespread availability of immunizations, and the availability of government-sponsored health insurance for the poorest of the poor—all of the mechanisms that had been thought to explain the gap in the middle part of the century (Kadushin, 1964). Link and Phelan (1995) draw on this observation, as well as on Lieberson's (1985) notion of a basic cause, to argue that proximal-level interventions are incapable of altering the socioeconomic distribution of disease because they ignore the underlying causal processes that generate it.

In today's context, individual health-related behaviors such as smoking, exercise, and the like appear to be the causes of the socioeconomic gap in mortality. People in lower status groups do smoke more and exercise less, those unhealthy behaviors are associated with the risk of mortality, and, in fact, a statistical model would show that controlling those behaviors explains some of the socioeconomic gap in health (e.g., Ross & Wu, 1995). Despite these findings, however, Link and Phelan contend that programs designed to help people quit smoking and exercise more would have little effect on the socioeconomic gap in mortality because new mediational processes would replace them.

There is precedent for their claim. Lack of health insurance was once a major explanation for the socioeconomic gap in mortality, in theory, policy, and statistical models. However, giving more people health insurance did not alter the gap (and they would argue not just because a lot of people still don't have insurance and the quality of care differs by SES). Once that problem was taken care of, other causal mechanisms emerged to maintain it. For example, smoking used to be more common among higher status groups; once the dangers of smoking became evident, the socioeconomic distribution of smoking reversed (Centers for Disease Control, 2005; U.S. Department of Health and Human Services, 2001). Much as addressing problems in living conditions, insurance, and the like did not alter the socioeconomic gradient in health in the 20th century, helping lower-status persons stop smoking and exercise more would not alter the gradient in health. People in lower status positions would still be disadvantaged in myriad other ways that would then become the most powerful explanations for the socioeconomic gradient in health. In short, if we try to fix problems at the proximal level, we will be chasing a moving target.

According to Link and Phelan, the reason that this is true is that SES and other dimensions of stratification determine access to fundamental forms of power, knowledge, material resources, prestige, and social capital, all of which can be used to avoid health-related risks or minimize the consequences of disease when it occurs. Importantly, these types of resources are transportable from one context to another. As health-related risks change, those persons who command the most resources will always be in the best position to avoid those new risks.

The observed socioeconomic gap in school readiness may be amenable to a similar logic. Regardless of the specific context under consideration, families with greater access to knowledge, power, material resources, and the like will be better able to manage favorable outcomes for their children. Currently, school readiness is predicted powerfully by what happens in the family—the resources that parents make available to their children, the actions they take on their behalf, and the manner in which they interact with their children. If the context were to change, however—if we lived in a society that gave books to parents, the availability of books might no longer be an important determinant of variation in school readiness. Even in that context, however, advantaged parents would still have greater access to whatever resources were important for promoting the well-being of their children. In essence, the theory attempts to acknowledge the social and historical specificity of mediational processes, as well as to suggest the enduring relevance of social inequalities across those contexts.

There are a number of reasons that this argument may be informative in the case of school readiness. It shares the emphasis of dominant theoretical models on resources within the family as critical mediators of the effects of socioeconomic position. The knowledge, power, and resources that underlie Link and Phelan's approach conform to forms of human, cultural, and social capital that motivate much of the sociological research on school readiness. It resonates with what we know about effective educational interventions—they adapt to changes in the environment, they are sensitive to the local context. Moreover, the argument directs our attention to the complex reasons that people engage in behaviors that lead to poor outcomes, dependent to some extent on knowledge, but also on resources, power, and privilege.

I concede that the parallels to school readiness are not exact. In contrast to increasing socioeconomic disparities in health, disparities in school readiness have declined over the past 30 years, although they remain strong (Rouse, Brooks-Gunn, & McLanahan, 2005). So, indeed, something that has happened over the past 30 years has contributed to reducing the gap, although only time will tell whether the reduction persists. In addition, this argument will not hold if the processes responsible for the socioeconomic gap in school readiness are universal, trans-historical, unaltered by the social and historical context. If we really believe that what parents have to do to promote their children's school success is the same now as it was 30 years ago, and will be the same in 30 years as it is now, then we can feel secure that our interventions will be successful. Such a belief seems untenable, however, in light of evidence that the predictors of school readiness vary internationally even now (Hampden-Thompson & Pong, 2005; see Powell, Werum, & Steelman, 2004, for a review). Thus, if we really want to alter the distribution of school readiness, we have to alter access to knowledge, power, material resources, and the like. In essence, this argument suggests that we cannot achieve real lasting change in educational disparities without a fundamental reorganization of society.

The seeming impossibility of achieving that goal may explain the recommendations of some prominent scholars that the gap in school readiness can be closed most effectively by direct educational interventions that bypass parental education and training to teach children the skills that they need to succeed in school (Duncan & Magnuson, 2005). In other words, if we cannot change the structure of society and we cannot intervene at all of the points that we need to, perhaps we should ignore everything that happens between macro and micro, and simply attack the problem head-on. While sympathetic to the logic, I suspect that such interventions can only be effective if supported by changes in resources, cultures, and identities. Moreover, even if these interventions did equalize school readiness across groups, dominant social groups would work to maintain their educational advantages through other means

Although I have advocated this argument, I also want to note that there is a key limitation in this line of reasoning that is common to research on health disparities and perhaps on school readiness. In both lines of research, mediators are typically conceived of as resources; in the case of health, resources that can be applied to avoid risks and minimize their effects on disease; in the case of school readiness, resources that parents apply to their children's development. In other research not described here, Farkas (2003) clarifies that these resources can be of many different types—material, but also cultural and social. I submit that the parenting resources and actions that are the focus of school readiness research can also be conceptualized as symbols that indicate families' and children's knowledge of the rules of the game. Drawing on Weber's concept of style of life and on Bourdieu's concept of habitus[1] some health researchers contend that social groups develop characteristic profiles of health-related behaviors, health lifestyles if you will, that express group identities and affirm social hierarchies (see Cockerham, 2000, for a review; Pampel, 2005). Health lifestyles may be shaped by opportunities and constraints—essentially material resources—but they may also become automatic, passed on through the interaction of group members and internalized by individuals without consciously processing the current opportunity structure and knowledge of health risks. They may be used to express group differentiation, as the current emphasis on health lifestyles is used now by members of the middle and upper classes to express their superiority to members of lower-status groups.

In a similar manner, we can posit the existence of predictable patterns of achievement-related behaviors that disadvantage persons of lower status but that need not depend on differences in knowledge and resources as they are traditionally understood. According to this type of conceptualization, group-based differences in parenting choices may become ingrained into the lifestyles of those groups whether or not they differ in knowledge about the risks of the choices they have made or in their abilities to change. Achievement-related behaviors express group-based identities and values as much as they reflect current resource constraints. In other words, although it seems clear that parents' actions are important determinants of school readiness, those actions may or may not have their origins in access to knowledge, resources, and power.

In sum, a SSP approach to the study of disparities in school readiness encourages us to consider experiences across multiple levels of social life that are implicated in the creation and perpetuation of social inequalities. It has the advantage of forcing precision in our explanatory models and orienting us towards the widespread implications of social inequalities for human development. In the study of school readiness, as in SSP research more generally, we can also see limitations to the approach in its failure to attend to complexities of human action, the social and historical specificity of explanatory models, and the symbolic causes and consequences of social inequality.

Acknowledgments

Partial support for this work was provided by a grant from the National Institute of Child Health and Human Development, Grant No. R01 HD050288.

---

[1]The habitus is a framework of perceptions that adjusts people's aspirations and expectations to the obdurate realities of their lives.

References

Behrman, J. (2004). Family background, education determination, and policy implications: Some selected aspects from various countries. In D. Conley & K. Albright (Eds.), *After the bell – Family background, public policy, and educational success* (pp. 51–85). London and New York: Routledge.

Bryk, A. S., & Raudenbush, S. W. (1992). *Hierarchical linear models: Applications and data analysis methods*. Newbury Park, CA: Sage.

Centers for Disease Control. (2005). *MMWR—Cigarette smoking among adults—United States, 2003*. Available at: http://www.cdc.gov/tobacco/research_data/adults_prev/mm5420_intro.htm.

Cockerham, W. C. (2000). The sociology of health behavior and health lifestyles. In C. E. Bird, P. Conrad, & A. M. Fremont (Eds.), *Handbook of medical sociology* (pp. 159–172). Upper Saddle River, NJ: Prentice Hall.

Delamater, J. (Ed.) (2004). *Handbook of social psychology*. New York: Kluwer/Plenum.

Duncan, G. J., & Magnuson, K. A. (2005). Can family socioeconomic resources account for racial and ethnic test score gaps? *Future of Children, 15*, 35–54.

Emirbayer, M., & Mische, A. (1998). What is agency? *American Journal of Sociology, 4*, 962–1023.

Farkas, G. (2003). Cognitive skills and noncognitive traits and behaviors in stratification processes. *Annual Review of Sociology, 29*, 541–562.

Hampden-Thompson, G., & Pong, S. (2005). Does family policy environment moderate the effect of single-parenthood on children's academic achievement? A study of 14 European countries. *Journal of Comparative Family Studies, 36*, 227–248.

House, J. S. (1981). Social structure and personality. In M. Rosenberg & R. H. Turner (Eds.), *Social psychology: Sociological perspectives* (pp. 525–561). New York: Basic.

House, J. S., & Williams, D. R. (2000). Understanding and reducing socioeconomic and racial/ethnic disparities in health. In B. D. Smedley & S. L. Syme (Eds.), *Promoting health: Intervention strategies from social and behavioral research* (pp. 81–124). Washington, DC: National Academy Press.

Kadushin, C. (1964). Social class and the experience of ill health. *Sociological Inquiry, 35*, 67–80.

Lieberson, S. (1985). *Making it count: The improvement of social research and theory*. Berkeley and Los Angeles, CA: University of California Press.

Link, B. G., & Phelan, J. (1995). Social conditions as fundamental causes of disease. *Journal of Health and Social Behavior, Extra Issue*, 80–94.

McLeod, J. D., & Lively, K. A. (2004). Social structure and personality. In J. Delamater (Ed.) *Handbook of social psychology* (pp. 77–102). New York: Kluwer/Plenum.

Pampel, F. C. (2005). Diffusion, cohort change, and social patterns of smoking. *Social Science Research, 34*, 117–139.

Powell, B., Weum, R., & Steelman, L. (2004). Macro causes, micro effects: Linking public policy, family structure, and educational outcomes. In D. Conley & K. Albright (Eds.) *After the bell – Family background, public policy, and educational success* (pp. 111–144). London and New York: Routledge.

Preston, S. H., & Elo, I. T. (1995). Are educational differentials in adult mortality increasing in the United States. *Journal of Aging and Health, 7*, 476–496.

Robert, S. A., & House, J. S. (2000). Socioeconomic inequalities in health: An enduring sociological problems. In C. E. Bird, P. Conrad, & A. M. Fremont (Eds.) *Handbook of medical sociology* (pp. 79–97). Upper Saddle River, NJ: Prentice Hall.

Ross, C. E., & Wu, C. (1995). The links between education and health. *American Sociological Review, 60,* 719–745.

Rouse, C., Brooks-Gunn, J., & McLanahan, S. (2005). Introducing the issue. *Future of Children, 15,* 5–13.

Schorr, L. B. (2003). *Determining "what works" in social programs and social policies: Toward a more inclusive knowledge base.* Washington, DC: Brookings. www.brook.edu/views/papers/sawhill/20030226.pdf. Downloaded September 16, 2005.

Schwartz, S. (1994). The fallacy of the ecological fallacy: The potential misuse of a concept and the consequences. *American Journal of Public Health, 84,* 819–824.

Sorlie, P. D., Backlunc, E., & Keller, J. (1995). U.S. mortality by economic, demographic, and social characteristics: The national longitudinal mortality study. *American Journal of Public Health, 85,* 949–956.

U.S. Department of Health and Human Services. (2001). *Women and smoking: A report of the Surgeon General.* Rockville, MD: Department of Health and Human Services.

Williams, D. R., & Collins, C. (1995). U.S. socioeconomic and racial differences in health: Patterns and explanations. *Annual Review of Sociology, 21,* 349–386.

4

COMMENTS ON FARKAS AND HIBEL: A TRANSACTIONAL/ECOLOGICAL MODEL OF READINESS AND INEQUALITY

Lynne Vernon-Feagans
Erica Odom
Nadya Pancsofar
Kirsten Kainz
University of North Carolina at Chapel Hill

Introduction

The chapter by Farkas and Hibel is provocative and wide-ranging in its search for correlates of "unreadiness". Although they admit the limitations of the data set they use to examine unreadiness, they argue, as have others (see, e.g., Lee & Burham, 2002) that the ECLS-K is a relatively new and important national data set that can help answer important policy-relevant questions focused on entry into formal schooling and later success in school. Farkas and Hibel's contribution, through their chapter, is in examining a wide range of child, family, and family resource variables that are related to children's unreadiness for school, emphasizing the children who scored in the lowest 20% on a variety of academic 'readiness' tests at kindergarten entry. The authors also examined the possible role of mediators within the child and family that might account for variance in school outcomes and diminish the importance of more distal demographic variables. In addition, their chapter presented a cumulative risk model reminiscent of the work of others such as Sameroff (Rutter, 2000; Sameroff & Chandler, 1975; Sameroff & Fiese, 2000) who also have demonstrated the power of the accumulation of risks in predicting child outcomes in comparison to one or a few risks.

Although the chapter offers many important results, we choose to focus on four here. First, we try to develop a model of readiness within which to place many of the results presented in Farkas and Hibel. As part of the model, we suggest a more process-oriented approach to defining 'readiness' that situates it at the intersection of person, process, and context. Second, we suggest two analytic strategies that can be derived from this model of readiness. Third, we illustrate the usefulness of this conceptual model and one of the analytic strategies through discussion of a recent study. using the ECLS-K data. Fourth, we argue that some of the constructs linked to readiness are critically important to measure if we wish to understand inequalities among children as they enter school.

It may be helpful to provide some background on the importance of the topic of' readiness and why it is critical to our understanding of children's development. Almost all parents want their children to succeed in school (Fitzgerald, Spiegel, & Cunningham, 1991; Vernon-Feagans, 1996). Yet, many children are set on a trajectory of failure that begins at school entry and seems fairly stable after first grade (Entwisle & Alexander, 1996; Entwisle, Alexander, & Olson, 1997). Trying to disentangle the many factors within and outside the family that help children succeed is extremely complex, especially for the large group of poor and minority children who inevitably overrepresent the 'unready' children. Therefore, we agree that trying to identify factors related to the child's suboptimal development as they enter school may help us to better understand what Farkas calls 'unreadiness'.

Although child and family variables are certainly important in setting children's readiness and academic trajectories, a number of conceptually linked domains must be considered when examining children's academic success. For instance, Lee and Burkham (2002) also examined ECLS-K data and found that schools are also implicated in children's unreadiness since poor and minority children attend the worst quality schools, lowering their chances of success in comparison to success rates for other children. Thus, we present a model that includes classrooms and schools, as we draw from the work of Bronfenbrenner (1979) and others who have helped formulate an ecological model of development that emphasizes the influence of process and context on development. In addition, we emphasize the work of scholars who have examined the role of inequalities in our society (Garcia-Coll et al., 1996; Heath, 1983; Ogbu, 1991) and helped to construct models that include culture and discrimination as major factors that affect the development of many of our children. In Bronfenbronner's seminal work (1979), he described the ecology of the child as containing microsystems, which are activities and contexts in which the child participates directly. The most important microsystem for the young child is the home environment. The family context has a major influence on the child's cognitive and language functioning as has been reported in the NICHD study of early childcare (2000). Even though the quality of the childcare environment was shown to have significant impacts on child outcomes, the quality of the home environment was a much stronger predictor of child outcomes. The indepth study by Hart and Risley (1995), referred to in Farkas and Hibel, reported that the vocabulary input by middle-class parents was much greater than the vocabulary input by lower-income parents. The gap in diversity of vocabulary grew over time, putting lower-income children at a disadvantage as they entered school, since these vocabulary differences were linked to later academic outcomes for the children. Other studies suggest that these vocabulary differences between low- and middle-income children are not as apparent in children who talk with each other in the neighborhood setting (Feagans & Haskins, 1986; Heath, 1983; Vernon-Feagans, 1996) and/or in the home (Tizard & Hughes, 1984), suggesting that not all low-income children have poorer vocabulary and language. Yet, even in these studies that found no home or neighborhood language use differences between low- and middle-income children, the findings suggested that low-income children performed more poorly in school. Therefore, the examination of home variables may be extremely important but they need to be put in the context of a larger conceptual framework if we are to understand their impact.

The Definition of Readiness within an Ecological and Transactional Framework

In order to put the Farkas and Hibel information into a theoretical framework, the most important construct is to define 'readiness' or 'unreadiness', as Farkas and Hibel have done. The definition that they have operationalized includes the children's reading, math, general knowledge, and approaches to learning (behaviors in the classroom) at the beginning of kindergarten. These are certainly the marker variables used by most studies to define readiness. We would like to present for discussion what we believe to be a better definition of 'readiness'—one that has implications for how we conceptualize the role of the family. We argue that readiness is a transactional construct from an ecological perspective and is at the intersection of person, process, and context. This puts the definition of readiness not within the child but at the interaction and fit between the child and his/her family and the 'readiness' of the classroom/school to teach that child. This fit between the individual and the context results in developmental processes that change over time. Thus, we define readiness by the processes that change as children acquire important school skills in the first few years of schooling. This includes not only the level of skill at school entry, as Farkas and Hibel examined, but also the slope or growth in those skills over time, as a function of child and family characteristics as well as of classroom characteristics and school context. It seems to us that the interest in readiness is not due to the desire to focus on the static skills at school entry, but how those skills interact with many facets of the child's life in understanding his/her learning. As part of this process of 'readiness' Pianta and Cox (1999) called for "Ready Schools", and Vernon-Feagans (1996) called for schools to be ready for all of our children. Both have emphasized the importance of the interaction between the child and the classroom in understanding readiness. We believe this definition reflects the interests of educators and developmentalists because we are not just interested in the initial skills of children as they enter school. What we are really interested in is the learning of children and how this is a function of various complex systems.

Figure 4.1 depicts our less-elaborated conceptual model of readiness which places it at the intersection of person, process, and context. As can be seen in this transactional and ecological model of readiness, the child outcomes are not static scores but processes over time within an ecological framework. These trajectories are not only a function of child and family characteristics but also of classrooms and schools. Thus, this model expands the domains that are important in understanding readiness.

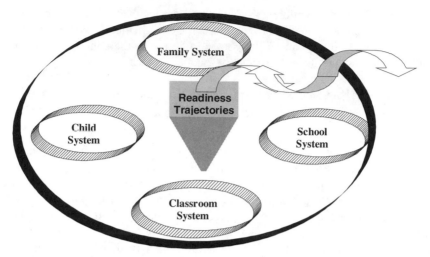

Figure 4.1. An ecological/process oriented model of 'readiness'.

Two Methodological Approaches

The ecological model presented here is particularly appropriate for children who may come to school with fewer resources than other children. These less advantaged children may profit from the classroom and school context. This underscores the transactional nature of development, in which processes in the home, classroom, and school and within the child interact over time to produce developmental trajectories for children. The analytic and theoretical perspective lends itself to a more person-oriented approach to development, especially when the goal is to understand individual differences, not normative development. The term person approach was coined by Block (1971) and has been used as a perspective by many theoretically oriented studies of individual differences in development (Kagan, 1994; Magnusson & Allen, 1983; Meehl, 1992). Magnusson and Stattin (1998) defined the theoretical orientation for this perspective:

> The person is conceptualized as an integrated, hierarchically organized totality, rather than the sum of variables. The goal is to discover the distinctive configurations of operating factors that characterize each individual's functioning and development, at different levels of the total hierarchical system . . . a great advantage of the person approach is that generalizations of empirical results refer to persons, not to variables (p. 51).

Cairns and his associates further developed this person-centered approach and have included the use of the construct of correlated constraints on development (Cairns, Elder, & Costello, 2001; Cairns, MacCombie, & Hood, 1983; Cairns, McGuire, & Gariepy, 1993). This is defined as "a network of associations among social, environmental, and biological forces. The upshot is that ontogeny is considerably more conservative than has been usually appreciated" (Magnusson & Cairns, 2001, p. 20). Using this construct helps to more clearly understand that families who have one characteristic usually have others that are highly correlated. For instance, families with low education generally have jobs with less income, more mental health and health problems, less access to resources, and poorer outcomes for children. Trying to disentangle each of these factors may be interesting but since they are so bound together in the real world, their unique contribution may not be as valuable to understand as the constellation of factors together. Thus, grouping together of individuals or children who are similar in a multivariate way may be a more important contribution to our understanding of the constellation of factors associated with these rather unique groups of people. This approach is intuitively appealing and has spawned a host of strategies, such as cluster analysis, latent class analysis, and growth mixture modeling (Cairns, Bergman, & Kagan, 1998; Cairns, Elder, & Costello, 2001; Muthen, 2004) that identify and characterize these multivariate groups of people. This seems to have been particularly productive in identifying "risk" groups that are characterized by aggressive behavior or drug and alcohol problems. Although Farkas and Hibel did not use cluster analysis, they did examine a risk group. They included a sample of children who scored at or below the 20th percentile in readiness, trying to identify the factors within this group that related to outcomes.

Other analytic strategies are complementary with this conceptual model and can be used when identifying a risk group. Latent curve models (LCM), an extension of structural equation modeling (SEM), have proven useful tools for examining the processes of change in multiple contexts. In LCM, individuals' growth trajectories are modeled as a function of the mean intercept and slope factors across the sample plus a residual term that stands for individual deviation from the mean trajectory. Variation around the mean intercept and slope factors represent individual differences in trajectories within the sample. Therefore, analytically, we are able to differentiate among a number of different patterns of growth or in this case readiness trajectories. Hussong et al. (2004) extended traditional LCM techniques and distinguished two underlying processes within a conditional LCM (i.e., an LCM with covariates as predictors). The first process is the individuals' growth trajectory. The trajectory is modeled as an intercept and growth factors underlying a set of repeated measures. When covariates are added as predictors of the intercept and growth factors, the resulting model indicates that the individuals' underlying growth trajectory mediates the relation between the covariates and the repeated measures. The second process reflects time-specific deviations from the individuals' growth trajectory. Time-specific deviations from the trajectory are represented as the direct effect of covariates on a test score at a specific time point above and beyond what can be accounted for by the individuals' growth trajectory.

The Conceptual Model, Analytic Strategy, and the ECLS-K Data

As an example of how the model and the analytic strategy can be useful, we look at a recent study (Kainz and Vernon-Feagans, in press) that examined the ECLS-K data to predict reading readiness trajectories over the first four years of school. Figure 4.2 depicts their model, which is an adaptation of our initial model but focuses instead on reading readiness trajectories.

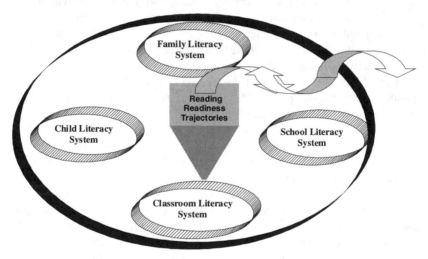

Figure 4.2. Reading 'readiness' trajectories.

Their study limited the sample to children who lived at 200% below the poverty threshold and those who had not changed schools over the four years, since they were interested in school-level variables. The risk sample differed from that used by Farkas and Hibel, but was clearly related to theirs—we used poverty while they used child performance. The variables used in our model are limited by the ECLS-K data. We admit, like Farkas and Hibel, that the measurement of all constructs has many limitations. Especially absent from a transactional framework is the lack of good family process data that would characterize the quality of the home environment emotionally and educationally. The ECLS-K contains good marker variables of the literacy environment of the home—both Farkas and Hibel and we have used them as important family variables. Figure 4.3 shows the set of variables used in the model. Without going into depth about each measure, there were child and family demographic measures, including a composite of the literacy environment of the home, along with classroom-level and school-level variables. These were all used in order to understand the simultaneous effects of these four systems on the children's reading readiness trajectories.

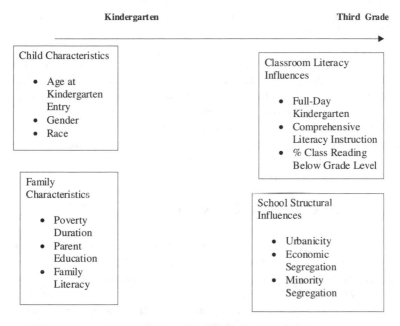

Figure 4.3. Variables used to understand 'readiness' trajectories.

At the outset, a restricted model allowed child and family characteristics to predict children's reading readiness trajectories, while fixing the effects from classrooms and schools to zero. The subsequent model, a full model, allowed children's classroom and school characteristics to predict time-specific reading performance beyond growth accounted for by children's expected trajectories and child and family characteristics. This full model produced a significantly better fit. When child, family, classroom, and school variables were considered simultaneously as predictors of children's reading trajectories, child and family variables more often were associated with children's initial skills at kindergarten entry than with patterns of growth over time. As expected, parent education, income, literacy practices, child older age, and child gender were all associated with higher reading scores at kindergarten entry. Classroom effects suggested that children's reading trajectories were a function of current comprehensive reading instruction as well as their previous comprehensive reading instruction. In addition, children in classrooms with higher percentages of students reading below grade level had lower reading scores. At the school level, neither geographic location nor economic segregation explained children's performance. However, minority segregation significantly accounted for children's reading performance at the end of kindergarten, first and third grades. This significant effect became stronger over time, with the effect size doubling from kindergarten to third grade.

By using this framework, we were able to determine the simultaneous effects of the home and the school in understanding children's readiness over a four-year period. It was not surprising that home characteristics predicted children's initial reading level at school entry. Interestingly, the home was not as predictive as we might have thought in understanding reading trajectories. Both classroom instruction and school environment were powerful predictors of children's performance above and beyond family predictors. Without examining the classroom and family contexts, we would have misrepresented the role of families in children's reading growth and what was of primary interest—the reading trajectories of the children. Thus, our conceptual model drove the analyses and supported the transactional and dynamic nature of readiness.

Additions to Our Conceptual Model

The last issue we wish to address is the variable omission problem discussed by Farkas and Hibel in their chapter. All studies have variables that are not measured due to constraints on data collection and our ability to measure important constructs. We would like to suggest that although some of these cannot always be measured in our studies, it is important to acknowledge their theoretical contribution to our understanding of readiness and inequality.

From an ecological perspective, children participate directly in important microsystem contexts that affect their development. We have shown some of these in our initial model. There are also exosystems or contexts in which the child does not participate but that may greatly influence the child. Also, more global influences called macrosystems, which include cultural beliefs, state and national policies, and other larger societal factors, impinge on families and children. We would like to briefly describe some additional exosystem and macrosystem factors that we should and can measure in studies of readiness as well as describe some constructs that we have not been very successful in measuring in studying readiness. Figure 4.4 contains our attempt to develop a better model of readiness from our ecological and transactional model.

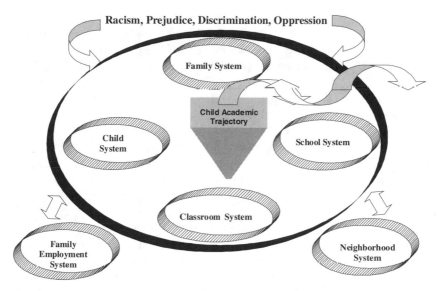

Figure 4.4. An ecological and process model of 'readiness'.

In Figure 4.4, we emphasize the importance of some additional exosystems and a macrosystem to our conceptual model. We would like to argue that these are critically important to measure in our understanding of the role of the family in helping children in the readiness process. We added the exosystems of the family work setting and the neighborhood/community setting. We also added the macrosystem-level influence that Garcia Coll and colleagues (1996) identified as insidious in their pervasive influence on many families and their children—discrimination and oppression of minority and poor families and children. We say only a few words about each of these influences but hope that future work will elucidate these systems in more detail.

The Family/Work Exosystem

The most immediately relevant context for the family that is important but not measured well in readiness studies is the parental work context and the associated related factors such as workplace characteristics, flexible hours, employer support of families with children, etc. Although very few researchers have seriously examined work/family relationships with respect to school 'readiness', this is likely an important source of variation across families that may impact children's readiness trajectories. For instance, parents who work unpredictable and variable work schedules that do not match the school hours not only may have less time to spend with their children at home but may be unlikely to be involved in school because of work schedules. In a recent study, using the NICHD study of early childcare (Han, 2005), it was found that the children of mothers who had variable and irregular work hours in the child's first year of life performed less well on cognitive and language measures at 24 and 36 months, than did those of mothers who had more predictable and regular work hours. Crouter and colleagues at Penn State showed that, with regard to older children, the work/family interface has important implications for family life and child outcomes (Crouter & Booth, 2004; Crouter, Head, McHale, & Tucker, 2004).

A recent project has some data to support the importance of examining the work/family interface, although we are just at the point of analyzing the data from the study, since the children are still in infancy. The Family Life Project is an interdisciplinary collaboration in which faculty are examining the lives of 1,292 families and their children in a non-urban context. This representative sample of babies born to mothers in three rural counties in North Carolina and three rural counties in Pennsylvania have some data to suggest the ways in which work, even when children are very young, may influence families' lives and children's development. Two thirds of the families in this project are living at below the 200% poverty threshold. For this sample, over 40% of the mothers were back in the workforce when their children were two months of age. By the time the children were six months of age, over 50% of the mothers were back in the workforce. Of those women who worked, only 60% had fixed daytime schedules. Twenty percent had evening or night work schedules and another 20% had irregular or rotating shifts. Given this small bit of data on work, if this trend continues as children enter school, many of these mothers may have a hard time being involved in parent-teacher associations that meet at night or helping children with homework and other school-related projects. The ways in which work settings promote or impede families' ability to participate in their child's schooling, and teachers and schools adapt to family work schedules and demands, are important to understand.

Community and Neighborhood Exosystems

Another important exosystem is the neighborhood and community. Many extra-familial aspects of children's environment may exert an influence on their early literacy development and readiness for early schooling. These extra-familial elements may have particular importance in explaining the achievement gap between low-income and middle-income children when looking at early readiness skills. In examining readiness, we believe that access to print in their neighborhood/community, community violence, and physical hazards may all be important and seem to coalesce in communities characterized by poverty.

Neuman and Celano (2001) investigated the access to print in low-income and middle-income urban communities. They found major differences in access to print between neighborhoods with different average incomes. Families in low-income neighborhoods had far fewer options for purchasing books, magazines, or comic books of any quality than did families from middle-income communities. Signs and logos in the low-income community were fewer and less readable than in the middle-income communities. Low-income neighborhoods were less likely to provide the resources, comfort, and ambience that supported reading activity in public spaces. Local preschools in the low-income neighborhoods had fewer books for their children and accessible books were of a lower quality than were found in preschools in the middle-income neighborhoods. School libraries in the lower-income neighborhoods had lower-quality books and fewer computers, and were open fewer days than were school libraries in middle-income neighborhoods. Further, public libraries in the low-income communities had smaller overall collections, fewer books per child, and more limited nighttime hours than those in the middle-income communities. These findings support the need to expand the research focus on readiness to inequalities in access to readiness. This finding supports the findings of Lee and Burkham (2002) that children whose families are low-income attend poorer quality elementary schools. These correlated constraints on children's development appear to extend to a large and pervasive number of systems.

A growing body of research is linking exposure to community violence to socioemotional functioning during the preschool years (see, e.g., Farver, Xu, Eppe, Fernandez, & Schwartz, 2005; Jones, Foster, Forehand, & O'Connell, 2005). Again, these contexts are most likely to occur in low-income neighborhoods. While fewer studies have considered possible implications for early cognitive development, there is some evidence that community violence may contribute to certain physical ailments in children that, in turn, may negatively impact their early school performance and cognitive development (Jones et al., 2005). Jones et al. studied a sample of elementary school-aged African American children from low-income families in an urban setting. They found that mother and child reports of neighborhood violence were significantly related to child-reported physical symptoms, such as headache, stomach ache, and vomiting. In one of the few studies to consider the impact of community violence on early cognitive development, Farver, Natera, and Frosch (1999) examined 64 preschoolers and their mothers recruited from a Head Start program in an urban setting. They found links between families' exposure to community violence and a reduction in preschoolers' cognitive performance. This relationship was mediated by children's distress, which the authors hypothesize may influence children's ability to profit from their preschool programs and elementary education.

Low-income neighborhoods are also associated with aspects of the physical environment that may negatively impact children's cognitive development. For example, children living in poverty are more likely to live in closer proximity to toxic waste dumps and to experience greater prevalence of unsafe lead levels, pesticide exposure, poor indoor air quality, high levels of nitrogen dioxide, carbon monoxide and radon, poor drinking water, and allergen exposure associated with asthma (Evans, 2004). Families living in poverty also experience less access to healthy food than do middle-income families, with low-income neighborhoods having three times fewer supermarkets, comparable numbers of small grocers and convenience stores, and three times more bars and taverns as are found in middle- and upper-income neighborhoods (Evans, 2004).

Early childhood exposure to lead has been investigated in more depth. Sargent et al. (1995) examined data from lead screenings performed on 238,275 children from birth through age 4 in Massachusetts. They found that lead poisoning rates for children in communities with large numbers of young children living in poverty (>20%) were nearly nine times the rates for communities with childhood poverty rates below 5%. The greater the percentage of African Americans in neighborhoods, the higher the levels of children's lead poisoning rates. This significant relationship remained even after controlling for the effects of poverty and housing status. Nordin et al. (1998), in a study of a large metropolitan area, found that the lead levels for African American children were more than three times those for white children.

These studies suggest that the psychological, emotional, and physical characteristics of communities may have both direct and indirect effects on families and children. These effects may be especially important in understanding the interacting systems that produce "readiness" trajectories for children, especially our most vulnerable children.

The Macrosystem of Discrimination and Oppression

The final system is the macrosystem that contains the larger cultural values and policies in the community that affect children. Although many macrosystems that influence families and children might be placed in our model, the one that we would like to emphasize in understanding readiness is discrimination of ethnic minorities and the poor. The politics of discrimination in this country are bound together in a spiraling confluence of macrosystem factors that can profoundly affect the family and their children, especially as they enter the extrafamilial setting of the school. As was seen in Kainz and Vernon-Feagans (in press), minority segregation was a powerful predictor of readiness in kindergarten and became a more important predictor over time. This was somewhat surprising, given that economic segregation was not a significant predictor in this study, although the study only had a low-income sample. This also is connected to the other systems we have discussed that suggest that poverty, ethnicity, risky neighborhoods, risky schools, and risky jobs all go together to form an interacting system of oppression that make good readiness trajectories difficult for many of our children.

Despite improvements in racial attitudes towards minorities in America, African Americans have continued to be subject to prejudicial beliefs about their competence and abilities, often receiving differential treatment by others, including individuals as well as societal institutions. In fact, more than 50% of African Americans attribute substandard housing, lack of skilled labor jobs, and lower wages to ethnic discrimination (Sigelman & Welch, 1991). Although negative racial attitudes have become less overt, surveys continue to show that whites prefer to maintain a certain level of social distance from minority groups. As a consequence, African Americans are more likely to perceive discrimination than are whites (Sigelman & Welch, 1993). Although since 1958 the percentage of whites who support having their children attend an integrated school has increased (to 99% in 1990), this percentage declines as the number of black children in the school increases (Williams & Williams-Morris, 2000). Additionally, although whites indicate that they are committed to principles of equality, the percentage of whites supporting federal intervention in ensuring that blacks received fair treatment in employment has drastically declined since the 1960s (38% in 1964 and 28% in 1996; Williams & Williams-Morris, 2000).

The extent to which individuals perceive ethnic discrimination has been found to have implications for health status in the African American community. Research suggests that stress induced by experiences of racial bias is one way in which racism may affect health (Clark, Anderson, Clark, & Williams, 1999). Studies of the effects of racial discrimination on health have found a positive relationship between perceptions of discrimination and blood pressure (Williams, Neighbors, & Jackson, 2003). Klonoff, Landrine, and Ullman (1999) found that experiences of racism were strongly related to total psychiatric symptoms, somatization, obsessive-compulsive symptoms, interpersonal sensitivity, depression, and anxiety among African Americans.

These consequences of perceived discrimination along with institutional discrimination are risk factors that present a unique and formidable challenge for parenting within the African American community. Parenting must be conducted with the knowledge that children may be subject to the effects of discriminatory practices received by their parents, their own experiences of interpersonal discrimination, and discrimination as they progress through young adulthood, into the job market. Thus, discrimination pervades the everyday lives of the African American family unit.

Given the historical significance of racism in the United States, it remains one of defining contextual variables for families of African descent living in America. Bronfenbrenner (1986) argued that children's development must be examined within systems of influence. An overarching macrosystemic factor that may be experienced by children within families of color is racial discrimination. Socializing children about African American culture, preparing them for experiences with prejudice, and promoting out-group mistrust occur with increasing frequency from around age 4 to the teen years (Hughes & Chen, 1997). In families with young children, it may be more important to study parents' experiences with racism and children's well-being. It is hypothesized that parents' experiences with discrimination precede the child's birth; therefore, it is likely that these experiences may influence the parenting environment before the child reaches adolescence.

Very few studies have examined how parental experiences of discrimination operate on family functioning. Murry, Brown, Brody, et al. (2001) explored racial discrimination as a moderator of caregiver stress and caregiver-child relationship quality. Mothers experiencing higher levels of stress from a variety of sources presented with more symptoms of depression and anxiety. Maternal distress was linked directly to mother-child relationship quality and intimate partner quality; it was also linked indirectly with mother-child relationship quality through intimate partner relationship quality. Finally, for mothers experiencing higher levels of racial discrimination, stronger negative associations emerged among stressor pile-up, psychological distress, and the quality of the mothers' relationship with the child and intimate partner. Caughy, O'Campo, and Mutaner (2004) explored the relation among preschool children's mental health, parental experiences of racism, and parental coping behaviors. Higher total problem behaviors and higher externalizing behaviors were reported for children when parents denied personal experiences of racism. Additionally, higher reports of children's internalizing problems were reported when parents denied that racism affects those close to them or African Americans in general. Thus, even when racism is not acknowledged as a source of stress for African American parents, the potent effects remain and are salient in children's interactions and problem behaviors.

Conclusion

The concept of readiness is certainly linked to what families provide for their children. It is important to understand these links between families and children in a theoretical context that leads us to certain methodologies and to the examination of important constructs. We hope our thoughts have helped to put the Farkas and Hibel chapter in a larger perspective and have helped us think a bit differently about how to define "readiness". We believe a more transactional and process-oriented definition of 'readiness' helps place 'readiness' where it should be—at the intersection of important individual and contextual systems—and helps us to understand not just children's initial skills but also their growth in that skill, which we can call their learning or readiness trajectory. In our initial model, we found that children's reading skills were uniquely accounted for by child, family, classroom, and school characteristics. The addition to our model of exosystems of the family/ work environment and the neighborhood and community may prove to be equally important in understanding readiness. Finally, the overarching macrosystem of discrimination and oppression must be measured and used in future studies. The confounds of race, poverty and the myriad of other factors that co-occur may have the most profound effects on 'readiness' for children and have the greatest policy implications if we take these constraints on families and children seriously. We end our remarks from a quote from Lee and Burkham (2002), whose conclusions from their analysis of the ECLS-K data set mirror some of the Farkas and Hibel findings and call for us to take seriously the interaction of children and schools and the urgent need for schools to be ready to teach all of our children.

The poorest children in economic terms, those from black and Hispanic families, from families where parents are less educated and children attending school in large cities and rural areas, attend the lowest-quality schools. These findings translate into a sobering conclusion: The children who need the best schooling actually start their education in the worst public schools (Lee & Burkham, 2002, p. 84).

76   VERNON-FEAGANS, ODOM, PANCSOFAR, & KAINZ

References

Block, J. (1971). *Lives through time.* Berkeley, CA: Bancroft.

Bronfenbrenner, U. (1979). *The ecology of human development.* Cambridge, MA: Harvard University Press.

Bronfenbrenner, U. (1986). Ecology of the family as a context for human development: Research perspectives. *Developmental Psychology, 22,* 723–742.

Cairns, R. B., Bergman, L. R., & Kagan, J. (1998). *Methods and models for studying the individual.* Thousand Oaks: Sage.

Cairns, R. B., Elder, G. H., & Costello, E. J. (1996). *Developmental science.* New York: Cambridge University Press.

Cairns, R. B., MacCombie, D. J., & Hood, K. E. (1983). A developmental-genetic analysis of aggressive behavior in mice. *Journal of Comparative Psychology, 97,* 69–89.

Cairns, R. B., McGuire, A. M., & Gariepy, J. L. (1993). Developmental behavior genetics: Fusion, correlated constraints, and timing. In D. F. Hay & A. Angold (Eds.), *Precursors and causes in development and psychopathology* (pp. 87–122). New York: Wiley.

Caughy, M. O., O'Campo, P. J., & Muntaner, C. (2004). Experiences of racism among African American parents and the mental health of their preschool-aged children. *American Journal of Public Health, 94,* 2118–2124.

Clark, R., Anderson, N. B., Clark, V. R., & Williams, D. R. (1999). Racism as a stressor for African Americans. *American Psychologist, 54,* 80–816.

Crouter, A., Head, M., McHale, S., & Tucker, C. (2004). Family, time, and the psychosocial adjustment of adolescent siblings and their parents. *Journal of Marriage and Family, 66,* 1361–1377.

Crouter, N., & Booth, A. (2004). *Work-family challenges for low-income parents and their children.* Mahwah. NJ: Erlbaum.

Entwisle, D. R., & Alexander, K. L. (1996). Family type and children's growth in reading and math over the primary grades. *Journal of Marriage and the Family, 58,* 341–355.

Entwisle, D., Alexander, K., & Olson, L. (1997). *Children, schools, & inequality.* Boulder, CO: Westview Press.

Evans, G. W. (2004). The environment of childhood poverty. *American Psychologist, 59,* 77–92.

Farver, J. M., Xu, Y., Eppe, S., Fernandez, A., & Schwartz, D. (2005). Community, violence, family conflict and preschoolers socioemotional functioning. *Developmental Psychology, 41,* 160–170.

Farver, J. M., Natera, L. X., & Frosch, D. L. (1999). Effects of community violence on inner-city preschoolers and their families. *Journal of Applied Developmental Psychology, 20,* 143–158.

Feagans, L., & Haskins, R. (1986). Neighborhood dialogues of black and white 5-year-olds. *Journal of Applied Developmental Psychology, 7,* 181–200.

Fitzgerald, J., Spiegel, D., & Cunningham, J. (1991). The relationship between parental literacy level and perceptions of emergent literacy. *Journal of Reading Behavior, 23,* 191–213.

Garcia Coll, C., Lamberty, G., Jenkins, R., McAdoo, H. P., Crnic, K., Wasik, B. H., & Vasquez Garcia, H. (1996). An integrative model for the study of developmental competencies in minority children. *Child Development, 67,* 1892–1914.

Han, W. (2005). Maternal nonstandard work schedules and child cognitive outcomes. *Child Development, 76*, 137–154.

Hart, B., & Risley, T. R. (1995). *Meaningful differences in the everyday experience of young American children.* Baltimore: Paul H. Brookes.

Heath, S. B. (1983). *Ways with words: Language, life, and work in communities and classrooms.* New York: McGraw-Hill; Oxford University Press.

Hughes, D., & Chen, L. (1997). When and what parents tell children about race: An examination of race-related socialization among African American families. *Applied Developmental Science, 1*, 200–214.

Hussong, A. M., Curran, P. J., Moffitt, T. E., Caspi, A., & Carrig, M. M. (2004). Substance abuse hinders resistance in young adults' antisocial behavior. *Development and Psychopathology, 16*, 1029–1046.

Jones, D. J., Foster, S., Forehand, G., & O'Connell, C. (2005). Neighborhood violence and psychosocial adjustment in low-income urban African American children: Physical symptoms as a marker of child adjustment. *Journal of Child and Family Studies, 14*, 237–249.

Kagan, J., Snidman, N., & Arcus, D. (1994). The value of extreme groups. In R. B. Cairns, L. R. Bergman & J. Kagan (Eds.), *Methods and models for studying the individual* (pp. 65–80). Thousand Oaks, CA: Sage.

Kainz, K. (2005). *Reading development trajectories from kindergarten to third grade: Untangling effects from child, family, classroom, and school literacy systems for children living in poverty.* Unpublished doctoral dissertation, University of North Carolina at Chapel Hill.

Kainz, K., & Vernon-Feagans, L. (in press). The ecology of early reading development for children in poverty. *The Elementary School Journal.*

Klonoff, E. A., Landrine, H., & Ullman, J. B. (1999). Racial discrimination and psychiatric symptoms among Blacks. *Cultural Diversity and Ethnic Minority Psychology, 5*, 329–339.

Lee, V. E., & Burkham, D. T. (2002). *Inequality at the starting gate.* Washington, DC: Economic Policy Institute.

Magnusson, D., & Allen, V. (1983). *Human development: An interactional perspective.* New York: Academic Press.

Magnusson, D., & Cairns, R. B. (2001). Developmental science: Toward a unified framework. In R. B. Cairns, G. H. Elder, & E. J. Costello (Eds.), *Developmental science.* New York: Cambridge University Press.

Magnusson, D., & Stattin, H. (1998). Person-context interaction theory. In W. Damon & R. M. Lerner (Eds.), *Handbook of child psychology (5th ed.): Theoretical models of human development* (pp. 685–760). New York: Wiley.

Meehl, P. E. (1992). Factors and taxa, traits and types, differences of degree and differences in kind. *Journal of Personality, 60*, 117–174.

Murry, V. M., Brown, P. A., Brody, G. H., Cutrona, C. E., & Simons, R. L. (2001). Racial discrimination as a moderator of the links among stress, maternal psychological functioning, and family relationships. *Journal of Marriage and the Family, 63*, 915–926.

Muthen, B. (2004). Latent variable analysis. Growth mixture modeling and related techniques for longitudinal data. In D. Kaplan (Ed.), *The Sage handbook of quantitative methodology for the social sciences* (pp. 345–368). Newbury Park, CA: Sage.

Neuman, S. B., & Celano, D. (2001). Access to print in low-income and middle-income communities: An ecological study of four neighborhoods. *Reading Research Quarterly, 36*, 8–26.

National Institute of Child Health and Human Development (NICHD). (2000). *Report of the National Reading Panel. Teaching children to read: an evidence-based assessment of the scientific research literature on reading and its implications for reading instruction: Reports of the subgroups* (NIH Publication No. 00-4754).Washington, DC: U.S. Government Printing Office.

Nordin, J., Rolnick, S., Ehlinger, E., Nelson, A., Arneson, T., Cherney-Stafford, L., & Griffin, J. (1998). Lead levels in high-risk and low-risk young children in the Minneapolis-St Paul Metropolitan Area. *Pediatrics, 101*, 72–76.

Ogbu, J. (1991). Minority coping responses and school experience. *Journal of Psychohistory, 18*, 433–456.

Pianta, R. C., & Cox, M. J. (1999). *The transition to kindergarten.* Baltimore: Paul H. Brookes.

Rutter, M. (2000). Resilience reconsidered: Conceptual considerations, empirical findings, and policy implications. In J. P. Shonkoff & S. M. Meisels (Eds.), *Handbook of early childhood intervention* (pp. 651–682). New York: Cambridge University Press.

Sameroff, A. J., & Chandler, M. J. (1975). Reproductive risk and the continuum of caretaking causality. In F. D. Horowitz (Ed.), *Review of child development research, Vol. 4* (pp.187–244). Chicago: University of Chicago Press.

Sameroff, A. J., & Feise, B. H. (2000). Transactional regulation: The developmental ecology of early intervention. In J. P. Shonkoff & S. J. Meisels (Eds.), *Handbook of early intervention, 2nd ed.* (pp. 135–159). Cambridge, UK: Cambridge University Press.

Sargent, J. D., Brown, M. J., Freeman, J. L., Bailey, A., Goodman, D., & Freeman Jr., D. H. (1995). Childhood lead poisoning in Massachusetts communities: Its association with sociodemographic and housing characteristics. *American Journal of Public Health, 85*, 528–534.

Sigelman, L., & Welch, S. (1993). The contact hypothesis revisited: Black-white interaction and positive racial attitudes. *Social Forces, 71*, 781–795.

Sigelman, L., & Welch, S. (1991). *Black Americans' views of racial inequality: The dream deferred.* New York: Cambridge University Press.

Tizard, B., & Hughes, M. (1984). *Young children learning.* Cambridge, MA: Harvard University Press.

Vernon-Feagans, L. V. (1996). *Children's talk in communities and classrooms.* Cambridge, MA: Blackwell.

Williams, D. R., Neighbors, H. W., & Jackson, J. S. (2003). Racial/ethnic discrimination and health: Findings from community studies. *American Journal of Public Health, 93*, 200–208.

Williams, D. R., & Williams-Morris, R. (2000). Racism and mental health: The African American experience. *Ethnicity and Health, 5*, 243–268.

5
REPLY TO LOPEZ AND BARRUECO

George Farkas
Jacob Hibel

We are grateful to the volume editors for permitting us to draft this reply. Our points in reply may be grouped as follows: a restatement of our original goal, issues with non-experimental studies like the ECLS-K, and methodological issues. We discuss each of these in turn, below.

Restating Our Goal

Lopez and Barrueco begin their discussion by interpreting our goal as an "examination of potential racial/ethnic disparities in children's school readiness." Our stated goal, however, was to provide a wide-ranging "empirical summary" of trends in the "resources possessed, and the stresses experienced, by parents and their children", and the effects of these many factors on children's school readiness. This intent is further seen in how our regression analyses were structured. For example, in Table 1.2 and subsequently, the four race/ethnicity dummy variables were entered alongside 25 other predictor variables. This is because we sought to separate the net effects of all 29 variables in an even-handed way. In such an analysis, any net effects of race/ethnicity are over and above the other measured variables, and, as we stated in the chapter, remain to be explained by additional resource or risk factors. Had we intended to focus on racial/ethnic disparities, we would have begun all our analyses by including only the race/ethnicity variables as predictors, in order to estimate the total effects of these variables.

Lopez and Barrueco suggest that we focused on estimating the effects of social programs such as Head Start. They indicate that our analyses would be improved by restricting our sample to lower-income students who are targeted by these programs. This was not the primary goal of our study. Rather, in preparing the introductory chapter for this volume, we were casting a wide net to assess the relative impact of different resources and stressors on school readiness. By including fully 29 variables in even our simplest prediction equations, we adjusted for a broad array of differences between families, and permitted a reasonable test for difficult-to-estimate effects such as those associated with social programs.

We also stated that an experimental study, such as the Head Start Impact Study of which Dr. Lopez was a co-author, provides more reliable inferences than a regression study such as ours. It is interesting to note, however, that the findings of the Head Start Impact Study for 4-year-olds do not differ substantially from our findings for 5-year-olds. Table 5.1 below presents these findings.

Table 5.1

Significant Effects and Effect Sizes for 4-Year-Olds, Head Start Impact Study
(June 2005: Exhibit 1 of the Executive Summary)

Effect	Effect Size
Test Scores	
Woodcock-Johnson Letter-Word ID	.22
Letter Naming	.24
McCarthy Draw-A-Design	NS
Woodcock-Johnson Spelling	.16
PPVT Vocabulary	NS
PPVT Color Naming	NS
Problem Behaviors	
Total Behavior Problems	NS
Hyperactive Behavior	NS
Aggressive Behavior	NS
Withdrawn Behavior	NS
Social Skills and Approaches to Learning	NS
Social Competencies	NS

(NS = Not significant)
Source: http://www.acf.hhs.gov/programs/opre/hs/impact_study, downloaded 12/1/05

We see that of six test scores, Head Start had no significant effects on half of them, and an average effect size of about .2 on the other half. Of six behaviors, Head Start had significant effects on none of them.

ECLS-K Data Issues

Lopez and Barrueco raise several concerns regarding regression analysis of survey data, including the potential for bias associated with retrospective data collection and nonrandom data missingness. However, we believe that the standard for such criticism has moved from simply saying that a particular situation *might* bias a coefficient, to the more demanding requirement that Lopez and Barrueco specify *why* they believe a particular issue produces a *large* bias, and whether the biased coefficient is *biased upward or downward.* (In the latter case, our results may be conservative.)

One example of this is Lopez and Barrueco's discussion of the ECLS-K's screening-out of Latino children with poor oral English skills from testing on reading and other skills, and their consequent exclusion from our sample. Since these excluded children come from particularly at-risk contexts, however, their absence tended to make our estimates of the Hispanic effect on unreadiness conservative. That is, the positive effects of Hispanic ethnicity on unreadiness that we showed in Table 1.4 would have been even larger if these students had been included in the study. (Perhaps not too much larger, however, since the excluded students were a minority of Hispanics, and we partially controlled for this effect by including a measure of Non-English Speaking Home.) In sum, even if we had undertaken more elaborate calculations focused on this issue, our conclusions would likely have been unchanged.

Similar results are likely for many other regression analysis issues raised by Lopez and Barrueco—measurement error, omitted variables, and multicollinearity. We do not have the space to address every issue, but note that many of these concerns are ameliorated by the large number of control variables we used (including, in particular, controls for both continuous family income and a dummy variable that allows for a differential effect for families in poverty, as well as dummy variables for non-linear effects of both the mother's and father's education), the typically modest correlations among our predictors, and our large sample size (which acts in opposition to any increase in standard errors due to multicollinearity).

Methodological Concerns

Lopez and Barrueco suggest that we should have studied the data longitudinally, yet the explicit goal of this and the other studies in this volume was to measure *school readiness*, which is best measured when school begins in the fall of kindergarten. A study of children's educational growth trajectories, as Lopez and Barrueco recommend, represents an entirely different endeavor. The authors express concern about variation in our sample size across regressions, but there were none—all analyses were conducted on the sample described in Table 1.1 of our paper. Finally, Lopez and Barrueco raised concerns about the way dummy variables are used to represent a categorical variable in regression analysis. Dummy variables are used by setting one category as the base for comparison—for example, whites, mothers with at least a college education, two-parent households, or residents of the North—and then entering in the regression only the dummy variables for the remaining categories. Each dummy variable's coefficient in a regression equation is calculated relative to the reference category, not to all other categories in the model (Agresti & Finlay, 1997). Contrary to Lopez and Barrueco's suggestion, we did not omit the reference categories from our analyses. Our interpretation of regression coefficients for dummy variables is correct.

In conclusion, we appreciate the many worthwhile points raised by Lopez and Barrueco relating to directions for more detailed future research on factors affecting school readiness. We hope that the issues they raised regarding our study have been clarified in this reply.

Reference

Agresti, A., & Finlay, B. (1997). *Statistical methods for the social sciences* (3rd ed.). Upper Saddle River, NJ: Westview Press.

II

Effects of Family Processes on Early Brain Development and Academic Skills Acquisition

6

FAMILY PROCESSES THAT SUPPORT SCHOOL READINESS: SPECIFIC BEHAVIORS AND CONTEXTUAL CONDITIONS THAT SET THIS PROCESS IN MOTION

Susan H. Landry
University of Houston-Health Science Center

Karen E. Smith
University of Texas Medical Branch

Considerable national attention is currently focused on improving young children's readiness to learn as they enter the formal school years. As a large number of children enter kindergarten without the foundational skills necessary to succeed in school, educators and policy makers are discussing how to change this discouraging picture (Landry, 2004). Research investigating this national crisis describes the inequality in school readiness for children from varying economic backgrounds (Keating & Hertzman, 1999). Advances in the neuroscience of brain development have accelerated interest and investments in the early years of life as these advances delineate the critical nature of development in the early years and the role of the child's environment (Levitt, 2004; McCain & Mustard, 2002). Studies of the developing brain demonstrate how the pathways through which physical brain development occurs are susceptible to sources of stimulation both inside and outside the home (McCain & Mustard, 2002). For example, synapses in the developing brain are created through input from a child's interactions with people and objects in their environment. Thus, much of the "wiring" process in the brain is dependent upon a child's activities and experiences with others. As parents represent, perhaps, the single most influential factor in children's development, a close examination of the research delineating the influence of parenting on the skills necessary for school readiness reveals areas in need of further attention in order to change our national picture.

In this chapter, we first review different theoretical frameworks describing parents' role in children's development and the mechanisms by which parenting is expected to influence school readiness. The parenting behaviors identified in these frameworks provide the foundation for a body of research that examines the influence of a comprehensive style of "responsive parenting" for the promotion of school readiness. Thus, our second goal is: (1) to describe empirical support for the importance of behaviors within this style in fostering optimal developmental trajectories, and (2) establish a causal link between responsive parenting and children's development through experimental research. Finally, factors known to moderate parents' use of responsive behaviors and their ability to learn such behaviors from intervention programs will be discussed.

Theoretical Frameworks for Understanding Parental Influences

Over the years, a number of theories have guided the research on parenting behaviors in order to determine those most important for understanding more optimal child outcomes during early childhood. Thus, an overview of theories of parenting is important. While theories explain different mechanisms by which parents' behaviors may influence children and highlight the role of different parenting behaviors, there is consistency across theories in the need for high quality parent-child interactions for the most optimal outcomes. Support for the different theories described below has been documented across gender, culture, ethnicities, and social status. The key parenting behaviors associated with each theory are predictive of later school age cognitive and social outcomes.

Ethological and attachment theories posit a special role for the early caregiving environment in understanding children's development. Early responsive styles are thought to provide a foundation that allows children to feel secure and develop a basic trust of caregivers and their environment (Ainsworth, Blehar, Waters, & Wall, 1978). This is in contrast to theories emphasizing the influence of parenting experienced after infancy (Kagan, 1984; McCall, 1981) or those that consider consistency in responsive parenting across childhood as equally important (Bornstein & Tamis-LeMonda, 1989; Coates & Lewis, 1984, Landry et al. 2001). It is important to note that while attachment theory places a special emphasis on infancy, a consistency across childhood in warm responsive parenting is inferred. While this theory recognizes general stimulation and language input as important for cognitive development, the critical parenting behaviors associated with this theory involve warmth, acceptance, and responses that are contingent to children's needs. Attachment theory describes the importance of acknowledging the child's individuality and accommodating to their needs and emphasizes the quality of the relationship across caregiving activities (Ainsworth et al., 1978). As a child develops an attachment relationship with a parent, internal representations of relationships are formed that support independence in coping and competency in social and cognitive functioning (Main, Kaplan, & Cassidy, 1985; Van IJzendoorn, Dijkstra, & Buss, 1995). For example, secure attachment has been associated with greater social competence with peers in the preschool period in a Head Start population that included peer acceptance and the child's proscocial skills in play groups (Bost et al., 1998). A history of secure attachment also was associated with greater peer affiliation in the preschool period (LaFreniere & Sroufe, 1985). Although cognitive outcomes are less frequently examined from an attachment framework, long term relations between attachment security in infancy with school age cognitive skills have been reported (Stams, Juffer, & Van IJzendoorn, 2002).

Theories that emphasize how early *learning is first embedded and supported by a social context* are attributed to Mead (1934) and Vygotsky (1978) and are the focus of investigations concerned with early communication and cognitive development (e.g., Bakeman & Adamson, 1984; Bruner, 1975; Wertsch, 1979). Central to Vygotsky's theory, or a socio-cultural framework, is the concept of the "zone of proximal development" where the child's learning is thought to occur at a significantly higher level in the context of a supportive social interaction. Demonstrations of this phenomenon are reported in numerous studies (e.g., Fagot & Gauvain, 1997; Henderson, 1984; Rogoff, 1990). For effective learning to occur the parent needs to support, or "scaffold", the child's learning needs in ways that would not be possible through independent exploration. In contrast to attachment theory, the socio-cultural framework does not emphasize a critical period in which this supportive parenting needs to occur. However, investigations tend to begin about 6 months of age when infants become capable of jointly attending to objects with others. Shared engagement with objects and others is a complex attentional process since young children must shift attention from person to object and back to person as well as coordinate gestures, vocalizations and affect to communicate their interest and respond appropriately (Bakeman & Adamson, 1984). As the child increases in competency, parents' scaffolding optimally will shift and decrease in direct support to allow the child to move from a greater dependency on the parent to taking a more active role in learning.

The influence of scaffolding that matches children's developmental needs has been shown to enhance preschooler's object exploration. Evidence for this comes from a study where children who independently showed low levels of exploration showed comparable levels to those of high independent explorers when given this type of support (Henderson, 1984). Research also demonstrates that this specialized early parental support may be particularly important for children with greater biological risk (e.g., prematurity, Down's Syndrome) (Landry, Garner, & Pirie, 1994; Landry, Smith, Miller-Loncar, & Swank, 1998) and this may be due to their greater difficulties in attention and behavioral regulation (e.g., Landry, 1995). Evidence for the importance of this parental support being provided early in childhood is documented in studies linking provision of high levels of scaffolding during preschool with stronger vocabulary and mathematic skills (Fagot & Gauvain, 1997) and verbal and nonverbal reasoning skills (Smith, Landry, & Swank, 2000a) at school entry.

The role of the parent also has been described as a *cognitive agent* in the child's learning, a role that shares some similarities to the importance of supportive parent interactions posited by the socio-cultural framework. In this role, the parent provides opportunities for learning with appropriate modeling of language and engagement with objects (Hart & Risley, 1995; Royce, Darlington & Murray, 1983). Research examining parents' role in children's early literacy development documents the importance of children having access and experiences with books in their homes, rich language input, as well as interactions that focus their attention on letters and sounds in words (Bloom, Rocissano, & Hood, 1976; Neuman, 1996; Snow, 1986; Whitehurst & Lonigan, 1998). The evidence for a long term impact on children's cognitive skills as late as 7th grade was found for enhanced maternal verbal stimulation through a randomized intervention conducted through the Mother-Child Home Study (Lazare & Darlington, 1982; Royce, Darlington, & Murray, 1983).

A critical role parents can play across early childhood for promotion of school readiness is reading to their children on a regular basis in ways that model language and require children to think and provide information about the story (Payne, Whitehurst, & Angell, 1994; Whitehurst & Lonigan, 1998). During the preschool years these experiences are particularly beneficial when coupled with an early childhood classroom that promotes similar language and literacy rich experiences (Whitehurst et al., 1994). In a well-documented longitudinal study of an early childhood classroom intervention that included a parenting component, Reynolds and colleagues (1996) showed that parent involvement in school, together with children's cognitive readiness, were important in mediating the impact of a preschool intervention on later school achievement. Rich language experiences in the home also promote cognitive readiness for children with biological risk factors and can help buffer the negative effects on cognitive skills of early severe medical complications (e.g., respiratory distress) associated with premature birth even when it occurs in children from poverty homes (Landry et al., 2001).

As cognitive readiness needs to develop in parallel with social competence, the role of the parent also involves being an agent of *socialization* (Maccoby & Martin, 1983). In this framework, beginning in early childhood, the most optimal parenting style is one that moves away from external constraints and avoids punishment, commands, and other forms of high external control. This, in turn, is shown to support the child's ability to regulate and inhibit their own behavior. The child's ability to develop independence in regulating their behavior is more likely to occur when parents provide clear expectations and consistency in behavioral guidance (Baumrind, 1989). In this vein, different styles of reacting to children's behavioral difficulties are associated with variability in social competence including cooperation. For example, authoritative parenting combines warm responsiveness with discipline that emphasizes reasoning and results in higher social skills. In contrast, an authoritarian style, involves power-assertive disciplinary tactics and results in decreased socialization skills (Hart, DeWolf, & Burnts, 1993; Kennedy, 1992). Better cooperation also has been associated with parents who allow their children to share control in interactions in terms of taking initiative in problem solving and demonstrate a willingness to follow the children's lead (Parpal & Maccoby, 1985). The mechanism by which this is expected to promote social competence includes a greater willingness on the child's part to "give and take" because their experience with their parents provides them with a trust that their needs and interests will be acknowledged.

In addition to social competence, children's ability to develop emotional competence is important for school readiness. A consistently strong finding is that when parents explicitly teach about emotions, their children display better regulation in their own emotions and understand more about the emotions of others (Dunn & Brown, 1991; Laible, 2004; Zahn-Waxler, Iannotti, Cummins, & Denham, 1990). Other supports parents provide to assist children's development of emotional competence include acceptance of children's emotions, modeling of effective management of emotions, and avoidance of frequent displays of highly negative emotions, particularly anger (Denham, 1998; Halberstadt, 1991).

Key Responsiveness Behaviors for Parenting

When considering the behaviors included across the frameworks described above, at least four key aspects of responsiveness can be identified: (1) contingent responding, (2) emotional/affective support, (3) support for infant and children's foci of attention, and (4) rich language input (Landry, Smith, & Swank, 2004). These four aspects often are considered in theoretical frameworks to be distinct and important for specific areas of child development such as cognition or social-emotional skills. However, rarely have these four aspects of responsiveness been examined in terms of how they may be related to a broader responsiveness construct and the extent to which they work together to provide the most optimal influence for cognitive and social skills. In a recent investigation of this issue, this conceptualization has been supported through factor analysis with each of the four aspects identified as separate factors. Moderate correlations, across the four factors that were stable over time and across contexts, provide some support for considering them as part of a broader responsiveness construct, or style (Landry et al., 2004).

The first of these aspects, contingent responding, comes from an attachment framework, and has been described as a three term chain of events where the child shows an action, the parent responds promptly and sensitively to the action, and, in turn, the child experiences a supportive consequence (Bornstein & Tamis-LeMonda, 1989). Contingent responding is thought to require parents to perceive their children as individuals with their own needs and interests. When parents were grouped using cluster analyses regarding the extent to which they used these behaviors across infancy and the preschool period, four groups were identified (Landry et al., 2001). The most optimal social and cognitive developmental trajectories were found for children whose mothers displayed higher levels of contingent responding across both developmental periods and the least optimal was found for those whose mothers showed minimal responsiveness during either period. There was some developmental advantage for children whose mothers showed some responsiveness during either period as these children's development was significantly better than those with mothers in the minimally responsive group. These findings contribute to our understanding of contingent responding by highlighting the need for this behavior to be at relatively high levels across early childhood. Further evidence for the importance of consistency in early responsiveness was found by following these families through 8 years of age where responsiveness across infancy and the preschool period continued to be important above and beyond responsive parenting in the school age years (Landry, Smith, & Swank, 2003).

Avoidance of inappropriate parental reactions to children's behavior including lower levels of restricting interests, physical intrusiveness, and harsh voice tone also was found on the contingent responding factor (Landry et al., 2004). Across 6, and 12, and 24 months of age, we found clusters of mothers who differed in their use of restrictiveness with and without warm responsiveness and linked these to children's preschool outcomes (Smith, Landry, & Swank, 2000b). The most devastating pattern included high levels of restrictiveness that increased across early childhood together with minimal levels of warmth as this pattern was associated with the lowest levels of preschool cognitive and social skills. In contrast, better cognitive and social outcomes were associated with mothers' use of a more optimal pattern that included relatively high warm responding with lower levels of restrictiveness. Although restrictiveness in this cluster of mothers increased over time, it remained low relative to other groups of mothers in the sample (Smith et al., 2000b).

Our research also has demonstrated that high levels of restrictiveness are most detrimental for children born at very low birth weight with greater neonatal medical complications (e.g., chronic lung disease, severe intracranial insult). In the presence of very low restrictive caregiving environments, children with this high-risk medical status showed social initiative at comparable and often higher levels than their term peers by preschool ages (Landry, Smith, Miller-Loncar, & Swank, 1997). In contrast, if their caregiving environments were highly restrictive, they had the worst social outcomes with trajectories of social initiative that decreased dramatically by three years of age. Although restrictiveness in this study could include harsh and physically intrusive behaviors, it also included any attempt by parents to stop their children from doing or saying something and thus, may not have appeared highly negative. In some cases, it was the high frequency rather than the high negative quality of parental restrictiveness that predicted poorer outcomes.

Another behavior associated with parental control that shows inconsistent associations with children's outcomes is directiveness or high structure. However, consideration of how directiveness is defined or characterized and the developmental period when it is measured is necessary in order to better understand its potential influence. Marfo (1990) has described how higher levels of directiveness may be an appropriate form of support for children with developmental problems across childhood as it provides structure and clear information abut what is expected from the child. In our work, we have documented how across the first two years of life, directiveness may provide support for healthy and "at risk" children, but can become a negative influence on initiative and executive processing abilities if it remains at high levels after this age point (Landry, Smith, Swank, & Miller-Loncar, 2000). In support of this finding we also documented that high levels of directiveness in the preschool years showed negative, direct effects on children's executive processing skills at 3 years of age that, in turn, predicted a lower trajectory of skill development through 6 years of age. In another study, when directiveness occurred at high levels in the preschool years, it had negative indirect effects on children's math skills at 8 years of age through its negative direct effects on earlier executive processing skills (Assel et al., 2003). These findings demonstrate the need for some parenting behaviors to change in relation to the child's changing developmental needs. For example, in the case of directiveness, its influence appears to be positive when the immature attention, motoric, and problem-solving skills of the infant require more structure and information about how to carry out an action or task. However, with increasing competency in these and other skill domains, the child requires support for their efforts to become more autonomous and to learn to take greater initiative, and high directiveness does not provide this type of support.

A second aspect of a responsive parenting style is the parents' use of warm sensitivity and positive affect during interactions, as this is thought to communicate affectively the caregiver's interest and acceptance (e.g., Darling & Steinberg, 1993). This form of positive emotional support is described as having an important role for children's development of cooperation and regulation of affect (Grusec & Goodnow, 1994; Maccoby & Martin, 1983). Warm sensitivity including positive affect was identified as a distinct factor from that of contingent responding while the absence of negative emotionality loaded on the same factor as contingent responding. The separation of these behaviors on different constructs is consistent with other theoretical descriptions. For example, while contingent responding and avoidance of negative emotionality from an attachment framework has a special role for supporting children's distress, warmth is important for its support of positive engagement (MacDonald, 1992).

In our longitudinal study, warm sensitivity in the toddler period predicted higher levels of cooperation by preschool ages (Miller-Loncar, Landry, Smith, & Swank, 2000) and greater increases in mothers' use of this behavior across early childhood was associated with greater increases in social responsiveness (Landry et al., 1998). Higher levels of early warm sensitivity across infancy also were associated with higher levels of cognitive and language skills during the preschool period (Smith et al., 2000b). Thus, while warm sensitivity has been more frequently described for its importance to social-emotional development, findings from this longitudinal study demonstrate its importance for both cognitive and social aspects of school readiness.

Supporting children's foci of attention was a third aspect of responsive parenting that included parents' attempts to maintain and build upon their children's interest rather than redirecting their attention (e.g., Ahtkar, Dunham, & Dunham, 1991; Landry, 1995; Tomasello & Todd, 1983). In the socio-cultural framework, this is expected to be particularly important in early development as it provides support for the young child's immature attentional and cognitive capacities. Such support, in turn, allows the child to focus and organize responses that allow them to better integrate information from the shared, or joint, interaction. In our longitudinal study, we found that when provided across early childhood, parenting behaviors such as maintaining and building on interests that can be considered "other regulation", predicted faster rates of language growth through 8 years (Landry et al., 2003). We have assessed changes in maternal maintaining across early childhood that were responsive to children's changing skills, as we expected they would be important in understanding children's rates of social development (Landry et al., 1998). As children increased in signaling to their mothers regarding their attentional interests, those with mothers who adapted to these changing signals by increasing their maintaining strategies had faster increases in their ability to initiate social interactions.

Parents' provision of rich verbal stimulation that includes labeling of objects and actions, explanations about how objects work and verbal encouragement is the fourth aspect of responsiveness important for children's development. Early language development is most likely to be supported from the parenting environment rather than the early childhood classroom environment while early literacy skills (e.g., phonological awareness) receive the strongest support from classroom experiences (Whitehurst & Lonigan, 1998). Other research has demonstrated children's need for this rich language input to occur in the context of supportive social interactions that maintain children's attention focus (Ahtkar et al., 1991; Tomasello & Farrar, 1986). Of concern is that children from lower economic backgrounds are the least likely to experience this type of rich language input (Hart & Risley, 1995). In their classic study, through observation of parent-child interactions from 9 through 36 months of age, children from lower-income families heard less than 100 unique vocabulary words per hour as compared to 500 per hour for children from more affluent families (Hart & Risley, 1992). Not only was the quantity of words heard low for children in poverty but the informational content of the parents' language input was extremely limited. These differences in quality of verbal parental input were strongly correlated with children's intelligence in the elementary school years.

In our longitudinal study, families from the poorest backgrounds used a high frequency of what Hess and Shipman (1965) referred to as "empty language". For 50% of our sample, over half of the utterances they heard from their families were words that carried very limited meaning and information (e.g., "this", "that", "here", "huh"). These children also heard, at high proportions, verbalizations that were meant to restrict their behavior (e.g., "stop", "don't", "get away from there").

Additionally, across the whole sample, rich language input that provides information about links between objects and actions rather than just the label for an action or object occurred in only 30% of the parents' utterances (Smith et al., 2000a). We examined later reading outcomes in relation to this paucity of rich language input as it occurred in early childhood and found, using structural modeling, a significant path between the quality of language input at 3 years of age with reading comprehension outcomes at 10 years of age. This occurred indirectly through the direct influence of parents' language input on child language skills at 4 years of age and their decoding skills at 8 years of age (Dieterich et al., in press).

Evidence for the Causal Influence of Responsive Parenting on Development

While there is a general appreciation for responsive parenting to support optimal development, this comes primarily from a broad base of descriptive research. To fully document the expectation that responsive parenting has a causal influence on development, findings are needed from experimental research. We recently examined this causal role in a randomized intervention in which changes were evaluated in a range of maternal responsive behaviors with growth in children's skills. In a home-based intervention, Playing and Learning Strategies (PALS), 133 mothers received coaching to enhance their skills in using behaviors within the four aspects of responsive parenting described in the previous section of this chapter. This was contrasted to a second group of 131 mothers who, in a comparable number of home visits, received information about their infant through weekly developmental assessments (DAS), but not how to promote more optimal skills for their young children (Landry et al., 2004). The infants varied in early biological characteristics (term, $n = 120$; very low birth weight [VLBW], $n = 144$) and the two intervention groups had comparable numbers of children with these biological risk factors and were comparable on a broad range of family demographic factors and infant characteristics.

Support for a causal role for responsive behaviors was expected to come from: (1) greater positive changes in PALS, as compared to DAS, mothers' use of the key aspects of responsiveness that, in turn, (2) resulted in greater gains for children's social and cognitive development when their mothers received PALS. The key ingredients for the 10-session PALS intervention included: (1) a review and discussion of key responsive behaviors using educational videotapes developed to highlight demographically similar mothers using these with infants, (2) coaching of mothers practicing behaviors with their infant in a variety of every day situations, (3) videotaping of the practice that is for mothers to review their own behavior and infant reactions, and (4) problem solving about how mothers could implement practice of these behaviors throughout the week. The intervention was constructed to assure a trusting relationship would develop between mothers and their coaches through the session format. In particular, the coach supported mothers' development of these supportive behaviors through a similar scaffolding approach to the one mothers would use with their infants. Mother-and-child-targeted behaviors were examined from videotaped measures of mother-child toy play, daily activity, and book reading (toddler/preschool period only) activities assessed just prior to the start of the intervention, during the middle of the intervention, two weeks following the end of the intervention and one month later. Children also were observed at these time points in interactions with a novel adult (i.e., research assistant) and in independent exploratory play to determine the extent to which infants whose mothers showed greater increases in responsiveness would generalize the benefit of this caregiving style by showing more optimal skills when not interacting with their mothers. Increases in mothers' responsiveness behaviors and child skills were analyzed using growth curve modeling procedures.

As expected, PALS mothers demonstrated significantly greater increases in their use of the four aspects of responsiveness. These, in turn, supported greater increases in their infants' social, cognitive, and language skills. Mothers and infants across the two groups were comparable on all pre-intervention measures. Of note, infants with PALS, as compared to DAS, mothers showed strong increases in their use of words and cooperation in interacting directly with their mothers as well as in interactions with an examiner. They also showed significantly greater increases in the complexity of their independent exploratory play than the control infants. When mothers were randomized again into these two groups in the toddler/preschool period, we found that greater growth in responsiveness across both developmental periods was particularly important for children's language development (Landry & Smith, in press).

The strongest test of a casual role of these maternal responsive behaviors on infant outcomes comes from evidence that positive change in these behaviors correlated with child outcomes and that the maternal behaviors mediated the effectiveness of the intervention on infant outcomes (Landry et al., 2004). For example, responsive behaviors from three of the four aspects (i.e., contingent responsiveness, rich language input, emotional support), together completely mediated the intervention influence on infants' cooperation. This finding may serve to advance the way responsiveness is thought to support social development as it highlights the need for multiple types of responsive support on this important skill area.

Factors Moderating Family Support for Children's Development

Decades of research provide consensus regarding the parenting characteristics during early childhood that predict individual differences in children's development. Children of parents with lower income, less education (e.g., Elder, Nguyen, &

Caspi, 1985; Huston, McLoyd, & Garcia-Coll, 1994; McLoyd, 1990; McLoyd, Jayaratne, Ceballo, & Borquez, 1994; Martin, Ramey, & Ramey, 1990; Campbell & Ramey, 1994), and greater psychosocial risk (e.g., substance abuse, domestic violence) (e.g., Huston et al., 1994; McLoyd, 1990; St. Pierre & Layzer, 1998) are more likely to have poorer developmental outcomes (e.g., lower skills in cognition, literacy, math, social interaction, coping resources). Two of the most consistently reported demographic predictors of child cognitive outcomes are maternal intelligence and years of education. However, the importance of these factors can decrease as intervention becomes more intensive. For example, the relation between maternal intelligence and child outcomes was lower beginning at 24-months than the relation between cognitive outcomes and an intensive education intervention (Ramey, Yeates, & Short, 1984). The mechanisms by which maternal intelligence and/or education influences children's development are not completely understood. Research supports that it is both environmental and genetic factors as well as an interaction between the two that are important in understanding these influences.

Often family economic and education level are described as markers for specific aspects of the caregiving environment (e.g., parenting behaviors) that have a more direct influence on children's development. When considering factors beyond demographic characteristics, there is a range of parental personal and social characteristics that provide information on the process by which parenting influences children's development. Personal characteristics of parents such as beliefs regarding children's developmental needs, and the parents' own childrearing history (Fish, Stifter, & Belsky, 1993; Liaw & Brooks-Gunn, 1994; McGroder, 2000) consistently show relations with parent behaviors and, in turn, child outcomes. Mothers who are more likely to believe that children need high levels of restrictiveness and direction regarding what is expected (i.e., degree of structure) are less likely to respond to children's needs in ways that provide appropriate nurturance and stimulation (Landry et al., 2001). Additionally, the level of complexity with which parents understand children's development influences a range of parent interactive behaviors and child outcomes (Miller-Loncar et al., 2000). Specifically, parents who are flexible in their thinking and use transactional explanations that consider multiple and reciprocal influences for their children's behavior are more likely to react to children in sensitive, responsive ways (Holden & Edwards, 1989; Sameroff & Feil, 1985). Another belief system that relates to whether parents provide behaviors described in this chapter is related to their perception of their own role in their children's cognitive development. Caregivers who do not believe they are important as a "teacher" for their child but rather attribute this role to others (i.e., teachers, childcare workers) or to "luck" are less likely to provide cognitively rich experiences (Hess & Shipman, 1965).

Research also shows a concordance between adults' views of their developmental history and the quality of the relationship they share with their own children (Ainsworth & Eichenberg, 1992; Fonagy, Steele, & Steele, 1991; Main et al., 1985). In general, studies reveal that positive relationships with parents in childhood are predictive of a later parenting style that is warm, flexible, and responsive to children's bids for attention. There is somewhat less consistency between negative developmental histories and parenting styles that lack emotional responsivity. Factors such as cultural diversity, life changing events, and child characteristics are thought to explain exceptional findings (Fonagy et al., 1991). For example, mothers with abusive and hostile child rearing histories show positive parenting behaviors but only when their infant is biologically high risk (Hammond, Landry, Swank, & Smith, 2000). These studies highlight the critical nature of understanding multigenerational influences on children's development.

Another personal characteristic predictive of children's outcomes is parents' psychological well-being (e.g., self-esteem, depression), as the availability of sufficient psychological resources has a positive effect on parenting behavior (e.g., Brody & Flor, 1997; McLoyd, 1998; Smith et al., 2001). Much of this research has examined the effects of parental depression (Assel et al., 2002; Lee & Gotlib, 1991; Lovejoy, Graczyk, O'Hare, & Neuman, 2000). For example, depressed mothers often report that their depression makes it difficult for them to be nurturant, patient, and involved in the parenting process (McLoyd, 1990; Taylor, Roberts, & Jacobson, 1997). This body of research clearly documents the debilitating effects of low self-esteem and high-risk mental health conditions on parents' ability to parent effectively and, ultimately, on children's outcomes.

Social support, including the level, amount, and type of support, is a predictive, external rather than internal, influence associated with more successful parenting (McLoyd, 1990; Melson, Ladd, & Hsu, 1993; Simons, Lorenz, Wu, & Conger, 1993; Stevens, 1988). Social networks that provide models for flexibility in interpersonal interactions, respect for others' ideas, and acceptance promote parenting views that consider the child's interest and abilities (Miller-Loncar et al., 2000). Parental warmth, responsiveness, and role satisfaction are related to the extent and amount of support (Crittenden, 1985). In a recent random assignment intervention targeting aspects of responsive parenting, social support uniquely predicted the likelihood that mothers would move from a poorer to higher quality of responsive parenting across the intervention period (Guttentag, Pedrosa-Josic, Landry, Smith, & Swank, in press). Given that social support is a determinant of children's outcomes (Cochran & Brassard, 1979), targeting change in this area is important, particularly given that it may be more open to modification than has been shown when trying to foster increases in family income or education.

The quality of the home environment also is an important predictor of school readiness and later academic and social competence. Children's development is influenced by factors beyond direct interactions with the parent. Until more recently, research has not accounted for the larger social and environmental context influencing caregiver's interaction with their children. Caldwell and Bradley have been responsible for studies looking at the influence of factors in the broader home and community context. Using the HOME scale (Caldwell & Bradley, 1984), they examined a broad range of factors in the home environment on children's cognitive (e.g., intelligence, language, reading and math achievement) and social outcomes (e.g., social competence with peers and teachers). Aspects of the home environment that are reported to predict better outcomes include availability of resources that potentially provide cognitive stimulation for the child (e.g., amount of books, play materials such as magnetic alphabet letters on the refrigerator), trips to a park or zoo. Interactions beyond parents (e.g., grandparents, friends) are also important for explaining children's school readiness.

Influences Beyond the Caregiving Environment

More recently there has been a movement to go beyond a focus of primary caregivers to include a broader social context such as the neighborhood or community in understanding children's development. Research examining parameters of the community such as access to children's books (Neuman, 1996), the quantity and quality of interactions between the neighborhood schools and parents (Reynolds et al., 1996), and racial socialization practices within families (Caughy, O'Campo, Randolph, & Nickerson, 2002) can expand our understanding of the complexity of environmental influences on children's cognitive readiness.

Research examining the influence of qualitative aspects of the broader social context on child development often uses ethnography, a methodology that requires systematic observation of children in natural settings. Building off of work by Bruner (1977) and Snow (1986), Norton (1996) examined the relation between children's language experiences and their academic achievement. By attending to the broader social system in the family and child's life, they addressed questions such as whether the child's language behaviors reflected what was expected in their own cultural context and the extent to which children adapted their language upon entry into the school environment. An important outcome of this research is its identification of the importance of environments that provide the child with a high degree of decontextualized language rather than language that is very contextualized in nature. High levels of decontextualized language meant that the child heard language (i.e., vocabulary, question, comment) that included information that went beyond the family environment or culture versus language that was closely linked only to the child's direct environment. Across similar poverty environments, children only hearing highly contextualized language decreased dramatically in their language and intelligence from preschool into middle school years to show functioning in the borderline range. In contrast, early exposure to decontextualized language was linked to average cognitive development and academic outcomes in school age years (Norton, 1996).

Another aspect of a families' social context is the number of people living together and this factor has significant effects on a parents' behavior with their child, above beyond that of economic status. For example, parents in crowded homes were found to speak in less complex ways to their children including the number of unique nouns, adjectives, and adverbs spoken per hour. An interesting aspect of this work was that the effect of crowded homes on the use of less rich language was mediated by the parents' verbal responsiveness to their children such that parents with lower levels of responsiveness were more likely to use diminished amounts of complex verbal utterances. Thus, this type of residential density results in parental social withdrawal that we know has negative impacts on a child's outcome (Evans, Maxwell, & Hart, 1999).

Although not directly linked to child outcomes, a better understanding of the negative impact of economic and social deprivation in neighborhoods on families' ability to access resources and receive social support from others may help us better understand the influence of the larger social context on the family and the child (Caughy, O'Campo, & Brodsky, 1999). In a recent study, the perception of neighborhood safety was associated with inconsistency in maternal discipline practices but not to displays of positive affect. The impact of the neighborhood on disciplinary practices was mediated by symptoms of maternal depression for both African American and Euro-American mothers (Hill & Herman-Stahl, 2002). Thus, parents who felt less safe in their surroundings had more difficulty responding to their children's misbehavior and this seemed to be due, in part, to a heightened level of depression. As noted previously in this chapter, maternal depressive symptoms have a negative impact on parents' use of responsive behaviors with their children. In general, across studies neighborhood factors account for less variance than parenting factors but are still important because they contribute to our understanding of the broader social context on children's school readiness (Leventhal & Brooks-Gunn, 2000).

Over the past decade greater attention has been paid to cultural influences on parenting behaviors and children's outcomes. Recent research has suggested that the impact of specific types of parenting on child outcomes may vary depending upon the family's ethnic background (Deater-Deckard & Dodge, 1997). However, this often is difficult to discern from that of poverty given that minority status is highly correlated with economic status. In a recent study of low-income families this was illustrated for maternal intrusiveness. Mothers who showed high levels of this behavior with their 15-month-old infants found their children at 2 years of age to exhibit greater negativity; this was true for all study families that comprised three ethnic backgrounds. In contrast, decreases in child engagement in relation to intrusiveness were only seen for children from Euro-American backgrounds. Thus, these results suggest that particular parent behaviors may have different meanings depending upon the family's culture and the meaning of the parenting behavior in the culture will determine its impact on a child (Ispa et al., 2004).

Integrating Science and Policy and Program Application

Developmental science often is not well integrated into policy or program application. The research described above outlines a range of factors during early childhood that are important for school readiness. Some of these, such as education and levels of poverty, are assumed to be markers for how parents interact and behave towards their children. Others are more direct indicators of the quality of the parenting environment, such as how parents understand children's needs and parents' internal (e.g., psychological health) and external (e.g., social support in the home and community) resources. These factors are shown to influence children indirectly, through a direct influence on parents' behaviors with their children. One avenue by which this research can inform policy and practice decisions is the information it provides on parents who are most at-risk. It suggests that interventions that attempt to facilitate change in parents' behaviors may need to consider factors such as parenting beliefs, mental health status, and level of social support in order to maximize effectiveness.

Additionally, better synthesis of relevant research concerning policy decisions will be important as research results currently fail to support popular programmatic policies. Recent advances in understanding the neurobiological mechanisms that drive development have promoted new interest in the role of early experience in brain development. This is understandable as the activation of neurons that direct the type and organization of connections in the brain are influenced by the type and frequency of a child's early experiences. However, while it is important to continue to examine this critically important link, direct connections between the recent neuroscience findings and child development research need to be more fully explored (DiPietro, 2000). The growing emphasis on accountability for publicly funded services for children and families should serve to push programs in the direction of giving greater consideration to the factors described above as program effectiveness is examined. New investments in programs need to call for a systematic evaluation of the components of programs (i.e., content, delivery approaches, use of technology to scale up programs) that are necessary in order to get sustained positive effects for families. For example, in a recent early childhood center-based intervention study, improved school readiness was obtained only when three major components were in place. These included research-based language/literacy curricula, web-based professional development courses with mentoring, and valid approaches for monitoring child developmental gains with feedback to inform instruction. With only one or two of these components, gains suggestive of school-readiness were not obtained (Landry, Swank, & Anthony, 2005). This work could be extended to determine whether there was an additive impact for school readiness if a parent component was also included. Related to this investment is the need to better understand the conditions, such as parent, child, and community factors, under which better program outcomes can be achieved rather than determining if the program "works" or not (Brooks-Gunn, Berline, Leventhal, & Fuligni, 2000). For example, are multi-faceted programs more important for families with higher and more risk factors (i.e., single-parent families, low education, severe poverty) while families at lower risk are able to take good advantage of programs that are highly focused on facilitating parent skills but not on improving other family risk factors? In order for these important questions to be answered federal, state and private fundors will need to agree that these are high priority areas that deserve careful and extensive investigation.

Acknowledgments

Some of the research in this chapter was supported by NIH grant nos. HD25128 and HD36099.

References

Ahtkar, N., Dunham, F., & Dunham, P. (1991). Directive interactions and early vocabulary development: The role of joint attention focus. *Journal of Child Language, 18*, 41–49.

Ainsworth, M. S., Blehar, M. S., Waters, E., & Wall, S. (1978). *Patterns of attachment: A psychological study of the strange situation.* Hillsdale, NJ: Erlbaum.

Ainsworth, M. D., & Eichenberg, S. H. (1992). Effects on infant-mother attachment of mother's unresolved loss of an attachment figure or other traumatic experience. In P. Marris, J. Stevenson-Hindle, & C. Parkes (Eds.), *Attachment across the life cycle* (pp. 160–183). New York: Routledge.

Assel, M. A., Landry, S. H., Swank, P. R., Steelman, L., Miller-Loncar, C., & Smith, K. E. (2002). How do mothers' childrearing histories, stress, and parenting affect children's behavioral outcomes? *Child: Care, Health and Development, 28*, 359–368.

Assel, M. A., Landry, S. H., Swank, P. R., Smith, K. E., & Steelman, L. (2003). Precursors to mathematical skills: Examining the roles of visual spatial skills, executive processes, and parenting factors. *Applied Developmental Science, 7*, 27–38.

Bakeman, R., & Adamson, L. B. (1984). Coordinating attention to people and objects in mother-infant and peer-infant interactions. *Child Development, 55*, 1278–1289.

Baumrind, D. (1989). Rearing competent children. In W. Damon (Ed.), *Child development today and tomorrow* (pp. 349–378). San Francisco, CA: Jossey-Bass.

Bloom, L., Rocissano, L., & Hood, L. (1976). Adult-child discourse: Developmental interaction between information processing and linguistic knowledge. *Cognitive Psychology, 8*, 521–552.

Bornstein, M., & Tamis-LeMonda, C. S. (1989). Maternal responsiveness and cognitive development in children. In M. H. Bornstein (Ed.), *Maternal responsiveness: Characteristics and consequences* (pp. 49–61). San Francisco: Jossey-Bass.

Bost, K. K., Vaughn, B. E., Washington, W. N., Cielinski, K. L., & Bradbard, M. R. (1998). Social competence, social support, and attachment: Demarcation of construct domains, measurement, and paths of influence for preschool children attending Head Start. *Child Development, 69*, 192–218.

Brody, G. H., & Flor, D. L. (1997). Maternal psychological functioning, family processes, and child adjustment in rural, single-parent, African-American families. *Developmental Psychology, 33*, 1000–1011.

Brooks-Gunn, J., Berline, L. J., Leventhal, T., & Fuligni, A. (2000). Depending upon the kindness of strangers: Current national data initiatives and developmental research. *Child Development, 71*, 257–268.

Bruner, J. (1975). The ontogenesis of speech acts. *Journal of Child Language, 2*, 1–9.

Caldwell, B., & Bradley, R. H. (1984). *Home observation for the measurement of the environment.* Little Rock: University of Arkansas at Little Rock.

Campbell, F. A., & Ramey, C. T. (1994). Effects of early intervention on intellectual and academic achievement: A follow-up study of children from low-income families. *Child Development, 65*, 684–698.

Caughy, M. O., O'Campo, P. J., & Brodsky, A. E. (1999). Neighborhoods, families, and children: Implications for policy and practice. *Journal of Community Psychology, 27*, 615–633.

Caughy, M. O., O'Campo, P. J., Randolph, S. M., & Nickerson, K. (2002). The influence of racial socialization practices on the cognitive and behavioral competence of African American preschoolers. *Child Development, 73*, 1611–1625.

Coates, D. L., & Lewis, M. (1984). Early mother-infant interaction and infant cognitive status as predictors of school performance and cognitive behavior in six-year-olds. *Child Development, 55*, 1219–1230.

Cochran, M. M., & Brassard, J. A. (1979). Child development and personal social networks. *Child Development, 50*, 601–616.

Crittendon, P. M. (1985). Social networks, quality of child rearing, and child development. *Child Development, 56*, 1299–1313.

Darling, N., & Steinberg, L. (1993). Parenting style as context: An integrative model. *Psychological Bulletin, 113*, 487–496.

Deater-Deckard, K., & Dodge, K. A. (1997). Externalizing behavior problems and discipline revisited: Nonlinear effects and variation by culture, context, and gender. *Psychological Inquiry, 8*, 161–175.

Denham, S. A. (1998). *Emotional development in young children.* New York: Guilford Press.

Dieterich, S. E., Assel, M. A., Swank, P. R., Smith, K. E., & Landry, S. H. (in press). The impact of early maternal verbal scaffolding and child language abilities on later decoding and reading comprehension skills. *Journal of School Psychology.*

DiPietro, J. A. (2000). Baby and the brain: Advances in child development. *Annual Review Public Health, 21*, 455–471.

Dunn, J., & Brown, J. (1991). Relationships, talk about feelings, and the development of affect regulation in early childhood. In J. Garber & K. Dodge (Eds.), *The development of emotion regulation and dysregulation.* Cambridge: Cambridge University Press.

Elder, G., Nguyen, T., & Caspi, A. (1985). Linking family hardship to children's lives. *Child Development, 56*, 361–375.

Evans, G. W., Maxwell, L. E., & Hart, B. (1999). Parental language and verbal responsiveness to children in crowded homes. *Developmental Psychology, 35*, 1020–1023.

Fagot, B. I., & Gauvain, M. (1997). Mother-child problem-solving: Continuity through the early childhood years. *Developmental Psychology, 33*, 480-488.

Fish, M., Stifter, C., & Belsky, J. (1993). Early patterns of mother-infant dyadic interaction: Infant, mother, and family demographic antecedents. *Infant Behavior & Development, 16*, 1–18.

Fonagy, P., Steele, H., & Steele, M. (1991). Maternal representations of attachment during pregnancy predict the organization of infant-mother attachment at one year of age. *Child Development, 65*, 684–698.

Grusec, J. E., & Goodnow, J. J. (1994). Impact of parental discipline methods on the child's internalization of values: A reconceptualization of current points of view. *Developmental Psychology, 30*, 1–19.

Guttentag, C. L., Pedrosa-Josic, C., Landry, S. H., Smith, K. E., & Swank, P. R. (in press). Individual variability in parenting profiles and predictors of change: Effects of an intervention with disadvantaged mothers. *Journal of Applied Developmental Psychology.*

Halberstadt, A. G. (1991). Socialization of expressiveness: Family influences in particular and a model in general. In R. S. Feldman & S. Rime (Eds.), *Fundamentals of emotional expressiveness* (pp. 106–162). Cambridge: Cambridge University Press.

Hammond, M. V., Landry, S. H., Swank, P. R., & Smith, K. E. (2000). Relation of mothers' affective developmental history and parenting behavior: Effects on infant medical risk. *American Journal of Orthopsychiatry, 70*, 95–103.

Hart, C. H., DeWolf, D. M., & Burnts, D. C. (1993). Parental disciplinary strategies and preschoolers' play behavior in playground settings. In C. H. Hart (Ed.), *Children on playgrounds: Research perspectives and applications* (pp. 271–313). Albany, NY: State University of New York Press.

Hart, B., & Risley, T. R. (1992). American parenting of language-learning children: Persisting differences in family-child interactions observed in natural home environments. *Developmental Psychology, 28*, 1096–1105

Hart, B. & Risley, T. R. (1995). *Meaningful differences in the everyday experiences of young American children.* Baltimore: Paul Brookes.

Henderson, B. B. (1984). Parents and exploration: The effects of context on individual differences in exploratory behavior. *Child Development, 55*, 1237–1245.

Hess, R. D., & Shipman, V. C. (1965). Early experience and the socialization of cognitive modes in children. *Child Development, 36*, 869–886.

Hill, N. E., & Herman-Stahl, M. A. (2002). Neighborhood safety and social involvement: Associations with parenting behaviors and depressive symptoms among African-American and Euro-American mothers. *Journal of Family Psychology, 16*, 209–219.

Holden, G. W., & Edwards, L. A. (1989). Parental attitudes toward child rearing: Instruments, issues, and implications. *Psychological Bulletin, 106*, 29–58.

Huston, A. C., McLoyd, V. C., & Garcia-Coll, C. (1994). Children and poverty: Issues in contemporary research. *Child Development, 65*, 275–282.

Ispa, J. M., Fine, M. A., Halgunseth, L. C., Harper, S., Robinson, J., Boyce, L. et al. (2004). Maternal intrusiveness, maternal warmth, and mother-toddler relationship outcomes: Variations across low-income ethnic and acculturation groups. *Child Development, 75*, 1613–1631.

Kagan, J. (1984). *The nature of the child.* New York: Basic Books.

Keating, D. P., & Hertzman, C. (1999). *Developmental health and the wealth of nations.* New York: Guilford Press.

Kennedy, J. H. (1992). Relationship of maternal beliefs and childrearing strategies to social competence in preschool children. *Child Study Journal, 22*, 39–60.

LaFreniere, P. J. & Sroufe, L. A. (1985). Profiles of peer competence in the preschool: Interrelations between measures, influence of social ecology, and relation to attachment theory. *Developmental Psychology, 21*, 56–69.

Laible, D. (2004). Mother-child discourse in two contexts: Links with child temperament, attachment security, and socioemotional competence. *Developmental Psychology, 40*, 979–992.

Landry, S. H. (2004). *Effective early childhood programs: Turning knowledge into action.* Houston, TX: James Baker Institute for Public Policy, Rice University.

Landry, S. H. (1995). The development of joint attention in premature, low birth weight infants: Effects of early medical complications and maternal attention-directing behaviors. In C. Moore & P. Dunham (Eds.), *Joint attention: Its origins and role in development* (pp. 223–250). Hillsdale, NJ: Erlbaum.

Landry, S. H., Garner, P., & Pirie, D. (1994). The effect of social context and mothers' requesting strategies on Down Syndrome children's responsiveness. *Developmental Psychology, 30*, 293–302.

Landry, S. H., & Smith, K. E. (in press). Parent's support of children's language provides support for later reading competence. In R. K. Wagner, A. Muse, & K. Tannenbaum (Eds.), *Vocabulary acquisition and its implications for reading comprehension*. New York: Guilford Press.

Landry, S. H., Smith, K. E., Miller-Loncar, C. L., & Swank, P. R. (1997). Predicting cognitive-linguistic and social growth curves from early maternal behaviors in children at varying degrees of biologic risk. *Developmental Psychology, 33*, 1–14.

Landry, S. H., Smith, K. E., Miller-Loncar, C. L., & Swank, P. R. (1998). The relation of change in maternal interactive styles with infants' developing social competence across the first three years of life. *Child Development, 69*, 105–123.

Landry, S. H., Smith, K. E., & Swank, P. R. (2003). The importance of parenting during early childhood for school age development. *Developmental Neuropsychology: Special Issue 24*, 559–590.

Landry, S. H., Smith, K. E., & Swank, P.R.. (in press). Responsive parenting: Establishing early foundations for social, communication, and independent problem solving skills. *Developmental Psychology*.

Landry, S. H., Smith, K. E., Swank, P. R., Assel, M. A., & Vellet, S. (2001). Does early responsive parenting have a special importance for children's development or is consistency across early childhood necessary? *Developmental Psychology, 37*, 387–403.

Landry, S. H., Smith, K. E., Swank, P. R., & Miller-Loncar, C. (2000). Early maternal and child influences on children's later independent cognitive and social functioning. *Child Development, 71*, 358–375.

Landry, S. H., Swank, P. R., & Anthony, J. (2005). *Findings supporting the effectiveness of comprehensive professional development programs for pre-kindergarten teachers of at-risk children*. Paper presented at the Interagency Education Research Initiatives meeting, Washington, DC.

Lazare, I., & Darlington, R. (1982). Lasting effect of early education: A report from the Consortium for Longitudinal Studies. *Monographs of the Society for Research in Child Development, 47* (2, Suppl.3), 1–151.

Lee, C. M., & Gotlib, I. H. (1991). Adjustment of children of depressed mothers: A 10-month follow-up. *Journal of Abnormal Psychology, 100,* 473–477.

Leventhal, T., & Brooks-Gunn, J. (2000). The neighborhoods they live in: The effects of neighborhood residence on child and adolescent outcomes. *Psychological Bulletin, 126*, 309–337.

Levitt, P. (2004). *The neuroscience of child development: Policy implications*. Presentation to the James A. Baker III Institute for Public Policy, Rice University.

Liaw, F., & Brooks-Gunn, J. (1994). Cumulative familial risks and low-birthweight children's cognitive and behavioral development. *Journal of Clinical Child Psychology, 23,* 360–372.

Lovejoy, M. C., Graczyk, P. A., O'Hare, E., & Neuman, G. (2000). Maternal depression and parenting behavior: A meta-analytic review. *Clinical Psychology Review, 20,* 561–592.

Maccoby, E., & Martin, J. A. (1983). Socialization in the context of the family: Parent-child interactions. In P. H. Mussen (Series Ed.) & E. M. Hetherington (Vol. Ed.), *Handbook of child psychology: Vol. 4. Socialization, personality, and social development* (4th ed., pp. 1–102). New York: Wiley.

Main, M., Kaplan, N., & Cassidy, J. (1985). Security in infancy, childhood, and adulthood: A move to the level of representation. In I. Bretherton & E. Waters (Eds.), *Growing points in attachment theory and research.* Monographs of the Society for the Research in Child Development, 50(1-2, Serial No. 209).

Marfo, K. (1990). Maternal directiveness in interactions with mentally handicapped children: An analytical commentary. *Journal of Child Psychology & Psychiatry, 4,* 531–549.

Martin, S. L., Ramey, C. T., & Ramey, S. (1990). The prevention of intellectual impairment in children of impoverished families: Findings of a randomized trial of educational day care. *American Journal of Public Health, 80,* 844–847.

McCain, M. N. & Mustard, J. F. (2002). *The Early Years Study three years later.* Toronto, ON: The Founders' Network.

McCall, R. (1981). Nature-nurture and the two realms of development: A proposed integration with respect to mental development. *Child Development, 52,* 1–12.

MacDonald, K. (1992). Warmth as a developmental construct: An evolutionary analysis. *Child Development, 63,* 753–773.

McGroder, S. M. (2000). Parenting among low-income African American single mothers with preschool-age children: Patterns, predictors, and developmental correlates. *Child Development, 71,* 752–771.

McLoyd, V. C. (1990). The impact of economic hardship on black families and children: Psychological distress, parenting, and socioemotional development. *Child Development, 41,* 311–346.

McLoyd, V. C. (1998). Socioeconomic disadvantage and child development. *American Psychologist, 5,* 185–204.

McLoyd, V. C., Jayaratne, T. E., Ceballo, R., & Borquez, J. (1994). Unemployment and work interruption among African American single mothers: Effects on parenting and adolescent socioemotional functioning. *Child Development, 65,* 562–589.

Mead, G. H. (1934). *Mind, self, and society.* Chicago: University of Chicago Press.

Melson, G. F., Ladd, G. W., & Hsu, H. (1993). Maternal support networks, maternal cognitions, and young children's social and cognitive development. *Child Development, 64,* 1401–1417.

Miller-Loncar, C. L., Landry, S. H., Smith, K. E., & Swank, P. R. (2000). The influence of complexity of maternal thoughts on sensitive parenting and children's social responsiveness. *Journal of Applied Developmental Psychology, 21,* 335–356.

Neuman, S. B. (1996). Children engaging in storybook reading: The influence of access to print resources, opportunity, and parental interaction. *Early Childhood Research Quarterly, 11,* 495–513.

Norton, D. G. (1996). Early linguistic interaction and school achievement: An Ethnographical, ecological perspective. *Zero to Three, 16,* 8–14.

Parpal, M., & Maccoby, E. E. (1985). Maternal responsiveness and subsequent child compliance. *Child Development, 56,* 1326–1334.

Payne, A. C., Whitehurst, G. J., & Angell, A. L. (1994). The role of home literacy environment in the development of language ability in preschool children from low-income families. *Early Childhood Research Quarterly, 9,* 427–440.

Ramey, C. T., Yeates, K. O., & Short, E. J. (1984). The plasticity of intellectual development: Insights from prevention intervention. *Child Development, 55,* 1913–1925.

Reynolds, A. J., Mavrogenes, N. A., Bezruczko, N., & Hagemann, M. (1996). Cognitive and family-support mediators of preschool effectiveness: A confirmatory analysis. *Child Development, 67*, 1119–1140.

Rogoff, B. (1990). *Apprenticeship in thinking.* New York: Oxford University Press.

Royce, J. M., Darlington, R. B., & Murray, H. W. (1983). Pooled analyses: Findings across studies. In Consortium for Longitudinal Studies (Eds.), *As the twig is bent: Lasting effects of preschool programs* (pp. 411–459). Hillsdale, NJ: Erlbaum.

Sameroff, A. J., & Feil, L. A. (1985). Parental concepts of development. In I. E. Sigel (Ed.), *Parental belief systems* (pp. 83–105). Hillsdale, NJ: Erlbaum.

Simons, R. L., Lorenz, F. O., Wu, C., & Conger, R. D. (1993). Social network and marital support as mediators and moderators of the impact of stress and depression on parental behavior. *Developmental Psychology, 29*, 368–381.

Smith, K. E., Landry, S. H., & Swank, P. R. (2000a). Does the content of mothers' verbal stimulation explain differences in children's development of verbal and nonverbal cognitive skills? *Journal of School Psychology, 38*, 27–49.

Smith, K. E., Landry, S. H., & Swank, P. R. (2000b). The influence of early patterns of positive parenting on children's preschool outcomes. *Early Education and Development, 11*, 147–169.

Snow, C. E. (1986). Conversations with children. In P. Fletcher & M. Garmen (Eds.), *Language acquisition: Studies in first language development* (pp. 69–89). New York: Cambridge University Press.

Stams, G. J. M., Juffer, F., & van IJzendoorm, M. H. (2002). Maternal sensitivity, infant attachment, and temperament in early childhood predict adjustment in middle childhood: The case of adopted children and their biologically unrelated parents. *Developmental Psychology, 38*, 806–821.

Stevens, J. H. (1988). Social support, locus of control, and parenting in three low-income groups of mothers: Black teenagers, black adults, and white adults. *Child Development, 59*, 635–642.

St. Pierre, R. G., & Layzer, J. I. (1998). Improving the life chances of children in poverty: Assumptions and what we have learned. *Social Policy Report, Society for Research in Child Development, 5.*

Taylor, R. D., Roberts, D., & Jacobson, L. (1997). Stressful life events, psychological well-being, and parenting in African-American mothers. *Journal of Family Psychology, 11*, 436–446.

Tomasello, M., & Farrar, M. (1986). Joint attention and early language. *Child Development, 57*, 223–229.

Tomasello, M., & Todd, J. (1983). Joint attention and early language. *Child Development, 4*, 197–212.

Wertsch, J. V. (1979). From social interaction to higher psychological processes: A clarification and application of Vygotsky's theory. *Human Development, 22*, 1–22.

Whitehurst, G. J., Epstein, J. N., Angell, A. L., Payne, A. C., Crone, D. A., & Fischel, J. E. (1994). Outcomes of an emergent literacy intervention in Head Start. *Journal of Educational Psychology, 86*, 542–555.

Whitehurst, G. C., & Lonigan, C. J. (1998). Child development and emergent literacy. *Child Development, 68*, 848–872.

van IJzendoorn, M. H., Dijkstra, J., & Buss, A. G. (1995). Attachment, intelligence, and language: A meta-analysis. *Social Development, 4*, 115–128.

Vygotsky, L. (1978). *Mind in society.* Cambridge, MA: Harvard University Press.

Zahn-Waxler, C., Iannotti, R. J., Cummins, E. M., & Denham, S. A. (1990). Antecedents of problem behaviors in children of depressed mothers. *Development & Psychopathology, 3*, 271–292.

7

STUDY OF THE EFFECTS OF PARENTING ON ASPECTS OF BRAIN GROWTH AND DEVELOPMENT RELEVANT TO SCHOOL READINESS: A WORK IN PROGRESS

Clancy Blair
Pennsylvania State University

The chapter by Susan Landry (this volume) provides a valuable framework for organizing a variety of aspects of parenting important for developing competence and well-being in children. Under the heading of 'responsive parenting', she arrays large and sometimes disparate literatures, skillfully integrating multiple theoretical perspectives. One aspect of the responsive parenting framework that serves as the primary focus of this commentary concerns interrelations among the various aspects of responsive parenting. Given Landry's approach, two overarching issues emerge: the extent to which distinct aspects of responsive parenting tend to covary, and the extent to which each is likely to demonstrate unique relations with various child outcomes. Is rich language stimulation frequently accompanied by high levels of contingent responding? Does support for attention frequently occur in combination with emotional/affective support? And is there naturally occurring variation among the different aspects of responsive parenting that can allow for some empirical conclusions about each on its own? Can we examine each aspect of responsive parenting in relation to child outcomes and come to some conclusions about that aspect of parenting irrespective of other aspects? Or are they inextricably intertwined such that this expectation is really more a theoretical than empirical reality? Landry's work suggests that this separation does exist and provides some indication of relations of specific aspects of responsive parenting to specific aspects of child development.

The attempt to relate specific aspects of responsive parenting to child development outcomes sets the stage for the examination of potential contributions of parenting to early brain growth and development important for school readiness. Here, one can begin to sketch out a developmental neuroscience model of school readiness that builds on the rich history of work on high-quality care in infancy and early childhood. In doing so, however, it is worth noting that while such a model is conceptually quite rich, in certain respects it tends to be empirically poor in humans and relies to some extent on data that are suggestive of the framework or that come from extremely well-developed nonhuman animal models. For the nonhuman animal work there are important considerations of applicability to humans.

The overarching theoretical orientation for this examination of parenting, brain development, and school readiness is based on a general developmental psychobiological model provided by Gilbert Gottlieb (1991). This model, presented in Figure 7.1, is familiar to many and provides a straightforward and picturesque description of expected relations among genetic, physiological, behavioral, and environmental levels of influence on development. Its central point is the idea that action at any given level influences and is influenced by action at all other levels.

Bidirectional Influences

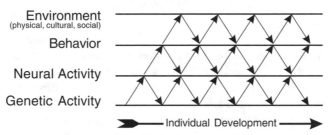

Reprinted from Gottlieb (1992) with permission. Copyright 1992 by Oxford University Press.

Figure 7.1. A system view of psychobiological development.

The model in Figure 7.1 is particularly valuable in the study of school readiness in providing multiple entry points for an area of study that can and has been examined from many different levels. By focusing explicitly on relations among variables at multiple levels, the model allows for the examination of diverse influences on school readiness with an eye to relations between various sets of indicators. For present purposes, this amounts to an examination of those associated with parenting and those associated with processes of child neural and physiological development important for certain competencies associated with school readiness. Stated simply, the model suggests that in the study of development it is important to examine how what occurs outside the child in the parent-child relationship affects processes inside the child important for school readiness; and on the flipside of this, how what occurs inside the child affects what transpires between parent and child, outside of the child. In colloquial terms, we are examining how the outside gets in and the inside gets out.

Beginning with how the outside gets in, this approach builds on well-established research traditions in psychology, the study of environmental enrichment/impoverishment and the study of stress early in the life course, particularly the study of stress in infancy. The best-known and perhaps definitive of the human studies of enrichment include the Abecedarian (Ramey & Campbell, 1984), Perry Preschool (Schweinhert et al., 1985), and Chicago Parent-Child Center (Reynolds & Temple, 1998) projects. From the impoverishment end of the spectrum, recent work on child development after early care experiences in the orphanages of Romania (O'Connor, Rutter, Beckett, Keaveney, & Kreppner, 2000; Zeanah, Nelson, Fox, Smyke, Marshall, Parker, & Koga, 2003) provides what is perhaps the clearest indication of the effects of care at the extreme low end of what might be considered the "normal" range, that is, care that stops short of the extreme abuse and neglect as is seen most frequently in literatures on developmental psychopathology.

Findings from human studies of early enriched care suggest initial effects on general intelligence and early school achievement. Data from the Abecedarian Project, for instance, demonstrate effects on intelligence through early childhood and longer-term impacts on school achievement in reading and math, decreased grade retention and reduced special education placement (Campbell, Pungello, Miller-Johnson, Burchinal, & Ramey, 2001). Similarly, both Perry Preschool and the Chicago study findings clearly indicate improved school achievement as well as improved life outcomes, including high school completion, decreased criminality, and various other indicators of health and well-being.

Findings from studies of impoverished rearing and extreme privation are equally clear and essentially the opposite of those from enrichment, indicating deficits in cognitive, social, and emotional outcomes early in the life course. However, there is considerable heterogeneity in outcomes following impoverishment as well as considerable evidence of remediation of deficits and developmental improvements following placement in high quality care environments (Rutter et al., 1998; Zeanah et al., 2003).

Without question, the early intervention and early privation studies are foundational and highly insightful. But it is necessary to make just one obvious and simple point about them. Namely, they provide little information specifically about mechanisms of effects. These studies, as strong and valuable as they are, tend to provide global "good-bad" indicators of early care. They lack specificity along the dimensions of responsive parenting in which we are interested. Were the caregiving environments of the early intervention studies primarily characterized by rich language input? Were they also characterized by contingent responding and support for attention? Without doubt they were, but these specific aspects of care were unmeasured per se. Similarly, with the effects of extreme privation on child outcomes, were these environments uniformly bad? Almost certainly they were, along multiple dimensions of responsive parenting and several others as well, such as nutrition and basic health, for example. But few or no studies, whether of enrichment or privation, offer empirical insight into the relation of variation in dimensions of care to variation in aspects of child outcomes.

Lack of specificity in the measurement of early care is something of a problem for efforts to substantiate a developmental neuroscience model of high-quality parenting and school readiness. This is seen when we turn to the nonhuman animal literature on enriched versus impoverished early care. A number of nonhuman animal studies provide some very interesting data on the neurobiological consequences of rearing in enriched environments, that is, environments that are physically materially stimulating, versus impoverished environments—those that are lacking in material stimulation. Work on environmental enrichment and impoverishment in nonhuman animal models, in rodents in particular, indicates that highly physically stimulating or conversely highly unstimulating environments are associated with changes in brain growth and development. Data from these studies indicate that rats reared in environmentally stimulating housing demonstrate increased brain size, brain weight, synaptic density, dendritic branching, neurogenesis, gene expression and a variety of other indicators of brain growth and development. (Lewis, 2004; Rosenzweig, 2003).

Findings from the study of enriched rearing in nonhuman animals suggest effects from general increases in stimulation in humans, such as parents providing opportunities for exploration, but lack specificity with regard to what might generally be considered parenting effects. This is particularly so in light of findings indicating that one relevant factor in changes in brain growth in rats in enriched environments is physical activity (van Praag et al., 2003). Enriched environments provide rats with greater opportunity for movement and exploration, through tunnels, mazes, etc. The habitat is more complex. This is in contrast to the completely unstimulating environment of standard laboratory housing. As a consequence, these rodent studies perhaps have more to say about animal care protocols than they do about parental care, per se. The primary independent variable manipulation is not in the quality of parental care but in a distinction between high or low level of physical material stimulation. Here, comparison of effects to the human studies of the extreme privation of institutional rearing may be apt. However, it is necessary to distinguish between material stimulation and social stimulation. Studies with rodents have noted distinct effects on cognitive and behavioral outcomes associated with rearing among littermates versus isolation rearing that are distinct from those associated with enriched versus impoverished physical and material stimulation (Schrijver et al., 2004). These studies suggest the need to closely examine both physical and social aspects of the early care environment.

Despite the cautions presented by the nonhuman animal literature on early experience and brain growth, it is still very tempting to ask whether there might be a relation between generally higher quality parental care, of any responsive type, and generally larger and heavier brains that could link high-quality care to early schooling outcomes in humans. Many behavioral scientists would very much like to make this empirical leap of faith but unfortunately the evidence is not particularly compelling. For one thing, it is not clear that the physical and social environmental manipulations of the rodent studies are on the same psychosocial level with something as complex as parenting. And for another, the links between brain volumes and intelligence have been around for over 100 years, some with a very checkered history (Gould, 1996). The theoretical link between brain volumes and intelligence has recently received some impressive support, however, from brain imaging research. Volumetric analyses of whole brain gray matter and gray matter volumes in the frontal cortex in particular have been linked to measures of intelligence. Furthermore, like general intelligence, gray matter volumes have been shown to be highly heritable (Thompson et al., 2001). The link between gray matter volumes and frontal cortex is particularly impressive given functional MRI evidence linking increases in activation in the frontal cortex to measures of general intelligence (Gray, Chabris, & Braver, 2003). Therefore, given evidence of experience-dependent synaptic plasticity in the brain and findings of links between high-quality early educational care and IQ in disadvantaged human populations, it is at least conceivable that high-quality care, of a nonspecific variety, is affecting brain volumes in ways that lead to cognitive advantage and increased school achievement.

No doubt this is part of the story, but there continues to be a frustrating lack of specificity in the link between high-quality care and brain volumes on both sides of the equation. On the care side we lack specificity both in theory and research on what aspects of care are most important. On the brain side of the equation we lack specificity in relations of brain size and brain function to cognitive abilities and behavior, particularly when we examine the specific instance of school readiness. There is no clear nonhuman animal model analogue of school readiness other than perhaps general competence at being a rodent or nonhuman primate. In both the short and long run, it would seem that a general association among early experience, brain development, and behavioral outcomes important for school readiness is too simplistic to be of great value. Perhaps the idea that better environments lead to faster, more efficient brains is correct in its general form but it leaves little in the way of hard and fast scientific conclusions. We cannot stop there.

The question is this: Are there specific aspects of early care experience that affect specific brain systems and functions important for school readiness? No doubt there are and it should be possible to provide as least one example of relations between certain aspects of early care and certain child outcomes. To do this, it is necessary to turn again to the nonhuman animal literature but this time to the study of early stress; specifically, to separation paradigms in rodents. These studies have for many years indicated that brief intermittent separation of the rat pup from the dam (the mother) leads developmentally to an enhanced hypothalamic-pituitary-adrenal (HPA) axis stress response in the pup (Levine, 1957; Meaney et al., 1989). Rat pups experiencing brief separation, also referred to as handling in the literature, exhibit a higher threshold for activation of the stress response and exhibit an appropriate increase and decrease in the regulation of the glucocorticoid stress hormone, corticosterone in the rodent, cortisol in the human. Those experiencing extended separation exhibit outcomes that are the opposite of these—low threshold for activation and problems with reactivity and regulation of glucocorticoid.

The finding of an early experience effect on the regulation of the stress response system in the rat is fascinating in that problems with the regulation of the stress response and resulting high levels of glucocorticoids are associated with a variety of social and behavioral problems, not only in rats, but in humans, too. Chronically high levels of glucocococrticoids work to establish a hyper-reactive stress response system. In turn, hyper-reactivity of the stress response system leads to increased levels of anxiety-like behaviors, hyperactivity, and problems with social behavior and learning and memory fairly early in development (Francis et al., 1999; Kaufman & Charney, 2001).

Could the study of separation from the mother in rodents have a relation to early care and the development of brain systems important for school readiness in humans? The answer is, quite possibly, although in a specific and perhaps not obvious way. The first step in the relation has to do with the working out of the relation of brief separation from the mother to HPA stress reactivity and later developmental outcomes. It is a story of high-quality maternal care in rodents that is expertly detailed by Michael Meaney and colleagues. In short, what Meaney and others have shown is that what transpires following the brief separation of the pup from the dam is an increase in stimulating types of behaviors from the mother upon reunion. That is, upon reunion the rat mothers demonstrate higher levels of licking and grooming (LG) and a type of nursing referred to as arched back nursing (ABN). These two behaviors are highly correlated, so much so as to indicate a single behavioral parenting construct in the rat. Furthermore, these behaviors have been shown to vary naturally among rat dams. In naturalistic studies, Meaney and his colleagues have demonstrated relations between variation in LG/ABN and the stress response and behavior in the offspring (Meaney, 2001). Furthermore, they have shown nongenomic transmission across generations of this maternal style using cross fostering paradigms (Francis et al., 1999). They have also shown that the behavioral effects of rearing by a low LG/ABN mother are reversible through environmental enrichment (Francis et al., 2002). Although offspring reared by low LG/ABN mothers continue to look like stressed-out rats at the physiological level, behaviorally they look like their high LG/ABN counterparts after experiencing environmental enrichment. That is, effects appear to be reversible at the behavioral but not at the physiological level (Bredy et al., 2003).

Meaney and his colleagues' work presents a well-developed model of what it means to be a good mother—if you are a rat, that is. However, the obvious question is, what could possibly be the parenting analogue in humans? Likely not grooming, but maybe something similar, along the lines of contingent responding and emotional/affective support from Landry's framework. Might contingent responding and emotional/affective support be distinct aspects of parenting separate from more informational, attention-directing aspects of responsive parenting? Moreover, are aspects of parenting that can be shown to have a specific influence on child developmental outcomes important for school readiness? Quite likely, and toward this goal one can offer hypotheses about some distinct effects of contingent responding/nurturing sensitivity on child development outcomes versus types of parenting that may be more informational, i.e., language stimulation and direct provision of information. To do so leads us to a second step in this analysis, one concerning the relation of HPA and glucocorticoid function to aspects of cognition referred to as executive functions (EF). Executive functions are aspects of cognition associated with a response to novel or to be learned information. Although of course related to and to some extent dependent on knowledge and information, they refer to time limited and effortful processes of holding information in mind, of shifting and sustaining attention, and inhibiting extraneous or prepotent types of information and responses (Diamond, 2002; Zelazo & Müller, 2002). Here, EF can also be thought of as being important for planning and problem solving and for abstraction, for understanding complex relations among hierarchically related items.

There are large literatures on EF in which two important issues concern the extent to which the distinct aspects of EF are separable or are essentially one entity (unity versus diversity of EF) and the extent to which EF is separable from general intelligence. For present purposes, it is sufficient to say that although the dimensions of EF are distinct (Miyake et al., 2000), data indicate that they do tend to go together within persons and that as such are clearly distinct from the general factor of intelligence (Blair, 2006). Furthermore, most relevant present interest is evidence indicating that aspects of EF are dependent in predictable ways on the HPA stress response system and levels of circulating glucocorticoids (Blair, Granger & Razza, 2005; Lupien, Gillin, & Hauger, 1999) and are important correlates of school readiness and academic ability in the early elementary grades (Blair & Razza, in press). In fact, in the rat one of the outcomes of variation in maternal behavior that has been examined by a number of investigators is the EF of WM, particularly spatial WM. Findings in the rat indicate that high levels of stress reactivity interfere with WM ability and do so through problems with synaptogenesis in the hippocampus (Liu et al., 2000). Indeed, the model is one that is highly consistent with the known effects of problems with the regulation of stress reactivity and high levels of circulating glucocortioids. In the stress response, a cascade is triggered leading from the hypothalamus to the pituitary to the adrenals that signal to the body to produce the fuel, glucocorticoid, needed for a stress response. The brain structure that plays an important role in signaling the HPA axis to start the cascade is the amygdala, which is associated with vigilance and the fear response. Once the cascade is in motion, the brain structure associated with signaling to the amygdala to halt the HPA cascade is the hippocampus. Signaling from the hippocampus is dependent on the level of circulating glucocorticoid; a negative feedback loop, like the home heating thermostat on the wall. However, unlike the thermostat on the wall, in response to chronic stress or in individuals in which the system is biased toward an increase rather than regulation of the response, the negative feedback fails in an important way and ultimately inhibits aspects of brain function and synaptic growth, particularly in the hippocampus (McEwen, 2000).

Work on environmental influences on the HPA response to stress provides a powerful model for how what occurs external to the organism affects the internal milieu and behavioral and cognitive phenomena dependent on this milieu. But of course, what is perhaps well known in the rodent is less well known in the human. Data from studies of child abuse, extreme neglect, and extreme stress indicate hippocampal shrinkage, problems with HPA axis regulation, and problems with cognitive functions similar to EF (Bremner et al., 1995; Kaufman & Charney, 2001). However, whether such a psychobiological model might apply to child outcomes occurring within care environments at the low end of the normal range, a type more likely to occur in the conditions of poverty, remains unknown. In our work, we have shown relations between HPA stress reactivity and EF and self-regulation in children from low-income homes and have also demonstrated relations between EF and early progress in school in these children (Blair, Granger, & Razza, 2005; Blair & Razza, in press). These findings are aspects of the larger model we have been working on for some time that is now linking early care experience with development of the regulation of stress and emotionality and the development of EF and school readiness. What remains to be accomplished involves some very important questions, namely: Is poor quality care stressful or just unstimulating? Can nurturant/sensitive care be unstimulating from an informational standpoint or from an affective standpoint? What is the variation in care in low-income environments, what are the influences on this variation, and how are they related to school readiness?

This all leads to a further and for now concluding step in the examination of relations among parenting, brain growth and development, and school readiness, one that has to do with the idea that what transpires physiologically and psychologically in the child may affect the parent-child relationship and the quality of care. In short, the question is whether highly stress reactive mothers have highly stress reactive babies. This likely possibility raises the further possibility of reciprocal causation such that the combination of the highly reactive baby with the highly reactive mother leads most consistently to problems with caregiving and thereby to problems with stress regulation, EF, and later school outcomes in the child. The rodent model investigated by Michael Meaney and colleagues strongly suggests this to be the case (Meaney, 2001). In their work, rat dams who are more stress reactive engage in a maternal style that tends to pass on the highly reactive profile, a mechanism of transmission that has been demonstrated through experimental cross-fostering manipulations (Liu et al., 1997), and is of particularly wide-ranging implication in that it has been shown to produce its effect at the level of the gene. As shown in the rat, high level of maternal LG/ABN chemically alters the expression of a segment of the genome important for the regulation of the HPA axis, leading to stable and potentially lifelong effects of early care on physiology and behavior (Weaver et al., 2004).

The model of early care and stress reactivity in the rat provides an example of a truly Gottliebian process consistent with the model in Figure 7.1 in which multiple levels of influence, including genes and early experience, combine to determine development. We believe that the model of early care in the rat has valuable implications for the study of school readiness, and calls particular attention to the early care and early school environments as contexts that support or hinder the developing integration of cognition and emotion important for early adaptation to school. Attention to the child within context is central to efforts to promote school readiness and the many developmental benefits that children accrue from early success in school. Without doubt, further articulation of responsive parenting and expected effects on child development important for school readiness is needed. To this end, we are currently collecting data with approximately 1,200 children and their families, beginning at birth, to examine the developmental relation among stress reactivity, emotion regulation, and the aspects of cognition that comprise EF. Through home visits conducted at child ages 6, 15, 24, and 36 months, we will relate measures of emotionality and HPA response to stress to the development of EF and to social and cognitive self-regulation the underline school readiness. By examining these relations within the context of the family and relating them to measures of parenting behavior, we can assess the extent to which the highly reactive child is more frequently seen in the chaotic home characterized by less sensitive parenting and also the extent to which this reactivity is more likely to be maintained through age 3 years. By then following the children and families into school, we can further examine the extent to which this more reactive child and family configuration may be associated with problems with early school adjustment, but also the extent to which the school context may further increase or decrease problems associated with reactivity.

References

Blair, C. (2006). How similar are fluid cognition and general intelligence? A developmental neuroscience perspective on fluid cognition as an aspect of human cognitive ability. *Behavioral and Brain Sciences, 29,* 109–125.

Blair, C., Granger, D., & Razza, R. P. (2005). Cortisol reactivity is positively related to executive function in preschool children attending Head Start. *Child Development, 76,* 554–567.

Blair, C., & Razza, R. P. (in press). Relating effortful control, executive function, and false-belief understanding to emerging math and literacy ability in kindergarten. Manuscript submitted for publication. *Child Development.*

Bredy, T. W., Humpartzoomian, R. A., Cain, D. P. & Meaney, M. J. (2003). Partial reversal of the effect of maternal care on cognitive function through environmental enrichment. *Neuroscience, 118,* 571–576.

Bremner, J. D., Randall, P., Scott, T., Capelli, S., Delaney, R., McCarthy, G. & Charney, D. (1995). Deficits in short-term memory in adult survivors of childhood abuse. *Psychiatry Research, 59,* 97–107.

Campbell, F.A., Pungello, E.P., Miller-Johnson, S., Burchinal, M., & Ramey, C.T. (2001). The development of cognitive and academic abilities: Growth curves from an early childhood educational experiment. *Developmental Psychology, 37,* 231–242.

Diamond, A. (2002). Normal development of the prefrontal cortex from birth to young adulthood: Cognitive functions, anatomy, and biochemistry. In D. Stuss & R. Knight (Eds.), *Principals of frontal lobe function* (pp. 466–503). Oxford, UK: Oxford University Press.

Francis, D., Caldji, C., Champagne, F., Plotsky, P. M., & Meaney, M. J. (1999). The role of corticotropin-releasing factor-norepinephrine systems in mediating the effects of early experience on the development of behavioral and endocrine responses to stress. *Biological Psychiatry, 46,* 1153–1166.

Francis, D., Diorio, J., Liu, D., & Meaney, M. J. (1999). Nongenomic transmission across generations of maternal behavior and stress responses in the rat. *Science, 286,* 1155–1158.

Francis, D., Diorio, J., Plotsky, P. M., & Meaney, M. J. (2002). Environmental enrichment reverses the effects of maternal separation on stress reactivity. *The Journal of Neuroscience, 22,* 7840–7843.

Gottlieb, G. (1991). Experiential canalization of behavioral development: Theory. *Developmental Psychology, 27,* 4–13.

Gould, S. J. (1996). *The mismeasure of man–revised and expanded.* New York: Norton.

Gray, J. R., Chabris, C. F. & Braver, T. S. (2003). Neural mechanisms of general fluid intelligence. *Nature Neuroscience, 6,* 316–322.

Kaufman, J., & Charney, D. (2001). Effects of early stress on brain structure and function: implications for understanding the relationship between child maltreatment and depression. *Development and Psychopathology, 13,* 451–471.

Levine S. 1957. Infantile experience and resistance to physiological stress. *Science, 126,* 405–406.

Lewis, M. (2004). Environmental complexity and CNS development and function. *Mental Retardation and Developmental Disabilities Research Reviews, 10,* 91–95.

Liu, D., Diorio, J., Day, J. C., Francis, D. D., & Meaney, M. J. (2000). Maternal care, hippocampal neurogenesis, and cognitive development in rats. *Nature Neuroscience, 3,* 799–806.

Lupien, S. J., Gillin, C. J., & Hauger, R. L. (1999). Working memory is mores sensitive than declarative memory to the acute effects of corticosteroids: A dose-response study in humans. *Behavioral Neuroscience, 113,* 420–430.

McEwen, B. S. (2000). Effects of adverse experiences for brain structure and function. *Biological Psychiatry, 48,* 721–731.

Meaney, M. J. (2001). Maternal care, gene expression, and the transmission of individual differences in gene expression across generations. *Annual Review of Neuroscience, 24,* 1161–1192.

Meaney, M. J., Aitken, D. H., Viau, V., Sharma, S., & Sarrieau, A. (1989). Neonatal handling alters adrenocortical negative feedback sensitivity and hippocampal type II glucocorticoid receptor binding in the rat. *Neuroendocrinology, 50,* 597–604.

Miyake, A., Friedman, N. P., Emerson, M. J., Witzki, A. H. & Howerter, A. (2000). The unity and diversity of executive functions and their contributions to complex "frontal lobe" tasks: A latent variable analysis. *Cognitive Psychology, 41,* 49–100.

O'Connor, T. G., Rutter, M., Beckett, C., Keaveney, L., & Kreppner, J. M. (2000). The effects of global severe privation on cognitive competence: extension and longitudinal follow-up. English and Romanian Adoptees Study Team. *Child Development, 71,* 376–390

Ramey, C. T., & Campbell, F. A. (1984). Preventive education for high-risk children: Cognitive consequences of the Carolina Abecedarian Project. *American Journal of Mental Deficiency, 88,* 515–523.

Reynolds, A. J., & Temple, J. A. (1998). Extended early childhood intervention and school achievement. *Child Development, 69,* 231–246.

Rosenzweig, M. (2003). Effects of differential experience on brain and behavior. *Developmental Neuropsychology, 24,* 523–540.

Rutter, M., & the English and Romanian Adoptees Study Team. (1998). Developmental catch-up, and delay, following adoption after severe global early privation. *Journal of Child Psychology and Psychiatry, 39,* 465–476.

Schrijver, N., Pallier, P., Brown, V., & Wurbel, H. (2004). Double dissociation of social and environmental stimulation on spatial learning and reversal learning in rats. *Behavioural Brain Research, 152,* 307–314.

Schweinhart, L. J., Berrueta-Clement, J. R., Barnett, W. S., Epstein, A. S., & Weikart, D. P. (1985). Effects of the Perry Preschool program on youths through age 19. *Topics in Early Childhood Special Education, 5,* 26–35.

Thompson, P., Cannon, T., Narr, K., van Erp, T., Poutanen, V., Huttunen, M., Lonnqvist, J., Standertskjold-Nordenstam, C., Kaprio, J., Khaledy, M., Dail, R., Zoumalan, C. & Toga, A. (2001) Genetic influences on brain structure. *Nature Neuroscience, 4,* 1253–1258.

van Praag, H., Christie, B. R., Sejnowski, T. J., & Gage, F. H. (1999). Running enhances neurogenesis, learning, and long-term potentiation in mice. *Proceedings of the National Academy of Sciences USA, 96,* 13427–13431.

Weaver, I., Cervoni, N., Champagne, F., Alessio, A., Sharma, S., Seckl, J., Dymov, S., Szyf, M., & Meaney, M. (2004). Epigenetic programming by maternal behavior. *Nature Neuroscience, 7,* 847–854.

Zeanah, C. H., Nelson, C. A., Fox, N. A., Smyke, A. T., Marshall, P., Parker, S. W., & Koga, S. (2003). Designing research to study the effects of institutionalization on brain and behavioral development: the Bucharest Early Intervention Project. *Development and Psychopathology, 15,* 885–907.

Zelazo, P. D., & Müller, U. (2002). Executive function in typical and atypical development. In U. Goswami (Ed.), *Handbook of childhood cognitive development* (pp. 445–469). Oxford: Blackwell.

8

GENETIC SOURCE OF READING DISABILITY AND A PROPOSAL TO USE NLSY-CHILDREN TO STUDY GENETIC AND ENVIRONMENTAL INFLUENCES ON READING DISABILITY

Guang Guo
Jonathan Daw
University of North Carolina at Chapel Hill

Introduction

Reading disability, also known as dyslexia, is defined as difficulty in learning to read despite adequate intelligence, customary instruction, and typical patterns of family and social support. It can have a major influence on the cognitive, emotional, and social development of affected individuals. Depending on the defining criteria, reading disability affects 5–15% of school children (Paulesu et al., 2001; Shaywitz et al., 1998) and accounts for more than 80% of all learning disabilities (Lerner, 1989). Reading disability is the most common neuro-behavioral disorder that affects children and is a major social, educational, and mental health problem.

This chapter contains a review of molecular studies of linkage and association analysis on reading disability and a plan for collecting DNA data for the existing National Longitudinal Study of Youth (NLSY). Reading disability is one of the first complex quantitative behavioral traits geneticists have attempted to map and more than a decade of molecular genetic studies on reading disability have repeatedly pointed to a small number of chromosomal regions that may contain the genes responsible for reading disability (e.g., Cardon et al., 1994; Fisher et al., 2002; Smith et al., 1991). The NLSY is a traditional large-scale social and demographic study of children's well-being including reading skills. Since 1979, the NLSY has conducted a yearly follow-up of about 4800 women aged 14–21 in 1979 and about 11,000 of these women's children. As the children reach ages 4 to 5, they are given a battery of cognitive tests, including tests on readings skills and verbal cognitive ability, every two years. The collection of DNA data for the NLSY would yield a large nationally representative and longitudinal sample for studies of reading disability and other child outcomes. The wealth of information on the environments of the children that already exists in the NLSY will aid future analyses of how children's social environment may compensate for reading disability.

Figure 8.1 shows a conceptual framework for how genes, caregiving environment, extra caregiving environment, and their interactions influence reading disability over the life course. Amongst environmental and non-genetic factors we distinguish between caregiving environmental factors and extra caregiving environmental factors. Potential caregiving environmental factors include the Home Scale, Maternal Intelligence, Maternal Education, and Parenting Behaviors. Possible extra caregiving environmental factors include child's age, race/ethnicity, sex, socioeconomic status, and contextual conditions. The influences on reading disability from caregiving environmental factors tend to be direct, whereas the extra caregiving environmental factors typically influence reading disability indirectly by operating through the caregiving environmental factors. The arrow from genetic disposition to reading disability refers to the Mendelian cases in which genes and mutations cause reading disability. The interactive effects are illustrated by two arrows: one that travels from the line linking extra caregiving environmental factors and genetic predisposition to caregiving environmental factors, and the other that connects the line linking the caregiving environmental factors and genetic predisposition to the longitudinal measures of reading disability.

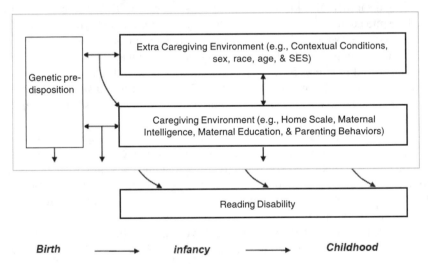

Figure 8.1. Influences of genes and caregiving environment and extra-caregiving environment & their interactions on reading disability.

Identification of the Phenotype

Diagnosis of dyslexia usually derives from the results of a standardized word-recognition test and an IQ test. A frequently used definition requires a discrepancy of negative 2 standard deviations between the reading score and the IQ score. Certain factors may complicate diagnostic efforts. For example, the observed IQ of dyslexic children declines with age and is negatively related to socioeconomic status, so that children who are older or of lower socioeconomic status are less likely to be diagnosed by the discrepancy criterion. Alternative methods that make no assumptions about IQ–reading relationships define reading disability as a significant lag in reading age.

Unfortunately, most diagnosis criteria for dyslexia rely upon an arbitrary diagnostic threshold. This is difficult to justify because the question of whether dyslexia is a pathological condition indicating a qualitatively different category or the tail of a normal distribution of individuals remains unresolved. With reading disability, as with other complex traits, there probably is considerable phenotypic variability among subjects designated as affected. Further complicating the issue is the fact that different developmental stages may yield different levels of reading skills. Adolescents and adults with reading disability can 'compensate'; such persons appear to have normal word recognition skills, but the underlying deficits persist. These deficits can be detected with appropriate tests that tap spelling, reading rate or phonological skills. Therefore, global diagnosis of dyslexia might not always prove optimal for genetic research, as these tests do not differentiate the variability of the phenotypes.

These problems can be overcome to a certain extent by the use of quantitative measures of reading-related processes instead of categorical diagnostic measures. In addition, standardized tests may be constructed to measure the hypothesized components of the reading process, such as phoneme awareness (PA), phonological decoding (PD), and orthographic coding (OC). Affected children usually show deficits in one or more of these component measures. Phoneme awareness is defined as the ability to reflect on the individual speech sounds that make up a word (phonemes). This ability is assessed using oral tasks that do not involve any visual processing of print. Phonological decoding, the ability to convert written sublexical letter units (graphemes) into their corresponding phonemes, is measured by the oral reading of pronounceable non-words that lack real meaning, like 'torlep.' Orthographic coding is defined as the ability to recognize the specific letter patterns (orthography) of whole words. This is assessed by forced-choice tasks (OC-choice) that require rapid recognition of a target word compared with a phonologically identical non-word (such as rain versus rane).

Genetic Source of Reading Disability

Family Studies Using Siblings

Familial clustering of reading disability has been repeatedly demonstrated over the last century, and numerous segregation and twin studies have consistently supported a significant role for genetic factors in the disorder (DeFries & Fulker, 1985; Hallgren, 1950; Olson et al., 1989; Pennington, 1995; Pennington et al., 1991). Recent results of a large Colorado-based study reported a proband-wise concordance rate of 68% in MZ twins versus 38% in DZ twins (DeFries & Gillis, 1993). Gilger et al. (1991) reported that the risk for dyslexia for children with an affected parent is about eight times that of children in the general population. Twin and other family studies have established that 40–70% of the variance in these reading-related measures is due to genetic factors.

Linkage Analysis

Linkage analysis is a technique to map genes for specific traits by attempting to find DNA sequences that are more likely to be shared among affected relatives and differ between affected and unaffected relatives. When specific chromosomal regions are already suspected, mapping efforts can be tailored to these areas. Otherwise, a genome-scan can be conducted in search of novel chromosomal loci contributing to the phenotype. The next step is to fine-map the most promising regions in order to narrow down the linked chromosomal region. Once the chromosomal location of a gene is known, molecular methods can be used to find markers that are even closer to the gene, eventually identifying the exact piece of DNA carrying the gene. At this point the exact sequence can be determined, facilitating the identification of the gene's precise function.

Since genes are strung together in a specific order on the chromosome, genes that are close together on the same chromosome tend to be inherited together as the chromosome is transmitted to the offspring. Such genes are said to be linked. However, when homologous chromosomes pair at meiosis, there can be an exchange of DNA between the two chromosomes that can separate alleles that were previously together. The probability that this recombination will occur is positively related to the distance between the two linked loci. For this reason, the frequency of recombination is used as a measure of the distance between the genes. The chromosomal location of a gene causing a disorder can be found using linkage analysis. For instance, if reading disability is found to be transmitted together with a known marker allele, this is evidence that the reading disability is influenced by a gene that is close to the marker locus.

Two general approaches of linkage analysis have been used in the search for genes influencing reading disability. The first method is the traditional LOD score analysis of extended families, or parametric linkage analysis. In this method large three generation, autosomal dominant families are selected for study and a variety of genetic markers are typed, including restriction fragment length polymorphisms (RFLPs), minisatellites, microsatellites, and single nucleotide polymorphisms (SNPs). The transmission of these markers through each family is compared to the transmission of reading disability. LOD analysis seeks to identify which genetic markers are near polymorphisms that differentially impact the expression of the trait in question. The identified markers resulting from this analysis is referred to as a quantitative trait locus, or QTL. The probability of linkage to a QTL is expressed as LOD score, an acronym for log10 of the odds of linkage. Traditionally, a linkage has been accepted as proven if it registers a LOD score greater than 3.0 and is rejected with a score less than -2.0.

Another approach for linkage analysis is the sib pair, or nonparametric, method. These methods are particularly appropriate for complex traits such as reading disability because they do not require assumptions about monogenic inheritance, penetrance, and mode of inheritance because they only require that reading disability be measured for the siblings under study. The downside is that this method requires a larger sample size.

Reported Linkage Results

Nearly two decades of linkage studies have identified a number of potential loci for reading disability: chromosome 6 (Cardon et al., 1994, 1995; Fisher et al., 1999; Grigorenko et al., 1997, 2000; Gayán et al., 1999; Kaplan et al., 2002; Smith et al., 1991), chromosome 15 (Grigorenko et al., 1997; Morris et al., 2000; Nothen et al., 1999; Smith et al., 1983), chromosome 2 (Fagerheim et al., 1999; Fisher et al., 2002), chromosome 3 (Nopola-Hemmi et al., 2000), and Chromosome 18 (Fisher et al., 2002). See Fisher and Defries (2002) for a recent overview. Table 8.1 briefly shows these linkage results for reading disability. For each study, it lists the locus at which a linkage is present; the scope of search, which is either targeted at a specific chromosomal region or genome-wide; the authors; the population from which the sample was drawn; a description of the sample; the treatment of phenotype; the analytical method used; and the reported LOD score or P-value.

In many of the linkage analyses, investigators targeted the human leukocyte antigen (HLA) region on chromosome 6 because of a suspected association between reading disability and autoimmune disorders (Cardon et al., 1994). Many dyslexic children have asthma, hay fever, or other immune system problems. There is now converging evidence from several independent studies that a QTL on 6p21.3 contributes to multiple components of dyslexia. The region of 6p21.3 was first implicated by Smith et al. (1991). Cardon et al. (1994, 1995) targeted the same region and defined the putative QTL as a two cM region within the HLA complex. Grigorenko et al. (1997) reported significant linkage results for the phonological awareness phenotype for the region of 6p21.3, thus providing a partial replication of the earlier results by Smith et al. (1991) and Cardon et al. (1994). These results were further replicated by Gayán et al. (1999). In 2000, Grigorenko et al. expanded their early study (Grigorenko et al., 1997) and the findings were consistent with those from three other independent studies that a QTL at 6p21.3 influences various dyslexia-related phenotypes. The locus is now named *DYX2* (OMIM 600202). It should be noted that Field and Kaplan (1998) failed to replicate linkage to the 6p23-6p21.3 region using a sample of 79 Canadian families.

Table 8.1
Selected Findings of Molecular Genetic Studies of Reading Disability

Locus	Scope of Analysis	Reference	Population	Sample	Treatment of Phenotypes	LOD or P-value
6p21.3	Targeted	Smith et al. (1991)	U.S.	19 ()	Qualitative/global Quantitative/global	P<0.02 P<0.0001
6p21.3	Targeted	Cardon et al. (1994)	U.S.	19 (); 46 DZ twin pairs	Quantitative/global Quantitative/global	P=0.04 P=0.009
6p22.3-6p21.3	Targeted	Grigorenko et al. (1997)	U.S.	6 ()	Qualitative components	P<0.005 P<0.000001
No linkage	Targeted	Field & Kaplan (1998)	UK	79 ()	Qualitative/global	
No linkage	Targeted	Schulte-Korne et al. (1998)	Germany	7 ()	Qualitative/global	
6p21.3	Targeted	Fisher et al. (1999)	UK	82	Quantatitive components	P=0.004–0.0006
6p21.3	Targeted	Gayan et al. (1999)	U.S.	79 ()	Quantatitive components	LOD=3.1
6p21.3	Targeted	Grigorenko et al. (2000)	U.S.	8 ()	Qualitative components	
6p21.3	Targeted	Petryshen et al. (2000)	Canada	79 ()	Quantatitive components	P=0.07
15q15-Qter	Targeted	Smith et al. (1991)	U.S.	18 families	Qualitative/global	
15q21	Targeted	Grigorenko et al. (1997)	U.S.	6 families N=94	Qualitative components	
15q21	Targeted	Schulte-Korne et al. (1998)	Germany	7 families N=67	Qualitative/global	
15q21	Targeted	Morris et al. (2000)	UK	178 parent-proband trios	Qualitative/global	
15q21	Genome-wide	Nopola-Hemmi (2001)	Finland	2 families		
2p15-16	Genome-wide	Fagerheim et al. (1999)	Norway	1 large extended family	Qualitative/global	LOD: 2.92, 3.54, 4.32 P: 0.016, 0.023, or 0.0009
3p12-q13	Genome-wide	Nopola-Hemmi et al. (2001)	Finland	1 large extended family	Qualitative/global	LOD: 3.84 P=0.00006
18p11.22 p16 3p13	Genome-wide	Fisher et al. (2002)	UK	89 ()	Quantitative components	P<0.0001
18p11.22 2p15 3q13			U.S.	119 ()	Quantitative components	P<0.0004
18p11.2			UK	84 ()	Quantitative components	P<0.0005

Smith et al. (1983) reported the first linkage for reading disability to the short arm of chromosome 15. In 1991, Smith et al. reported another locus in the long arm of chromosome 15 as well as a susceptibility locus on the short arm of chromosome 6. Grigorenko et al. (1997) studied six independent families and were able to map a potential risk locus to 15q21 with a LOD score greater than 3. Schult-Körne et al. (1998) obtained additional evidence supporting linkage between chromosome 15q21 markers and a putative dyslexia locus (*DYX1*, OMIM 127700).

Fagerheim et al. (1999) investigated a genome-wide linkage to reading disability in a large Norwegian family with 36 dyslexic family members and reported a locus on 2p15-p16 cosegregating with reading disability. This finding has been replicated by Fisher et al. (2002) and the locus has been labeled *DYX3* (OMIM 604254). Nopola-Hemmi et al. (2001) reported a linkage to chromosome 3 (*DYX5*; OMIM 606896) in an extended Finnish family of 28 dyslexic individuals. The reading deficits in the family included phonological awareness, verbal short-term memory, and rapid naming. Other families in the same study showed no evidence of linkage in this region. Fisher et al. (2002) later replicated this result in a genome-wide investigation.

Fisher et al. (2002) performed genome-wide scans in two large sets of nuclear families with dyslexic members from the United Kingdom and the United States. Among other potential risk loci, they reported strong linkage to 18p11.2 in the UK sample. Using single-point analysis, linkage to marker D18S53 was found to be one of the most significant results (p<0.0004) for single-word reading disability in each of the two samples. Multipoint analysis yielded stronger evidence of 18p11.2 linkage for single-word reading with p values of 0.00001 in the UK sample and 0.0004 in the U.S. sample. Measures related to orthographic and phonological processing also showed linkage at this locus. Fisher et al. (2002) confirmed the results at 18p11.2 with a third independent sample from the UK. Analysis combining the two independent samples from the UK verified the 18p QTL (OMIM 606616). The independent verification in multiple data sets suggests a probable general risk factor for reading disability operating through several reading related processes.

Association or Candidate Genes Studies

Despite encouraging linkage results, the identification of the particular genetic variants that influence dyslexia has proven difficult. Linkage analysis usually implicates chromosomal regions that contain hundreds of candidate genes. In order to achieve greater specificity, association studies can be used to either locate the gene associated with reading disability in the implicated region or test the hypothesis that one or more polymorphisms in the region are associated with reading disability. The latter type of studies is usually based upon prior knowledge of the gene's biological function.

An association study of reading disability (when treated as a binary outcome) typically requires a sample of individuals both with and without the condition. The genotype of these individuals must be determined by sequencing the same stretch of DNA or polymorphism in the individuals. Then, the frequency of the genotype at the locus of interest among those with reading disability (cases) is compared with that among those without the condition (controls); a higher frequency of the genotype in cases is taken as evidence that genotype is associated with increased risk of reading disability. A statistically significant result indicates that the polymorphism under consideration either affects risk of reading disability directly or is a marker correlated with some nearby genetic variant that affects the condition directly.

Reported Results from Association Studies

Genetic hunts for the forms of speech and language disorder more rare and severe than dyslexia have been more successful. In 1998, Fisher et al. reported linkage results from an analysis of a three-generation family on a severe speech and language impairment with an apparently autosomal dominant mode of inheritance. The researchers managed to map the locus to a small interval at 7q31. Subsequent studies (Lai et al., 2000, 2001) were able to sequence *FOXP2* in the family and demonstrated a point mutation in all affected individuals. The disorder associated with *FOXP2* is severe and involves difficulty in controlling the fine muscle movements in the mouth required for speech. The results serve as an example of how current investigations on dyslexia might eventually shed light on the underlying processes.

Using 178 proband-parent trios from Great Britain, Morris et al. (2000) in a family-based association mapping study reported a highly significant association between reading disability and a three-marker haplotype (D15S994/D15S214/D15S146) on chromosome 15q. More recently, Taipale et al. (2003) reported the results of the characterization of a novel gene, which they refer to as *DYXC1*. This gene is located on 15q21, near the locus previously reported in a number of linkage studies of dyslexia. Its specific function in humans is unknown. Taipale et al. analyzed the structure of the gene and identified two sequence changes in *DYXC1* that appear to be associated with dyslexia.

In a linkage disequilibrium screen of the genes including *VMP, DCDC2, KIAA0319, TTRAP,* and *THEM2* in a 575-kb region of chromosome 6p22.2 in an independent sample, incorporating family-based and case-control designs, Cope et al. (2005) found an association between developmental dyslexia and two SNPs (*rs4504469* and *rs6935076*) in the *KIAA0319* gene. The haplotype formed by these two markers was also significantly associated with dyslexia (P=0.00001 in the case-control sample and P=0.02 in the trios). The data strongly implicate *KIAA0319* as a susceptibility gene for dyslexia. The expression of the gene product is found in the brain, but its biological function is not understood.

Use of the NLSY to Study Genes and Environment of Dyslexia

The NLSY Study

The proposed study will piggy-back on the existing National Longitudinal Survey of Youth and their Children (NLSY). The NLSY is a multi-purpose panel survey that originally included a nationally representative sample of 12,686 men and women who were all 14–21 years of age on December 31, 1978. With primary support from the National Institute of Child Health and Human Development (NICHD), all children born to NLSY female respondents have been independently followed and interviewed in various ways starting in 1986, greatly expanding the breadth of child-specific information collected. In addition to all of the mother's information from the NLSY, the child survey includes assessments of each child as well as additional demographic and development information collected from either the mother or child.

Starting in 1986, the children of the NLSY female respondents have been assessed every two years. The assessments measure cognitive ability, temperament, motor and social development, behavior problems, and self-competence of the children as well as the quality of their home environment. As of 2000, a total of 11,205 children have been identified as having been born to the original 6,283 NLSY female respondents. As of the 2000 interview round, all the women had attained the ages 35–43. An estimated 90% of the total offspring of the sampled women were represented in the sample.

Reading Disability and Other Related Measures

The child assessments that are particularly relevant to our purpose include Peabody Individual Achievement Test for Reading Recognition (PIATR), Peabody Individual Achievement Test for Reading Comprehension (PIATC), Peabody Individual Achievement Test for Math (PIATM), and the Peabody Picture Vocabulary Test-Revised (PPVT-R). Previous linkage analysis has frequently used the three PIAT tests, especially the PIATR to measure the phenotypes of reading disability.

The Peabody Individual Achievement Test (PIAT) is a measure of academic achievement for children aged five and over and is widely known and used in research. It is among the most widely used brief assessments of academic achievement, having demonstrably high test-retest reliability and concurrent validity. The NLSY used three subsets of the full PIAT battery: the Reading Recognition, Reading Comprehension, and Mathematics assessments.

The PIAT Reading Recognition subset measures word recognition and pronunciation ability—essential components of reading achievement. Children read a word silently and then say it aloud. PIAT Reading Recognition contains 84 items, each with four options, which increase in difficulty from preschool to high school levels. Skills assessed include matching letters, naming names, and reading single words aloud. The basic goal of the subtest is to measure skills in translating sequences of printed alphabetic symbols into speech sounds that can be understood as words. The PIAT Reading Comprehension subset measures a child's ability to derive meaning from sentences that are read silently. This subtest goes beyond the meaning of individual words; it focuses on comprehending passages that is more representative of practical reading ability. For each of 66 items of increasing difficulty, the child silently reads a sentence once and then selects one of four pictures that best portrays the meaning of the sentence.

The PIAT Mathematics subscale measures a child's attainment in mathematics as taught in mainstream education. It consists of 84 multiple-choice items of increasing difficulty. It begins with such early skills as recognizing numerals and progresses to measuring advanced concepts in geometry and trigonometry. Essentially, the child looks at each problem and then chooses an answer by pointing to or naming one of four options. In the Colorado Reading Disability Project, the PIAT Reading Recognition (Dunn & Markwardt, 1970) was the primary measure for reading skills and the Wechsler's test was used to tap intelligence quotient (Wechsler, 1974, 1981).

The Peabody Picture Vocabulary Test (PPVT) "measures an individual's receptive (hearing) vocabulary for Standard American English and provides, at the same time, a quick estimate of verbal ability or scholastic aptitude" (Dunn & Dunn, 1981, p. 2). The English language version of the assessment consists of 175 vocabulary items of generally increasing difficulty. The child listens to a word uttered by the interviewer and then selects one of four pictures which best describes the word's meaning. A child's entry point into the assessment is based on his or her PPVT age. This assessment, designed for ages 3 and over, has been administered, with some exceptions, to NLSY children between the ages of 3–18. The PPVT-R is among the best-established indicators of verbal intelligence and scholastic aptitude across childhood.

The NLSY has valid measures of reading skills and verbal IQ for the large majority of the children included in the study. Many of these measures were also obtained repeatedly. Table 8.2 shows that 8,061 children in the study have at least one valid PIAT score, and most have two or more scores over time. The same table shows that 8,465 children have at least one PPVT score and most of these children have two more valid PPVT scores.

Table 8.2

The Distribution of the Number of Valid PIAT and PPVT Scores:
Children Assessed in Any Year, 1986–2000

Number of Valid Scores Available	Number of Children Having PIAT	Number of Children Having PPVT
One	1,256	3,038
Two	1,438	2,144
Three	1,359	3,138
More than Three	4,008	145
Total	8,061	8,465

Measures of Children's Home Environment

The NLSY incorporates an excellent set of longitudinally measured socioeconomic indicators for each child. Among these is a special measure of home environment, the composite scale of HOME, a subset of the Home Observation for Measurement of the Environment (HOME) (Bradley & Caldwell, 1977). The original HOME was created for identifying high-risk environments and for facilitating early intervention efforts to reduce developmental problems. Only a subset of the original HOME was included in the NLSY HOME because of the time and administrative restrictions in the study. The score on the HOME has been shown to be closely tied to family income (Garrett, Ngandu, & Ferron, 1994) and HOME predicts performance on standard cognitive tests (Duncan et al., 1994).

To obtain DNA data for the NLSY subjects. DNA samples can be obtained from blood or buccal cells. We propose to obtain DNA from the entire sample of the NLSY children and their mothers totaling about 15,000 individuals using the buccal cell methods. One similar undertaking has been carried out before. The Wave III of the National Longitudinal Study of Adolescent Health successfully obtained DNA for the sibling subsample of about 2,600 individuals using the buccal cell methods (Harris et al., 2003). The human genomic DNA is traditionally obtained from peripheral blood samples for genetic studies. However, new technologies have demonstrated that DNA can be obtained much less invasively through the use of cheek cells from rubbing the inside of the cheek with a cotton swab or by a mouth rinse (Freeman et al., 1997; Meulenbelt et al., 1995). Moreover, the DNA samples can be obtained through the mail, making the buccal cell method much less expensive than the traditional blood sampling. The buccal cell method is especially suitable for our NLSY sample since it is nationally representative and geographically scattered. In addition, the inexpensiveness and convenience of obtaining DNA by mail makes it possible to acquire additional cheek swabs from respondents who have provided a low yield and who have failed to return the kit in the previous attempt.

Simple, reliable, and inexpensive methods have been developed for obtaining DNA from the samples collected by mail using the buccal cell method. Freeman et al. (2003) developed a method that can be applied directly to the tissue samples received by mail and thereby normally yield DNA sufficient for several thousand PCRs (polymerase chain reaction). These researchers also investigated the impact of storage on DNA quantity and purity. There are two types of storage: first, that used during the length of time between sample collection and DNA extraction; and second, long-term storage of extracted DNA afterwards. The first type of storage was evaluated by comparing a sample that had been collected by mail and stored at room temperature for one year before extraction, with a sample that had been extracted within one week of receipt by mail. The two samples were found to be comparable. The second type of storage was assessed by comparing a sample that had been extracted four years ago with a sample prepared at the time of the experiment. The comparison suggests that the long-term stored samples were as robust in providing PCR templates as the short-term samples.

Though the quantity of the genomic DNA yielded from the buccal cell collection methods can be considerably less than that obtained from blood sampling, it is usually sufficient for all but the most demanding genotyping projects. Buccal cell methods routinely obtain 30–40 ìg of DNA per individuals, which is generally sufficient for 4000 individual PCRs (Anchordoquy et al., 2003; Freeman, 1997). In comparison, blood extractions typically yield in excess of 100 ìg of DNA. There are at least two reasons why the genomic DNA from cheek swabs may prove insufficient. First, a genome-wide scan with SNPs may require 50,000 or more genotyping per individual. Second, for certain individuals, the yield of DNA can be as low as 1 or 2 ìg. In both cases, the primer extension pre-amplification (PEP) can amplify the entire genome non-preferentially by 100-fold or more (Anchordoquy et al., 2003; Zhang et al., 1992). The allele calls with the pre-amplified DNA correspond to those of the genomic DNA almost 99% of the time. The rates of erroneous calls and missing data are almost identical between the two types of DNA. The problems encountered in the genotyping using the two types of DNA are comparable. The PEP is a simple, practical, and cost-effective method for routinely pre-amplifying genomic data for ambitious projects or for individual samples of especially low yield when it is difficult to return to subjects for additional cheek swabs.

Child-mother, sibling, aunt-child, and cousin samples. Many of the individuals in the NLSY are genetically related, providing opportunities for specialized genetic analysis. The entire sample of NLSY is composed of women first recruited in 1979 and their biological children, so child-mother pairs are an essential feature of the sample. Since the NLSY generally recruited all children born to the original women subjects, most of the children have siblings in the sample. Most women interviewed have had more than one child, including a rather large sample of women who have had three or more children, as they reach the end of their childbearing years. Table 8.3 displays the distribution of sibship size among the NLSY children. When the sample selection for NLSY was made, all individuals living in the selected households who were between the ages of 14 and 21 on December 31, 1978 were selected for sample inclusion. In many instances, sibling sisters were included in the original sample, meaning that many of the offspring studied have cousins and aunts included in the sample as well as mothers and siblings, and all of these relationships can be readily identified. Over the course of the survey years, more than 3,000 children in the sample have been identified as having an aunt in the main NLSY sample (Table 8.4). Table 8.5 shows that 2,663 children in the NLSY have one or more cousins, and many have three or more.

Table 8.3

The Distribution of Sibship Size Among NLSY Children Interviewed

Sibship Size	Children Interviewed
Single Child	1,203
Two Siblings	3,892
Three Siblings	3,273
Four Siblings	1,660
Five Siblings	675
Six Siblings	222
Seven Siblings	161
Eight Siblings	72
Nine Siblings	27
Ten Siblings	20
Total	11,205

Table 8.4

The Distribution of Number of Nieces and/or Nephews Among NLSY Mothers Having Sister(s)

Number of Nieces/Nephews	Number of Mothers Having Sister(s)	Number of Children Having an Aunt
0	229	0
1	173	173
2	370	740
3	250	750
4	147	588
5	60	300
6	39	234
7	31	217
8 or more	32	286
Total	1,331	3,288

Table 8.5
The Distribution of Number of Cousins Among NLSY Children

Number of Cousins	Number of Children
1	397
2	866
3	614
4	373
5	152
6	94
7	85
8 or more	68
Total	2,663

Significance

Most dyslexics who are diagnosed as children remain dyslexic throughout their lives and their reading skills stay behind non-dyslexic adults (Felton et al., 1990; Pennington et al., 1991). However, a portion of children diagnosed as dyslexics eventually develop normal reading skills. These are referred to as compensated dyslexics (Pennington & Lefly, 2001). Compensation rates across different studies are remarkably similar (22–25%) with higher rates for females than males (Pennington, 1991; Scarborough, 1984).

The reports on sex differentials in dyslexia prevalence are mixed. Some studies found a higher prevalence of dyslexia for males than female with a ratio between 1.4 and 1.8 (Lefly & Pennington, 1991; Wolff & Melngailis, 1994). Others, however, reported approximately equal prevalence rates for both sexes (Shaywitz et al., 1990). These differences in sex ratio across different studies may reflect higher compensation rates observed in adult female, since the studies reporting a higher sex ratio tend to be based on both children and adults (Lefly & Pennington, 1991) and the studies reporting an equal sex ratio tend to be based on children only (Shaywitz et al., 1990). Compensation may add complexity to studies of dyslexia, but it also indicates the effectiveness of environmental intervention.

Identifying specific gene variants contributing to dyslexia has important ramifications. It could lead to early identification of those at higher risk and the diagnosis of phenotypically ambiguous cases, allowing environmental intervention at a young age. Concordance rates of reading disability for MZ twin are about two-thirds, so the room for environmental intervention is likely to be large. The observation that a significant proportion of child dyslexics manage to acquire normal or near-normal reading skills also demonstrates the possible effect of environmental intervention. Identifying crucial genes influencing dyslexia will facilitate additional work that will further understanding of the molecular pathology of dyslexia.

References

Anchordoquy, H. C., McGeary, C., Liu, L., Krauter, K. S., & Smolen, A. (2003). Genotyping of three candidate genes after whole-genome preamplification of DNA collected from buccal cells. *Behavioral Genetics, 33,* 73–78.

Bradley, R. H., & Caldwell, B. M. (1977). Home observation for measurement of the environment: a validation study of screening efficiency. *American Journal of Mental Deficiency, 81,* 417–420.

Cardon, L. R., Smith, S. D., Fulker, D. W., Kimberling, W. J., Pennington, B. F., & DeFries, J. C. (1994). Quantitative trait locus for reading disability on chromosome 6. *Science, 266,* 276–279. Note: Erratum: *Science, 268,* 1553 (1995).

Cope, N., Harold, D., Hill, G., Moskvina, V., Stevenson, J., Owen, M. J., O'Donovan, M. C., & Williams, J. (2005). Strong evidence that *KIAA0319* on chromosome 6p is a susceptibility gene for developmental dyslexia. *American Journal of Human Genetics, 76,* 581–591.

Critchley, M. (1970). *The dyslexic child.* Springfield, IL: Charles C. Thomas.

Defries, J. C., & Fulker, D. W. (1985). Multiple regression analysis of twin data. *Behavioral Genetics, 15,* 467–473.

DeFries, J. C., & Gillis, J. J. (1993). Genetics of reading disability. In R. Plomin & G. McClearn (Eds.), *Nature, nurture, and psychology* (pp. 121–145). Washington, DC: APA.

Dib, C., Faure, S., Fizames, C., Samson, D., Drouot, N., Vignal, A., Millasseau, P. et al. (1996). A comprehensive genetic map of the human genome based on 5,264 microsatellites. *Nature, 380,* 152–154.

Dunn, L., & Dunn, L. (1981). *PPVT-R manual.* Circle Pines, MN: American Guidance Service, Inc.

Dunn, L. M., & Markwardt, F. C. (1970). *Examiner's manual: Peabody Individual Achievement Test.* Circle Pines, MN: American Guidance Service.

Duncan, C. C., Rumsey, J. M., Wilkniss, S. M., Denckla, M. B., Hamburger, S. D., & Odou-Potkin, M. (1994). Developmental dyslexia and attention dysfunction in adults: Brain potential indices of information processing. *Psychophysiology, 31,* 386–401.

Fagerheim, T., Raeymaekers, P., Tonnessen, F. E., Pedersen, M., Tranebjaerg, L., & Lubs, H.A. (1999). A new gene (DYX3) for dyslexia is located on chromosome 2. *Journal of Medical Genetics, 36,* 664–669.

Felton, R. H., Naylor, C. E., & Wood, F. B. (1990). Neuropsychological profile of adult dyslexics. *Brain Language, 39,* 485–497.

Field, L. L., & Kaplan, B. J. (1998). Absence of linkage of phonological coding dyslexia to chromosome 6p23-p21.3 in a large family data set. *American Journal of Human Genetics, 63,* 1448–1456.

Fisher, S. E., Francks, C., Marlow, A. J., MacPhie, I. L., Newbury, D. F., Cardon, L. R., Ishikawa-Brush, Y., Richardson, A. J., Talcott, J. B., Gayan, J., Olson, R. K., Pennington, B. F., Smith, S. D., DeFries, J. C., Stein, J. F., & Monaco, A. P. (2002). Independent genome-wide scans identify a chromosome 18 quantitative-trait locus influencing dyslexia. *Nature Genetics, 30,* 86–91.

Fisher, S. E., Marlow, A. J., Lamb, J., Maestrini, E., Williams, D. F., Richardson, A. J., Weeks, D. E., Stein, J. F., & Monaco, A. P. (1999). A quantitative-trait locus on chromosome 6p influences different aspects of developmental dyslexia. *American Journal of Human Genetics, 64,* 146–156.

Fisher, S. E., & Defries, J. C. (2002). Developmental dyslexia: genetic dissection of a complex cognitive trait. *Nature Reviews, 3,* 767–780.

Freeman, B., Powell, J., Ball, D., Hill, L., Craig, I., & Plomin, R. (1997). DNA by mail: An inexpensive and noninvasive method for collecting DNA samples from widely dispersed populations. *Behavioral Genetics, 27,* 251–257.

Freeman, B., Smith, N., Curtis, C., Huckett, L., Mill, J., & Craig, I. (2003). DNA from buccal swabs recruited by mail: evaluation of storage effects on long-term stability and suitability for multiplex polymerase chain reaction genotyping. *Behavioral Genetics, 33,* 67–72.

Garrett, P., Ngandu, N., & Ferron, J. (1994). Poverty experiences of young children and the quality of their home environments. *Child Development, 65,* 331–345.

Gayán, J., Smith, S. D., Cherny, S. S., Cardon, L. R., Fulker, D. W., Brower, A. M., Olson, R. K., Pennington, B. F., & DeFries, J. C. (1999). Quantitative-trait locus for specific language and reading deficits on chromosome 6p. *American Journal of Human Genetics, 64,* 157–164.

Gilger, J. W., Pennington, B. F., & DeFries, J. C. (1991). Risk for reading disability as a function of parental history in three family studies. *Reading & Writing, 3,* 205–217.

Grigorenko, E. L., Wood, F. B., Meyer, M. S., Hart, L. A., Speed, W. C., Shuster, A., & Pauls, D. L. (1997). Susceptibility loci for distinct components of developmental dyslexia on chromosomes 6 and 15. *American Journal of Human Genetics, 60,* 27–39.

Grigorenko, E. L., Wood, F. B., Meyer, M. S., & Pauls, D. L. (2000). Chromosome 6p influences on different dyslexia-related cognitive processes: further confirmation. *American Journal of Human Genetics, 66,* 715–723.

Hallgren, B. (1950). Specific dyslexia (congenital word-blindness), a clinical and genetic study. *Acta Psychiatrica et Neurologica Supplement, 65,* 1–287.

Harris, K. M., Florey, F., Tabor, J., Bearman, P. S., Jones, J., & Udry, J. R. (2003). The National Longitudinal Study of Adolescent Health: Research Design [WWW document]. URL: http://www.cpc.unc.edu/projects/addhealth/design.

Haseman, J. K., & Elston, R. C. (1972). The investigation of linkage between a quantitative trait and a marker locus. *Behavioral Genetics, 2,* 3–19.

Kaplan, D. E., Gayan, J., Ahn, J., Won, T.-W., Pauls, D., Olson, R. K., DeFries, J. C., Wood, F., Pennington, B. F., Page, G. P., Smith, S. D., & Gruen, J. R. (2002). Evidence for linkage and association with reading disability, on 6p21.3-22. *American Journal of Human Genetics, 70,* 1287–1298.

Kruglyak L., & Lander, E. S. (1995). Complete multipoint sib-pair analysis of qualitative and quantitative traits. *American Journal of Human Genetics, 57,* 439–454.

Lai, C. S. L., Fisher, S. E., Hurst, J. A., Levy, E. R., Hodgson, S., Fox, M., Jeremiah, S., Povey, S., Jamison D. C., Green E. D., Vargha-Khadem, F., & Monaco, A. P. (2000). The *SPCH1* region on human 7q31: Genomic characterization of the critical interval and localization of translocations associated with speech and language disorder. *American Journal of Human Genetics, 67,* 357–368.

Lai, C. S. L., Fisher, S. E., Hurst, J. A., Vargha-Khadem, F., & Monaco, A. P. (2001). A forkhead-domain gene is mutated in a severe speech and language disorder. *Nature, 413,* 519–523.

Lerner J. W. (1989). Educational interventions in learning disabilities. *Journal of the American Academy of Child and Adolescent Psychiatry, 28*, 326–331.

Meulenbelt, I., Droog, S., Trommelen, G. J., Boomsma, D. I., & Slagboom P. E. (1995). High-yield noninvasive human genomic DNA isolation method for genetic studies in geographically dispersed families and populations. *American Journal of Human Genetics, 57*, 1252–1254.

Morris, D. W., Robinson, L., Turic, D., Duke, M., Webb, V., Milham, C., Hopkin, E., Pound, K., Fernando, S., Easton, M., Hamshere, M., Williams, N., McGuffin, P., Stevenson, J., Krawczak, M., Owen, M. J., O'Donovan, M. C., & Williams, J. (2000). Family-based association mapping provides evidence for a gene for reading disability on chromosome 15q. *Human Molecular Genetics, 9*, 843–848.

Nopola-Hemmi, J., Taipale, M., Haltia, T., Lehesjoki, A. E., Voutilainen, A., & Kere, J. (2001). Two translocations of chromosome 15q associated with dyslexia. *Journal of Medical Genetics, 37*, 771–775.

Nothen, M. M., Schulte-Korne, G., Grimm, T., Cichon, S., Vogt, I. R., Muller-Myhsok, B., Propping, P., & Remschmidt, H. (1999). Genetic linkage analysis with dyslexia: evidence for linkage of spelling disability to chromosome 15. *European Child & Adolescent Psychiatry, 3*, 56–69.

Olson, R., Wise, B., Conners, F., Rack, J., & Fulker, D. (1989). Specific deficits in component reading and language skills: genetic and environmental influences. *Journal of Learning Disabilities, 22*, 339–348.

Paulesu, E., Demonet, J. F., Fazio, F., McCrory, E., Chanoine, V., Brunswick, N., Cappa, S. F., Cossu, G., Habib, M., Frith, C. D.,& Frith, U. (2001). Dyslexia: Cultural diversity and biological unity. *Science, 291*, 2165–2167.

Pennington, B. F., Gilger, J. W., Pauls, D., Smith, S. A., Smith, S. D., & Defries, J. C. (1991). Evidence for major gene transmisson of developmental dyslexia. *Journal of the American Medical Association, 266*, 1527–1534.

Pennington, B. F. (1995). Genetics of learning disabilities. *Journal of Child Neurology Supplement, 10*, S69–77.

Pennington, B. F., & Lefly, D. L. (2001). Early reading development in children at family risk for dyslexia. *Child Development, 72*, 816–833.

Scarborough, H. S. (1984). Continuity between childhood dyslexia and adult reading. *British Journal of Psychology, 75*, 329–348.

Schulte-Korne, G., Grimm, T., Nothen, M. M., Muller-Myhsok, B., Cichon, S., Vogt, I. R., Propping, P., & Remschmidt, H. (1998). Evidence for linkage of spelling disability to chromosome 15. (Letter) *American Journal of Human Genetics, 63*, 279–282.

Shaywitz, S. E., Shaywitz, B. A., Fletcher, J. M., & Escobar, M. D. (1990). Prevalence of reading disability in boys and girls. Results of the Connecticut Longitudinal Study. *Journal of the American Medical Association, 264*, 998–1002.

Shaywitz, S. E., Shaywitz, B. A., Pugh, K. R., Fulbright, R. K., Constable, R. T., Mencl, W. E., Shankweiler, D. P., Liberan, A. M., Skudlarski, P., Fletcher, J. M., Katz, L., Marchione, K. E., Lacdadie, C., Gatenby, C., & Gore, J. C. (1998). Functional disruption in the organization of the brain for reading in dyslexia. *Proceedings of the National Academy of Sciences USA, 95*, 2636–2641.

Smith, S. D., Kimberling W. J., Pennington B. F., & Lubs, H. A. (1983). Specific reading disability: identification of an inherited form through linkage analysis. *Science, 219*, 1345–1347.

Smith, S. D., Kimberling, W. J., & Pennington, B. F. (1991). Screening for multiple genes influencing dyslexia. *Reading & Writing, 3,* 285–298.

Taipale, M., Kamine, N., Nopola-Hemmi, J., Haltia, T., Myllyluoma, B., Lyytinen, H., Muller, K., Kaaranen, M., Lindsberg, P. J., Hannula-Jouppi, K., & Kere, J. (2003). *Proceedings of the National Academy of Sciences USA, 100,* 11553–11558.

Wechsler, D. (1974). *Wechsler Intelligence Scale for Children – Revised (WISC-R).* New York: Psychological Corporation.

Wechsler, D. (1981). *Wechsler Adult Intelligence Scale – Revised (WAIS-R).* New York: Psychological Corporation.

Willcutt, E. G., Pennington, B. F., Smith, S. D., Cardon, L. R., Gayan, J., Knopik, V. S., Olson, R. K., & DeFries, J. C. (2002). Quantitative trait locus for reading disability on chromosome 6p is pleiotropic for attention-deficit/hyperactivity disorder. *American Journal of Medical Genetics, 114,* 260–268.

Wolff, P. H., & Melngailis, I. (1994). Family patterns of developmental dyslexia: clinical findings. *American Journal of Medical Genetics, 54,* 122–131.

Zhang, N., Threadgill, N. W., & Womack, J. E. (1992). Synteny mapping in the bovine: Genes from human chromosome 4. *Genomics, 14,* 131–136.

9

PROXIMAL PROCESSES IN SCHOOL READINESS

Kyle L. Snow

National Institute of Child Health and Human Development

In 1979, *The ecology of human development* was first published (Bronfenbrenner, 1979). Historically, the state of theory in human development was reasonably, if somewhat arbitrarily, divided into those positions that placed development as a largely within-person process and those that placed the mechanisms of development largely outside of the individual. The nature-nurture debate was raging, and it was expedient to assign models of development into one camp or the other, even when there were some that blurred the lines. For example, the work of Vygostky, who had long since died, was just becoming known to American and European developmentalists. Even in its initial state (and more so as it evolved into its current state), the ecological model of human development was a transactional model, one that considered development to be due to both internal and external forces, and in the process continued to transform the debate between nature-nurture into a question of how these two forces interact (see, e.g., Bronfenbrenner & Ceci, 1994), rather than which is dominant, as Anne Anastasi had done nearly 20 years before (Anastasi, 1958).

As initially articulated by Bronfenbrenner (1979), the transactional nature of the ecological theory is captured in what he identified as Proposition 1:

> In ecological research, the properties of the person and of the environment, the structure of environmental settings, and the processes taking place within and between them must be viewed as interdependent and analyzed in system terms (Bronfenbrenner, 1979, p. 41).

While the beginnings of what became known as the ecological model of development were largely considered to be focused on the contexts for development (and the now-iconic concentric circles of micr-, meso-, exo-, and macro-system), the model evolved to focus largely on the processes taking place within these contexts, but this same proposition had been recast in much more complex terms:

> Especially in its early phases, but also throughout the life course, human development takes place through processes of progressively more complex reciprocal interaction between an active, evolving

biopsychological human organism and the persons, objects, and symbols
in its immediate external environment (Bronfenbrenner & Morris, 1998,
p. 996).

These processes taking place within the child's primary environmental context,
that which he or she is immediately experiencing, became known as proximal
processes, what Bronfenbrenner and Ceci (1994, p. 572) called "the primary engines
of effective development." The nature of proximal processes, at first vague, gradually
came into focus. Bronfenbrenner (1989, p. 5) argued that "in order to develop –
intellectually, emotionally, socially, and morally – a child requires, for all of them,
the same thing: participation in progressively complex reciprocal activity," and, in
its near final form, Bronfenbrenner and Morris (1998, p. 996) added that these
processes occur "on a fairly regular basis over extended periods of time." These
processes, though, work within a complex web of external and internal factors,
as Bronfenbrenner and Ceci (1994, p. 572) proposed: "The form, power, content,
and direction of the proximal processes effecting development vary systematically
as a joint function of the characteristics of the developing person, of the
environment...in which the processes are taking place, and the nature of the
developmental outcomes under consideration." With the incorporation of
development (or time-dynamic forces), the model reached its current state in the
person-process-context-time (PPCT) model (Williams & Ceci, 1997).

Since declaring their importance, however, Bronfenbrenner sought examples
of proximal processes to demonstrate the power of the conceptual framework
he helped to put in place (see, e.g., Bronfenbrenner & Morris, 1998), and to explicitly
test the proposition that these processes should vary systematically as a function
of person and contextual factors. Although the ecological model has been adopted
as an organizational framework through which to call for a program of research on
child care (Belsky, 1980b) and families (Bronfenbrenner, 1986), as well as to view
a wide range of phenomena, including child maltreatment (Belsky, 1980a, 1993),
parenting (e.g., Bornstein, 2002), and school readiness (Pianta, Rimm-Kaufman
& Cox, 1999), the identification of proximal processes that could be examined
through rigorous ecological designs has been far more limited. One notable
exception often used by Bronfenbrenner (e.g., Bronfenbrenner, 1989;
Bronfenbrenner & Ceci, 1994; Bronfenbrenner & Morris, 1998) is the pioneering
work of physician Cecil Mary Drillien (1964), which coincidentally was also based
upon a study of low birthweight children.

In a similar, more systematic effort, Landry and Smith (this volume) summarize
their work with low birthweight babies and their mothers that supports a central
role for parental responsiveness in supporting early academic skills. In doing so,
they identify four independent factors within a larger responsiveness construct:
contingent responding, emotional support, attentional support, and language input.
This chapter examines these processes, and in fitting them into a PPCT model,
identifies a number of additional research questions.

The Construct of Responsiveness

As a construct, maternal responsiveness, especially during early and middle infancy, has a rich theoretical and empirical history. Ribas, de Moura, and Ribas (2003) conducted a literature search of PsychInfo and found 231 articles addressing maternal responsiveness published between 1967 and 2001. It is beyond the scope of this chapter to provide a full review of the findings with regard to maternal responsiveness, a review that can be found elsewhere (e.g., Bornstein, 1989). Instead, several findings about the nature and variability of responsiveness bear mentioning. First, there are data that suggest naturally occurring cultural differences in responsiveness (e.g., Burchinal, Follmer & Bryant, 1996; Richman, Miller & LeVine, 1992). Second, data show associations between responsiveness and specific developmental outcomes throughout the early years (e.g., Bornstein & Tamis-LeMonda, 1997; Tamis-LeMonda, Bornstein, Baumwell & Damast, 1996). Finally, there is literature on the effectiveness of interventions to specifically change maternal responsiveness, with resulting changes on children (e.g., Riksen-Walraven, 1978). It should be noted that the literature on responsiveness is split between studies within normative populations, and studies of children, families, or parents that are at some form of developmental risk (e.g., Beckwith & Cohen, 1989; Wakschlag & Hans, 1999), creating a literature that is at least partially based upon a deficit model of development. This brief overview of responsiveness is an important background for the research findings summarized by Landry and Smith (this volume) that places responsiveness as a candidate proximal process for school readiness.

Responsiveness as Parental Style or Proximal Process

Landry and Smith present the construct of responsiveness as a primary process in supporting school readiness, referring to it as an aspect of parenting style (see also Darling & Steinberg, 1993). Their data suggest four independent, but related, processes: contingent responding, emotional support, attentional support, and language input. On their own, these are not new constructs in the literature. Indeed, most have a rich theoretical and empirical basis, the scope of which cannot be captured here, and are beginning to be integrated into coherent models that reduce the confusion possible in among these ambiguously, and frequently differentially, defined constructs (Snow, Canfield & Ricciuti, 2005). What is innovative about this approach, however, is the examination of characteristics of parent-child interaction under the rubric of parenting style (cf. Grolnick & Ryan, 1989), much like Baumrind's well known use of the term to capture distinctive patterns of authoritative, authoritarian, and permissive parental behaviors, and even more similar to Maccoby and Martin's (1983) identification of parenting styles. Landry and Smith use the concept of parental style much as Darling and Steinberg (1993), treating it not as a process descriptor, but as a characteristic of the parent (see also Belsky, 1984). However, it must be noted that, in their derivation of a responsiveness style, Landry and Smith cannot fully heed Darling and Steinberg's (1993, p. 492) warning that "researchers must maintain the distinction between practice and style." Certainly, it is reasonable to infer (or statistically determine) a style from a set of practices and behaviors in ways which maintain the distinction, even though they are clearly related. However, basing a style of parenting on patterns of behaviors that occur during interaction between parent and child will lead to instability in parenting style insomuch as the pattern of behaviors during interaction are a joint function on parent and child. Darling and Steinberg (1993) note that parenting style, although related to behaviors, owes its origin to parenting goals, beliefs, and values, as does parenting practice. In their model, parenting style will be insulated against instability by the stabilizing forces of beliefs, and goals, through their acting on parenting practices. This conceptualization, however, neglects the bidirectional nature of interaction between parents and infants and young children, the implications of which are discussed below.

Regardless of whether or not responsiveness, as it is used by Landry and Smith (this volume) represents a parenting style or a collection of proximal processes, Landry and Smith use parental style as a construct to lend coherence to a rich and diverse literature. First, in conceptualizing the responsive parenting style, critical constructs such as encouragement of attention (Tamis-LeMonda & Bornstein, 1989), joint attention, including follow-into and redirection (Tomasello, 1988, 1992), stimulation, responsiveness, and contingency (e.g., Dunham, 1990) must be reconciled. In so doing, several distinctions must be made that map onto Landry and Smith's model. First, as Cohen (1972) argued, there is a distinction between motivating an infant's attention to an object and maintaining it on that object, a distinction which is both behavioral and neurocognitive in nature (e.g., Johnson, Posner & Rothbart, 1991). As the child develops, the degree to which the child is resistant to parental efforts at directing their attention becomes formalized within the construct of executive function. As noted by Landry and Smith, a parenting style that balances the interplay between directing and responding to a child's signals is ultimately the most beneficial to the child.

Second, specific aspects of parenting behavior map onto specific outcomes. For example, in one of the earliest experimental manipulations of parenting, Riksen-Walraven (1978) found that stimulation and responsiveness mapped onto independent measures of infant functioning (processing speed and contingency learning). When we consider the range of outcomes relevant to early school success, it is not surprising that multiple parenting behaviors, even if associated with discrete outcomes, must be employed to support school readiness.

Finally, in modeling the role of parents in supporting early development, Landry and Smith provide the parents with the role of cognitive agent. In this role parents are responsible for supporting the child's development through both action (e.g., stimulation) and reaction (e.g., contingent responsiveness). Such a conceptualization is consistent with efforts to apply a Vygotskian perspective on school readiness (e.g., Berk & Winsler, 1995; Carlton & Winsler, 1999) calling for scaffolding of early development. An important question that has remained unaddressed, however, based upon these views of parenting styles as evidenced in complex behavioral patterns, is the origins of these differences in style. While data show the efficacy of interventions to promote these modes of interaction, there is still a need to understand the degree to which experience and genetics contribute to the parent's tendency to adopt a responsiveness style. In the context of the literature on attachment formation, there have been recent calls on the need to further understand the complexities of the caregiving system, including its origins and motivations (e.g., Bell & Richard, 2000; Cassidy, 2000).

Several specifics within the model of responsiveness provided by Landry and Smith may be overly restrictive. For example, they focus on the role of oral language stimulation. While there is good reason for this (e.g., Hart & Risley, 1995), especially when consideration is given to language skills as an outcome, it may be that other forms of stimulation, such as visual and tactile, which have been heavily explored in early infancy, may be important for young children as well. Critically, when this model is translated into practice, we must be cautious to note that stimulation alone is not the goal, but when coupled with responsiveness and emotional and attentional support, what results is not reading aloud, but rather an approach to reading with young children more akin to dialogic reading, a distinction that may be lost among parents who just several years ago were extolled to read to their children (without guidance on how best to support their emergent literacy).

Significance of the Landry and Smith Paper

The findings presented by Landry and Smith (this volume; see also Landry, Smith, & Swank, 2003; Landry, Smith, Swank, Assel & Vellet, 2001) are significant to the literature base that contributes to our understanding of school readiness in several respects. First, and most generally, it expands the discourse on school readiness beyond consideration of designer programs and interventions to a focus on family level processes. Second, by identifying the four processes described above, Landry and Smith have stretched, perhaps inadvertently, the more typical chronological window of factors important to school readiness into earlier development. There is a substantial literature on responsiveness, attention regulation, emotion regulation, and stimulation in early infancy through the preschool period. The importance of this literature cannot be overstated because, to this point in the field, much of the discussion about school readiness has relied upon studies of children aged 3 to 5 years, drawn primarily from Head Start programs. The result is a dramatic expansion of the population of interest.

The Landry and Smith paper also projects the window forward through the central role given to responsiveness. Certainly, responsiveness and sensitivity during earlier development contributes to the formation of secure attachments (Bowlby, 1969; DeWolf & Van Ijzendoorn, 1997; Egeland & Farber, 1984), and these attachments have enduring positive effects on child socioemotional and cognitive competence at least into early elementary school (Cohn, 1990; Jacobsen, Edelstein & Hofmann, 1994; Moss & St-Laurent, 2001; Pianta & Harbers, 1996). Additionally, Pianta (Hamre & Pianta, 2001; Pianta, 1997, 1999; Pianta, Nimetz & Bennett, 1997) has argued and provided data for the importance of positive relationships between child and teachers in fostering school readiness and transition outcomes. For example, Hamre and Pianta (2005) found that students identified as being at-risk in kindergarten performed comparably to the low-risk peers in first grade when they were is classrooms with teachers offering them high levels of emotional support. The result is that responsiveness, as a construct, appears to be a central theme throughout early development into the elementary school years (at least).

Landry and Smith do not directly address issues concerning neurobiological ramifications of their findings, but drawing on Blair's (2002) excellent review, there is strong evidence to support the contention that parental efforts to support their child's attentional efforts do indeed interact with neurobiological factors in development and may contribute to more efficient hard-wiring of cognitive and regulatory processes. Still, the relationship between patterns of social experience in neurobiological development continues to be a rich avenue of potential study.

Finally, the model proposed by Landry and Smith provides a prescription for interventions to enhance school readiness, especially among at-risk children or children in high-risk ecological contexts. The mapping of specific effects to specific modes of parent-child interaction certainly demonstrates the need for multifaceted interventions. Additionally, on the basis of the Bakersman-Kranenburg, van Ijendoorn, and Juffer (2003) meta-analysis, parental sensitivity and responsiveness are amenable to intervention, suggesting that such efforts may well be effective in promoting both secure attachments as well as supporting the emergence of a range of school readiness outcomes. Indeed, Brooks-Gunn and Markman (2005) argued that the racial gap in school readiness is reduced by as much as half when parenting factors are accounted for; clearly there is the potential for a high return on the investment of intervention. Despite this promise, a number of research questions, driven from the PPCT model, need to be addressed.

Future Directions for Research

Starting with Bronfenbrenner's (1986) provocative paper laying out a research agenda for the roles of families in child development, a number of further research questions present themselves. First, it is important to further test the central premise of the PPCT model, that is, that the effects of a given proximal process will vary as a function of characteristics of the child, the contexts within which the process occurs, and the timing of the process in the child's development. Landry and Smith provide a good start, but several additional child factors present themselves as potentially important, especially given the nature of the processes in question. The first may be the degree to which the child is inhibited or uninhibited (Shamir-Essakow, Ungerer, Rapee & Safier, 2004), and infant temperament generally (e.g., Gauvain & Fagot, 1995; Halpern, Garcia Coll, Meyer & Bendersky, 2001; Van den Boom, 1994). With regard to context, there is a growing literature on the impact of maternal depression on mother-child interaction that can be exploited and expanded (e.g., Lovejoy, Graczyk, O'Hare & Neuman, 2000). Similarly, single-parenthood is an apparent risk-factor for child school readiness, at least in some racial and ethnic contexts (Ricciuti, 1999), but would not itself seem to be a factor in the degree to which that parent can be responsive to the child. Further explorations must be made regarding the potential mediating role of parenting factors on the association between socioeconomic and race and ethnicity factors and school outcomes (e.g., Connell & Prinz, 2002; Raviv, Kessenich & Morrison, 2004).

Bronfenbrenner (1989) introduced the concept of chronosystem models of development to call attention to the need for research designs to consider consistency and change over time in both the individual and his or her environment. The need for such designs is especially important during life transitions, such as occurs at a child's transition to school (see also Sameroff & Haith, 1996), events that may "…alter the existing relation between person and environment, thus creating a dynamic that may instigate developmental change" (Bronfenbrenner, 1989, p. 201). From this perspective, a number of questions regarding time emerge, such as, is there a critical period during which responsiveness must be established as a pattern of interaction within families? Given the multidimensional aspects of responsiveness as presented here, do these factors remain stable over time, and if not, how do they change within the system over time? There is good data from Landry et al. (2001) and Steelman, Assel, Swank, Smith, and Landry (2002) to suggest the importance of developmental timing with regards to responsiveness, including good data summarized by Landry and Smith (this volume) that interventions to enhance responsiveness show the predicted effect, but interventions early seem to have a greater impact on the child. The need to more thoroughly explore the timing of the process of responsiveness is underscored by the importance of time with regards to child development, as well as the stability of parenting behaviors over time (e.g., Dallaire & Weinraub, 2005; Fagot & Gauvain,

1997), which suggests either a synergistic effect of changes in parenting processes or a sensitive period during which specific processes are of particular importance (regardless of their stability following this period (see also Baumrind, 1989). These questions and more are not ripe for addressing within the field.

It must be noted that the central construct of responsiveness described by Landry and Smith (this volume) is itself a collection of a number of candidate proximal processes. While their paper contains an elegant description of how the four components interconnect in the larger construct, additional processes have been implicated in school readiness, especially academically oriented aspects of school readiness, primarily adult instructional style (e.g., Burchinal et al., 2005; Dopkins-Stright, Neitzel, Garza Sears & Hoke-Sinex, 2001; Pianta & Habers, 1996; Rimm-Kaufman, LaParo, Downer & Pianta, 2005; Supplee, Shaw, Hailstones & Hartman, 2004). Few studies examine responsiveness simultaneously with instructional processes. In their study of kindergarteners at risk for school failure, Hamre and Pianta (2005) found that the best outcomes for at-risk children occurred in classrooms characterized as being high in emotional and instructional support, although there were also strong direct effects for each individually. These findings suggest the need to closely examine whether these processes are additive or synergistic in nature. Additionally, the limited longitudinal nature of the design does not allow for an examination of the importance of developmental timing as called for in the PPCT model, although such analyses are surely forthcoming.

Landry and Smith have provided a provocative description of what may prove to be a central developmental process in enhancing child school readiness. This chapter, and the studies with which it connects, provide a rich, longitudinal examination of parenting factors as they affect children born at risk or at low risk, within a given ecological niche. However, as Bronfenbrenner (1986) challenged, once we understand the dynamics of a developmental process within a given ecological niche, we must then consider the degree to which this process operates in a comparable manner across developmental niches, not just those characterized as being of high risk, but also those considered to be of moderate or nominal risk. Certainly, if responsiveness is indeed a proximal process, its importance should be evidence across the human condition. This importance has begun to be studied as a means of ameliorating risk, but its role in promoting positive development has not yet been explored.

Finally, the work of Landry and her colleagues demonstrates the impact of manipulations of the caregiving environment, at least along a circumscribed set of dimensions, which then impact important early childhood outcomes (in this case, school readiness). Bronfenbrenner and Ceci (1994) noted the importance of such studies because they directly confront some arguments coming from a behavioral genetics stance, the arguments most typically associated with Scarr (1992; Scarr & McKartney, 1983) that the environment parents provide for their children is in part genetically driven, both through the influence of genes on the parent directly, and from the influence of the child's genes that may be implicated in how the child elicits or otherwise constructs aspects of his or her environment, which is, by necessity, also related genetically to the parents. In this context, Bronfenbrenner's (e.g., 1989) distinction between developmentally instigative characteristics, those attributes of the developing child that elicit specific reactions from the environment, and developmentally structuring attributes, those that lead the developing child to seek out or specifically structure his or her environment further complications the inter-relationships between genotype and phenotype, both within and across parent and child. It is beyond the scope of this chapter to address the behavioral genetics of school readiness (cf., Dickens, 2005; Hohnen & Stevenson, 1999), however, given the intent of this chapter to argue that responsiveness be examined as a proximal process, the arguments made by Bronfenbrenner and Ceci (1994, p. 574) that "proximal process can produce appreciable differences in developmental outcomes that cannot be attributed to genetic selection...any effects of proximal processes on heritability...cannot be interpreted solely as the products of a genetic component in proximal process," open wide the doors for complex behavioral genetic studies that will examine how person factors (which are to varying degrees genetically loaded), environmental factors (which may also be partially genetically loaded) and process factors (which also may have genetic loadings) interact both at the phenotype and genotype level to produce outcomes for children.

In conclusion, the outstanding work reported by Landry and Smith is evocative rather than provocative. While illuminating the importance of maternal responsiveness in promoting school readiness, and showing the efficacy of interventions to enhance maternal responsiveness as a means of ameliorating early risk for school difficulties, their findings set the foundation for a range of additional research questions that can ultimately guide policies and practices that bear on children's preparation for the transition to school and throughout development. It seems fitting, then, to end a chapter dedicated to the life work of Urie Bronfenbrenner, to give him the last word: "...it is essential to determine which policies and programs can do most to enable families to perform the magic feat of which they alone are capable: making and keeping human beings human" (Bronfenbrenner, 1986, p. 738).

References

Anastasi, A. (1958). Heredity, environment, and the question "how?" *Psychological Review,* *65,* 197–208.

Bakermans-Kranenburg, M. J., van Ijzendoorn, M. H., & Juffer, F. (2003). Less is more: Meta-analyses of sensitivity and attachment interventions in early childhood. *Psychological Bulletin, 129,* 195–215.

Baumrind, D. (1989). The permanence of change and the impermanence of stability. *Human Development, 32,* 187–195.

Beckwith, L., & Cohen, S. E. (1989). Maternal responsiveness with preterm infants and later competency. *New Directions for Child Development, 43,* 75–87.

Bell, D. C., & Richard, A. J. (2000). Caregiving: The forgotten element in attachment. *Psychological Inquiry, 11,* 69–83.

Belsky, J. (1980a). Child maltreatment: An ecological integration. *American Psychologist, 35,* 320–335.

Belsky, J. (1980b). Future directions for day care research: An ecological analysis. *Child Care Quarterly, 9,* 82–99.

Belsky, J. (1984). The determinants of parenting: A process model. *Child Development, 55,* 83–96

Belsky, J. (1993). Etiology of child maltreatment: A developmental ecological analysis. *Psychological Bulletin, 114,* 413–434.

Berk, L. E., & Winsler, A. (1995). *Scaffolding children's learning: Vygotsky and early childhood education.* Washington, DC: National Association for the Education of Young Children Press.

Blair, C. (2002). School readiness as propensity for engagement: Integrating cognition and emotion in a neurobiological conceptualization of child functioning at school entry. *American Psychologist, 57,* 111–127.

Bornstein, M. H. (Ed.) (1989). *Maternal responsiveness: Characteristics and consequences.* San Francisco: Jossey-Bass.

Bornstein, M. H. (Ed.). (2002). *Handbook of parenting (2nd ed.). Volume 2: Biology and ecology of parenting.* Mahwah, NJ: Erlbaum.

Bornstein, M. H., & Tamis-LeMonda, C. S. (1997). Maternal responsiveness and infant mental abilities: Specific predictive relations. *Infant Behavior and Development, 20,* 283–296.

Bowlby, J. (1969). *Attachment and loss. Volume 1: Attachment.* New York: Basic Books.

Bronfenbrenner, U. (1979). *The ecology of human development: Experiments by nature and design.* Cambridge, MA: Harvard University Press.

Bronfenbrenner, U. (1986). Ecology of the family as a context for human development: Research perspectives. *Developmental Psychology, 22,* 723–742.

Bronfenbrenner, U. (1989). Ecological systems theory. *Annals of Child Development,* Vol. 6 (pp. 187–249). Greenwich, CT: JAI Press.

Bronfenbrenner, U., & Ceci, S. J. (1994). Nature-nurture reconceptualized in developmental perspective: A bioecological model. *Psychological Review, 101,* 568–586.

Bronfenbrenner, U., & Morris, P. A. (1998). The ecology of developmental processes. In R. M. Lerner (Vol. Ed.), *Handbook of Child Psychology (5th ed.). Volume 1: Theoretical models of human development* (pp. 993–1028). New York: Wiley.

Brooks-Gunn, J., & Markman, L. B. (2005). The contribution of parenting to ethnic and racial gaps in school readiness. *The Future of Children, 15*, 139–168.

Burchinal, M., Follmer, A. & Bryant, D. (1996). The relations of maternal social support and family structure with maternal responsiveness and child outcomes among African American families. *Developmental Psychology, 32*, 1073–1083.

Burchinal, M., Howes, C., Pianta, R. C., Bryant, D., Early, D., Clifford, R., et al. (2005). Predicting child outcomes at the end of kindergarten from the quality of pre-kindergarten teaching, instruction, activities, and caregiver sensitivity. Manuscript under review.

Carlton, M. P., & Winsler, A. (1999). School readiness: The need for a paradigm shift. *School Psychology Review, 28*, 338–352.

Cassidy, J. (2000). The complexity of the caregiving system: A perspective from attachment theory. *Psychological Inquiry, 11*, 86–91.

Cohen, L. B. (1972). Attention-getting and attention-holding processes of infant visual preferences. *Child Development, 43*, 869–879.

Cohn, D. A. (1990). Child-mother attachment of six-year-olds and social competence at school. *Child Development, 61*, 152–162.

Connell, C. M., & Prinz, R. J. (2002). The impact of childcare and parent-child interactions on school readiness and social skills development for low-income African American children. *Journal of School Psychology, 40*, 177–193.

Dallaire, D. H., & Weinraub, M. (2005). The stability of parenting behaviors over the first 6 years of life. *Early Childhood Research Quarterly, 20*, 201–219.

Darling, N., & Steinberg, L. (1993). Parenting style as context: An integrative model. *Psychological Bulletin, 113*, 487–496.

DeWolff, M. S., & Van Ijzendoorn, M. H. (1997). Sensitivity and attachment: A meta-analysis on parental antecedents of infant attachment. *Child Development, 68*, 571–591.

Dickens, W. T. (2005). Genetic differences in school readiness. *The Future of Children, 15*, 55–69.

Dopkins-Stright, A., Neitzel, C., Garza Sears, K., & Hoke-Sinex, L. (2001). Instruction begins in the home: Relations between parental instruction and children's self-regulation in the classroom. *Journal of Educational Psychology, 93*, 456–466.

Drillien, C. M. (1964). *Growth and development of the prematurely born infant.* Edinburgh and London: Livingston.

Dunham, P. J. (1990). Temporal structure of stimulus maintains infant attention. In J. E. Enns (Ed.), *The development of attention: Research and theory* (pp. 67–85). New York: Elsevier Science Publishers.

Egeland, B., & Farber, E. (1984). Infant-mother attachment: Factors related to its development and changes over time. *Child Development, 55*, 753–771.

Fagot, B., & Gauvain, M. (1997). Mother-child problem solving: Continuity through the early childhood years. *Developmental Psychology, 33*, 480–488.

Gauvain, M., & Fagot, B. (1995). Child temperament as a mediator of mother-toddler problem solving. *Social Development, 4*, 257–276.

Grolnick, W. S., & Ryan, R. M. (1989). Parental styles associated with children's self-regulation and competence in school. *Journal of Educational Psychology, 81*, 143–154.

Halpern, L. F., Garcia Coll, C. T., Meyer, E. C., & Bendersky, K. (2001). The contributions of temperament and maternal responsiveness to the mental development of small-for-gestational-age and appropriate-for-gestational-age infants. *Applied Developmental Psychology, 22,* 199–224.

Hamre, B. K. & Pianta, R. C. (2001). Early teacher-child relationships and the trajectory of children's school outcomes through eight grade. *Child Development, 72*, 625–638.

Hamre, B. K., & Pianta, R. C. (2005). Can instructional and emotional support in the first-grade classroom make a difference for children at risk of school failure? *Child Development, 76*, 949–967.

Hart, B., & Risley, T. R. (1995). *Meaningful differences in the everyday experiences of young American children.* Baltimore, MD: Brookes.

Hohnen, B., & Stevenson, J. (1999). The structure of genetic influences on general cognitive, language, phonological, and reading abilities. *Developmental Psychology, 35*, 590–603.

Jacobsen, T., Edelstein, W., & Hofmann, V. (1994). A longitudinal study of the relation between representations of attachment in childhood and cognitive functioning in childhood and adolescence. *Developmental Psychology, 30*, 112–124.

Johnson, M. H., Posner, M. I., & Rothbart, M. K. (1991). Components of visual orienting in early infancy: Contingency learning, anticipatory looking, and disengaging. *Journal of Cognitive Neuroscience, 3*, 335–344.

Landry, S. H., Smith, K. E., & Swank, P. R. (2003). The importance of parenting during early childhood for school-age development. *Developmental Neuropsychology, 24*, 559–591.

Landry, S. H., Smith, K. E., Swank, P. R., Assel, M. A., & Vellet, S. (2001). Does early responsive parenting have a special importance for children's development or is consistency across early childhood necessary? *Developmental Psychology, 37*, 387–403.

Lovejoy, M. C., Graczyk, P. A., O'Hare, E., & Neuman, G. (2000). Maternal depression and parenting behavior: A meta-analytic review. *Clinical Psychology Review, 20*, 561–592.

Maccoby, E. E., & Martin, J. A. (1983). Socialization in the context of the family: Parent–child interaction. In P. H. Mussen (Series Ed.) & E. M. Hetherington (Vol. Ed.), *Handbook of child psychology: Vol. 4. Socialization, personality, and social development* (4th ed., pp. 1–101). New York: Wiley.

Moss, E., & St-Laurent, D. (2001). Attachment at school-age and academic performance. *Developmental Psychology, 37*, 863–874.

Pianta, R. C. (1997). Adult-child relationship processes and early schooling. *Early Education and Development, 8*, 11–26.

Pianta, R. C. (1999). *Enhancing relationships between children and teachers.* Washington, DC: American Psychological Association.

Pianta, R. C., & Harbers, K. L. (1996). Observing mother and child behavior in a problem-solving situation at school entry: Relations with academic achievement. *Journal of School Psychology, 67*, 307–322.

Pianta, R. C., Nimetz, S., & Bennett, L. (1997). Mother-child relationships, teacher-child relationships and outcomes in preschool and kindergarten. *Early Childhood Research Quarterly, 12*, 263–280.

Pianta, R., Rimm-Kaufman, S., & Cox, M. (1999). An ecological approach to conceptualizing the transition to kindergarten. In R. Pianta & M. Cox (Eds.), *The transition to kindergarten* (pp. 3–10). Baltimore, MD: Brookes.

Raviv, T., Kessenich, M., & Morrison, F. J. (2004). A mediational model of the association between socioeconomic status and three-year-old language abilities: The role of parenting factors. *Early Childhood Research Quarterly, 19*, 528–547.

Ribas, A. F. P., de Moura, M. L. S., & de Castro Ribas, R. (2003). Maternal responsiveness: A Review of the literature and a conceptual discussion. [Portuguese]. *Psicologia: Reflexao e Critica, 16*, 137–145.

Ricciuti, H. N. (1999). Single parenthood and school readiness in White, Black and Hispanic 6- and 7- year-olds. *Journal of Family Psychology, 13*, 450–465.

Richman, A. L., Miller, P. M. & LeVine, R. A. (1992). Cultural and educational variations in maternal responsiveness. *Developmental Psychology, 28*, 614–621.

Riksen-Walraven, M. (1978). Effects of caregiver behavior on habituation rate and self-efficacy in infants. *International Journal of Behavioral Development, 1*, 105–130.

Rimm-Kaufman, S. E., LaParo, K. M., Downer, J. T., & Pianta, R. C. (2005). The contribution of classroom setting and quality of instruction to children's behavior in the kindergarten classroom. *Elementary School Journal, 105*, 377–309.

Sameroff, A., & Haith, M. (Eds.). (1996). *The five to seven year shift: The age of reason and responsibility.* Chicago: University of Chicago Press.

Scarr, S. (1992). Developmental theories for the 1990s: Development and individual differences. *Child Development, 63*, 1–19.

Scarr, S., & McKartney, K. (1983). How people make their own environments: A theory of genotype-environment effects. *Child Development, 54*, 424–435.

Shamir-Essakow, G., Ungerer, J. A., Rapee, R. M., & Safier, R. (2004). Caregiving representations of mothers of behaviorally inhibited and uninhibited preschool children. *Developmental Psychology, 40*, 899–910.

Snow, K. L., Canfield, R. C., & Ricciuti, H. N. (2005). Scaffolding of attention during infancy: A review and integration. Paper submitted.

Steelman, L. M., Assel, M. A., Swank, P. R., Smith, K. E., & Landry, S. H. (2002). Early maternal warm responsiveness as a predictor of child social skills: Direct and indirect paths of influence over time. *Applied Developmental Psychology, 23*, 135–156.

Supplee, L. H., Shaw, D. S., Hailstones, K., & Hartman, K. (2004). Family and child influences on early academic and emotion regulatory behaviors. *Journal of School Psychology, 42*, 221–242.

Tamis-LeMonda, C. S., & Bornstein, M. H. (1989). Habituation and maternal encouragement of attention in infancy as predictors of toddler language, play, and representational competence. *Child Development, 60*, 738–751.

Tamis-LeMonda, C. S., Bornstein, M., Baumwell, L., & Damast, A. (1996). Responsive parenting in the second year: Specific influences on children's language and play. *Early Development and Parenting, 5*, 173–183.

Tomasello, M. (1988). The role of joint attention in early language development. *Language Sciences, 11*, 69–88.

Tomasello, M. (1992). The social bases of language acquisition. *Social Development, 1*, 67–87.

Van den Boom, D. C. (1994). The influence of temperament and mothering on attachment and exploration: An experimental manipulation of sensitive responsiveness among lower-class mothers with irritable infants. *Child Development, 65*, 1457–1477.

Wakschlag, L. S., & Hans, S. L. (1999). Relation of maternal responsiveness during infancy to the development of behavior problems in high-risk youths. *Developmental Psychology, 35*, 569–579.

Williams, W. M., & Ceci, S. J. (1997). A person-process-context-time approach to understanding intellectual development. *Review of General Psychology, 1*, 288–310.

III

Parental Conceptualization and Organization of Non-Familial Experiences for Children

10

THE CONTEXT OF SCHOOL READINESS: SOCIAL CLASS DIFFERENCES IN TIME USE IN FAMILY LIFE

Annette Lareau
University of Maryland, College Park

Elliot B. Weininger
SUNY Brockport

In a brief turn of two words, "school readiness," we are immediately drawn into a complex nexus of interactions between families and schools—a nexus that has garnered attention for many decades (Baker & Stevenson, 1986; Bronfenbrenner, 1989; Entwisle, Alexander, & Olson, 1997; Epstein, 1987, Epstein & Sanders, 2000; Leichter, 1979; Lightfoot, 1978; Stevenson & Baker, 1987; Waller, 1961; see also Diamond, 2000). As with any complex pattern of interactions, people look at it from multiple perspectives. Classroom teachers often ask, as other chapter authors in this volume note, "Can children sit still in my classroom so that they are prepared to listen to me?" "Do children know the letters of the alphabet?"

But, in important respects, this approach to school readiness is too narrow and, it could be argued, moralistic. Often researchers look at readiness as a discrete set of tasks, such as knowing the alphabet or being able to maneuver scissors, that are either present or absent. If they are absent, as they are more likely to be among children whose parents have little education, then they are seen as deficient.[1] But teaching children school-related skills is part of a broader approach to child rearing that appears to vary by social class (Alwin, 1984; Bernstein, 1975; Bronfenbrenner, 1966; Gecas, 1979; Hart & Risley, 1995; Heath, 1983; Hofferth, 1999; Kohn & Schooler, 1983; Kohn, Slomczynski, & Schoenback, 1986, Lynd & Lynd, 1929; Medrich et. al., 1981). Notably, there are signs that parents differ in the degree to which they believe it is their duty to provide direct literacy training to their children and to develop their children's talents and skills.

---

[1] On the basis of data in the Condition of Education (U. S. Department of Education, 1995) it is clear that children who are four years old vary in their acquisition of pre-literacy skills, including knowing the alphabet, knowing how to write out their name, being able to count to 100, and other skills. Children whose mothers are college graduates are much more likely than children whose mothers are high school drop-outs to have these skills. More recently, the National Center for Education Statistics (2000) has altered how it reports the data, basing it on "risk factors" (i.e., being in a single-parent home, receiving food stamps, English is a second language, and mother is a high-school drop-out) rather than mother's education per se (U.S. Department of Education, 2005). http://nces.ed.gov/programs/coe/2000/essay/e03f.asp#info. This categorization, which is far from ideal, shows a similar pattern to the older data.

Indeed, in recent work Lareau (2003) argued the existence of class differences in the logic of child rearing. She identified contrasting orientations to child rearing. She termed the approach used by middle-class parents "concerted cultivation." According to this view of child rearing, mothers and fathers believe that they have an obligation to foster the growth and development of children's talents and skills. This approach contrasts with "the accomplishment of natural growth," in which parents actively provide for children but then allow them to grow spontaneously. Here, for example, parents presume that educational skills are best transmitted by educational professionals who have specific college training for these important tasks. The accomplishment of natural growth was observed in working-class and poor families.

These approaches to child rearing have important strengths and limitations. In the valorization of a narrowly conceived set of literacy skills as part of the school readiness literature, researchers fail to acknowledge important drawbacks to middle-class family life and important strengths of working-class and poor children's family lives. Notably, as middle-class parents adopt a project of developing their child through organized activities and literacy development, they create a pace of family life that is heavily adult-structured and hectic, even frenetic. While children can learn valuable skills in these encounters, they also can be exhausted, cranky, and deprived of opportunities for creative peer interaction. By contrast, in viewing their job as one of caring for and protecting their children, but then allowing schools to educate them (Lareau, 2000), working-class and poor parents adopt a different approach to child rearing. While these activities may not promote literacy skills in the same way as in middle-class families, working-class and poor children were spared the disadvantages of many middle-class children's lives. Notably, in the ethnographic study, we found that working-class and poor children were not as exhausted and worn down as the middle-class children. Middle-class children often only saw their relatives on holiday occasions in holiday clothes, even when they had cousins within a twenty-minute drive, while working-class and poor children developed deeper connections with kinship groups as they saw them several times per week. Middle-class children often had little time for creative, self-initiated play. When faced with an afternoon, or even a few minutes, without a planned activity, we observed middle-class children proclaim themselves to be bored and demanded that their parents do something to entertain them. Middle-class children also seemed sometimes to have an air of ennui and did not show the pleasure and enthusiasm that we observed in working-class and poor families in organized activities, when they occurred, or with little events such as pizza or eating out in a fast food restaurant.

In short, the development of literacy skills is embedded in different logics of child rearing that, in turn, imply a different use of time and a different pace and rhythm of daily life. In recent years, particular attention has been paid to the involvement of children in organized forms of leisure such as soccer, baseball, art and dance lessons, scouting, and other adult-organized and controlled activities.

These activities have come to occupy a substantial amount of time, at least for some children, and there is evidence that young children are enrolled in programs such as "Tot tumbling" or "Kindergym" before they enter kindergarten.[2] In the popular press, discussions have emerged concerning the potential value of these activities, as well as their negative impact on the family dinner hour and the pace of family life (Belluck, 2000; Doherty, 2002). Some psychologists have decried *The Hurried Child* (Elkin, 2001) or the *The Over-Scheduled Child* (Rosenfeld & Wise, 2000). Among social scientists, there is an emerging interest in these activities and the impact on literacy and school readiness (see especially Farkas & Hibel, this volume). There are striking parallels between organized activities and the structure of schooling. While the activities are designed for leisure and fun, they also have an institutionalized character. For example, they have a clear starting time. Children are expected to line up, be quiet, and follow directions given by adults, and are publicly assessed in terms of their performance. Children also have the potential to learn work-related skills, such as interacting with adults and working on a team. Yet, relatively little is known about organized activities and their place in family life; nor has there been sufficient study of the role of class in shaping children's time use, especially with respect to children's organized activities. It is this topic that we develop in this chapter, using an ethnographic study of 88 children and their families as well as analyses of the Panel Study of Income Dynamics Child Development Supplement. As we note, the children in this study are school-aged, being in third and fourth grade in the ethnographic study and from 6–12 in the quantitative analysis. Thus, this chapter does not directly address the issue of school readiness. Yet, detailed examinations of children's daily lives and organized activities are rare and we believe that there are useful conceptual implications of this study for the issues discussed in this volume.

Here, we first argue that the pace of family life differs by social class. For middle-class children, organized leisure activities can dominate and constrain the rhythm of daily family life. Dinner hours, weekend, vacations, and other family routines are mediated and transformed by kids' schedules. Second, middle-class families face formidable scheduling challenges because middle-class kids' schedules routinely clash with other family obligations. One key arena of conflict is parents' work schedules and children's leisure activities. At times, parents' work schedules preclude children's participation; other times middle-class parents squeeze in work tasks while waiting in cars during soccer practices and piano lessons. Third, across all social classes there is a "predictably unpredictable" character of life, but the

---

[2] Although beyond the purview of this paper, there is ample evidence of important historical shifts in child rearing practices from basic conceptions of children's economic or sentimental value (Zelizer, 1985) to ideas by professionals about how children should be raised (Bronfenbrenner, 1966; Wrigley, 1988). There is also evidence of importance changes in parents' time use, especially women's labor force participation (Presser, 1989) although there are signs of mothers spending more time with children rather than less (Bianchi, 2000; Bianchi & Robinson, 1997). Sharon Hays also writes of the rise of a new standard of "intensive mothering" (Hays, 1996). For a review of historical changes in family life see Skolnick (1991).

uncertain nature of children's leisure activities gives these hurdles a distinctive character. "Hectic" "nuts" "crazy" are words that middle-class parents often use in describing aspects of daily parenting routines.

By contrast, working-class and poor families exhibit a different rhythm of life, largely because children participate in far fewer organized activities. Here, rather than being determined by children's leisure, resource constraints and the management of economic challenges shape the texture of life. Thus, key family events are contingent upon the influx of resources, such as the date of a paycheck, the ability of a boyfriend to provide a ride, the availability of a transportation pass, or other arrangements. In addition, work obligations are more rigid and are more strictly centered on the work place; parents in working-class and poor families are less likely to squeeze in work during children's activities or, for that matter, during their time away from the job. Another striking difference is that in the working-class and poor families we studied, kinship obligations appeared palpably stronger and more important in daily life. Time conflicts did arise, especially regarding kin obligations. Overall, the pace of life was less time-pressured for parents and more resource-pressured. Nevertheless, working-class and poor parents often felt time pressured in their schedules. Finally, as in middle-class families, working-class and poor parents also struggled with the "predictably unpredictable" character of life; however, once again, these challenges often swirled around resource issues, or the lack thereof. Parents had fewer degrees of freedom to resolve the conflicts that surfaced.

This chapter begins with a review of the research methodology used in the ethnographic data and quantitative data. Then, as further background, we provide a summary of the concepts of concerted cultivation and natural growth. We then discuss the experience of middle-class families before turning to that of the working-class and poor families in the studies. As we show, we found differences by social class in the role of children's organized leisure activities in driving the pace and rhythm of family life, in the qualitative nature of conflicts that surfaced between children's lives and other aspects of family life, and in the nature of the "predictably unpredictable" shifts that all families encountered. There were, however, important aspects of family life where class seemed quite unimportant.

Methods

We use two data sets for this paper: an ethnographic data set (collected by the first author and a set of research assistants), and an analysis of the Panel Study of Income Dynamics Child Development Supplement (carried out by the second author).

The Ethnographic Data

Our ethnographic results are drawn from an extensive study directed by the first author of social class differences in childrearing. Much of the analytic focus of the study was on parents' organization of their children's time. Data were gathered on the families of 88 children between the ages of 8- and 10-years old from middle-class, working-class, and poor families (see Table 10.1 for a definition of terms). Thirty-two of the families resided in a medium-sized Midwestern city, while the remaining 56 lived in a large city on the East Coast (or the surrounding area). In both cases, the families were selected from a small number of elementary schools that cooperated with the study after a period of observation in third and fourth grade classrooms. Over 90% of the families that were approached agreed to participate in an in-depth interview that usually took place in their home. These interviews (first with the mothers and then the fathers) lasted about two hours. While they followed a specified format, respondents were offered ample opportunity to direct the conversation. Approximately one-half of the families were white and one-half black; one girl was interracial. The children included an equal number of boys and girls.

Table 10.1

Distribution of Children in the Lareau Study by Social Class and Race

Social Class	White	African American	Total
Middle class*	Melanie Handlon Garrett Tallinger 18	Stacey Marshall Alexander Williams 18	36
Working class#	Wendy Drivei Billy Yanelli 14	Tyrec Taylor Jessica Irwin+ 12	26
Families in poverty^	Katie Brindle Karl Greeley 12	Tara Carroll Harold McAllister 14	26
Total	44	44	88

*Middle-class children are those who live in households in which at least one parent who is employed in a position that either entails substantial managerial authority or that draws upon highly complex, educationally certified skills (i.e., college level)

#Working-class children are those who live in households in which neither parent is employed in a middle-class position and at least one parent is employed in a position with little to no managerial authority and that does not draw on complex, educationally certified skills. This category includes lower-level white-collar workers.

^Poor children are those whose households have parents who are on public assistance and do not participate in the labor force in a regular, continuous basis.

+Inter-racial girl: black father and white mother

In addition to the interviews, detailed observational data was gathered on a subset of twelve of the children and their families. The families were selected so as capture different combinations of class, race, and gender across the children. Nine of the twelve children came from the classrooms where we had observed, but three, including both middle-class black children, came from other settings (i.e., another school and an informal social network of the researcher; the poor white boy was referred by a social service program the researchers contacted.) Nineteen families were approached, and 12 agreed to participate, yielding a response rate of 63%. The observations entailed daily visits to the participating families by the second author and/or her assistants. Approximately 20 visits were made to each family, usually over the course of one month. During the visits, which typically lasted about three hours (though they sometimes took longer), fieldworkers, carrying tape recorders, accompanied the children wherever they went, including check-ups, games, shopping trips, etc. In every case, at least one of the fieldworkers who regularly visited belonged to the same racial groups as the child, and in most instances, at least one fieldworker was also of the same gender. Additionally, in most families there was one overnight stay by a fieldworker. The families who participated were paid $350. A pizza party was held to mark the end of the fieldwork. Although there is no question that the researchers altered family dynamics, there were signs that families did adjust to their presence, as yelling and cursing often increased after the third visit. In addition, children and parents reported that they had behaved normally or that their behavior had been altered in highly specific ways (e.g., in one family the children reported that the house was cleaner than usual; in another family that the mother talked more). Most, but not all, of the children enjoyed being in the study. They reported that it made them feel "special."

The Quantitative Data

While the majority of our chapter draws on qualitative data, we periodically supplement our analysis with figures derived from the Child Development Supplement (CDS) to the 1997 wave of the Panel Study of Income Dynamics (PSID), a nationally representative quantitative data set. The PSID is a well-known survey that has been used to collect a wide variety of data (primarily relating to work and finances) from a sample of U.S. families since 1968 (Hill, 1982). The sample has evolved by following not only the original families, but their offshoots as well—that is, the families formed by the children of members of the initial sample. The CDS gathered data from a subsample of PSID families that had children between the ages of 0 and 12 in 1997.

The various instruments that made up the CDS contained a multitude of questions pertaining to family life, to children's experiences, and to things like their schooling. The data are generally structured at the child level. Specifically, the CDS contains information on 3,563 children in 2,380 families (implying that 66.4% of the children are siblings of another child in the subsample; however, no more than two children were sampled from a given family). The data include a number of details provided by the primary caregiver concerning the focal child's education and daily life. Also important to our purposes, one module of the CDS is made up of time diaries that were used to record the full range of each child's activities for a 24-hour period on one weekday and one weekend day. The CDS includes 2,904 completed diary sets. The activities that the children engaged in on diary days were recorded via a highly elaborate and detailed coding system. For this paper, we created a child-level data set that combined time diary information on children's leisure activities with information provided by the primary caregiver and a number of familial SES variables. Our data set is restricted to children who are at least 6 years old, in order maintain as much comparability as possible with our qualitative data. We further limit the sample to children who are black or white, on the grounds that with the age restriction in place, the number of children of other races is relatively small.

Our foremost interest is in a measure of children's participation in organized leisure. We understand this to be comprised of activities that are generally viewed as leisure (and therefore are voluntary), but which have a schedule (replete with deadlines) and are adult-directed. (Many—but not all—organized leisure activities also have some kind of participation fee.) We made use of two measures. The first is survey question posed to each child's primary caregiver: "Does (CHILD) participate in any extracurricular activities such as gymnastics, scouts, music lessons, a sports team, or a boys' or girls' club?" The possible responses were "yes" and "no." Our second measure is an estimate of the amount of time devoted to involvement in organized leisure derived from the time diaries. This measure was created by summing the amount of time recorded in the diary that the child spent on activities that we could confidently identify as falling into this category. These include all sports that have formal enrollment requirements (such as membership on a baseball team or karate lessons), as well as cultural pursuits (such piano lessons) and certain "organizational activities" (such membership in a church youth group). In a few cases—such as horseback riding and photography— it is impossible for us to determine whether an activity took place in a formal or informal setting. With two exceptions, these ambiguous codes have been excluded from our measure.[3] To construct the measure, we first summed the amount of time spent in organized activities for each time diary. We converted it to a meaningful

---

[3] In the case of playing a musical instrument, we assume that children are most likely rehearsing for a formal lesson, and therefore treat this as organized leisure. We also ultimately decided to include religious services on the grounds of their scheduled nature. It should be noted that the code for religious services includes participation in a religious choir, an activity that was not infrequently reported among middle-class children in the ethnographic study.

metric by using Hofferth and Sandberg's (2001) procedure for constructing a weekly estimate from the time diary data: the weekday total was multiplied by five, the weekend total was multiplied by two, and the results summed.

In order to examine variations in children's participation in organized leisure and the amount of time they spend in it, we used a small number of demographic and SES variables. These include the child's gender, his or her race (although this is limited to a comparison of blacks and whites, as other groups are poorly represented in the data), the mother's education (categorized as less than high school, high school degree, some college, and bachelor's degree and above), and her employment status (categorized as non-employed, employed less than 35 hours per week, and employed 35 hours or more).

Concerted Cultivation and Natural Growth

In the middle-class families that participated in the ethnographic study, busy schedules were common.[4] The middle-class families, black and white, appeared to be committed to childrearing strategies that favored the individual development of each child, sometimes at the expense of family time and group needs. By encouraging involvement in activities outside the home, middle-class parents position their children to receive more than an education in how to play soccer, baseball, or piano. These young sports-enthusiasts and budding musicians acquire skills and dispositions that help them navigate the institutional world. They learn to think of themselves as special and as entitled to receive certain kinds of services from adults. They also acquire a valuable set of white-collar work skills, including how to set priorities, manage an itinerary, shake hands with strangers, and work on a team. We have described this cultural logic of childrearing, in which there is a sustained effort to develop children's talents and skills, as *concerted cultivation*. This logic of childrearing can be seen in the enrollment of children in many organized activities, a tendency to reason with children in extensive verbal negotiation, and a pattern of close supervision of children's lives in institutions outside of the home.

In working-class and poor families in the study, there was a different cultural logic of childrearing, one that Lareau (2003) termed *the accomplishment of natural growth*. The limited economic resources available to working-class and poor families make getting children fed, clothed, sheltered and transported time-consuming, arduous labor. Parents tend to direct their efforts toward keeping children safe, enforcing discipline and, when they deem it necessary, regulating their behavior in

---

[4] National data also suggest that children of highly educated parents have more organized activities and busier schedules. See especially Hofferth and Sandberg (2001), as well as Lareau, Elliot, and Bianchi (2005). There are also a number of older studies on children's organized leisure activities, including the classic piece by Janet Lever (1976), as well as Elliot Medrich et al. (1981), and Fine (1987). For discussions of children's cultures see Cahill (1992), Corsaro (1998), Opie and Opie (1991), and Thorne (1992). For more general discussions of families and time use see Daley (2001), and Robinson and Godbey (1999).

specific areas. However, within these boundaries, working-class and poor children are allowed to grow and to thrive. They are given the flexibility to choose activities and playmates and to decide how active or inactive to be as they engage in these activities. Thus, whereas middle-class children often are treated as a project to be developed, working-class and poor children are given boundaries for their behavior and then allowed to grow.

The greater emphasis on kinship in working-class and poor families means that children spend much more time interacting with family members and providing important goods and services to kin than do their middle-class counterparts. The cultural logic of the accomplishment of natural growth grants children an autonomous world, apart from adults, in which they are free to try out new experiences and develop important social competencies. Working-class and poor children learn how to be members of informal peer groups. They learn how to manage their own time. They learn how to strategize. Children, especially boys, learn how to negotiate open conflict during play, including how to defend themselves physically. Boys are also given more latitude to play further away from home than are girls.

These social competencies are as real as those acquired by middle-class children. The two sets of competencies are not the same, however; and they are not equally valued in the institutional worlds with which *all* children must come in contact (e.g., schools, healthcare facilities, stores, workplaces). Unlike middle-class children, working-class and poor children do not have opportunities to start developing the kinds of skills that reap the greatest benefits in institutional settings outside the home. For example, children from working-class and poor families typically do not learn how to choose among conflicting organizational commitments, read trip itineraries, sign identification cards, or travel out of state or work on an adult-led team with formal, established rules. Nor do they have the same experience as middle-class children of thinking of themselves as entitled to receive customized attention from adults in positions of institutional authority. In fact, working-class and poor children are regularly instructed to defer to adults.[5]

To be sure, there are some important differences between the lives of children in working-class families and those in poor families. Compared to poor children, working-class children have greater stability; their lives are less contingent, especially in terms of the availability of food, transportation, money for treats, and other economic resources. There are also differences by race and by gender. Although working-class and poor children pursue the same or similar activities and organized their daily lives in much the same way, they generally do so in racially segregated groups. This pattern held even among children who lived only a few blocks from one another and who went to the same school and were in the same class. Middle-class black parents were also quite anxious about the possibility

---

[5] Elijah Anderson (1999) documents the importance of complying with codes of respect, particularly in children's relations with adults.

that their children would experience racial discrimination in school and other settings away from home. Parents, especially the mothers, kept a sharp eye out for such problems. Additionally, as other studies have shown, we found gender to be a very powerful force in shaping the organization of children's daily life. Despite some active moments, girls are more sedentary, play closer to home, and have their physical bodies more actively scrutinized and shaped by others than do boys. Nevertheless, the greatest gulf we observed is one that has not been fully recognized in the existing literature: a class-rooted difference in the organization of daily life whereby middle- and upper-middle-class children pursue a hectic program of adult-controlled leisure activities while working-class and poor children follow a more open-ended schedule that is not as heavily managed by adults.

As childrearing strategies, concerted cultivation and natural growth entail very different temporal experiences. In particular, organized leisure activities—which middle-class parents generally view as a way of fostering the development of their children's unique talents and interests—can dramatically impact the rhythm and pace of family life. It to this that we now turn.

Children's Activities Help to Create a Hectic Rhythm for Middle-Class Family Life

Organized activities are generally common in middle-class families. This can be seen in the Lareau data on 88 children (Table 10.2) and, more significantly, in the national data (Tables 10.3 and 10.4). In addition, the number of activities that middle-class children participate in and the time that they devote to them can be considerable. Using the time dairies from the CDS, we estimate that children of highly educated mothers (i.e., those with at least a bachelor's degree) spend 4 hours and 49 minutes per week in organized leisure (Table 10.5). For families with two children, this implies almost ten hours per week.[6] These organized activities, which have rigid deadlines, limited duration, and various requirements for participation, can easily come to dominate the rhythm and pace of family life in middle-class families. For example, one middle-class family that we observed,

---

[6] Echoing other studies of the division of labor (e.g., Hochschild, 1989), in both the ethnographic data and the PSID data there is compelling evidence that mothers, much more than fathers, bear the responsibility for managing the daily rhythms of children's lives and for managing any subsequent conflicts that develop (Lareau, Weininger, & Bianchi, 2005; Thompson, 1999). Extensive amounts of "invisible" labor or "mental" labor are expended by middle-class mothers working out the schedules of all of the various family members. In some instances, especially for single fathers, men do play an active role. Yet, even when men play very active roles in children's organized activities, for example by being soccer coaches, they receive important "hidden" assistance from their wives. See Berhau, Lareau, and Press (2005). Many middle-class fathers in the ethnographic study felt that they were active participants in their children's lives, and observations did confirm their salience; but overwhelmingly, the fathers in the ethnographic study were far less informed, engaged, and responsible for managing the details of children's lives than were the mothers. As a result, the fathers were not particularly valuable informants on the subject of their children's schedule of organized activities. See Lareau (2000b). But see Steir and Tienda (1993) for evidence of in-kind gifts by the kinfolk of non-custodial fathers.

the Tallingers consists of two parents who both work in high-level managerial jobs, and three boys: Garrett in fourth grade, Spencer in second grade, and Sam, a 4-year-old in pre-school. In the Tallinger family, the older children's schedules set the pace of life for all family members. Mr. and Ms. Tallinger often have limited time between work and the start of an activity. They rush home, rifle through the mail, prepare snacks, change out of their work clothes, make sure the children are appropriately dressed and have the proper equipment for the upcoming activity, find their car keys, put the dog outside, load the children and equipment into the car, lock the door, and drive off. This pattern repeats itself, with slight variations, day after day. Garrett has the most activities. Thus, it is his schedule, in particular, that determines where the adults must be and when they must be there, sets the timing and type of meals for everyone, and even shapes the family's vacation plans.

Table 10.2

Average Number of Organized Leisure Activities Child Participates in by Social Class: Lareau Data on 88 Children[1]

	Poor	Working Class	Middle Class
All Children			
Organized Activities	1.5	2.5	4.9
Items with Missing Data[2]	2.0	3.0	2.5
Count	26	26	36
Gender			
Organized Activities: Boys	1.5	2.6	5.1
Items with Missing Data: Boys[2]	2.1	3.8	3.4
Count	11	14	18
Organized Activities: Girls	1.5	2.5	4.7
Items with Missing Data: Girls[2]	1.9	2.1	1.5
Count	15	12	18
Race			
Organized Activities: Whites	1.4	2.3	4.6
Items with Missing Data: Whites[2]	0.9	2.3	2.9
Count	12	14	18
Organized Activities: Blacks	1.6	2.8	5.2
Items with Missing Data: Blacks[2]	2.9	3.8	2.0
Count	14	12	18

[1]Organized activities include: Brownies or Cub Scouts, music lessons, team sports (soccer, Little League, etc.), non-team sports (gymnastics, karate, etc.), Tot Tumbling, dance lessons (ballet, tap, etc.), religious classes, choir, art classes, and any activity offered through a recreational center that requires formal enrollment.

[2]Not every respondent was asked about all of the activities that were eventually coded (though each was asked if his/her child participated in any activities not explicitly mentioned).

Table 10.3

Children's Participation in Organized Leisure (yes/no) by Mother's Education, Gender, and Race: National Data

| | | Mother's Education | | | |
	LT HS	HS Degree	Some College	Bachelor's or Higher	Total
All Children					
% who Participate	57.1	69.1	82.1	93.6	77.6
Count	253	630	460	290	1,633
Gender					
% Boys who Participate	62.5	69.1	75.8	93.6	75.8
Count	132	313	224	139	808
% Girls who Participate	50.4	69.0	88.3	93.6	79.4
Count	121	317	236	151	825
Race[1]					
% Whites who Participate	59.9	75.1	87.9	94.0	83.4
Count	66	294	240	243	843
% Blacks who Participate	54.2	51.8	59.0	88.3	57.0
Count	187	336	220	47	790

Source: 1997 Child Development Supplement to the Panel Study of Income Dynamics. Data are weighted. Includes children between the ages of six and twelve years old.

[1]Data reported on blacks and whites only due to low cell frequencies for other categories.

Table 10.4

Children's Average Weekly Hours in Organized Leisure by Mother's Education, Gender, and Race: National Data

	LT HS	HS Degree	Some College	Bachelor's or Higher	Total
		Mother's Education			
All Children					
Mean Weekly Hours	2.02	2.91	3.38	4.82	3.45
Count	179	509	387	250	1,325
Gender					
Mean Weekly Hours: Boys	1.59	2.84	3.72	5.53	3.59
Count	91	258	187	121	657
Mean Weekly Hours: Girls	2.56	2.99	3.04	4.21	3.31
Count	88	251	200	129	668
Race[1]					
Mean Weekly Hours: Whites	0.90	3.25	3.52	5.03	3.73
Count	44	249	212	212	717
Mean Weekly Hours: Blacks	3.02	1.84	2.81	2.02	2.40
Count	135	260	175	38	608

Source: 1997 Child Development Supplement to the Panel Study of Income Dynamics. Data are weighted.
Includes children between the ages of six and twelve years old.
[1]Data reported on blacks and whites only due to low cell frequencies for other categories.

Table 10.5

Children's Average Weekly Hours in Organized Leisure by Mother's Education and Employment Status: National Data

	LT HS	HS Degree	Some College	Bachelor's or Higher	Total
		Mother's Education			
Mother's Employment Status					
Not Employed	2.80	4.35	3.79	5.96	4.28
Count	79	104	55	42	280
Employed less than 35 hrs/wk	2.58	3.74	3.30	5.31	4.03
Count	35	120	108	89	352
Employed 35 hrs/wk or more	0.95	2.01	3.29	3.92	2.76
Count	65	285	224	119	693

Source: 1997 Child Development Supplement to the Panel Study of Income Dynamics. Data are weighted.
Includes children between the ages of six and twelve years old.

For example, during the month of May, Garrett participates in baseball, Forest soccer (a private soccer club), Intercounty soccer (an all-star, elite team of boys drawn from various soccer clubs), swim team practice, piano lessons, and saxophone. Only the saxophone lessons take place at school; all of the rest are extracurricular activities that Garrett's parents have enrolled him in, with his consent. This list does not include Spencer's activities, nor does it fully reflect the parents' commitments. During the week of May 23rd, when Garrett has his regular baseball, soccer, and swim team events, Mr. Tallinger is scheduled to umpire a game on Monday evening, and Spencer has a baseball game Tuesday and a Cub Scout meeting Thursday. On the weekend, the entire family drives four hours to an out-of-state soccer tournament. They are gone Friday, Saturday, and Sunday and return home Monday. On Tuesday, Garrett has swim team practice, soccer tryouts, and Intercounty soccer practice. On Wednesday, he has swim team practice (which he can ride his bike to) and a baseball game. On Thursday, when Garrett has practice for swim team and for Forest soccer, Spencer has a baseball game at 5:45 p.m.. Then, on Saturday, Spencer has another baseball game (at 9:15 a.m.) and Garrett has two soccer games, one at 10:15 a.m. and one at 3:00 p.m. When a conflict arises, as between his cousin's college graduation party (held at his house) and a soccer game, Garrett is given the choice of what to do; he chooses to attend the soccer game. Not all middle-class families, of course, were as sports-oriented––or as busy—as the Tallingers. Still, many middle-class children in the study had a hectic schedule of activities. Middle-class children participated in substantially more activities than did working-class and poor children (Table 10.2). There were some gender differences in the type of activities in which children were involved (Tables 10.2–10.4); interviews suggested, for example, that boys were more heavily oriented to athletics than were girls.

Other families had similar schedules. Particularly for families with more than one child, scheduling conflicts were routine. As Ms. Handlon complained, it was "nuts:"

> One year we had all three playing and we started T-ball like at 5:30 and then the other one started at 6:00 and the other one started at 6:30. So there were three different fields in three different parts of the township. It was nuts.

Third- and fourth-grade children also have to make choices, such as when an activity they enjoyed a previous year, such as Scouts summer camp, conflicts with other summer activities:

> He went to Day camp with Scouts last summer. He has a schedule conflict this summer. He can't go…..It conflicted with his soccer camp where he is going for a week and he's got, what else, science. He is going to be in the science program……Everything is in July.

Since children's activities are seasonal, and many programs at townships or recreational centers are offered sporadically throughout the year, things that families wanted to happen sometimes could not, as in this white middle-class family:

> I: Has he ever had karate?
> Yes. And that's one of those other things that I wanted to follow through on and what happens with karate is it always ends up being during soccer season. It's just too hectic trying to get him to both [soccer] practices, and a game, and she has it [soccer practices] twice a week and a game .... [Karate] was at the wrong time. It interfered with the soccer practices so he had one session and that was it.

Indeed, institutional offerings were not necessarily coordinated, as Mr. Williams complained:

> I got all the brochures ... because I knew he wanted to go to a basketball camp. And, ... that all four of them had basketball camp the week of, I think it was June 23rd. You would think that the schools would have them at different times. And that is the week that he wanted to go on a canoe trip.

The Interweaving of Children's Organized Activities with Other Aspects of Family Life

The propensity of middle-class parents to enroll their children in organized leisure activities can have dramatic consequences for family life. In particular, tensions often result from the competing commitments that ensue. These are triggered both by the children's school obligations and by the parents' work obligations.

In contrast to their working-class and poor counterparts, most of the middle-class children we studied participated in more than one organized activity. They also attended school, of course, and most had homework that needed to be done (as did their brothers and sisters). And their organized activities were usually not within walking distance. As Ms. Wallace, the mother of an eighth grader, a fourth grader, and a third grader, said: "There's an awful lot of driving involved in being a mother around here." The fourth grader's soccer practice was at 6 p.m.; he did his homework at his grandmother's while he and his mother waited for his older sister to take her piano lesson:

> Today I also have to pick up my older daughter and her friend over at the library. So I'll pick the kids up from school, go to the library and pick those kids up. Go down and drop her off at her piano and go hang out at my mother's who doesn't live too far away for the half hour that she's

there. [Don, the fourth grader] usually sits down and does some homework at my mother's house. Go pick her back up, come home, have dinner, take Don over to [soccer practice] by 6:00 so there's about an hour and ten minutes that we have to come home and finish up homework. Eat dinner and then get over there.

Getting everyone dinner, getting homework done, and getting everyone where they needed to be was complex on Tuesday nights:

> My husband is taking a night class right now on Tuesday nights so a lot of times he would be the one to go over and pick Don up at nine. And sometimes he does. Sometimes he's out in time to do that. If not—and then Sarah's got a Bible class in there from 7:30 to 8:30 so I usually take her. Tuesday night is—I mean, that's the busiest night where I really do feel like I'm in the car the whole time because the three kids have gone in three different directions. Sometimes we try and car pool but there's not a whole lot of kids in this area who play for Forest soccer. A lot of the kids just play the township league. So, there's not any car-pooling for that. The little girls are in Girl Scouts—the two girls are in Scouts, too, so sometimes I think that's a little much, but ....

When asked to elaborate, Ms. Wallace added:

> Well, see, because sometimes I think, "If I have to get in this car one more time!" My day is very fragmented. Sometimes I feel that what I do is chauffeuring back and forth but, yet, I don't feel—it's just that I happen to have three kids who, even if they are maybe only in two activities each, which they pretty much are, then that takes you six different places.

The schedule was highly variable and the next night would be quieter, but only temporarily:

> You know, on Tuesday night I'm thinking, this is crazy. But it's really not that bad. Wednesday night will be fine. In fact, I don't think anybody will be going out. His Scouts has changed from Thursday to Wednesday, but, anyway, that's part of having kids.

At times, homework entailed especially complex "projects" that the children were expected to work on over a period of time. Often these projects involved special materials, such as poster board, fabric, and glue that they asked their parents to help them procure. In some families last-minute crises occurred when a child, having not kept pace with the project, needed help to get it in on time. If the middle-class families had empty stretches of time in the afternoon or evening, then resolving these crises would have been easier; but, in most cases, children also had competing obligations of lessons and practices that made finding time for homework substantially more difficult.

The sheer logistics of getting through the afternoon and evening—with snacks, homework, dinner, and bedtime—was difficult. Sometimes parents felt that they could not take advantage of particular activities for their children. For example, when asked about a special form of musical training that requires parents to sit during the weekly lesson of one hour and also monitor daily practices, the Suzuki method, Mrs. Hopewell saw it as an ideal form of instruction for her daughter:

> I like the way of teaching. It's more by ear which is the way for her. In fact, it teaches piano lessons the way she learns best. She learns best by ear.

Other family obligations, however, made it impossible, even though Ms. Hopewell was a full-time homemaker:

> [Suzuki] requires a great deal of parental involvement and I can't do it, I really can't. There is no way that I can sit at Suzuki for an hour in the afternoon when there are other kids who need homework, snack, dinner started and it's 4:30 in the afternoon. And then the parent has to be involved in the lesson … I cannot go up there and sit. I just can't do that. I really like the idea. If I didn't have so many children I would definitely pursue that.

Most of the mothers, however, were not homemakers (Table 10.4). In the observational study, many children with elaborate schedules like Garrett Tallinger's had mothers who worked in high-pressure, professional jobs. Thus despite mothers' and fathers' formidable work commitments, children still had multiple organized activities. At times, these middle-class parents would squeeze in work obligations during the time surrounding children's activities. Mr. Tallinger, for example, had a 45-minute work-related conversation (with someone on the West Coast) in his car in the dirt parking lot of a soccer field during a 7 p.m. practice. Other parents would take care of job-related reading or work on reports while attending practices, games, and lessons. Still, in the interviews, middle-class parents often reported conflicts between their work obligations and the demands of their children's activities that precluded the children from participating in some events. As one African American attorney, a single father, reported:

> He can't do things that are scheduled at three and four in the afternoon … Karate is Wednesday night; he was going at six o'clock. Since [his older step-brother] started working days, I've been having him take him at five o'clock. Now this week he can't take him at five because he has a class he has to take for work. I can't get him in time to take him for

the five o'clock class which is the class in his age range. So we have to go to the six o'clock class which is a younger group. But in order for me to get home for the six o'clock class I have to leave work by around 4:30 which is very difficult. I just can't manage it.

Other mothers reported similar conflicts. They would note, "I can't manage it," or, "I can't do it with my schedule." Indeed, the PSID data indicate that full-time maternal employment is associated with less participation by the child, as compared to part-time employment or non-employment on the part of the mother (Table 10.5).

To be sure, middle-class parents often found the deadlines posed by children's activities to be stressful and difficult. Mr. Tallinger, for example, complained bitterly about having to leave work at 3:30 on a Friday to get his son to a soccer game, located an hour from home, that started at 5:00. He was annoyed and found the soccer schedule "arrogant." But he was able to make an adjustment in the work schedule without, for example, risking being fired. Working-class parents, on the other hand, reported that they did not have this type of flexibility available to them.

Still, even for middle-class parents, an event such as a job change could reverberate through family life, altering parents' availability to their children. This is apparent in the case of the mother of an African American middle-class family:

I have to really get better with this. I've been on my job for two and a half months. Things went kind of awry for us back in May [when her husband was laid off]. Then I got this job … just as school was starting for them and I really been putting a lot of time [in] on my job trying to ensure that I can keep my job. A lot of the areas that I used to be really involved with them I have to admit that I haven't been that much over the past couple of months.

Predictably Unpredictable Schedules: Middle-Class Families

Most children's sports have a post-season. Often, tournaments follow a "double elimination" format (in which the team has to lose twice to be eliminated from the tournament). Regardless of the format, however, the schedule of games is typically contingent on performance in some manner, and thus uncertain. For example, in the McNamara family, on a Tuesday night, the plan for the week was indeterminate but involved the mother going to practice with the fourth-grader first, and then proceeding to watch the end of the older boy's tournament game, which was forty-five minutes away:

> We're gonna have to [car pool] tonight because Drew has practice so [my wife] will take Drew to practice. And somehow I think I'll try to get a ride for [his brother] and I to go up with one of the other players. And [my wife] will drive and we'll come back [together] rather than taking two cars.

The rest of the week was also uncertain as both boys played in tournaments that were each forty-five minutes to an hour away from the house, but in opposite directions:

> I guess we'll all go tomorrow and then [we'll go] depending on what they do. They could play Wednesday or Thursday. See, [his brother] is playing in [another] tournament. They [his brother's team] play tonight and play Wednesday for sure. So if they both play Wednesday night we'll have to split up. One will have to go to one and one will have to go to the other. I don't know how we'll figure out who goes where.

These kinds of conflicts were routine.

Other disruptions were more unpredictable. In the Midwest and East, for example, soccer, baseball, and football practices can be routinely disrupted by rain or by threatened rain. Since play can go on in a light drizzle and thunder showers can roll in relatively quickly, the decision to have a practice or a game is usually not made until the very last minute. Often, parents had to drive to the field to find out if the event was on or off. Then, if it was rained out, typically a make-up game would need to be scheduled. One rainy spring, seven different soccer games were rained out and had to be made up. One mother had six soccer games in one weekend. Similarly, snow, ice, and other weather interrupted school schedules; parents would then need to scour around to learn if children's organized activities––such as scout meetings, piano lessons, or choir practices––would also be cancelled.[7]

---

[7] Other factors altered family schedules. Children often, for example, pleaded with parents to have overnights, rendering the next day's schedule complex, as this mother, Ms. Wolman, reported one summer morning with her 9-year-old daughter and her 12-year-old son. Ms. Wolman worked in a family business; her hours were therefore flexible but, but it was essential that she make it to work:

> It's like this morning. Both of them had a friend stay overnight because it was the Fourth of July. And then [I'm] trying to get rid of two of them so [the babysitter] didn't have four children. And the little girl that stayed all night was leaving. And a friend of Jamie's called and she was supposed to go over there. And Aaron said he wanted to go to the Mall and [the babysitter] wanted to take off early and ... (Laughter). So then I had to call and check out and make sure that Jamie was, in fact, invited to this friend's because I know his mother is babysitting. It gets really complicated.

Race and the Rhythm of Daily Life

In the in-depth interview data and family observations, both white and black middle-class parents reported enrolling their children in numerous organized activities. Conversely, in working-class and poor families, both white and black children participated in substantially fewer organized activities than their middle-class counterparts. There were, however, key ways that race made a difference in daily life: Black fathers were vulnerable to insults in street life, they complained of difficulties at work connected to race, the families lived in racially segregated neighborhoods, and many black parents reported that they wanted their children to have a positive racial identity, taking them to middle-class African American churches as part of an effort to promote that goal. Black parents also, as noted earlier, closely monitored schools for signs of racial discrimination. Nevertheless, with respect to the number and kind of activities their children were enrolled in, and with respect to other aspects of concerted cultivation (especially use of reasoning and intervening in institutions), the ethnographic data did not show clear and striking differences between the 18 middle-class white families and the 18 middle-class black families. However, the PSID data suggest the possibility of race differences (Tables 10.3 and 10.4). White children spend more time in organized activities than black children at all but the lowest level of maternal education, with a particularly dramatic difference apparent for children of mothers who have a bachelor's degree (although the number of cases in the cell for blacks is fairly low, and therefore should be interpreted with caution). While a full exploration of this finding would require additional research, we were struck in interviews by the job uncertainty, job anxiety, and job worries expressed by middle-class black parents. It could be, as some have argued (Oliver & Shapiro, 1997), that the position of the black middle-class is quite precarious. If economic uncertainty and fear of being fired are pervasive, then black parents may feel less confident about taking on the challenges raised by children's participation in organized leisure activities.

Working-Class and Poor Families: Economics and Time

The working-class and poor children in the ethnographic study and in the PSID study had fewer organized activities than their middle-class counterparts (Tables 10.2–10.4). Furthermore, poor children had fewer activities than did working-class children. As a result, the daily crises and negotiations that were ubiquitous in middle-class homes did not surface in observations and interviews in working-class and poor homes. Even in rare cases where children did have three organized activities (as with one white working-class girl we observed, Wendy Driver), the rhythm of life had a different feel. For example, in middle-class homes, the parents saw themselves as having a duty to develop children's talents. After an organized activity, middle-class parents often quizzed their children, trying to determine what the children had learned. They sought to make leisure experiences educational ones; they sought to enrich children's lives. In working-class and poor homes, however, parents seemed to view children's activities simply in terms of the pleasure and enjoyment doing so created for the children. They did not see them as particularly significant. We did not observe conversations or efforts to extract "teachable moments" out of what children learned in their lessons.

> [Fieldworker] asked how she thought CCD was. Wendy said, "Boring."
> Mr. Driver said [to fieldworker], "She always says that."
> Mr. Driver asked Wendy, "what'd you do tonight?"
> Wendy said, "The Saints."
> Mr. Driver did not ask for any further explanation—what they learned about the Saints or which Saints. Wendy does not provide any more information.

When children sought themselves to draw a "teachable moment" out of their experiences in an organized activity, parents listened to what they had to say but did not develop, elaborate, or build on it.

Indeed, in the interviews and in family observations, it became clear that school had a more central role in children's lives. As with middle-class families, parents had to oversee getting children up, dressed, fed, and ready for school. Many children procrastinated on homework and thus did it in the mornings, as in this observation of an early morning at the home of Katie Brindle, a white girl, in a family living on public assistance, who did her homework on the couch, in her pink nightgown:

> Katie holds up the piece of paper and says, "I'm done!" She says, "It took me nineteen minutes to do it." (It is now 7:19 p.m.) She says she has to copy it over. Her mother says, "drink your hot cho - cold chocolate now." … Katie then slides off the couch and leaning over with head close to the rug she flings her arm up and over her head with the paper in it and hands it backwards towards her mom (without looking to see if she was close to her mom). She passes the pencil too. Her mom looks at the paper and without saying anything, signs it with the pencil.

When Katie came home from school, she had a snack, watched television, went on errands with her mother, and played with children in the neighborhood. She also often visited her grandmother who lived a few minutes away by bus. Occasionally, on a Friday night, she attended a church program for underprivileged children; a van came by on the street corner to pick up a group of neighborhood kids. She did not always attend, however, on Friday evenings. Nor, when she did attend, did anyone ask her questions about what she had learned there. In short, as with many working-class and poor children, parents saw childhood as a chance to relax and "be a kid." An effort was made to protect the children from the economic challenges and difficulties that lay ahead.

Most working-class and poor children were keenly aware, however, of the scarcity of economic resources in their homes. The infusion of economic resources often set the pace for life. For example, the Drivers, a white working-class family, went shopping every other Friday night—partly because they got paid on that day and partly because Mr. Driver had to work every other weekend, and he was the person who drove them to the grocery store. When children needed money for school, or clothes for summer camp, there was a period in which the parents would scrape the resources together. Children were often aware of this "accumulation" delay.

Indeed, the lack of economic resources was a constant topic of conversation in the homes we visited. For example, in Katie Brindle's family, a white poor family on public assistance, the key events were managing the tasks of daily life: getting clothes washed when the washing machines were broken in the building, going to collect food stamps, and getting to the super market. Most poor families did not have a car, which made the simplest trips far more complicated than they were for middle-class families. Waiting on busy street corners in the winter was not only cold but, in times of melting snow and rain, could mean getting soaked as cars splashed through large pools of dirty, slushy water that gathered at street corners due to poor drainage systems. It was difficult to get to some places on buses. And, since all members of the Brindle family were struggling economically, the ability of others to provide rides was highly contingent: Ms. Brindle's brother's car sometimes was broken, her mother had to take care of another brother who was schizophrenic, and the occasions on which she had to travel sometimes did not mesh with others' schedules, even if they were available. Katie knew about many of these issues; in particular, she was keenly aware of her mother's trips to collect food stamps, since food shortages were chronic in the days leading up to these trips.

Even in working-class families, where resources were more plentiful, events that middle-class families took for granted, such as eating out in a fast food restaurant, were scheduled around paychecks. When asked when they tended to eat out, Mr. Irwin knew in advance:

> It's a Friday. So she gets paid every other week. And since this is new, her working every day, she is getting strapped and I said, well, OK, you're strapped and I'm coming home and doing dishes, I'm strapped. Why don't we just say, OK, when you get paid that's payday for the extra stress, too, so we all go out.

In the Irwin family, as in other working-class and poor families, there was constant talk of money, lack of money, cost of items, and squeezing money out for extras. The children were aware of it, and would sometimes ask their mother, after a trip to a grocery store, if there was any money "left over."

In this context, expenditures for enrollment in organized activities—often entailing fees that were purely nominal from the perspective of middle-class families (such as the $25 required to play soccer)—constituted an immense challenge to working-class and poor families. Even two dollars for school trips, money for hot dogs while out at a baseball game, and money for bus fare to get to practices, were strains on the limited budgets of these families. Sometimes it was not the cost per se but the threat of a large cost if something went wrong that dissuaded parents, as in this white working-class family where the mother refused to allow her daughter to take violin lessons (which were free) at school:

> She wanted to take violin last year really bad and we said, "No."...She begged. And, she's not responsible. The flyer came home from school and it said that if anything happened to the violin it was $200. Well he [the dog] loves chewing wood. And she doesn't put anything away and she's not old enough to be responsible for something that big.

Another white working-class mother, who did permit her daughter to take up the violin, reported the cost to be $30, but then noted that, "I had to go out and buy her a book and a chin thing ... I guess it is a chin pad and then this thing, it looks like a stone that you rub on the strings to make it sound better." These ancillary expenditures were not even mentioned by middle-class parents in interviews.

In sum, not all working-class and poor parents wanted their children to participate in organized activities, but when they did, the lack of resources often made it impossible to do so.

Managing Conflicts

The working-class and poor children in the ethnographic study had more time for childhood activities than their middle-class counterparts. They spent less time waiting for adults to take them places, order them around, and praise them in the course of organized activities. They were free to watch television for extended periods of time or to engage in child initiated free-play. In most neighborhoods, children played outside after school and on weekends with other neighborhood children. Some boys would be outside the entire afternoon and evening, coming in only for meal times and chores.

While organized activities were not as common in working-class and poor families as in middle-class ones, they certainly existed. Many children and their parents found participation to be fun, as when Billy Yanelli played baseball in the spring and summer. His parents and grandparents would turn out to see him play. In addition, the parents would consider themselves to be "extremely busy" when they had a week with one practice and one game, a schedule that was considered very light in the Tallinger household.

Still, when the working-class and poor families faced scheduling conflicts between organized activities and other aspects of family life, the organized activity would sometimes be cancelled. For example, the working-class Farringer family had only one car. The children had played soccer the previous year. However, a change in the father's work schedule, combined with the lack of availability of transportation, precluded them from playing again:

> They were playing soccer but this year I didn't sign them up because I couldn't take them to practice. It's too far up ....
> I: What happened when you all decided that they couldn't do it this year?
> Well, there wasn't really much to decide. I just couldn't do it. I had no way to get up there to take them and with him working nights .... Their practices were Tuesday and Thursday nights and I couldn't take them. They would have been able to do Saturday mornings but at the time his hours just changed again. He's still doing night hours but he was working Saturdays and I couldn't take them because most Saturdays he was going in early. Now he's off Saturdays and Sundays but he's still going in on the weekends for the overtime so there was just no way that I could take them. I can't just sign them up when they can't go to practice and just play in the game because it wouldn't be fair to the other kids. So ... but they're not complaining.

In noting that "there wasn't really much to decide," Ms. Farringer pointedly expresses the limited degrees of freedom that the family has in resolving scheduling issues. This distinguishes them from the Tallingers and other middle-class families in which the parents have two cars and flexible work schedules that can tolerate the unpredictability of children's leisure schedules.

Parents in working-class jobs were resigned in their belief that some activities were simply not possible, as is indicated by this mother who works at the desk of a local motel:

> I: Has he ever been in Cub Scouts?
> Ms. Chase: No. But he does want to be......He's asked me a couple of times if he could join Cub Scouts and because of my schedule we haven't had time.

Another mother, who was going to school, had enrolled her son in piano lessons but realized he needed to quit: "Just getting busy. I just couldn't. It was just too much for me."

In addition, extended family ties had a critically important role in the texture of daily life in the working-class and poor families in the ethnographic study. For the children, their cousins were often their playmates and best friends. Birthday parties, for example, tended to include only extended family members or possibly one friend from school (unlike middle-class children, who reported routinely being invited to birthday parties of classmates). In the working-class and poor families, family events were of the utmost importance. Birthday parties, wedding, first communions, and other family gatherings dominated the conversation of family members. With so many relatives planning so many parties and gatherings, scheduling conflicts were inevitable. So, too, were "hurt feelings," as Wendy Driver's stepfather explains during a discussion over breakfast one morning before school:

> "There's a wedding and a First Communion that day. My cousin has a wedding, and then my brother's kid is making the First Communion…and we're going to the Communion—there'll be some feelings hurt." Debbie adds, "Yeah, but it's between a brother and a cousin, so … " (she trailed off, implying that the fieldworker would automatically understand which is the more important engagement).[8]

In the middle-class families, relatives often lived far away; however, even if they were close by, middle-class children often attended soccer games and other organized activities rather than extended family gatherings. Thus, no one seemed to complain when Garrett Tallinger missed his cousin's graduation party for a soccer game, something that would have been unheard of in the Driver family.

Predictably Unpredictable Schedules: Working-Class and Poor Families

As with the middle-class families, working-class and poor families experienced predictably unpredictable events. Children got sick, it snowed and school closed in the middle of the day, a babysitter couldn't work, and other such events intervened to disrupt family life. On the one hand, children who were in fewer organized activities caused fewer scheduling disruptions. However, because working class parents enjoyed considerably less autonomy vis-à-vis their jobs,

---

[8] On the day of the aunt's wedding, in which Wendy was participating, her brother Willie came down with the flu. Although he was unable to eat, Willie was required to attend the wedding reception so that "he wouldn't hurt [his aunt's] feelings."

any disruption could balloon into a major crisis. These parents had considerable less leeway in their schedules (some could not even receive a phone call at work), and taking off in the middle of the day in order to deal with an unexpected obligation was generally impermissible. Some had almost no control over their schedules:

> Ms. Yaeger: He doesn't have any set day off …. He doesn't know what his days off are going to be at all until they put up the schedule.

This father, who went to work at 3:00 or 4:00, could not attend any of his son's baseball games:

> I: So did he ever see any games in the season?
> Ms. Yaeger: Oh no. There was no way, no.

Nor, given the tight economic standing, could they afford to take off a day from work. This created more pressure. In the Yanelli family, the mother cleaned houses (riding in the car with her boss from house to house) and her husband painted the exterior of houses (in a non-union job). Taking off from work was an economic hardship. The regular, but sporadic, early dismissals that occurred at their son's school were a major source of stress:

> Well, tomorrow the school closes at 11:45. My Dad is going to take the bus from his house down to pick Billy up from school. And this is a major thing for me. I'm gonna be in work thinking, oh, my God, did he get him? Did they get the right bus? Cause my Dad can't read or write and Mom has to work. So it's the only thing—I never have anybody to pick Billy up from school or I don't have that kind of family where everybody chips in and helps with each other's kid. So I'm always stuck with this struggle––who's gonna pick him up from school if I've got to work and things like this. And my Dad is going to do it tomorrow and I'm nervous about it.

Her mother and father could not afford to have a car, nor could her mother afford to take off from work. These school disruptions were also difficult, of course, for middle-class mothers who worked full-time, but middle-class families usually had the resources to cover the cost of extra child-care or transportation to pick up the child. In working-class and poor families, by contrast, disruptions of this sort were major sources of anxiety.

For poor families, we observed that the predictably unpredictable character of life was more pronounced than in working-class families. Resources were scarcer than in working-class homes, and there was less latitude if something went wrong. Thus, as noted above, the breakdown of the washing machines in the Brindle's apartment was a major problem since the family did not have transportation to get the laundry to another laundromat (nor was there one close by). In addition, a large snow storm and bitterly cold weather, which made getting around difficult for persons regardless of social class, was particularly difficult for families below the poverty level such as Ms. Brindle, who had an 18-month-old child (without a stroller) as well as Katie, to manage as they walked to the bus stop, waited for buses (that sometimes didn't come as scheduled), and carried packages with them on the bus.

In addition, a number of the members of extended families also had difficult life circumstances. For example, in the poor African American family of Harold McAllister, food was scarce. Children secured permission to eat something before taking food out of the cupboard. One evening, Harold's cousin had not heard his aunt's directive to "eat up" at the birthday party; his request for food later that night (after they had returned home from the birthday party) was denied. Another evening, Harold's mother discovered that her twin sister (who was on drugs) had stolen some of the new clothes that Harold's father had bought for him for summer camp. While in middle-class families a last minute gap in clothes might have sent family members scurrying to a Target or Wal-Mart, in the McAllister family as in other poor families there was neither the transportation nor economic resources to replace the clothes before he departed the next day. Taken together, there were more often contingencies and fewer economic resources in the poor families than working-class families. Unlike middle-class families, however, where children's leisure schedules were a major source of the predictably unpredictable character of life, in working-class and poor families children's schedules were not a similar driving force; instead, it was the lack of economic resources that seemed critical.

Discussion

As Lareau (2003) noted elsewhere, important aspects of family life appear to be relatively immune to social class. Regardless of social class, for example, some of the family members in the ethnographic study seemed to have a sense of humor, while others did not. Some houses were tidy and neat; others were messy and dusty. Some mothers always planned their days in advance; others did not. Children, and their parents, also had different temperaments and, in particular, ease around strangers. All parents had to take care of 8- to 10-year-old children: they had to get them up, fed, clothed, and off to school. They celebrated birthdays and holidays with them. They dried their tears, and joined them in laughter. None of these variations were clearly tied to social class.

These threads of cross-class similarity should not distract us, however, from important aspects of the texture and pace of daily life that were clearly tied to social class. As we have shown, we found a hectic, sometimes frenetic, pace of life in many middle-class families. This pace was heavily, but not exclusively, driven by children's participation in multiple organized activities. As Ms. Wallace noted, if each of her three children had only two activities each, it was "six places" to which she needed to take them regularly. Many children were enrolled in far more than two activities. The tight deadlines and parents' lack of flexibility in the face of needs to adjust to other family demands—including homework, dinner, and bedtime—created pressure points in many middle-class homes on weekday afternoons and evenings. Weekends were often no better as parents raced from activity to activity, traveled to "away" games, and helped out with fundraising projects. By contrast, life in working-class and poor families proceeded at a more relaxed pace. Children played outside for long periods of time, watched television for hours on end, and developed games with their friends. In these families, however, the timing and rhythm of key economic moments shaped the texture of family life. The scarcity of economic resources was palpable as, for example, the Brindle family waited for food stamps to be replenished, or the Irwins looked forward to their evening out at McDonalds or Burger King when the paycheck arrived. But, unlike middle-class families, working-class and poor children's schedules did not drive the family schedule. Nor were adults' leisure time commitments focused on cultivating children's talents through organized activities.

The organized activities in which middle-class children participated intersected in a complex fashion with the demands of middle-class professional jobs. As Jacobs and Gerson (2004) have shown, the "long work hours" discussed in the literature in recent years are not characteristic of the entire labor force; rather, they are particularly common among managers and professionals. These positions create a paradox. On the one hand, they do offer the autonomy and flexibility to adjust to the time demands created by children's organized leisure activities (and other unpredictable events). On the other hand, the long hours, travel schedule, and work demands that they entail draw parents away from home and make it difficult for them to manage the demands of their children's lives. In contrast to this, our data suggest that working-class parents whose children participate in organized activities have considerably less scheduling flexibility, but spend fewer hours at work, freeing them for children's activities. Other blue-collar workers had rotating schedules, evening work, and other work demands that clashed with children's organized lives.

How do we understand these class differences in the texture and pace of daily life? Why do they matter? What do they mean? It is fruitful to embed discussion of school readiness in a broader context. School readiness is, in many ways, the study of family-school relationships more narrowly conceived. It is an effort to assess whether children are "ready" or "not ready" for a set of educational tasks. But rather than seeing working-class and poor children as deficient in a set of literacy tasks, it is important to look more broadly at the context of children's daily lives. Here, it is clear that there are important class differences. First, middle-class children spend more time observing interactions with institutional personnel. They learn about deadlines, conflicts between activities, itineraries, identification cards, and other routines similar to those that characterize managerial and professional work life. This differential exposure to institutions and to adults in positions of authority is likely helpful in their lives as working adults. But middle-class children spend less time on their own, organizing their own leisure time, playing with their siblings, and directing the pace of their own lives.

Second, there are striking differences in the dominance of kinship relations in daily life. Working-class and poor children's lives were thoroughly intertwined with kinship groups. This extended kin life often created pressures and conflicts. But in contrast to middle-class (where the organized schedule of activities changes several times a year), there is greater continuity with respect to the people they spend their time with and the activities they undertake.

Third, in his book *Hidden Rhythms*, Evitar Zerubavel (1981) suggested that higher-status individuals experience a greater interpenetration of public and private time, whereas their lower-status counterparts experience more rigidity and separation of public and private time.[9] The differences in the texture of time that Zerubavel raises seem to be echoed in the schedules of the lives of children in the third and fourth grades. Middle-class children, with their soccer games, baseball practices, and piano recitals, have a "public" element to their childhood experiences. They perform before adults; their skills are publicly assessed. Middle-class children also have "private" time, including waiting for their parents to take them places, or running around in circles on the soccer field before practice has started. But the boundaries of public and private interpenetrate more. In working-class and poor families, by contrast, the boundaries appear to be more rigid. Children have more time to control, their free time is more likely to be spent in and around home (rather than in settings away from home), and they do not need to perform for adults. Finally, there is an irony in the fact that working-class and poor children, despite tremendous economic strain, often seem "younger" and "more childlike" than their middle-class counterparts who, at the age of ten, sometimes display an air of ennui. Little events, such as having pizza, eating at Burger King, or going for a ride in the car, could be truly special for working-class and poor children. The working-class and poor children we observed also did not routinely complain of being "bored"—something which the middle class children would do in the occasional moments of "down time" that punctuated their otherwise hectic schedules.

It is striking that in the popular press and with childrearing experts (Belluck, 2000; Doherty, 2002; Rosenfeld & Wise, 2000), there has been a gathering critique of the invidious ways in which children's organized activities can corrupt and transform family life. Critiquing the "over scheduled child" (Rosenfeld & Wise, 2000), professionals call for a diminishment of organized activities. In addition, in other settings parents vociferously complain about the excessive amount of homework their children are receiving and its negative impact on family time (Lareau, 2003). Yet it is hard to see, from the perspective of educators, the potential for the

---

[9] For example, he suggests that an emergency room doctor is expected to be available for patients after his shift has ended (and in his time at home), whereas a lower status employee, such as an orderly, is presumed to be free to such demands.

negative costs of the family strategies that actively promote family literacy. Understanding the pluses and the minuses of promoting literacy skills, and embedding a discussion of "school readiness" in a broader context, is an important and challenging task for social scientists.

Acknowledgments

For funds for this research we are grateful to the Spencer Foundation; Annette Lareau also gratefully acknowledges the Sloan Foundation, ASA/NSF Grants for the Discipline, Temple Grant-in-Aid, and Southern Illinois University. Lareau is also indebted to the research assistants who helped with the family observations, including Christine Paul, Mimi Keller, Mary Woods, Gillian Johns, Caitlin Howley, Greg Seaton, Mark Freeman, Wendy Starr Brown and Robin Rogers-Dillon. Pat Berhau played a key role in the research process. An earlier version of this paper was presented at the Eastern Sociological Society meetings in 2003. For their helpful comments we are grateful to Nan Crouter, George Farkas, Karen Getzen, Erin Horvat, and Julia Wrigley. All errors, of course, are the responsibility of the authors.

References

Alwin, D. (1984). Trends in parental socialization values. *American Journal of Sociology,* *90*, 359–382.

Anderson, E. (1999). *Code of the street: Decency, violence, and the moral life of the inner city.* New York: Norton.

Arendell, T. (2000). *Soccer moms and the new care work.* Working Paper. Center for Working Families. Berkeley, CA: University of California, Berkeley.

Baker, D., & Stevenson, D. (1986). Mothers' strategies for school achievement: managing the transition to high school. *Sociology of Education, 59*, 156–167.

Belluck, P. (2000). Parents try to reclaim their children's time. *New York Times* on the Web.<http://www.nytimes.com/library/national/061300family-practices.html>. Accessed August 9, 2006.

Bernstein, B. (1975). *Class, codes and control.* New York: Schocken Books

Bianchi, S. M. (2000). Maternal employment and the time with children: dramatic change of surprising continuity. *Demography, 37*, 401–414.

Bianchi, S. M., & Robinson, J. (1997). What did you do today? Children's use of time, family compositions and the acquisition. *Journal of Marriage and the Family, 59*, 332–345.

Bronfenbrenner, U. (1989). Ecological systems theory. *Annals of Child Development, 6*, 187–249.

Brontenbrenner, U. (1966). Socialization and social class through time and space. In R. Bendix & S. M. Lipset (Eds.), *Class, status, and power* (pp. 362–377). New York: The Free Press.

Cahill, S. E. (1992). The sociology of childhood in an uncertain age. *Contemporary Sociology, 21*, 669–672.

Corsaro, W. (1988). Routines in the peer culture of American and Italian nursery school children. *Sociology of Education, 61*, 1–14.

Daley, K. J. (Ed.). (2001). *Minding the time in family experience: emerging perspectives and issues.* Contemporary Perspectives in Family Research, Vol. 3. New York: JAI Press.

Diamond, J. (2000). Beyond social class: Cultural resources and educational participation among low-income Black parents. *Berkeley Journal of Sociology, 44*, 15–54.

Doherty, W., & Carlson, B. (2002). *Putting family first: Successful strategies for reclaiming family life in a hurry-up world.* New York: Owl Books.

Elkind, D. (2001). *The hurried child: Growing up too fast too soon* (3rd ed.). New York: Perseus.

Entwisle, D. R., Alexander, K. L., & Olson, L. S. (1997). *Children, schools, and inequality.* Boulder: Westview Press.

Epstein, J. L. (1987). Toward a theory of family-school connections: Teacher practices and parent involvement. In K. Hurrelmann, F. Kaufmann, & F. Losel (Eds.), *Social interventions: Potential and constraints* (pp. 121–136). New York: Walter de Gruyter.

Epstein, J. L. & Sanders, M. G. (2000). Connecting home, school, and community: New directions for social research. In M. Hallinan (Ed.), *Handbook of the sociology of education* (pp. 285–306). New York: Kluwer Academic/Plenum.

Fine, G. A. (1987). *With the boys: Little league baseball and preadolescent culture.* Chicago: University of Chicago Press.

Gecas, V. (1979). The influence of social class on socialization. In W.R. Burr, R. Hill, F. I. Nye, & I. R. Reiss (Eds.), *Contemporary theories about the family* (pp. 365–404). New York: Free Press.

Hays, S. (1996). *The cultural contradictions of motherhood.* New Haven: Yale University Press.

Hart, B., & Risley, T. R. (1995). *Meaningful Differences in the Everyday Experiences of Young American Children.* Baltimore: Paul H. Brookes.

Heath, S. B. (1983). *Ways with words.* New York: Cambridge University Press.

Hertz, R., & Marshall, N. L. (2001). *Working families: The transformation of the American home.* Berkeley and Los Angeles: University of California Press.

Hill, M. S. (1992). *The Panel Study of Income Dynamics: A user's guide.* Newbury Park, CA: Sage.

Hochschild, A. (1989). *The second shift.* New York: Avon.

Hofferth, S. L. (1999). *Family reading to young children: Social desirability and cultural biases in reporting.* Paper presented at the Workshop on the Measurement of and Research on Time Use. Committee on National Statistics, National Research Council, Washington, DC.

Hofferth, S. L., & Sandberg, J. F. (2001). Changes in American children's time use, 1981-1997. In T. Owens & S. Hofferth (Eds.), *Children at the millenium: Where have we come from, where are we going?* (pp. 193–232). New York: Elsevier Science.

Jacobs, J. A., & Gerson, K. (2004). *The time divide.* Cambridge, MA: Harvard University Press.

Kohn, M. L., & Schooler, C. (1983). *Work and personality.* Norwood, NJ: Ablex.

Kohn, M. L., Slomczynski, K. M., & Schoenbach, C. (1986). Social stratification and the transmission of values in the family: A cross-national assessment. *Sociological Forum 1,* 73–102.

Lareau, A. (2003) *Unequal childhoods: Class, race, and family life.* Berkeley: University of California Press.

Lareau, A. (2000a). *Home advantage.* Updated edition. Lanham, MD: Rowman and Littlefield.

Lareau, A. (2000b). My wife can tell me who I know: Conceptual and methodological problems in studying fathers. *Qualitative Sociology, 23,* 407–433.

Lareau, A., Weininger, E., & Bianchi, S. (2005). *Gender, work-family conflicts, and children's organized leisure activities.* Department of Sociology, University of Maryland. Unpublished paper.

Leichter, H. J. (1979). Families and communities as educators: Some concepts of relationships. In H. J. Leichter (Ed.), *Families and communities as educators* (pp. 3–94). New York: Teachers College Program.

Lever, J. (1976). Sex differences in the games children play. *Social Problems, 23,* 478–487.

Lightfoot, S. L. (1978). *Worlds apart.* New York: Basic Books.

Medrich, E. et al. (1981). *The serious business of growing up.* Berkeley: University of California Press.

Oliver, T., & Shapiro, M. (1997). *Black wealth/white wealth: A new perspective on racial inequality.* New York: Routledge.

Opie, I., & Opie, P. (1991). The culture of children. In F. C. Waksler (Ed.), *Studying the social worlds of children* (pp. 123–144). London: Falmer Press.

Presser, H. B. (1989). Can we make time for children? The economy, work schedules, and child care. *Demography, 26,* 523–543.

Robinson, J. P., & Godbey, G. (1999). *Time for life: The surprising ways Americans use their time*. University Park, PA: The Pennsylvania State University Press.

Rosenfeld, A., & Wise, N. (2000). *The over-scheduled child*. New York: St. Martin's Griffin.

Skolnick, A. (1991). *Embattled paradise: The American family in an age of uncertainty*. New York: Basic Books.

Steir, H., & Tienda, M. (1993). Are men marginal to the family? Insights from Chicago's inner city. In J. Hood (Ed.), *Men, work, and family* (pp. 23–44). Thousand Oaks, CA: Sage.

Stevenson, D. L., & Baker, D. P. (1987). The familyschool relation and the child's school performance. *Child Development, 58,* 1348–1357.

Thompson, S. M. (1999). *Mother's taxi: Sport and women's labor.*. Albany: SUNY Press.

Thorne, B. (1992). *Gender play*. New Brunswick, NJ: Rutgers University Press.

U.S. Department of Education. (1995). *The condition of education, 1995*. Washington, DC: National Center for Educational Statistics.

U.S. Department of Education. (2001). *The condition of education, 2001*. Washington, DC: National Center for Educational Statistics. http://nces.ed.gov/programs/coe/2000/essay/e03f.asp#info Accessed August 9, 2006.

Waller, W. (1961). *Sociology of teaching*. New York: Russell and Russell.

Wrigley, J. (1988). Do young children need intellectual stimulation? Experts' advice to parents, 19001985. *History of Education, 29,* 41–75.

Zelizer, V. (1985) *Pricing the priceless child*. New York: Basic Books.

Zerubavel, E. (1981). *Hidden rhythms: Schedules and calendars in social life*. Berkeley: University of California Press.

11

CULTURAL VERSUS SOCIAL CLASS CONTEXTS FOR EXTRA-CURRICULAR ACTIVITY PARTICIPATION

Diane Hughes
New York University

"The Context of School Readiness Social Class Differences in Time Use in the Family" provides a refreshing and thought-provoking in-depth examination of daily routines among African American and white lower- and middle-class families with adolescent children. The patterns emergent in this study are not surprising, but the authors' interpretation of them turns on its head social scientists' tendency to privilege the practices of middle-class participants over those of their lower-class counterparts. Among middle-class families, both black and white, children's extra-curricular activity participation occupies a prominent place in organizing families' daily routines. Among lower-class families, other investments, such as in extended family and in relaxed leisure, are more prominent. Such high levels of participation have clear costs for families and parents according to Lareau's analysis. In this way, her analysis challenges traditional modes of thinking about race and social class patterns, and in particular the notion that practices among the mainstream middle class are generally preferable to participants who are less economically affluent.

In my comments, I first consider several study strengths as these might inform future research on adolescents and their families. These include (a) attention to unpacking race and social class; (b) attention to how families transverse the multiple and various settings in which they participate; (c) the combined use of in-depth interviews, ethnographic visits, and quantitative analyses; and (d) the focus on families' daily rhythms and routines. In attending to these strengths, I ultimately wish to argue that the analysis presented by Lareau is a cultural analysis in that the essential interpretation is that daily routines around extra-curricular activity participation reflect deeper underlying beliefs about the nature of childhood, which vary across social class groups. I then identify two missing pieces that may add additional insight into the cultural beliefs that are described. These include (e) the need to explicitly ask parents and others about the beliefs that underlie their common and divergent practices, and (f) attention to whether tendencies toward "concerted cultivation" versus "natural growth" are seen in other aspects of families' lives, including rhythms and routines around academics and school work. Finally, I consider the ongoing tension in the social sciences between the desire to respect and affirm the observed practices of multiple "cultural groups" and empirically based knowledge that some practices or styles of parenting are more conducive to success in dominant institutions such as school than are others.

Unpacking Social Class and Race

A persistent methodological issue in the literature on race and social class differences in achievement and other adolescent and family outcomes is that race and social class are confounded in most studies, as they are in the U.S. more generally. Specifically, comparative studies frequently include European American participants from middle-class backgrounds alongside ethnic minority participants from lower- or working-class backgrounds, precluding the ability to disentangle differences in outcomes that are due to race from those that are due to social class. Statistical controls for socioeconomic status do not completely alleviate these methodological concerns, because measures of social class are frequently imprecise, and unmeasured social class differences may account for observed differences in outcomes of interest. In particular, as scholars have argued, unmeasured variance in assets and wealth (Conley, 2002) and in variation in income across time (McLoyd, 1998; McLoyd & Ceballo, 1998) leave open the possibility that scholars will attribute to race or ethnicity variance that is due to socioeconomic factors.

The confounding of race and social class has been the focus of considerable debate because it has implications for whether differences in outcomes are understood as (a) differences in access to the resources that income and education provide, (b) differences in culturally embedded beliefs systems held by members of different racial or ethnic groups, or (c) attributable to some other factor. Lareau's effort to disentangle race and social class is quite notable in this regard. Although the design and sample selection do not bypass all of the issues mentioned above, inclusion of approximately equal numbers of black and white families who are lower-class, working-class, and middle-class represents a rare but desirable working model for how future studies should proceed. Interestingly, this study finds that middle-class black families look very much like the middle-class white families in their activity participation—with the exception that they worry about race and discrimination. At the same time, the working-class and lower-income white families look much like the working-class and lower-income black families in their levels of activity participation.

Interpreting the seeming greater similarity within class categories as compared to within racial groupings is not straightforward. One explanation is that patterns of participation are primarily a function of job structures and limitations in resources shared by working- and lower-class families. Resource and time constraints are highly salient to families, and one might surmise that if lower-class participants were given adequate time and financial resources, their extra-curricular activity participation would look much like that of their middle-class counterparts. Lareau takes the different, albeit plausible, position that social class differences in patterns of activity participation emanate from social class differences in fundamental belief systems about the nature of childhood. According to her analysis, middle-class parents believe that children need to be carefully nourished and cultivated, as evidenced by their deliberate efforts to indulge children in activities, conversation, and reflection on their experiences. Working- and lower-class families, in contrast, believe that children need to be protected and provided for, but that they should otherwise be left to grow naturally. Thus, families with similar social class backgrounds operate according to shared "cultural" scripts, shared blue prints for living, shared realities, and shared systems of understanding. These fundamental beliefs are manifested, in turn, in their patterns of activity participation.

Curiously, this high level of within-class similarity was not replicated in the analysis of data from the Panel Study of Income Dynamics. Here, extra-curricular activity participation was higher among whites than among blacks at each income level, with the exception of the poorest families. Thus, the equivalent levels of extracurricular activity participation among blacks and whites in the ethnographic sample may be unique to particular types of families in particular contexts. Differences in patterns of relationships may be due to sample or method differences or to differences in the measurement of social class or extra-curricular participation. Thus, it will be important for future studies to examine the conditions under which these sorts of similarities in practices and perhaps underlying beliefs can be documented.

Attention to How Families Transverse Settings

The idea put forth by the late Urie Bronfenbrenner (Bronfenbrenner, 1977, 1979) that development inherently takes place in the context of increasingly complex nested structures—the most immediate being the developmental dyad and the most distal being organizational principles and norms that operate at the level of the macrosystem—is by now one of the most widely embraced ideas of the past thirty years. Indeed, it is easy to identify studies that examine a single setting or microsystem vis-à-vis a particular child outcome, such as how development is influenced by processes within families, schools, or neighborhoods (Bowen, Bowen, & Ware, 2002; Ceballo, McLoyd, & Yoyokawa, 2004; Gutman, McLoyd, & Tokoyana, 2005; Leventhal & Brooks-Gunn, 2003; Petit, Bates, Dodge, & Meece, 1999; Voydanoff, 2004). One can also readily find studies of a mesosystem linkage––that is, linkages across two microsystems—such as work and family, or family and school. For instance, Lerner's (Lerner, 1983; Lerner, Palermo, Spiro, & Nesselroade, 1982) studies of the ways in which Puerto Rican families' lack of rhythmicity during the preschool years have consequences for children's experiences upon entering formal schooling (where demands for structure and routines are high) are particularly good examples of how such mesosystem linkages can influence school success. Studies of how parents' experiences at work influence their socialization practices or emotional availability to their children are readily available as examples of exosystem influences on development (Barling, Zacharatos & Hepburn, 1999; Crouter & Bumpass, 2001; Fortner, Crouter, & McHale, 2004; Repetti, 1994; Repetti & Wood, 1997; Stewart & Barling, 1996). See Figure 11.1.

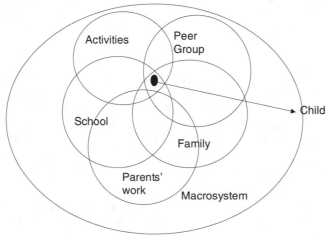

Figure 11.1. After Bronfenbrenner.

One of Bronfenbrenner's most consistent critiques of the developmental literature concerned the fact that studies rarely examine persons or processes across multiple systems and multiple levels (Bronfenbrenner, 1977, 1986), in part because it is challenging to empirically represent the complexity of these nested relationships. However, Lareau's investigation into the intersection between extra-curricular activity participation and multiple contexts, including work, family, extended family, and school, as presented in Figure 11.1, seems very close to what Bronfenbrenner had in mind. Children's activity participation is intimately linked to experiences in the family domain for the focal child, the parent, and siblings, including few or brief dinners and little time for relaxation. The activity participation-family time relationship is further complicated and shaped by demands of parents' jobs, which can facilitate or impede children's participation in extracurricular activities. Children's academic obligations are made more difficult by the need to accommodate jobs and activities. Finally, all of these inter-relationships among work, family routines, extracurricular activity participation, and schooling are shaped by larger structural forces that determine norms around expected linkages across these domains.

The advantages of an approach that has intersections between multiple contexts at its forefront are readily apparent. Specifically, Lareau's analysis enables us to see families' lives in the way families themselves actually experience them, rather than as parsed into behavioral tesserae (Barker, 1964) that are of interest to researchers. It also reminds us to look for outcomes in potentially unexpected places. For example, the literature on extra-curricular activity participation has primarily examined and documented beneficial effects of such participation on a range of outcomes, including school readiness, self-esteem, self-knowledge, skill development, positive peer relations, school connectedness, and academic outcomes (Dworkin, Larson & Hansen, 2003; Hansen, Larson & Dworkin, 2003; Mahoney & Stattin, 2000; Mahoney, Cairns, & Farmer, 2003; Mahoney, Larson, & Eccles, 2005; Zaff, Moore, Papillo, & Williams, 2003). The consequences of a target child's participation on family outcomes, regularity of family routines, sibling outcomes, or parenting satisfaction have rarely been examined and are potentially important directions for future study.

The Strengths of Multiple Methods

One cannot help but be struck by the intensity with which Lareau sought to describe and understand patterns of extra-curricular activity participation and its meaning in families' lives, using both large survey data and intensive ethnographic methods. Collecting and analyzing these sorts of data is tedious, time-consuming, and expensive. The advantages and challenges of integrating these methods, however, are clearly evidenced in Lareau's work. The quantitative PSID data are ideal for answering certain types of questions, such as how much time is spent in extra-curricular activities, by whom, and how often? The sample is relatively large and diverse. One can describe parents' or youth's activities and experiences on independently assessed constructs. And, one can test hypotheses about statistical relationships between constructs. However, the ethnographic data constitute a critical supplement to this approach. It enables us to better understand how family life, activity participation, work life, and the intersection among them are experienced by families as a unit and by individual family members. It enables us to follow families through transitions from one setting to the next. It enables us to see how these unfold during the course of families' and adolescents' daily lives. And finally, it enables us to better pinpoint the beliefs and parenting goals that underlie different practices and routines. These insights could not have been garnered through examination of the participation patterns in the PSID data alone.

The benefits of multimethod approaches are especially apparent when considering the high levels of activity participation among middle-class participants. For example, from the PSID we learn about the average number of hours spent across a nationally representative sample whereas the ethnographic data permit an up-close view of how such activities are managed. The challenges of multi-method approaches are evident as well, however. Specifically, it not easy to draw conclusions about phenomena of interest when findings based on different methods conflict with one another, as is the case here regarding within-class/between-race patterns of extra-curricular activity participation. The goal for researchers, then, as exemplified by Lareau's efforts, would be to determine what further questions need to be addressed or areas probed to resolve apparent inconsistencies.

Attention to Daily Routines as a Cultural Analysis

Observation of the choices families make about how daily time is spent and about the settings and activities to which children are exposed can provide critical insight into families' beliefs about children's development. As Weisner (2002) eloquently argued, daily routines are organized according to basic premises and goals pertaining to the constitution of a "good" life and the skills and practices necessary to attain it. In Super and Harkness's conceptualization of a child's developmental niche, it is through daily and repeated exposure to cultural practices and specific types of settings that children acquire the organized whole of a culture—its logic, rules, role relations, expectations (Super & Harkness, 1986, 1999)

Accordingly, it is in attention to daily routines and practices around extra-curricular activity participation that Lareau's argument takes on its cultural character. For instance, Lareau suggested that excessive extra-curricular activity participation is part of a larger pattern among middle-class parents in which children are carefully nourished and cultivated in ways that help them acquire the skills parents believe they need to succeed in adulthood. Less involvement in extra-curricular activity participation among working- and lower-class families is positioned as part of a larger tendency toward "natural growth", in which children are thought to develop independent of deliberate intervention from their parents. In essence, then, Lareau infers a deeper cultural meaning from observation of practices that, on the surface, appear to be similar within social class groupings. One might reasonably question how to evaluate whether or not extra-curricular activity participation does emanate, in fact, from larger cultural belief systems, since routines can also emerge as a function of restricted or excess resources. In this regard, I now turn to a discussion of two aspects of this work that could be strengthened by additional information: (a) the need for direct assessment of parental beliefs, and (b) evidence that particular belief systems are apparent in multiple aspects of childrearing.

Direct Assessment of Parental Beliefs

Although it may be appropriate to infer parental belief systems from redundancies across families within particular social strata in patterns of behavior and activities, it is also possible to inquire directly about the beliefs underlying parental practices. In Lareau's analysis, information about parents' own construction of their beliefs, particularly as these pertain to extra curricular activity participation, would have been informative. For instance, if asked, what do middle-class parents say about why children participate in an abundance of activities? How do parents describe its benefits for children? To what extent is such participation tied to long-term (getting a college scholarship) versus short-term (development of confidence and skills) childrearing goals? What do parents believe would happen if children were NOT involved in this multitude of activities? Similar questions might be asked of working and lower-class parents. Do their lower levels of participation in extra-curricular activities reflect childrearing beliefs that they actually articulate, if asked?

As part of the Center for Research on Culture, Development, and Education at New York University, Niobe Way and I are investigating how parental beliefs and practices pertaining to academics, ethnicity/race, and peers influence academic engagement and performance among early adolescents. We have found that although it is often true that practices emanate from parents' underlying beliefs, it is not always true. Parents often articulate beliefs that contradict their practices. When asked, we learn that a variety of factors, including lack of financial, instrumental, or psychological resources, can result in inconsistencies between beliefs and practices.

In these ways, Lareau's current work would benefit from asking parents explicitly about the beliefs underlying their levels of activity participation. Their answers may indeed support the sorts of belief strictures that have been inferred in this work. The arguments would be further bolstered if these were assessed directly.

Assessment of Evidence for "Concerted Cultivation" and "Natural Growth" in Other Domains of Parenting

Parents' cultural beliefs about childrearing are rarely, if ever, manifest in a single aspect of childrearing. As Super and Harkness (1986) argued, processes of "contemporary redundancy" and "thematic elaboration" are critical mechanisms through which cultural phenomenon are manifested in children's proximal environments. The term "contemporary redundancy" refers to the repetition of similar messages and influences from several parts of the child's environment during a single period of development. For instance, western cultural values promoting individualism are evident at any particular stage of development in the structure of schooling, the content of media messages, parenting practices, and elsewhere. The term "thematic elaboration" refers to the repetition and cultivation of similar themes across stages and domains of development at varying levels of intensity.

Based on the ethnography presented in the present study, Lareau identified multiple aspects of children's environments that support the cultural beliefs thought to underlie activity participation. For instance, whereas middle-class children are asked to reflect on their experiences and to perform for adults, lower-class children's experiences and ideas remain untapped by their parents. However, it would be fascinating to examine the extent to which, and the ways in which, notions of "concerted cultivation" versus "natural growth" are evidenced in other aspects of children's environments, such as the physical and social spaces they occupy, in management of other developmental tasks related to development, such as academics and peer relationships, or in explicit directives given to children. This sort of approach would serve as a useful model for elaborating the integrated nature of the broader cultural context of which youths' activity participation is one part.

Cultural Sensitivity Versus Science-based Knowledge

A substantial amount of social scientific attention has been paid in recent years to the researchers' need to acknowledge how cultural values and beliefs shape all aspects of the research process (Hughes, Seidman, & Williams, 1993; Trickett, 1996). Indeed, the Eurocentric perspective that pervades the research literature as a whole, privileging white middle-class values over those of other groups, has been deeply criticized. The work presented here, however, which validates the cultural practices of multiple groups raises other complicated issues. Based on the current analysis, Lareau emphasized the potential downside of the white middle-class pattern of activity participation. Specifically, children are fatigued and irritable. They are heavily dependent on adults for direction and approval. They are unable to create their own adventures or structure their own time. The complex issues underlying this approach concern the fact that although extra-curricular activity participation clearly has its limitations when it is excessive, the large majority of empirical research underscores its benefits for youth.

This issue is, of course, not unique to the present study. Researchers need to pay more attention overall to the tensions between our desire to uncover and elaborate deeply held cultural belief systems that underlie cultural practices that dominant institutions may view as "non-normative" and empirically based knowledge that particular practices, in this case low levels of extra-curricular activity participation, may place youth at a disadvantage in terms of their success in mainstream institutions. Nevertheless, the strengths of Lareau's current program of mixed-method research on an ethnically diverse sample that is stratified by both race and social class can serve as a model for how studies in other areas might move forward.

References

Barker, R. C. (1965). Explorations in ecological psychology. *American Psychologist, 20,* 1–14.

Barling, J., Zacharatos, A., & Hepburn, C. G. (1999). Parents' job insecurity affects children's academic performance through cognitive difficulties. *Journal of Applied Psychology, 84,* 437–444.

Bowen, N. K., Bowen, G. L., & Ware, W. B. (2002). Neighborhood social disorganization, families, and the educational behavior of adolescents. *Journal of Adolescent Research, 17,* 468–490.

Bronfenbrenner, U. (1986). Ecology of the family as a context for human development: Research perspectives. *Developmental Psychology, 22,* 723–742.

Bronfenbrenner, U. (1979). *The ecology of human development: Experiments by nature and design.* Cambridge, MA: Harvard University Press.

Bronfenbrenner, U. (1977). Toward an experimental ecology of human development. *American Psychologist, 32,* 513–531.

Ceballo, R., McLoyd, V. C., & Toyokawa, T. (2004). The influence of neighborhood quality on adolescents' educational values and school effort. *Journal of Adolescent Research, 19,* 716–739.

Conley, D. (2002). *Wealth and poverty in America: A reader.* Malden, MA: Blackwell.

Crouter, A. C., & Bumpus, M. F. (2001). Linking parents' work stress to children's and adolescents' psychological adjustment. *Current Directions in Psychological Science, 10,* 156–159.

Dworkin, J. B., Larson, R., & Hansen, D. (2003). Adolescents' accounts of growth experiences in youth activities. *Journal of Youth and Adolescence, 32,* 17–26.

Fortner, M. R., Crouter, A. C., & McHale, S. M. (2004). Is parents' work involvement responsive to the quality of relationships with adolescent offspring? *Journal of Family Psychology, 18,* 530–538.

Gutman, L. M., McLoyd, V. C., & Tokoyawa, T. (2005). Financial strain, neighborhood stress, parenting behaviors, and adolescent adjustment in urban African American families. *Journal of Research on Adolescence, 15,* 425–449.

Hansen, D. M., Larson, R. W., & Dworkin, J. B. (2003). What adolescents learn in organized youth activities: A survey of self-reported developmental experiences. *Journal of Research on Adolescence, 13,* 25–55.

Hughes, D., Seidman, E., & Williams, N. (1993). Cultural phenomena and the research enterprise: Toward a culturally anchored methodology. *American Journal of Community Psychology: Special Issue: Culturally Anchored Methodology, 21,* 687–703.

Lerner, J. V. (1983). The role of temperament in psychosocial adaptation in early adolescents: A test of a "goodness of fit" model. *Journal of Genetic Psychology, 143,* 149–157.

Lerner, R. M., Palermo, M., Spiro, A., & Nesselroade, J. R. (1982). Assessing the dimensions of temperamental individuality across the life span: The dimensions of temperament survey. *Child Development, 53,* 149–159.

Leventhal, T., & Brooks-Gunn, J. (2003). Children and youth in neighborhood contexts. *Current Directions in Psychological Science, 12,* 27–31.

Mahoney, J. L. Larson, R. W., & Eccles, J. S. (2005). *Organized activities as contexts of development: Extracurricular activities, after-school and community programs.* Mahwah, NJ: Erlbaum.

Mahoney, J. L., Cairns, B. D., & Farmer, T. W. (2003). Promoting interpersonal competence and educational success through extracurricular activity participation. *Journal of Educational Psychology, 95*, 409–418.

Mahoney, J. L., & Stattin, H. (2000). Leisure activities and adolescent antisocial behavior: The role of structure and social context. *Journal of Adolescence, 23*, 113–127.

McLoyd, V. C. (1998). Socioeconomic disadvantage and child development. *American Psychologist, 53*, 185–204.

McLoyd, V. C., & Ceballo, R. (1998). Conceptualizing and assessing economic context: Issues in the study of race and child development. In V. C. McLoyd & L. Steinberg (Eds.), *Studying minority adolescents: Conceptual, methodological, and theoretical issues.* Mahwah, NJ: Erlbaum.

Pettit, G. S., Bates, J. E., Dodge, K. A., & Meece, D. W. (1999). The impact of after-school peer contact on early adolescent externalizing problems is moderated by parental monitoring, perceived neighborhood safety, and prior adjustment. *Child Development, 70*, 768–778.

Repetti, R. L. (1994). Short-term and long-term processes linking job stressors to father–child interaction. *Social Development, 3*, 1–15.

Repetti, R. L., & Wood, J. (1997). Effects of daily stress at work on mothers' interactions with preschoolers. *Journal of Family Psychology, 11*, 90–108.

Stewart, W., & Barling, J. (1996). Fathers' work experiences effect children's behaviors via job-related affect and parenting behaviors. *Journal of Organizational Behavior, 17*, 221–232.

Super, C. M., & Harkness, S. (Eds.). (1999). *The environment as culture in developmental research.* Washington, DC: American Psychological Association.

Super, C. M., & Harkness, S. (1986). The developmental niche: A conceptualization at the interface of child and culture. *International Journal of Behavioral Development, 9*, 545–569.

Trickett, E. J. (1996). A future for community psychology: The contexts of diversity and the diversity of contexts. *American Journal of Community Psychology, 24*, 209–234.

Voydanoff, P. (2004). Work, community, and parenting resources and demands as predictors of adolescent problems and grades. *Journal of Adolescent Research, 19*, 155–173.

Zaff, J. F., Moore, K. A., Papillo, A. R., & Williams, S. (2003). Implications of extracurricular activity participation during adolescence on positive outcomes. *Journal of Adolescent Research, 18*, 599–630.

12

LINKING SOCIAL CLASS TO CONCERTED CULTIVATION, NATURAL GROWTH AND SCHOOL READINESS

Sandra L. Hofferth

University of Maryland

Introduction

The Lareau conceptualization of class differences in child-rearing approaches that reproduce inequality (Lareau, 2002, 2003), concerted cultivation versus natural growth, has four main elements:

	Concerted Cultivation	*Natural Growth*
1) Organization of daily life	Organized activities	Hanging out
2) Language use	Negotiation/reasoning	Directives
3) Social connections	Weak kin ties	Strong kin ties
4) Relationship to institutions	Active	Passive

In their chapter in this volume, Lareau and Weininger focus primarily upon the *organization of daily life* component of their theory, which they say is more relevant to the success of older children and less so to preschool children. I argue instead that the *framework* is useful in exploring the school readiness of young children. However, one must include other aspects of child rearing than the organization of daily life; these other dimensions are probably the most crucial for young children. Further, in contrast again with the Lareau framework, I argue that education is more important than social class in explaining how social advantage is replicated across generations. I start with language and return to the organization of daily life at the end of my discussion.

Language

Research suggests two types of generalizations. First, the amount of verbalization directed to children is associated with children's vocabulary growth in their early years (Huttenlocher et al., 1991). The amount of speech children hear at 11–18 months is correlated with speech they hear at age 3 years. There is a wide range of hourly parental utterances to children, ranging from 56 to 793, with a mean of 325 (Hart & Risley, 1995). The amount of talking was associated with vocabulary growth and school readiness in this study. A second study found large differences in the number of occasions in which mothers talked to 18- to 29-month-old children during everyday activities, the richness of the vocabulary, and types of interactions. Children whose mothers talked more had larger vocabularies, indicating the importance of integrating conversation throughout the day (Hoff-Ginsberg, 1991). A third study found that a scale of parental communication with children accounted for over 60% of variance in the rate of children's vocabulary growth to age 3 and vocabulary at age 3 (Hart & Risley, 1995).

There is some evidence that parental vocalizations differ by the socioeconomic status of the family. If socioeconomic status is defined by parental education, this result would not be too surprising, because mothers with less education are likely to have poorer vocabularies themselves. Research shows a strong positive association between maternal vocabulary and that of their child (Hofferth, Curtin, & Sandefur, 2005). Educational level is associated with scores on a test such as the passage comprehension test of the Woodcock Johnson Test of Basic Achievement. Thus, if social class is defined by educational level of parents, we should expect language and communication differences in children across social class at school entry. Economic and employment circumstances may change over the life of a child and social status may also change. Consequently, research has focused on the relationship between socioeconomic circumstances in different periods of the child's life and children's achievement, with findings generally showing that early circumstances have larger effects than later ones (Duncan & Brooks-Gunn, 1997). The major question for policy research is whether these social class differences decline as children move through school and whether early intervention can reverse some of the potential consequences of initial disadvantage (Ramey & Ramey, 2000).

Another aspect of language is the content or nature of the communications. Research has found that criticism and directive comments reduce motivation and discourage children from learning. This holds true at home as well as in the classroom setting (Stipek & Greene, 2001). More research needs to be conducted on differences in parenting styles by maternal education.

What evidence is there for language differences? In general, in our qualitative research (to be described shortly), we found middle-class parents to be much more articulate in their goals for their children than were the working-class parents. Parents wanted the same things for their children. For example, most parents greatly valued physical activity (both exercise in general and sports in particular), but they expressed it differently:

> One of the things that we really encourage in our household is that you take care of your body as well as your mind. (Judy, mother of Serena [9] – middle-class community)

> The exercise from some of the things are [sic] good for her. (Lynn, mother of Ann [12] – working-class community)

Middle-class parents were more articulate in expressing their understanding of the linkage between physical and mental health. Working-class parents agreed but were able to articulate only a general sense of the value of exercise.

As children enter school, communication problems may be exacerbated if left untreated. Teachers may be more responsive to verbally-adept children, and research shows that children whose teachers talk with them more frequently have higher scores on verbal tests (NICHD Early Child Care Research Network, 2000). Vocabulary scores are important components of later cognitive growth and functioning. Children's scores at kindergarten entry are associated with later academic performance in the first three years and beyond (National Research Council, 1998). It is likely that the schools reinforce rather than alter early communication problems. However, this depends upon parental involvement with their child's school.

Institutional Interventions

If parents also have difficulty communicating with teachers and schools, teachers may not be sensitized to problems children have and children may not develop the motivation and/or skills to succeed in school. Thus, another of the four dimensions of social class differences in the Lareau framework is that of parental intervention in institutions to help and promote the well-being of their children. We saw in *Unequal childhoods* that Garrett Tallinger's parents were actively involved in promoting the child to schools, coaches, and other institutions. Billy Yanelli, in contrast, did not have parents who were able to interact in ways that helped their child navigate the school system with his behavior problems. As a consequence, the Yanellis felt powerless in attempting to improve their child's experiences at school and their son, Billy was suspended for fighting.

Social Connections

A third characteristic of the childrearing patterns of families is whether they rely primarily upon kin or nonkin networks. Middle-class families, "concerted cultivators," are likely to have moved some distance away from immediate kin to pursue employment opportunities. Consequently, they are unlikely to reside in close proximity, limiting their interaction. Working-class families, in contrast, are quite likely to live near kin, and therefore are more involved with them on a daily basis. I agree with Lareau that close family ties characterize working-class compared with middle-class families. This appears to be the case in qualitative data that I have collected as well as in the Lareau data. I do not necessarily agree that this reflects preference; rather, it often results from employment and career decisions that move individuals from their home towns.

Organization of Children's Activities

Although I agree that there are some differences between working- and middle-class families in the organization of children's activities, I think that the difference is one of degree and not of kind. There are elements of concerted cultivation in the working-class model just as there are elements of natural growth in the childrearing patterns of middle-class parents.

The qualitative data I present here are based on personal interviews conducted by my collaborators Janet Dunn and David Kinney with parents and children from 43 families living in two different medium-sized communities in Michigan (Dunn, Kinney & Hofferth, 2003; Hofferth, Kinney & Dunn, 2006). Twenty families were interviewed in "Riverview" (fictional name), a middle-class community, between November 1999 and May 2000. Twenty-three families were interviewed in "Parkside" (fictional name), a working-class community, between May 2000 and February 2001. For this study, we targeted families with children aged 9–12.

My definition of social class is primarily based on the educational level of the parents, and, in particular, whether one or both parents had completed some college. In our "upper-middle-class" community (Riverview), each parent had completed at least some college, and in most cases each parent in the family had a college degree. Most of the parents worked in professional occupations. In our "working-class" community (Parkside), one quarter of the men had not received any college education; nearly all of the mothers had completed some college, but less than one third had completed a four-year degree. The fathers worked primarily in blue-collar jobs, and the mothers in pink-collar jobs or administrative positions. Based upon Lareau's conceptualization of social class as primarily linked to occupation, we expected that communities would differ in the level of children's activities because of the differing class-linked characteristics of the communities: Riverview being upper middle class, populated by professionally employed parents, and Parkside being working class, with parents employed in blue-collar jobs.

The results showed that the average number of activities in which children were engaged (2–3 per week), did not differ across communities. Consistent with Lareau's theory, the *types* of activities differed. Parkside children tended to be involved in community activities such as scouting and church activities whereas the Riverview children were involved in multiple sports and music lessons. In addition, extended family activities were more prevalent in Parkside. However, in contrast to Lareau's theory, *both* middle- *and* working-class parents were concerned about having too much structure in the lives of their children. The following quote from a working-class Parkside parent with a child in the high activity category expresses this sentiment:

> She had something to do every night.... And we had, you know, every
> day we had something to do.... .... [I]t was too much so I cut back to just
> a couple of things. So, she had two nights of activities, but then she had,
> you know, two nights that she could play without having anything to do.
> (Maureen, mother of Jodi [9] – Parkside - 4 activities).

Before making a conscious decision to cut back to two activities, Billie, a middle-class parent, said:

> Her kids ... were tired. I was irritable. You know rushing here, rushing
> there. And it just, it just seemed like too much pressure and it just didn't
> seem to make sense. (Billie, mother of Tara [11], Riverview – 2 activities)

On the other hand, having no activities was not a solution either. Working-class and middle-class parents worried when children did not have any activities. One child (David) was in the sixth grade and his only activity during the school year was a church group. Although he seemed to be quite content, his father was concerned. David's father was disappointed that his son had stopped taking guitar lessons, and thought his son would benefit from the social aspect of being involved in a team sport, but did not want to push him too hard.

> The only thing he did this year was my wife did make him go to church on
> Wednesday nights, they have a youth group program. And basically
> once she got him there, he was okay and had a good time. But you know,
> getting him there was a little tough at times . . . (Robert, father of David
> [12] – Parkside).

Consistent with much research and in contrast to our initial expectations that there would be broad community-based differences, we found that maternal education within community was THE factor differentiating the high- and low-activity families. Through our multivariate analyses, we found that in both communities, the number of activities increased with maternal education up to 16 years of schooling (college degree) and then declined with education above that point. This is consistent with the expressed objectives of the most educated parents, and also with the awareness of the most articulate among them about the limits to which children can or should be pushed. Family structure and maternal employment did not explain activity level, and neither the age nor the gender of child was associated with the number of activities in which a child participated.

Today, it is true that parents are putting their children in organized activities at younger and younger ages, so the organization of activities is not a trivial issue even for kindergartners. In our study several children started soccer, dance, and gymnastics at age 5 years. Although most children had substantial input into their schedules, at such a young age participation is likely to be parent- rather than child-directed.

Conclusion: The Limits of Social Class Explanations for Childrearing Practices

Differing educational levels of parents, particularly mothers, is the most likely explanation for differences in childrearing across social classes. What is the rationale for attributing differences to a vague and abstract concept such as "class" when it is really a result of differential parental education? Education levels are more amenable to modification than social class, and there is more opportunity for intervention. Focusing on parental education seems especially important because of the critical role played by language in childrearing and by the institutional interference that parents run to support their children's schooling. Helping parents obtain additional education is about the best support for child development. Thus, of some concern is the differential access to a college education across social groups.

I am currently engaged in looking more closely at differences in some of these dimensions of parenting by parental education level as well as by other factors. I find the overall theoretical perspective developed by Lareau useful for analyzing the intergenerational transmission of advantage, and applaud her for making it explicit. However, I worry, first, that a definition of social class based upon parental occupation or income is not very useful to finding solutions and, second, that the focus exclusively on activities obscures the critical importance of the other components of the theory for making unequal childhoods into unequal adulthoods.

References

Duncan, G., & Brooks-Gunn, J. (1997). *Consequences of growing up poor.* New York: Russell Sage Foundation.

Dunn, J. S., Kinney, D. A., & Hofferth, S. L. (2003). Parental ideologies and children's after-school activities. *American Behavioral Scientist, 46,* 1359–1386.

Hart, B., & Risley, T. (1995). *Meaningful experiences in the everyday experiences of young American children.* Baltimore, MD: Brookes.

Hoff-Ginsberg, E. (1991). Mother-child conversation in different social classes and communicative settings. *Child Development, 62,* 782–796.

Hofferth, S. L., Curtin, S., & Sandefur, G. (2005). Grade retention: Family disadvantage or poor performance. Paper presented at Annual Meeting of the Population Association of America.

Hofferth, S. L., Kinney, D. A., & Dunn, J. S. (2006). The "hurried" child: Social class and child stress. Manuscript submitted for publication.

Huttenlocher, J., Haight, W., Bryk, A., Seltzer, M., & Lyons T. (1991). Early vocabulary growth: Relation to language input and gender. *Developmental Psychology, 27,* 236–248.

Lareau, A. (2002). Invisible inequality: Social class and childrearing in black families and white families. *American Sociological Review, 67,* 747–776.

Lareau, A. (2003). *Unequal childhoods: Class, race, and family life.* Berkeley: University of California Press.

National Research Council. (1998). *Preventing reading difficulties in young children.* Washington, DC: National Academy Press.

NICHD Early Child Care Research Network. (2000). The relation of child care to cognitive and language development. *Child Development, 71,* 958–978.

Ramey, S. L., & Ramey, C. (2000). Early childhood experiences and developmental competence. In S. Danziger & J. Waldfogel (Eds.), *Securing the future: Investing in children from birth to college* (pp. 122–150). New York: Russell Sage Foundation.

Stipek, D., & Greene, J. (2001). Achievement motivation in early childhood: Cause for concern or celebration? In S. Goldbeck (Ed.), *Psychological perspectives on early childhood education.* Mahwah, NJ: Erlbaum.

13

ORGANIZED ACTIVITY PARTICIPATION FOR CHILDREN FROM LOW- AND MIDDLE-INCOME FAMILIES

Joseph L. Mahoney
Yale University

Jacquelynne S. Eccles
University of Michigan

Recent research demonstrates that how children spend their after-school time has implications for their development in multiple domains (Mahoney, Larson, & Eccles, 2005; National Research Council and Institute of Medicine, 2002). In this regard, it is noteworthy that the after-school experiences of children from low- and middle-income families differ. A salient difference is participation in organized activities (e.g., extracurricular activities, after-school and community programs). National estimates show that children's participation in school- and community-based sports, clubs, lessons, and after-school programs increase as family income rises (Ehrle & Anderson Moore, 1999; Lugaila, 2003; McNeal, 1998). Qualitative research resonates with these estimates (Lareau, 2003; Lareau & Weininger, this volume). The after-school lives of children from middle-income families typically involve more participation in organized activities than their low-income counterparts.

The economic-related discrepancy in rates of organized activity participation has generated different concerns for children from low- and middle-income families. Although research often demonstrates benefits of organized activity participation, one concern is that such participation is excessive for children from middle-income families. As a result, it has been proposed that organized activities may contribute to an "over-scheduling" for middle-class families and that this may be detrimental to family functioning and child adjustment. By contrast, for children from low-income families, the concern is that a lack of organized activities may result in failed opportunities to build competencies developed through participation and increases risks associated with after-school arrangements that are unstructured or unsupervised. In this chapter we consider the scientific evidence surrounding these concerns.

Are Children from Middle-Income Families
Over-Scheduled in Organized Activities?

> [Over-scheduled child rearing] unbalances families, damages marriages, and contributes to unhappy, overstressed children being diagnosed as learning disabled, ADD, bipolar, and depressed, and to adolescents getting involved with drugs, alcohol, and premature sex (Rosenfield, 2003, p. 1).

Whether children participate in organized activities depends, in part, on the behavior of their parents. Children are more likely to become involved and to stay involved in organized activities when parents value and encourage their participation, provide the necessary material resources, and are participants themselves (Fletcher, Elder, & Mekos, 2000; Simpkins, Davis-Kean, & Eccles, 2005). However, there is evidence that the time budgeting and schedule commitments required of parents to support their children's activity participation can be challenging—particularly for working parents with several children (Lareau, 2003).

There has been speculation in the popular media that families managing child participation in several organized activities are "over-scheduled", resulting in a disruption of family life and contributing to psychological distress for children (Gilbert, 1999; Noonan, 2001; Rosenfield, 2003). This contention has drawn on research showing that as children from relatively affluent families enter adolescence they may be at heightened risk for substance use, depression, and anxiety compared to their low-income counterparts (Luthar & Latendresse, 2005a). Factors such as achievement pressures and isolation from parents help to account for these findings (Luthar & Becker, 2002; Luthar & Latendresse, 2005b). Accordingly, as part of what we term the "over-scheduling" hypothesis (OS), children from middle-income families may experience a decline in parent-child relationships and an increase in psychological distress as organized activity participation increases.

In opposition to the OS hypothesis, a scientific basis exists to expect that increasing amounts of organized activity participation may be associated with incremental benefits for children and families. We refer to this as the "organized activity" hypothesis (OA). With some qualifications, the bulk of the evidence indicates that organized activity participation is linked with positive adjustment for children across a range of psychological, social, and educational outcomes and for samples diverse in socioeconomic status (for reviews see, e.g., Dubois, Holloway, Valentine, & Cooper, 2002; Eccles, Barber, Stone, & Hunt, 2003; Eccles & Templeton, 2002; Mahoney, Larson, & Eccles, 2005; National Research Council and Institute of Medicine, 2002; Vandell, Pierce, & Dadisman, 2005). However, only a few longitudinal studies have assessed directly whether the benefits hold for children participating in many organized activities. Moreover, little consideration has been given to whether it is normative for children from middle-income families to demonstrate excessive participation in organized activities.

To evaluate the OS and OA hypotheses we first examine the amount of time that children ordinarily devote to organized activity participation. Then we consider developmental consequences for children and families (i.e., parent-child relationships, psychological distress, social and educational adjustment) with increasing amounts of organized activity participation.

How Much Time Do Children Spend in Organized Activities?

A review of time use studies employing the Experience Sampling Method and/or time diary approach suggests that American children experience 40–50% of their waking hours as discretionary time (Larson & Verma, 1999). This amount of time has been fairly consistent over the past century and estimates of free time are only slightly greater for children from lower-income families. On average, organized activities such as sports, art, music, and clubs consume 50–80 minutes of middle-class adolescents' free time each day (about 13–16% of free time per week). National estimates of children ages 6–12 are slightly lower (i.e., 20–30 minutes per day; 5–7% of free time per week) (Lareau & Weininger, this volume)[1]. Accordingly, young persons spend the vast majority of their free time in pursuits other than organized activity participation (e.g., watching television, talking, household chores, or paid labor). Moreover, although participation in organized activities is a normative developmental experience for children (Ehrle & Anderson Moore, 1999; Lareau & Weininger, this volume; Lugaila, 2003), longitudinal investigations suggest that adolescents typically participate in about two organized activities per year (see below). Accordingly, organized activities do not ordinarily dominate the free-time experience of young persons.

Does Adjustment Decline with Increasing Amounts of Organized Activity Participation?

To address this question, we consider findings from three longitudinal studies that focus on children's organized activity participation and psychosocial adjustment. Our expectation is that increasing amounts of organized activity participation will not be associated with a decline in adjustment. The basis for this expectation derives from studies examining the mechanisms by which participation in organized activities relate to positive outcomes (e.g., Eccles & Templeton, 2002; Mahoney, Larson, & Eccles, 2005; National Research Council and Institute of

---

[1] Time is based on one child sampled in a given family. It may be misleading to estimate organized activity participation for all children in a family by multiplying a single child's estimate by the number of children. All children in a family do not necessarily spend the same amount of time on organized activities. It may also be misleading to assume that parents' time commitment to children's activities can be inferred from a single child's schedule. Children in the same family often have partially overlapping activity schedules and parents are unlikely to participate directly in every activity function for each child.

Medicine, 2002). Among other things, this work suggests that the organized activity context is rich with respect to: (1) structuring time in a conventional pursuit that is socially valued and that helps form linkages between family, school, and community; (2) providing opportunities for developing supportive social relationships with peers and adults; (3) creating a shared experience and point of communication for parents and children that may otherwise be unavailable; (4) facilitating parents' knowledge of child whereabouts, peer relationships, and free time pursuits; and (5) providing an avenue for identity development, initiative, belonging, and self-worth. To the extent that emphasis on any given mechanism varies, or is reinforced, across different activities, then children's positive adjustment should be expected to increase with greater amounts of participation.

To begin, the amount of organized activity participation was assessed in relation to aspects of the parent-child relationship and indicators of child psychological distress in a sample of 1,227 middle-class youth followed longitudinally across grades 8 and 9. The sample represents 92% of all students attending grade 8 from a middle-sized city located in central Sweden (population about 120,000). In both years, students reported the number of organized activities they participated in at least one day/week over the past year (e.g., sports, music, theatre, church, scouts, political, hobby clubs, etc.). At each assessment, they also responded to multi-item scales concerning *parental knowledge* of their free time (e.g., "Do your parents know what you do during your free time?"), *parent-child communication* through child disclosure (e.g., "Do you keep secrets from your parents about what happens during your free time?") and parent solicitation (e.g., "How often do your parents start a conversation with you about your free time?"), *parent-child trust* (e.g., "Do you parents trust that you will stay out of trouble during your free time?") and their frequency of psychological distress in terms of *depressed and anxious mood* (e.g., frequency of sadness, rumination, worries about the future, social anxiety). Average responses to the scales were standardized across the two assessments. The number of activities participated in at each grade was summed to create a 6-point scale (0 = no participation, 5 = participation in five activities or more). Too few participants (3.9%) reported involvement six activities or more to be considered as separate categories.

Aspects of the parent-child relationship and indicators of psychological distress were compared with the number of organized activities using an Analysis of Variance (ANOVA). Descriptive information is shown in Table 13.1. With the exception of parent-child trust, all results were statistically significant ($p < .05$). As the number of activities increased, parental knowledge and parent-child communication tended to increase in a linear fashion. The trend for parent-child trust was similar ($p < .10$). Moreover, both indicators of psychological distress decreased with greater amounts of participation. Thus, during early adolescence, the results indicate that increasing amounts of organized activity participation are positively associated with aspects of parent-child relationships and negatively linked to indicators of children's psychological distress.

Table 13.1

Organized Activity Participation, Parent-Child Relationships, and Indicators of Psychology Distress (N = 1227)

	Number of Organized Activities (Grades 8 and 9)[1] (Standardized Scores)										
	0		1		2		3		4		5+
	M	SD	M	SD	M	SD	M	SD	M	SD	M	SD
	(*N* = 136)		(*N* = 277)		(*N* = 397)		(*N* = 196)		(*N* = 109)		(*N* = 112)
Parent Knowledge of Child	-.20	.78	-.05	.63	-.01	.63	.00	.61	.11	.62	.11	.52
Parent-Child Communication												
Child Disclosure	-.17	.77	-.09	.69	-.01	.65	.01	.61	.14	.66	.15	.57
Parent Solicitation	-.29	.61	-.09	.62	.01	.61	.11	.59	.10	.54	.11	.57
Parent-Child Trust	-.14	.75	-.02	.65	-.02	.68	.03	.68	.04	.71	.11	.58
Anxious Mood	.12	.78	.06	.76	.01	.71	-.05	.65	.01	.76	-.18	.67
Depressed Mood	.15	.59	.01	.57	-.02	.49	-.05	.47	-.04	.47	-.03	.47

[1] Average number of activities for Grades 8 and 9 were 1.3 (SD = .93) and 1.2 (SD = .95), respectively.

For a long-term accounting of organized activity participation and serious maladjustment we consider findings from the Carolina Longitudinal Study (Cairns & Cairns, 1994) that tracked 695 children annually from early adolescence through young adulthood. The socioeconomic status (SES) of this sample was approximately average for American families when the study began (1981–1982). Participation in one form of organized activities—school-based extracurricular activities—was determined from school yearbook information gathered over a six-year interval (grades 6–12). For the following analyses, we first performed a median split of SES to identify participants below and above average. Next, we categorized the total number of extracurricular activities children were involved in during the six years of secondary school along a 5-point continuum (i.e., 0 = none, 1 = 1–5 activities, 2 = 6–10 activities, 3 = 11–15 activities, 4 = 16–20 activities, 5 = 21+ activities). Again, too few participants (5.8%) were involved in 22 or more extracurricular activities during secondary school to categorize participation further. Finally, we compared these activity-based categories to rates of school dropout and subsequent criminal arrests in young adulthood as determined, in part, by school records and State Bureau of Investigation records, respectively (c.f., Mahoney, 2000; Mahoney & Cairns, 1997; Mahoney, Cairns, & Farmer, 2003).

Descriptive information is shown in Table 13.2. For children from families below or above the median SES, findings from an ANOVA show that the likelihood of experiencing school dropout or criminal arrests in young adulthood decrease significantly (*p* < .01) with increasing amounts of extracurricular activity participation. Because the rates of dropout and criminal arrests decline to near zero (a floor effect) as extracurricular activity participation increases, there is no evidence that increasing amounts of extracurricular activity participation place children at-risk for these outcomes.[3] To the contrary, increasing amounts of extracurricular activities during secondary school are negatively associated with school failure and criminal offending.

Table 13.2

Extracurricular Activity Participation, School Dropout, and Criminal Arrests According to SES (N = 662)

	Number of Extracurricular Activities (Grades 6 through 12) [1]					
	0	1-5	6-10	11-15	16-20	21+
SES Below Average	(N = 76)	(N = 147)	(N = 55)	(N = 28)	(N = 21)	(N = 14)
SES Above Average	(N = 27)	(N = 105)	(N = 70)	(N = 47)	(N = 30)	(N = 42)
Proportion of Dropouts						
SES Below Average	.61	.23	.02	.00	.00	.00
SES Above Average	.44	.09	.00	.02	.00	.00
Proportion Arrested (ages 18-24)						
SES Below Average	.34	.16	.09	.07	.06	.07
SES Above Average	.26	.07	.04	.02	.00	.00

[1] Extracurricular activity participation increases across adolescence (Mahoney & Cairns, 1997). The average number of activities participated in across grades 6-12 was 1.3. At the peak – during Grade 12 – the average was 2.5.
Note. SES = Socioeconomic Status.

The third set of findings summarized here comes from the Michigan Study of Adolescent Life Transitions (MSALT). In this longitudinal study of working- and middle-class youth and their families in southeastern Michigan, adolescents were surveyed at school in grades 6, 7, 10, and 12 and again at ages 21 and 25 on a wide variety of indicators of psychosocial functioning, including participation in extracurricular and other out-of-school activities. Here we summarize the findings for the relation of grade 10 activity participation to adjustment and academic performance at grades 10, 11, and 12 and on post-high school educational and occupational outcomes (for full details see Barber, Eccles & Stone, 2001; Eccles & Barber, 1999; Eccles et al., 2003). First, as was true in the previous two studies, virtually no adolescents could be classified as over-scheduled. The majority of the youth participated in at least one activity, with the average being a little more than 2. Girls participated in more and a wider variety of activities than boys. Adolescents whose mothers had some college education participated in more activities than adolescents whose mothers had completed high school or less.

---

[3] Mahoney (2000) found similar results when the sample was disaggregated into homogeneous configurations differing in bio-social-academic adjustment and family economy (i.e., physical maturation, aggression, popularity with peers, academic competence, socioeconomic status).

Second, there were strong associations between activity participation and subsequent functioning, even when controlling for the adolescents' functioning at grade 10. For every type of activity participation, participants showed more improvement over time than non-participants in school achievement (GPA, high school completion, college attendance and completion), feelings of school belonging, and self-esteem. These effects were particularly strong for participation in competitive team sports but also emerged for participation in school clubs, school performing arts programs, and school leadership activities. Involvement in volunteer activities and faith based activity programs predicted higher high school achievement as well as lowered rates of drinking and drug use. All of these effects held even when grade 10 levels on the dependent measure, as well as scores on the Differential Aptitude Test and mother's education were controlled. Interestingly, high school sport participation also predicted higher income and better jobs at age 25.

Finally, there was no evidence of declines in the benefits of participation as adolescents participated in more activities. In every case except sports, there was a linear increase in the indicators of positive functioning with increasing numbers of activities. In addition, the benefits increased linearly as the range of activity types broadened. Participation in sports did show a leveling off of benefits following participation in two competitive team sports. Together, these last two results suggest that participating in a wider range of activities is more beneficial than participating in more team sports.

One troubling finding did emerge: participation in competitive athletics predicted increases in alcohol use during the high school years. This change, however, was not reflected in either drug use or cigarette smoking—both of which were less frequent among athletes than non-athletes. It is likely that the increase in drinking reflects the peer culture of athletes in U.S. high schools at the time of this study. Interestingly, this difference in alcohol consumption disappeared by two years post-high school for two reasons: the mean levels of all students going on to college caught up to the athletes' level of drinking, and the mean level of drinking declined for those high school athletes who did not go on to college.

Towards a reconciliation. The quantitative findings summarized above are consistent with the OA hypotheses suggesting that "more participation is better." How should these results be viewed in light of qualitative evidence demonstrating that the scheduling of organized activities presents a challenge for middle-class families (Lareau, 2003; Lareau & Weininger, this volume)? One obvious possibility is that the quantitative and qualitative research is not in conflict. It is entirely possible that children's organized activity schedules can be challenging—even burdensome—for some families and that such participation is beneficial nonetheless.

A second possibility is that the qualitative and quantitative methods consider somewhat different facets of the phenomenon. Quantitative research has seldom considered how activity participation affects family-level processes and the existing qualitative research provides a limited accounting of such processes across families with children who differ in their amount of participation or in terms of children's adjustment. Investigations that marry these approaches should be fruitful.

A final possibility is that parenting behaviors characterizing some middle-class families may lead to adjustment difficulties for children, and organized activities have been confused with these behaviors. For example, one recent study of affluent families (Luthar, Shoum, & Brown, 2006) shows that perceived parenting practices (e.g., criticism, achievement pressure), rather than organized activities, predict psychological distress and substance use in young persons. However, it seems reasonable to assume that if organized activities are a focus of such parenting, then participation could be a catalyst in the development of these negative outcomes. Research is available to show that for some young athletes, perceived pressure from parents to participate and meet expectations is a source of competitive stress (e.g., Averill & Power, 1995; Leff & Hoyle, 1995; Scanlan, 1984). Consistent with the idea of OS, this increased level of stress is particularly likely for children and adolescents who are participating at the highest levels of sport competition. Heightened stress and perceived parental pressure are two of the most common reasons athletes and musicians give for dropping out of their sports or music activities (Fredricks et al., 2002). However, this is not true of the majority of athletes and musicians. In fact, many high school athletes and musicians site support from their parents and peers as two of the main reasons they continue participating throughout their high school years. Other reasons for continued participation include high expectations for success, great intrinsic enjoyment of the activity, and the centrality of the activity for one's personal and social identities. Accordingly, an important direction to pursue is child and parent motivations, goals, values, and expectations concerning organized activity participation as they relate to family processes and child adjustment (e.g., Duda, 1996; Eccles, Wigfield, & Schiefele, 1998; Fredricks & Eccles, 2005; Jacobs, Vernon, & Eccles, 2005).

Is a Lack of Organized Activity Participation Detrimental for Low-Income Children?

We noted at the outset that children from low-income families are less likely to participate in organized activities. As an example, the 2000 Census shows that children in poverty are about half as likely to participate in sports, clubs, or lessons, compared to children from families at least 200% above the poverty threshold (Lugaila, 2003). Time use and ethnographic research provide converging evidence on this point (Lareau & Weininger, this volume; Larson & Verma, 1999).

Limited access, availability, and affordability of organized activities in low-income areas coupled with parents' work schedules are established barriers to participation (e.g., Casey, Ripke, & Huston, 2005; Lareau & Weininger, this volume; Mahoney, Larson, & Eccles, 2005). With reference to access and availability, for example, the gap in supply vs. demand of organized activities in low-income areas––both in terms of current provisions and the funding to sustain existing activities––is documented (e.g., Afterschool Alliance, 2005; Mahoney & Zigler, 2006). Thus, in many cases low-income parents and their children want to be more involved in organized activities but are not able (Lareau & Weininger, this volume). For instance, data from the Yale Study of Children's After-School Time (Y-CAST)—a longitudinal study of after-school time for children from poor families (Table 13.3)—shows that most parents believe their child should spend more time in organized activities (sports, clubs, lessons) (Table 13.4). Parents' belief that their child spends too much time in organized activities was nearly absent.

Table 13.3

Demographic Characteristics of Participants from the Yale Study of Children's After-school Time

Participants	1st- to 3rd-grade students from 3 public schools
Consent Rate / Sample Size	73% / N = 599
Study Design	4-year longitudinal; biannual assessments
Child Race/Ethnicity	
African American	36%
European American	10%
Hispanic	50%
Asian	02%
Other	02%
Poverty Threshold [1]	
Under 50%	22%
51–100%	35%
101–175%	27%
Above 175%	16%
Primary Caregiver Not Married	58%
Primary Caregiver Employed	54%
Public Assistance/Income Support	72%
Median Annual Household Income [2]	$16,794
Average Family Size	4.4

[1] Based on poverty thresholds from the 2002 Census.

[2] Includes all household income (earnings, public assistance, compensation, etc.)

Table 13.4
Parent Beliefs About Child's Time Spent in After-school Activities (N = 402)

	Parent Beliefs (Proportion of Parents)		
Activity	Not Enough Time	Right Amount of Time	Too Much Time
Homework	.16	.79	.05
Watching Television	.02	.64	.34
Household Chores	.23	.74	.03
Caring for Siblings	.16	.78	.06
Religious Activities	.33	.64	.03
Organized Sports	.59	.40	.01
Organized Clubs	.56	.42	.02
Organized Lessons	.56	.43	.01

The fact that children from low-income families show relatively low amounts of organized activity participation raises two interrelated concerns. First, organized activities can provide developmental supports for low-income children with working parents through the provision of a safe and supervised context. Second, participation in such activities is linked to a reduced likelihood that low-income children will develop certain adjustment problems associated with socioeconomic disadvantage. Drawing on recent findings from the Y-CAST study, we outline an empirical base for these concerns.

Children who spend relatively large amounts of their free time in unstructured activities (i.e., "hanging out", driving in cars, congregating at unstructured youth centers) are at risk for developing antisocial and criminal behaviors (e.g., Mahoney, Stattin, & Lord, 2004; Osgood et al., 1996; Richardson, Radziszewska, Dent, & Flay, 1993). The likelihood of such outcomes is greater for children whose after-school arrangement is predominated by a lack of adult supervision (i.e., self care) and those living in socioeconomic disadvantaged areas (Pettit, Bates, Dodge, & Meece, 1999). Although the amount of self care experienced by children from low- and middle-income families is not vastly different (Ehrle & Anderson Moore, 1999; Vandell & Shumow, 1999), this arrangement may be of greater consequence for poor children.

Lord and Mahoney (2006; Mahoney, 2005) examined the interaction between neighborhood crime levels and after-school supervision in relation to the development of academic performance and aggression. Official crime reports were used to classify the census blocks in which Y-CAST participants lived as either high or average with respect to the level of crime (no areas in the city could be characterized as low crime in comparison to regional or national crime rates). Over a two-year interval, children living in high-crime areas showed significant decreases in academic performance and increases in aggression compared to those in average crime areas. This was true after controlling for multiple demographic dimensions of the census blocks and children's social-academic adjustment at the outset of the study.

However, the risks associated with living in a high-crime area were especially marked for children whose primary after-school arrangement was self-care. By contrast, children whose primary arrangement was after-school program participation were significantly buffered against the risks of living in a high-crime area. For example, reading achievement differences between children in after-school programs and those in self-care were equivalent to about two thirds of a school year in expected gains. Mahoney (2005) showed the associated buffering also applies to the development of aggression. The findings suggest that organized activities provide an important safety and supervision function for low-income working families. In this circumstance, simple enrollment in organized activities appears beneficial compared to unsupervised after-school arrangements.

Beyond enrollment, children from low-income families may benefit most when organized activity participation is a regular part of their after-school experience. For example, the benefits of after-school program participation are more apparent when attendance is consistent (i.e., more than 1 or 2 days in an average week) and sustained for a year or longer (e.g., Kane, 2004; Simpkins, Little, & Weiss, 2004; Welsh et al. 2002). An example is provided by a longitudinal study of child obesity and after-school program participation using the Y-CAST data set (Mahoney, Lord, & Carryl, 2005a). Consistent with risks of poverty and minority status, 22% of children in this sample were clinically obese at age 5. By age 8, 29% of the sample was obese. However, the body mass index (BMI) of children who showed regular and sustained attendance in after-school programs increased significantly less compared to children in other after-school arrangements. The BMI difference translated into significant differences in rates of clinical obesity. The study also found evidence of a dosage-related effect whereby BMI decreased linearly over time with greater attendance in after-school programs. The explanation likely involves the controlled eating environment and/or physical exercise common to after-school programs (c.f., Vandell et al., 2005). An implication is that, for some outcomes, benefits of organized activities may not be evident *unless* participation is a regular part of children's after-school experience. On this score, the supportive role of parents seems critical (Simpkins, Davis-Kean, & Eccles, 2006).

Finally, the extent to which organized activities relate to positive development for children from low-income families can be expected to depend on their value and motivation for participation. To this end, discussion of a third aspect of participation—*engagement*—is pertinent. By engagement we refer to the child's level of enjoyment, interest, and effort in organized activities (and other developmental contexts) (Larson, 2000; Weiss, Little, & Bouffard, 2005). High levels of engagement (rather than psychological distress) are typical of organized activity participation; however, high engagement does not characterize the experience of all participants. Because individual differences in activity engagement predict the extent to which benefits are observed for poor children (Mahoney, Lord, & Carryl, 2005b), understanding the reasons behind this individual variability is important. Program quality and content relate to engagement for children from low-income families (Mahoney, 2005) and children's social experiences in such programs are also important (Pierce, Hamm, & Vandell, 1999). Yet, little is known about the role of family and parenting in this process. The Y-CAST data set shows that individual differences in after-school program engagement correlate positively with the frequency of parent involvement (i.e., parent meetings and conversations with program staff, attending program events) (r (113) = .32, p < .01) and how well parents and staff know one another (r (130) = .22, p = .01). Nonetheless, the lack of information about the ways in which parents contribute to the quality of children's experiences in organized activities represents a gap in the existing knowledge base. Filling the gap will require additional longitudinal research involving qualitative and quantitative methods designed specifically to do so.

Summary and Conclusion

The data reviewed here support three conclusions. First, there is little evidence that organized activity participation contributes to an over-scheduling of children that is detrimental to their psychological, social, or educational well-being. Indeed, most of the findings show that children's adjustment becomes increasingly positive with greater amounts of organized activity participation. Second, there is merit in the concern that children from low-income families are under-involved in organized activities. For these children, a lack of participation is linked to increased adjustment problems associated with socioeconomic disadvantage. Finally, support and encouragement from parents ordinarily play a positive role in children's activity enrollment, attendance, and engagement. However, when children experience stress and perceived pressure from parents connected to their participation they are more likely to drop out of organized activities. Future research will need to provide a better understanding of how the expectations and values that children and parents hold for organized activity participation interact with parenting styles, amounts of activity participation, and child adjustment.

Acknowledgment

Findings presented in this chapter were supported, in part, by grants to the first author from the National Institute of Child Health and Human Development (R01 HD MH39909) and the Smith Richardson Foundation.

References

Afterschool Alliance (2005). *Working families and afterschool. A special report from America After 3PM: A household survey on afterschool in America.* Retrieved September 18, 2005 from http://www.afterschoolalliance.org/press archives Working Families.Rpt.pdf.

Averill, P. M., & Power, T. G. (1995). Parental attitudes and children's experiences in soccer: Correlates of effort and enjoyment. *International Journal of Behavioral Development, 18,* 263–276.

Barber, B. L., Eccles, J. S., & Stone, M. R. (2001). Whatever happened to the jock, the brain, and the princess? Young adult pathways linked to adolescent activity involvement and social identity. *Journal of Adolescent Research, 16,* 429–455.

Cairns, R. B., & Cairns, B. D. (1994). *Lifelines and risks: Pathways of youth in our time.* New York: Cambridge University Press.

Casey, D. M., Ripke, M. N., & Huston, A. C. (2005). Activity participation and the well-being of children and adolescents in the context of welfare reform. In J. L. Mahoney, R. W. Larson, & J. S. Eccles (Eds.), *Organized activities as contexts of development: Extracurricular activities, after-school and community programs* (pp. 65–84). Mahwah, NJ: Erlbaum.

Dubois, D. L., Holloway, B. E., Valentine, J. C., & Cooper, H. (2002). Effectiveness of mentoring programs for youth: A meta-analytic review. *American Journal of Community Psychology, 30,* 157–197.

Duda, J. L. (1996). Maximizing motivation in sport and physical education among children and adolescents: The case for greater task involvement. *Quest, 48,* 290-302.

Eccles, J. S., & Barber, B. (1999). Student council, volunteering, basketball, or marching band: What kinds of extracurricular involvement matters? *Journal of Adolescent Research, 14,* 10–43.

Eccles, J. S., Barber, B. L., Stone, M., & Hunt, J. (2003). Extracurricular activities and adolescent development. *Journal of Social Issues, 59,* 10–43.

Eccles, J. S., & Templeton, J. (2002). Extracurricular and other after-school activities for youth. *Review of Educational Research, 26,* 113–180.

Eccles, J. S., Wigfield, A., & Schiefele, U. (1998). Motivation to succeed. In W. Damon (Series Ed.) & N. Eisenberg (Vol. Ed.), *Handbook of child psychology: Social, emotional, and personality development* (pp. 1011–1073). New York: John Wiley & Sons.

Ehrle, J., & Anderson Moore, K. (1999). *1997 NSAF benchmarking measures of child and family well-being.* Methodology Reports No. 6. Washington, DC: Urban Institute.

Fletcher, A. C., Elder, G. H., Jr., & Mekos, D. (2000). Parental influences on adolescent involvement in community activities. *Journal of Research on adolescence, 10,* 29–48.

Fredricks, J.A., Alfeld-Liro, C., Hruda, L., Eccles, J. Patrick, H., & Ryan, A. (2002). A qualitative exploration of adolescents' commitment to athletics and the arts. *Journal of Adolescent Research, 17,* 68–97.

Fredricks, J. A., & Eccles, J. S. (2005). Family socialization, gender, and sport motivation and involvement. *Journal of Sport & Exercise Psychology, 27,* 3–31.

Gilbert, S. (1999, August 3). For some children, it's an after-school pressure cooker. *New York Times* (p. 7).

Jacobs, J. E., Vernon, M. K., & Eccles, J. (1995). Activity choices in middle childhood: The roles of gender, self-beliefs, and parent's influence. In J. L. Mahoney, R. W. Larson, & J. S. Eccles (Eds.), *Organized activities as contexts of development: Extracurricular activities, after-school and community programs* (pp. 235–254). Mahwah, NJ: Erlbaum.

Kane, T. J. (2004). *The impact of after-school programs: Interpreting the results of four recent evaluations.* Retrieved July 27, 2005, from http://www.wtgrantfoundation.org/usr_doc/After-school_paper.pdf

Lareau, A. (2003). *Unequal childhoods: Class, race, and family life.* Berkeley: University of California Press.

Larson, R. W. (2000). Toward a psychology of positive youth development. *American Psychologist, 55,* 170–183.

Larson, R. W., & Verma, S. (1999). How children and adolescents spend time across the world: Work, play, and developmental opportunities. *Psychological Bulletin, 125,* 701–736.

Leff, S. S., & Hoyle, R. H. (1995). Young athletes' perceptions of parental support and pressure. *Journal of Youth and Adolescence, 24,* 187–203.

Lord, H., & Mahoney, J. L. (2006). Neighborhood crime and self care: Risks for aggression and lower academic performance. Manuscript submitted for publication.

Lugaila, T. A. (2003). A child's day: 2000 (Selected indicators of child well-being). *Current Population Reports, P70-89.* Washington, DC: U.S. Census Bureau.

Luthar, S. S., Shoum, K. A., & Brown, P. J. (2006).Extracurricular involvement among affluent youth: A scapegoat for "ubiquitous achievement pressures"? *Developmental Psychology, 42,* 583–597.

Luthar, S. S., & Becker, B. E. (2002). Privileged but pressured? A study of affluent youth. *Child Development, 73,* 1593–1610.

Luthar, S. S., & Latendresse, S. J. (2005a). Children of the affluent: Challenges to well-being. *Current Directions in Psychological Science, 14,* 49–53.

Luthar, S. S., & Latendresse, S. J. (2005b). Comparable "risks" at the socioeconomic status extremes: Preadolescents' perceptions of parenting. *Development and Psychopathology, 17,* 207–230.

Mahoney, J. L. (2000). Participation in school extracurricular activities as a moderator in the development of antisocial patterns. *Child Development, 71,* 502–516.

Mahoney, J. L. (2005, July). Beyond achievement: Possibilities for and outcomes of after-school program participation. Paper presented at the School of the 21st Century National Conference, New Haven, CT.

Mahoney J. L., & Cairns, R. B. (1997). Do extracurricular activities protect against early school dropout? *Developmental Psychology, 32,* 241–253.

Mahoney, J. L., Cairns, B. D., & Farmer, T. (2003). Promoting interpersonal competence and educational success through extracurricular activity participation. *Journal of Educational Psychology, 95,* 409–418.

Mahoney, J. L., Larson, R. W., & Eccles, J. S. (Eds.) (2005). *Organized activities as contexts of development: Extracurricular activities, after-school and community programs.* Mahwah, NJ: Erlbaum.

Mahoney, J. L., Lord, H., & Carryl, E. (2005a). Afterschool program participation and the development of child obesity and peer acceptance. *Applied Developmental Science, 9,* 202–215.

Mahoney, J. L., Lord, H., & Carryl, E. (2005b). An ecological analysis of after-school program participation and the development of academic performance and motivational attributes for disadvantaged children. *Child Development, 76,* 811–825.

Mahoney, J. L., Stattin, H., & Lord, H. (2004). Participation in unstructured youth recreation centers and the development of antisocial behavior: Selection processes and the moderating role of deviant peers. *International Journal of Behavioral Development, 28,* 553–560.

Mahoney, J. L., & Zigler, E. F. (2006). Translating science to policy under the No Child Left Behind Act of 2001: Lessons from the national evaluation of the 21st-Century Community Learning Centers. *Journal of Applied Developmental Psychology, 27,* 282–294.

McNeal, R. B. (1998). High school extracurricular activities: Closed structures and stratifying patterns of participation. *The Journal of Educational Research, 91,* 183–191.

National Research Council and Institute of Medicine. (2002). *Community programs to promote youth development.* Committee on Community-Level Programs for Youth. J. Eccles & J. A. Gootman (Eds.), Board on Children, Youth, and Families, Division of Behavioral and Social Science and Education. Washington, DC: National Academy Press.

Noonan, D. (2001, January 29). Stop stressing me: For a growing number of kids, the whirlwind of activities can be overwhelming. How to spot burnout. *Newsweek* (pp. 54–55).

Osgood, D. W., Wilson, J. K., O'Malley, P. M., Bachman, J. G., & Johnston, L. D. (1996). Routine activities and individual deviant behavior. *American Sociological Review, 61,* 635–655.

Pettit, G. S., Bates, J. F., Dodge, K. A., & Meece, D. W. (1999). The impact of after-school peer contact on early adolescent externalizing problems in moderated by parental monitoring, perceived neighborhood safety, and prior adjustment. *Child Development, 70,* 768–778.

Pierce, K. M., Hamm, J. V., & Vandell, D. L. (1999). Experiences in after-school programs and children's adjustment in first-grade classrooms. *Child Development, 70,* 756–767.

Richardson, J., Radziszewska, B., Dent, C., & Flay, B. (1993). Relationship between after-school care of adolescents and substance use, risk taking, depressed mood, and academic achievement. *Pediatrics, 92,* 32–28.

Rosenfield, A. (2003). Over-scheduling children and hyper-parenting. Retreived August 30, 2005 from http://www.hyper-parenting.com/talkbrick.htm

Scanlan, T. K. (1984). Competitive sports and the child athlete. In J. M. Silva III & R. S. Weinberg (Eds.), *Psychological foundations of sport* (pp. 118–129). Champaign, IL: Human Kinetics.

Simpkins, S. C., Little, P. M. D., & Weiss, H. B. (2004). *Understanding and measuring attendance in out-of-school programs.* Retrieved July 27, 2005, from http://www.gse.harvard.edu/hfrp/projects/afterschool/resources/issuebrief7.html

Simpkins, S. D., Davis-Kean, P. E., & Eccles, J. S. (2005). Parents' socializing behavior and children's participation in math, science, and computer out-of-school activities. *Applied Developmental Science, 9,* 14–30.

Simpkins, S. D., Fredricks, J., Davis-Kean, P., & Eccles, J. S. (2006). Healthy mind, healthy habits: The influence of activity involvement in middle childhood. In A. C. Huston & M. N. Ripke (Eds.), *Developmental contexts in middle childhood* (pp. 283–302). New York: Cambridge University Press.

Vandell, D. L., Pierce, K. M., & Dadisman, K. (2005). Out-of-school settings as a developmental context for children and youth. In R. Kail (Ed.) *Advances in child development.* Vol. 33. Oxford: Elsevier.

Vandell, D. L., & Posner, J. K. (1999). Conceptualization and measurement of children's after-school environments. In. S. L. Friedman & T. Wachs (Eds.), *Measuring environments across the lifespan: Emerging methods and concepts* (pp. 167–196). Washington, DC: American Psychological Association.

Vandell, D. L., Shernoff, D. J., Pierce, K. M., Bolt, D. M., Dadisman, K., & Brown, B. B. (2005). Activities, engagement, and emotion in after-school programs. In H. B. Weiss, P. M. D. Little, & S. M. Bouffard (Issue Eds.) & G. G. Noam (Editor-in-Chief), *New directions in youth development: Vol. 105. Participation in youth programs: Enrollment, attendance, and engagement* (pp. 121–129). San Francisco: Jossey-Bass.

Vandell, D. L., & Shumow, L. (1999). After-school child care programs. *The Future of Children, 9* (pp. 64–80). Los Altos, CA: The David and Lucile Packard Foundation.

Weiss, H. B., Little, P. M. D., & Bouffard, S. M. (2005). More than just being there: Balancing the participation equation. In H. B. Weiss, P. M. D. Little, & S. M. Bouffard (Issue Eds.) & G. G. Noam (Editor-in-Chief), *New directions in youth development: Vol. 105. Participation in youth programs: Enrollment, attendance, and engagement* (pp. 15–31). San Francisco: Jossey-Bass.

Welsh, M. E., Russell, C. A., Williams, I., Reisner, E. R., & White, R. N. (2002). *Promoting learning and school attendance through after-school programs: Student-level changes in educational performance across TASC's First Three Years.* Washington, DC: Policy Studies Associates, Inc.

IV

Effects of Child Risk Characteristics and Family Processes on the Development of Children's Behavioral Control

14

CHILD CHARACTERISTICS AND FAMILY PROCESSES THAT PREDICT BEHAVIORAL READINESS FOR SCHOOL

Susan B. Campbell
Camilla von Stauffenberg
University of Pittsburgh

Behavioral Challenges for Young Children During the Transition to School

Between the ages of 4 and 6, young children are expected to make a major life transition from the relative safety of the home, family day care, childcare center or preschool to elementary school. This transition involves many changes and challenges. Children must become integrated into a new and larger group of peers, build relationships with a new set of adults who have different roles and different expectations for the child's behavior than did caregivers or preschool teachers, and move into a new physical setting (and with bussing and magnet schools, sometimes even a new community). For some children, this transition may also involve riding on the school bus alone without the company of family members or familiar peers—a potentially intimidating experience. Despite the fact that most children today in North America have experienced some form of out-of-home care before they enter kindergarten, the demands placed on young children to adapt to far-reaching changes in their daily lives occasioned by the transition to school are daunting.

Children must possess a variety of regulatory strategies and social skills to cope successfully with these changing demands and expectations. For example, the transition to kindergarten or first grade requires a degree of independence and self-reliance that is not expected in child care or preschool, and often children must be able to function in a much larger group of peers with substantially less adult supervision. Children also must relate to a new peer group, make new friends, and learn to work cooperatively with others in a more focused and goal-directed way than in preschool. They must follow teacher directions and inhibit impulses not to call out, push ahead in line, demand teacher attention, or be aggressive with peers. They must be able to follow a lesson and focus attention on challenging cognitive tasks. Many children also must cope with shyness and anxiety as they make the transition to school. Although children gradually develop these social and regulatory skills in preschool and childcare, the transition to kindergarten or first grade sometimes taxes young children's abilities in these areas.

Moreover, children's entry into the school system is more often determined by age than by the acquisition of skills and competencies that indicate social and cognitive readiness for school. Thus, children enter school with widely varying social and self-regulatory skills, and not all children are behaviorally and emotionally ready for the transition to school. The successful transition from the more protected environment of childcare or preschool to primary school will in part be determined by child characteristics and also by how supportive the family is—by how well parents have prepared the child, both explicitly and implicitly, for the demands of school (Alexander & Entwisle, 1988; Ladd, Birch, & Buhs, 1999; NICHD Early Child Care Research Network [ECCRN], 2003a, b; 2004). The school environment will also matter (NICHD ECCRN, 2003b), as some classrooms provide more emotionally and academically supportive environments than others. Since classroom and teacher characteristics also have implications for children's early school adjustment (NICHD ECCRN, 2003b; Pianta, Steinberg, & Rollins, 1995), Pianta (1999) argued that we need to ask not only when children are ready for school, but which schools are ready for children. In addition, the peer group is an important contributor to early school adjustment; children with early peer difficulties have a harder time adjusting to school than do those who fare well in the peer group (Ladd, Kochenderfer, & Coleman, 1996, 1997). For example, Ladd and colleagues (Ladd, 1990; Ladd et al., 1996) have demonstrated that having a familiar and liked peer in the same classroom facilitates children's transition to kindergarten, presumably because a familiar peer serves as an additional source of social support in a new and challenging environment. Despite the importance of the network of relationships that may facilitate children's school adjustment (Ladd et al., 1999), children are called upon to be quite independent as they make the transition to school. Furthermore, their adaptation to the demands of kindergarten and first grade will be strongly determined by their prior adjustment and social skills (NICHD ECCRN, 2003b).

Although there has been an increased focus on school readiness over the last several decades, the recent emphasis has shifted almost exclusively to children's cognitive and academic readiness for school, defined in terms of language development, pre-literacy skills, and developing number concepts (Dorn, 1998; Wesley & Buysse, 2003). It is also well-recognized that children's control of attention and emotions, social competence, and overall regulatory skills are necessary components of school readiness (Kagan, Moore, & Bredekamp, 1995; Lin, Lawrence, & Gorrell, 2003; McClelland & Morrison, 2003; Shonkoff & Phillips, 2000; Wesley & Buysse, 2003). Indeed, much of the focus in preschool settings is on facilitating the behavioral and emotional control needed to meet the demands of the classroom once formal schooling begins. Preschool and kindergarten teachers emphasize skills and competencies such as following directions and classroom rules, focusing and maintaining attention, sitting still, controlling aggression and other impulses, and sharing and cooperating with other children. For example, McClelland and Morrison (2003) identified a set of behaviors that they called "learning-related social skills". These include independence, responsibility, self-regulation, and cooperation. They argue that these behaviors are fostered in preschool, are relatively stable, and are necessary for early school success. Teachers also recognize that they will be able to teach basic literacy and numeracy skills only to young children who have both the motivation and interest to acquire these academic competencies, and also the behavioral competencies that are necessary prerequisites for learning. It is obvious that children will not be able to learn to read if they cannot sit still, pay attention, and follow the teacher's directions. Certainly teachers cannot teach if they are spending their time trying to control a classroom of fidgety, noisy, unruly, and inattentive children.

There are, however, wide individual differences in children's self-regulatory skills when they enter school (e.g., Conduct Problems Prevention Research Group, 1999; Gadow, Sprafkin, & Nolan, 2001; NICHD ECCRN, 2003a, b; Pianta & McCoy, 1997) as kindergarten and first grade teachers will attest. Rimm-Kaufmann, Pianta, and Cox (2000) specifically recruited a large national sample of kindergarten teachers and assessed their perceptions of school readiness and problem behavior as exhibited by children entering their classrooms. Teachers reported that 52% of the children in their classrooms made a smooth transition to kindergarten from preschool, 32% had a few transition problems, and 16% were seen as having serious adjustment problems. In terms of specific difficulties, over 30% of the teachers reported that the majority of entering kindergarten children in their classrooms had problems following directions, working independently, and cooperating as part of a group; a similar proportion of teachers noted that over half the children in their classrooms entered kindergarten behind in basic academic skills. Teachers also noted a high prevalence of social skill and communication deficits. Not surprisingly neighborhood poverty and the proportion of minority children in the school population predicted all of these problems at kindergarten entry. These results highlight not only the fact that kindergarten teachers are quite concerned about entering children's regulatory skills, but also that problems with social interaction, self-regulation in the classroom, and academic deficits co-occur, a finding that is consistent with the clinical literature which shows that behavior problems tend to occur in tandem with learning problems (especially language delays and reading problems) and peer difficulties in young children (Campbell, 2002; Cohen, Davine, & Meloche-Kelly, 1989; Conduct Problems Prevention Research Group, 1992; Hinshaw, 1992; Spira & Fischel, 2005).

Individual Differences in Children's Behavior and Self-Regulation

Individual differences in children's ability to appropriately control their emotions, attention, and behavior emerge in the context of the family, and are also related to earlier indicators of temperament, especially individual differences in reactivity and regulation that may be manifest in high levels of arousal, poor regulation of negative affect, difficulty focusing and maintaining attention, and poor control over impulses (Rothbart & Bates, 1998; Rothbart, Posner, & Hershey, 1995). A somewhat related construct is effortful control (Kochanska & Knaack, 2003; Kochanska, Murray, & Harlan, 2000), an individual difference dimension that involves effortful attention and the suppression of a dominant response. Kochanska and colleagues have demonstrated that effortful control develops over the course of the preschool years, becomes more stable and traitlike with development, and is related to other aspects of self-control. These individual difference dimensions are considered to be biologically based and to reflect personality characteristics that influence behavior in a range of contexts, although they also can be modified by environmental input (Kochanska et al., 2000). Clearly young children who are highly reactive and poorly regulated, or to use Kochanska's terminology, low in effortful control, are likely to have a harder time adjusting to school, presumably because their poor impulse control, difficulty waiting their turn, fidgetiness, inattention, and tendency to be uncooperative will conflict with teacher expectations, classroom demands, and success in the peer group (Campbell et al., 1994; Denham et al., 2000; Zahn-Waxler et al., 1996).

Defined in terms of inhibiting a prepotent response, effortful control includes response inhibition, resistance to temptation, and delay of gratification. Other related constructs include controlling and maintaining attention (NICHD ECCRN, 2003a; Rothbart & Bates, 1998; Ruff & Rothbart, 1996). Research indicates that deficits in these skills are related to higher levels of behavior problems during the transition to school (Campbell et al., 1994; Denham et al., 2000; Eisenberg et al., 1996). For example, Campbell et al. (1994) studied a group of hard-to-manage preschool boys identified at age 4 on the basis of teacher and maternal reports of symptoms of attention deficit disorder. Children so identified were observed to be more non-compliant with the teacher and more disruptive with peers in preschool. At age 4, hard-to-manage boys also differed from controls on laboratory measures of resistance to temptation and delay of gratification, as well as measures of activity level (observer ratings, counts of out-of seat behavior, and actometer counts) during structured tasks and inattention (disorganized and unfocused play with frequent activity shifts) to toys during free play. When followed up at age 6, hard-to-manage boys were still more impulsive than controls on two measures of inhibition and more fidgety and active, as assessed by observer ratings and actometer scores. Inattention to toys during free play and activity level during structured tasks at age 4, and more impulsive responses on a delay task all predicted persistent problems at age 6 (Campbell et al., 1994). These data and those of others confirm that early difficulties controlling attention and delaying responses in age-appropriate contexts may be signs of more persistent regulatory problems that can interfere with adjustment to the demands of school, as children are expected to sit still, control impulses, and focus attention (see Campbell, 2002, for a review).

In addition, studies indicate clearly that individual differences in these regulatory skills are related to individual differences in families (NICHD ECCRN, 2003a,b, 2005).

Family Predictors and Correlates of Behavioral School Readiness

Although individual differences in children's regulatory skills are important predictors of school readiness, they are also associated with individual differences in families that are likewise linked to school readiness. Both distal family characteristics and specific aspects of parenting are important to consider when predicting children's adjustment to school, as illustrated by Farkas and Hibel (in press).

Distal Family Characteristics

Children with poorer regulatory skills often come from less advantaged home environments characterized by a lower educational level, more poverty, unemployment or low occupational level, and single parenthood, and many children living in these family contexts are minority group members; children in such family environments also live in less desirable neighborhoods and often attend schools with fewer resources, compounding their problems with lower levels of academic and social readiness for school (e.g., Barbarin, 1999; Duncan, Brooks-Gunn, & Klebanov, 1994; Farkas & Hibel, in press; Kohen, Brooks-Gunn, Leventhal, & Hertzman, 2002; Yeung, Linver, & Brooks-Gunn, 2002). Although small neighborhood effects have been detected in some studies of young children's adjustment (e.g., Chase-Lansdale & Gordon, 1996), process models tend to implicate maternal stress and depression, and specific styles of parenting as factors accounting for the links between low income and low education and children's social, emotional, and academic functioning during the transition to school (e.g., McLoyd, 1990, 1998; Yeung et al., 2002). McLoyd (1990, 1998) suggested that sociodemographic risk may lead to high levels of depressive symptoms in mothers, which in turn can undermine sensitive, involved parenting. It is to these more proximal family processes that we now turn.

Proximal Family Processes

Maternal Depression

Although proximal family processes are especially relevant to understanding the mechanisms by which sociodemographic risk translates into poorer regulatory skills in children, these are to some degree confounded. Research has emphasized maternal self-reports of stress and depression and there are numerous studies showing that depressive symptoms are correlated with lower educational and occupational status, low income, and single parenthood (Kohen et al., 2002; NICHD

ECCRN, 1999; Yeung et al., 2002). At the same time, many women with young children who are not experiencing high levels of sociodemographic risk also report feeling depressed (e.g., Campbell, Cohn, & Meyers, 1995; Cicchetti, Rogosch, & Toth, 1998, 1997; Zahn-Waxler, Iannotti, Cummings, & Denham, 1990).

Maternal depression, independent of demographic risk, has long been considered a risk factor for poor social adjustment in children (Cummings & Davies, 1994; Downey & Coyne, 1990; Hammen, 2002), although studies have generally not examined maternal depression as it relates to the transition to school. It is easy to imagine how maternal depression might interfere with a young child's adjustment to school, for example, because of lower maternal engagement and support for the child during a stressful life transition and/or greater impatience and negative affect. Numerous studies have documented links between higher levels of maternal depressive symptoms and less sensitive and engaged maternal behavior, more negativity, and less elaborated conversation. Thus, school readiness may also be affected by maternal depression through links between maternal depression and more general maternal involvement, to be discussed in more detail below.

Data from the NICHD Study of Early Child Care illustrate some of these issues and processes. Examining data from birth to 36 months, we found that depressive symptoms were more likely to be elevated in women with more demographic risk (NICHD ECCRN, 1999) and that level of depressive symptoms and maternal sensitivity were strongly negatively related. Moreover, women with high levels of depressive symptoms and low financial resources were significantly less sensitive with their young children, indicating that the combined effects of prolonged sad mood and financial pressures were reflected in particularly low levels of maternal sensitivity. Sensitivity in turn moderated the effects of maternal depressive symptoms on children's social and language development at 36 months, such that when mothers were both chronically depressed and insensitive their children had the highest levels of behavior problems and scored lower on a measure of expressive language development. Maternal depressive symptoms were also related to later indices of school readiness and academic achievement in first grade in other analyses using this data set (Campbell et al., submitted).

Parent-Child Relationship Quality and Childrearing Strategies

Direct aspects of the parent-child relationship and parent-child interaction are especially germane to understanding how children develop the self-regulatory skills necessary for a successful transition to school (Campbell, 2002; Denham et al., 2000; Kochanska, Aksan, & Nichols, 2003; Kopp, 1989; Zahn-Waxler, Radke-Yarrow, & King, 1979). Some research has focused on general qualities of the emotional relationship between parents and their young children that include connectedness, warmth, sensitivity and mutuality in the parent-child relationship (Clark & Ladd, 2000; Kochanska & Aksan, 2004; Maccoby & Martin, 1983). These relationship qualities are associated with attachment security (Ainsworth, Blehar,

Water, & Wall, 1972; Bretherton, 1990; DeWolff & van IJzendoorn, 1997; Sroufe & Fleeson, 1986) and with later self-esteem and self-regulation (Bretherton, 1991; Sroufe, 1983; Thompson, 1998). Other research has emphasized the specific strategies parents use to socialize children, including proactive and appropriate limit-setting (Crockenberg & Litman, 1990; Maccoby & Martin, 1983). Proactive limit-setting involves anticipating situations that may be difficult for the child, explaining the reasons for a prohibition, and using firm guidance only when necessary. Other research has focused on mother-child conversations that include shared positive affect and mutual responsiveness (Clark & Ladd, 2000; Laible & Thompson, 2000) and discussions about feeling states, including conversations that take the child's perspective into account, discuss causality (Brown & Dunn, 1996) and also make children aware of the consequences of their actions on others (Brown & Dunn, 1996; Zahn-Waxler et al., 1979). Studies have also examined how parents inculcate values (Kochanska, 1997; Kochanska, Aksan, Knaack, & Rhines, 2004), and help children differentiate right from wrong and appropriate from inappropriate behaviors (Zahn-Waxler et al., 1979). These positive aspects of parenting, both general parental interest that includes mutuality, affective engagement and involvement (Cole, Teti, & Zahn-Waxler, 2003; Gardner, 1987; Harrist, Pettit, Dodge, & Bates, 1994), and more specific proactive and supportive parenting behaviors (Brown & Dunn, 1996; Denham et al., 2000) have all been associated with children's social competence and ability to regulate their own behavior. In the NICHD Study of Early Child Care, maternal sensitivity has emerged consistently as a strong predictor of social and cognitive competence in the first grade (NICHD ECCRN, 2003b, 2004), and has also been linked specifically to measures of inhibition and attention.

This diverse set of parenting behaviors appears to be characterized by positive affect and warmth, respect for children's autonomy and emerging sense of self and inductive discipline that includes taking the child's perspective and developmental competencies into account. Shared positive affect is an important by-product of this parenting approach. Kochanska and Aksan (2004) suggested that this early parent-child mutuality is primarily parent-driven, but by toddlerhood shared goals and a more bidirectional relationship emerge, a relationship quality that Kochanska (1997) called a mutually responsive orientation and Maccoby and Martin (1983) referred to as a willingness to comply. These developmentalists argue that children are more cooperative, compliant, internally controlled, and self-reliant in the context of positive and responsive parent-child relationships. Although most research has focused solely on the mother-child relationship, there is also emerging evidence that sensitive and supportive father-child relationships also facilitate children's self-regulation and adjustment to school (Denham et al., 2000; NICHD ECCRN, 2004).

Why might these parenting strategies facilitate better school adjustment? According to attachment theory, children with warm, supportive relationships with parents, reflected in secure attachments, should also have more positive expectations about relationships with others and a positive sense of self (Bretherton, 1985; Sroufe & Fleeson, 1986); this style of parenting is also associated with the internalization of appropriate behaviors (Kochanska et al., 2004), and with a prosocial orientation (Clark & Ladd, 2000; Eisenberg & Fabes, 1998). According to Kochanska et al. (2004), a warm parent-child relationship should facilitate attention to the parent and result in the child's processing of parental messages about values, norms, and expected behaviors and also make the child more willing to comply with these expectations. In school this process would be reflected in better behavioral control, acceptance of classroom norms and teacher expectations, attention to the teacher, and prosocial behavior with peers.

In contrast to warm and supportive parenting, harsh and less involved parenting has been associated consistently with the emergence of behavior problems in young children, including poor regulation of negative affect, impulses, and attention—the hallmarks of behavior problems during the transition to school. Numerous studies have linked harsh, angry, inconsistent, and coercive parenting to children's behavior problems (Campbell et al., 1996; Deater-Deckard, Dodge, Bates, & Pettit, 1998; Kochanska, Aksan, & Nichols, 2003; Patterson, Reid, & Dishion, 1992; Rubin, Burgess, Dwyer, & Hastings, 2003). Kochanska et al. (2003) proposed that power-assertive discipline that includes negative angry affect, physical punishment, and threats, and fails to provide explanations about prohibitions (Zahn-Waxler et al., 1979) may challenge young children's sense of autonomy and also arouse anger and resentment, leading to the coercive exchanges described by Patterson et al. (1992). Children may then be less likely to internalize standards for behavior, be more likely to rely on external pressures for compliance, and also be more likely to model angry coercive behavior in other contexts. In school this might translate into less compliance with classroom rules and expectations, more need for direction and attention from the teacher, and more difficulty sharing and behaving prosocially with peers.

Parenting as a Moderator of Children's Temperamental and Regulatory Behavior?

The literature reviewed so far suggests that parenting and relationship quality are associated with child characteristics and behavioral readiness for school. However, it makes sense to assume that particular parenting behaviors may be more appropriate for children with particular personality characteristics and behavioral tendencies; children with particular personality characteristics also may elicit certain behaviors from parents with particular styles and may respond more positively to some aspects of parenting and more negatively to others. Although theoretical models have posited interactions between child characteristics and parenting styles for decades (Sameroff & Chandler, 1975; Thomas, Chess, & Birch, 1968), only a handful of studies have clearly demonstrated that parenting moderates child characteristics in predicting outcomes.

Belsky, Hsieh, and Crnic (1998) found that boys high in negativity were more susceptible to differences in parenting styles; harsh maternal discipline in toddlerhood predicted more externalizing behavior at age 3 among boys who were high in negative emotionality in infancy, but not among boys low in negativity. Bates, Pettit, Dodge, and Ridge (1998) likewise found that maternal limit-setting made a difference primarily among children who were resistant to control in toddlerhood. In this case, difficult and resistant toddlers had fewer problems in the early elementary school years when their mothers employed restrictive disciplinary control that was both firm and consistent, but children high in resistance showed more continuing problems in the absence of maternal limit-setting. Although these results might appear somewhat contradictory, they may be interpreted to underscore the importance of consistency and clear limit-setting, as well as positive proactive controls. Similarly, Kochanska (1997) reported that more anxious and inhibited children internalized controls more easily when mothers used gentle guidance, rather than power assertive strategies that only increased their anxiety. Denham et al. (2000) recently demonstrated that proactive behavior by both fathers and mothers was protective for children with elevated levels of behavior problems, studied from preschool age to third grade. Taken together, these studies and others suggest that parenting and child characteristics may interact to predict children's ability to regulate their behavior as they adjust to first grade. In particular children who are more poorly regulated at 54 months may be especially in need of proactive and sensitive control that provides structure while supporting autonomy. In contrast, less sensitive and supportive parenting may exacerbate problems in children who show impulsive and disorganized behavior in early childhood.

In summary, the literature suggests that behavioral readiness for school is multi-determined. Child characteristics, family context, and family process variables all contribute to children's readiness for school consistent with Bronfenbrenner's person-process-context model of development (Bronfenbrenner, 1986). In the current analyses we consider how well sociodemographic indicators, child functioning on earlier measures of behavioral self-regulation, maternal depression, and parenting quality differentiate among children who are and are not behaviorally ready for school. We also ask whether fathers' parenting behavior adds to prediction over mothers' and also whether maternal sensitivity, maternal depression, and the quality of the home environment moderate links between children's self-regulation at 54 months and behavioral adjustment to school.

We use data from the NICHD Study of Early Child Care to form readiness groups, based on teacher ratings of first grade children's behavioral adjustment to school, defined in terms of inattention, overactivity, aggression, and related problems. We then address the following questions:

1. Do earlier (36 months and 54 months) measures of poor regulatory skills predict behavioral readiness at first grade?
2. Do maternal and paternal parenting and other family environment measures predict behavioral readiness at first grade?
3. Do parenting and family measures predict first grade behavioral readiness over and above earlier indicators of children's self-regulatory skills?
4. Do parenting and family measures moderate the links between early self-regulatory skills and children's behavioral readiness for school?

Method

The data to be discussed here come from Phases I and II of the NICHD Study of Early Child Care, an ongoing multi-site longitudinal study of children's development from birth through age 15. Details on sample recruitment procedures, measures, and abstracts of published papers may be obtained at our study website (http:// public.rti.org/secc/).

Briefly, children participating in this study were born between 1990 and 1991 in hospitals at ten data collection sites across the U.S.: Little Rock, AR; Irvine, CA; Lawrence, KS; Boston, MA; Philadelphia, PA; Pittsburgh, PA; Charlottesville, VA; Morganton, NC; Seattle, WA; and Madison, WI. Participants came from a range of family contexts, but mothers younger than 18 were not included and multiple births or children with serious birth complications requiring prolonged hospitalization were also excluded; mothers had to be fluent in English to participate and their neighborhoods had to be deemed safe enough to send in research assistants for home visits. Women with a known history of substance abuse were also excluded. Therefore, the sample, by definition, excluded some very high-risk children and families.

Data to be reported in this chapter are based on 1,063 children and families on whom we obtained outcome data at first grade. Of these 82% (874) were Caucasian and 18% (189) were minority (African American predominantly, but also Hispanic, Asian, and mixed ethnicity). The sample consisted of 524 girls (49%) and 539 boys (51%); 67% lived in a stable two-parent family and 33% lived in either single-parent, divorced, or widowed families or other family arrangements. In addition, 752 fathers or father figures participated in the 54-month data collection (subsequently referred to as fathers for simplicity). Of these, 90% were the fathers of study children, 6% were the mothers' live-in partners, and the remaining 4% were other adults living in the home, including grandfathers.

Attrition analyses indicate that families who were not included in these analyses either because they dropped out or were missing data on child functioning did not differ from those included on sex of child or mothers' marital status. However, families who were not included were more likely than those who were to be a member of a minority group (26% versus 18%, $\chi^2_{(1)} = 9.35$, $p < .01$); they also were lower in maternal educational level (13.6 years versus 14.4 years, $t = 4.94$, $p < .001$) and income (3.11 versus 3.57, $t = 2.23$, $p < .03$). Participating fathers also were more likely to be white (88%) and to have higher incomes and educational levels than families without fathers available, and than available fathers who did not participate.

Overview of Data Collection

Data were initially collected when the children were 1-month-old and again at 6, 15, 24, 36, and 54 months, kindergarten, and first grade. Home visits were conducted when the study children were one-month-old. During this visit, demographic information was collected, including maternal age and years of education, mother's marital status, child ethnicity, and family income. Demographic data on the family were updated during phone calls and face-to-face contacts with mothers at regular intervals through first grade.

Maternal reports of depression were obtained using the Center for Epidemiological Studies Depression Scale (CES-D; Radloff, 1977) at assessments when children were 1, 6, 15, 24, 36, and 54 months. In addition, observations of the quality of mother-child interaction were obtained in the home at 6 and 15 months and in the laboratory at 24, 36, and 54 months. During home visits at 6, 15, 36, and 54 months, age-appropriate versions of the Home Observation for the Measurement of the Environment (Caldwell & Bradley, 1984) were completed.

Children's self-regulation was assessed during laboratory visits at 36 and 54 months. Children's cognitive and language functioning was assessed at 36 and 54 months, and first grade. Teacher/caregiver ratings of children's behavior in childcare or school were obtained at 54 months and in kindergarten and first grade.

Measures

Demographics

Maternal education and ethnicity. During the one-month interview, mothers reported on the number of years of school completed and their child's ethnicity (coded as white versus other for these analyses).

Mean income-to-needs ratio. When the children were 6, 15, 24, 36, and 54 months old, information about family income and family size was collected. The income-to-needs ratio was calculated as the total family income divided by the poverty threshold according to size of family.

Marital stability. The mother's marital status was assessed during interviews at regular intervals from 1 month through 54 months. Mothers who identified themselves as married at each time point were considered "stably married," whereas mothers who endorsed being single, divorced, widowed, or living with a domestic partner at any time during the study period were labeled as "not stably married." Of the 1,063 families in the final sample for this report, 67% were considered stably married through 54 months.

Family Functioning and Parenting

Maternal depressive symptoms. Maternal reports of depressive symptoms were assessed at each interview with the CES-D, a 20-item scale that assesses depressive symptoms manifested in the past two weeks. The reliability and validity of the CES-D have been well established (Radloff, 1977).

Maternal and paternal sensitivity. Mother-child interactions were videotaped in semi-structured 15-minute observations at 6, 15, 24, 36, and 54 months. Father-child interaction was observed at 54 months. The tasks provided a context for assessing age-appropriate qualities of sensitive, responsive parental behavior. The tasks at all ages are described in the Manuals of Operation for the NICHD SECC (http://public.rti.org/secc/); interaction involved a free play session at 6 months and developmentally appropriate play and problem-solving tasks at subsequent assessments (15, 24, 36, and 54 months).

Mother-child interactions were videotaped and tapes were sent to a central non-data collection site for coding. Coders were blind to other information about the families. At 6, 15, and 24 months, composite *maternal sensitivity* scores were created from the sums of three 4-point ratings (maternal sensitivity to child non-distress, intrusiveness [reversed], and positive regard). At 36 and 54 months the maternal sensitivity composite was the sum of three 7-point ratings of supportive presence, respect for autonomy, and hostility (reversed). Cronbach's alphas for the sensitivity composites ranged from .70 to .84. Inter-coder reliability was determined by assigning two coders to 19–20% of the tapes randomly drawn at each assessment period. Coders were not aware which tapes were double-coded and reliability was assessed throughout the coding period. Inter-coder reliability was calculated as the intra-class correlation coefficient. Reliability coefficients for the composite maternal sensitivity scores used in the current report ranged from .72 to .87. The scores from 36 and 54 months were transformed from a 7- to a 4-point scale to make them equivalent to the earlier measures and then averaged across age to form a *maternal sensitivity composite* from infancy through 54 months.

At 54 months, children and their fathers were observed interacting with a similar set of toys during the home visit and father sensitivity was coded from videotapes on the same 7-point rating scales and averaged to form a *paternal sensitivity composite*. The coefficient alpha for the father sensitivity composite at 54 months was .71 and the inter-rater reliability coefficient was .86.

Home environment. The HOME Inventory (Caldwell & Bradley, 1984) was used to assess the quality of the physical and social resources available to a child in the home. The HOME consists of both direct observations and a semi-structured interview with the mother and has age-appropriate versions for infancy and early childhood. The focus is on the child as a recipient of stimulation from objects, events, and interactions occurring in the family surroundings. The Infancy version of the HOME was completed at 6 and 15 months and the Early Childhood version was completed at 36 and 54 months. Scores were based on the sum of items at each age, with higher values denoting higher levels of caregiver responsiveness, child stimulation, and support for the child's development. Cronbach's alphas for the total score ranged from .76 to .87. For these analyses, scores were averaged across the four assessments to form a *composite HOME* score. All home visitors went through a rigorous training and certification process prior to data collection.

Measures of Children's Regulatory Skills at 36 and 54 Months and First Grade

Behavior and attention problems. At 54 months, caregivers or preschool teachers completed the Teacher Report Form (TRF; Achenbach, 1991). These were obtained for 730 children or 69% of the current sample at 54 months. Kindergarten and first-grade teachers also completed the TRF. Scores on the externalizing scale and the attention problems scale were examined in the analyses.

Attachment security at 36 months. Attachment to mother was assessed using a modified age-appropriate version of the Strange Situation at 36 months (details are in NICHD ECCRN, 2001). During the laboratory visit, children's responses to two separation and reunion episodes with mother were videotaped and coded into secure and insecure categories by observers unaware of any information about study children. Most tapes were coded independently by two coders and agreement on the secure-insecure designation was 80.3% (k=.63).

Impulsivity and inattention. Children's resistance to temptation was assessed in a forbidden toy situation at 36 months. Midway through a two-hour laboratory visit, the child was shown an attractive toy and allowed to play with it briefly (Ski Boat Crocs). Then the examiner told the child that she had some work to do, that the child could play with other toys (previously played with), but that she/he should not touch the attractive toy until told she could do so. The toy was then placed at arm's length from the child and the examiner sat in a corner of the room doing paperwork for 2.5 minutes. At the end of the 2.5 minutes, the examiner allowed the child to play with the toy. This procedure was videotaped and scored at a central site by individuals unaware of any information about study children. For this paper, the variable latency to first *active engagement* was included. Inter-rater reliability was .98.

At 54 months, children were observed in a standard delay of gratification task. In the middle of a laboratory visit, the child was offered a small immediate reward of candy (or other preferred food) or a larger reward later. The child was taught to ring a bell to summon the experimenter and then was left to play the "waiting game."

The child was given two plates: one with a small amount of food that could be eaten right away (but only after the experimenter was summoned by a ring of the bell) and another with a larger amount that could only be eaten at the end of the waiting game. Waiting time was calculated and used in the analyses.

The Continuous Performance Task (CPT; Rosvold et al., 1956) measured impulsivity and inattention during the 54-month visit. Children saw dot-matrix images on a 2-inch computer screen. The child was asked to press a button "as fast as you can" each time the target stimulus (i.e., a chair) appeared (44 times), but not to respond to the 176 non-target stimuli (e.g., butterfly, fish, flower). Stimuli (220) were presented in 22 blocks. The stimulus duration was 500 msec. and the inter-stimulus intervals were 1,500 msec. The target stimulus was randomly presented, appearing twice within each block. The test took approximately 7.5 minutes. *Impulsivity* (commission errors) was measured by the number of responses to the non-target stimuli. *Inattention* or omission errors were recorded whenever the child did not respond to a target stimulus, reflecting lapses in attention. Because scores were skewed, a square root transformation was applied to these variables.

Measures of Children's Language and Cognitive Functioning

At 36 months, children were administered the Bracken Tests of Basic Concepts (Bracken, 1984) and the Reynell Developmental Language Scale (Reynell, 1991). Standard scores on the Bracken total score and the Expressive and Receptive Vocabulary Scores were included in the analyses.

At 54 months, children were administered the Preschool Language Scale (Zimmerman, Steiner, & Pond, 1979) and the Woodcock-Johnson Psycho-Educational Battery (Woodcock & Johnson, 1989, 1990). The letter/word identification scale, assessing pre-reading skills, and the applied problems scale, assessing number concepts, were examined in this report.

Establishing Readiness Groups

In order to select an extreme subgroup of children who were having difficulty adjusting to the behavioral and regulatory demands of first grade, children who obtained elevated ratings, defined as one standard deviation above the mean of the standardization sample (i.e., a T-score of 60 or above), on teacher reports of externalizing problems and/or attention problems were considered to be showing poor regulatory behaviors. Items included on these scales reflect difficulties sitting still, paying attention, complying with teacher requests and classroom rules, getting along with other children, controlling impulses including aggression, and managing without extra attention from the teacher. A few children (*n*= 55 or 4% of the sample) were missing first grade TRF scores; kindergarten scores were carried forward for these children. It should also be noted that T-scores control for gender differences in behavior problems, as they are normed separately for boys and girls.

Results

Behavioral Readiness Groups

Based on cut-off scores of one *SD* above the mean on Attention and/or Externalizing Problems, 76% (*n* = 806) of the sample was considered behaviorally ready for first grade and 24% (*n* = 257) received T-scores of 60 or above according to their first-grade teachers.

Demographic Correlates of Readiness Groups

The two readiness groups were compared on demographic measures, summarized in Table 14.1. Although there were equal proportions of boys and girls in both groups as would be expected when T-scores are used to delineate groups, there were group differences in ethnicity ($\chi^2_{(1)}$ =32.24, p<.001); 29.6% of the children in the low readiness group were minority in contrast to 14% of the group showing adequate behavioral readiness. As can be seen in Table 14.1, the two readiness groups also differed on maternal educational level at 1 month, income-to-needs ratio averaged across the 6–54 month period, and marital status. Thus, consistent with other studies, the behavioral readiness groups differed on indicators of sociodemographic context, with poorer readiness associated with fewer resources.

Table 14.1

Demographic Characteristics of the Behavioral Readiness Groups

	Ready for School		Not Ready for School	
	M	(SD)	M	(SD)
Maternal Education*	14.69	(2.44)	13.55	(2.31)
Income-to-Needs*	3.82	(2.88)	2.80	(2.41)
	%	(Count)	%	(Count)
Child Ethnicity*				
Minority	14	(113)	29.6	(76)
White	86	(693)	70.4	(181)
Child Gender				
Male	50.1	(404)	52.5	(135)
Female	49.9	(402)	47.5	(122)
Marital Status*				
Stably married	72.5	(584)	49.0	(126)
Not stably married	27.5	(222)	51.0	(131)

F or χ^2 significant at * p < .001

Earlier Child Characteristics

Means and standard deviations of earlier measures of child and family functioning are summarized in Table 14.2. Two (group) by two (gender) ANCOVAs were conducted, controlling for maternal education and family income. Gender was examined because of the strong possibility that there would be gender by group interactions on a number of readiness measures, with girls faring better than boys.

Table 14.2

Means and Standard Deviations for Early Measures of Child and Family Functioning

Variables	Ready M	(SD)	Not Ready M	(SD)	F or χ^2
36-month Measures of Child Functioning					
Resistance to Temptation					
Latency to First					
Active Engagement	102.13	(66.04)	68.39	(68.79)	33.14*
Reynell					
Receptive Language	100.84	(15.29)	91.42	(15.40)	36.01*
Expressive Language	98.74	(13.74)	93.45	(15.64)	9.36*
Bracken School					
Readiness Composite	16.00[a]	(10.15)	11.72[a]	(8.43)	13.42**
Attachment Status					
Secure	64.7%		53.9%		
Insecure	35.3%		46.1%		9.20**
54-month Measures of Child Functioning					
Continuous Performance Task					
Commission Errors	11.35	(18.25)	22.52	(25.88)	37.56*
Omission Errors	8.11	(7.09)	12.24	(8.23)	39.29*
Delay of Gratification	4.81	(2.91)	3.56	(3.09)	15.96*
Preschool Language Scale	102.86	(19.25)	91.67	(21.06)	28.16*
Woodcock-Johnson					
Letter Word Identification	100.51	(13.14)	94.08	(13.36)	18.74*
Applied Problems	105.35	(15.04)	96.23	(15.46)	36.19*
Family Functioning					
Maternal Depressive Symptoms	8.75	(6.33)	11.43	(7.05)	13.47*
Maternal Sensitivity (0–4 scale)	9.66	(1.14)	9.07	(1.36)	17.11*
Paternal Sensitivity (0–7 scale)	17.74	(2.21)	16.99	(2.58)	7.13**
HOME	41.10	(4.17)	37.83	(5.36)	56.93*

[a] Interaction between group and gender; see text.

* $p < .001$; ** $p < .01$

N's for "Ready" group range from 577 to 805; for the Low Readiness group, from 177 to 257.

36-month measures. At 36 months, children were observed in the lab during a resistance to temptation task and during a modified strange situation; they were also administered the Bracken Test of Basic Concepts and the Reynell Developmental Language Scale. The two readiness groups, classified on the basis of first-grade teacher ratings of behavior, were already showing differences on these 36-month measures. After controlling for maternal education and family income, children in the low readiness group were faster to engage with the forbidden toy (i.e., less able to resist temptation), and they showed poorer receptive and expressive language development on the Reynell. Although gender differences were evident on both language measures and resistance to temptation, with girls scoring better than boys, only the Bracken showed a significant group by gender interaction ($F_{(1, 1006)}$ = 7.36, $p<.01$). Girls in the high readiness group performed significantly better than boys in the high readiness group (Ms = 18.05 and 13.95), and males and females in the low readiness group had similarly lower scores (Ms= 11.82 and 11.62).

Finally, children in the low readiness group were less likely to be securely attached to their mothers at 36 months (54% secure, 46% insecure) as compared to those in the high readiness group (65% secure, 35% insecure; $\chi^2_{(1)}$ =9.19, $p<.01$). When a logistic regression analysis was conducted to control for maternal education and income, insecure attachment still predicted membership in the low readiness group (OR = 1.41, p<.03).

54-month measures. Similarly, at 54 months, children in the low readiness group were less able to delay gratification and made more errors of both omission (lapses in attention) and commission (impulsive responses) on the CPT. They also performed more poorly on measures of language development and on the Woodcock-Johnson subtests of pre-academic skills. Caregivers rated them as having more attention and externalizing problems. Although significant gender main effects were evident on measures of language and school readiness, and on the CPT measure of commission errors, with girls outperforming boys, no significant group by gender interactions were obtained on 54 month measures.

Parenting and Family Functioning

These analyses were also conducted controlling for income and maternal education; mothers of children in the low readiness group reported more depressive symptoms and were observed to be less sensitive with their children during the semi-structured play interaction averaged across the 6-, 15-, 24-, 36-, and 54-month assessments than mothers whose children were seen as behaviorally ready for first grade. Participating fathers whose children were in the low readiness group were also observed to be less sensitive at 54 months than fathers whose children were seen as ready for school. Finally, groups differed in the expected direction on the HOME averaged across the 6-, 15-, 36-, and 54-month home visits; children in the lower readiness group received less stimulation, responsiveness, and overall support for development at home across early childhood.

Logistic Regression Analyses

The next sets of analyses were meant to identify *unique* predictors of readiness groups. Analyses were run with and without controls for 54-month behavior problems; controlling for 54-month teacher ratings allowed us to examine predictors after taking into account the stability of behavior problems from 54 months to first grade, which was modest (r's=.37 for attention problems and .48 for externalizing problems). However, as already noted, a number of children (n=333) did not have 54-month teacher/caregiver ratings. Rather than lose this many children, we opted to examine predictors with and without controls for earlier behavior.

Demographics. In Model 1 the demographic variables were entered as a block ($\chi^2_{(6)}$ =174.49, p<.001). Results, summarized in Table 14.3, indicate that with all demographic variables in the model only ethnicity and maternal education were significant predictors of readiness groups. This is because ethnicity was almost totally confounded with income and marital status in our sample. Therefore, we controlled maternal education and ethnicity in subsequent analyses.

Measures of children's functioning at 54 months. Model 2 then added child characteristics at 54 months including delay of gratification, errors of omission and commission on the CPT, the Preschool Language Scale, Woodcock-Johnson Letter-Word Identification and Applied Problems. Although the overall model was significant ($\chi^2_{(8)}$ =93.92, p<0001), only errors of omission and commission on the CPT differentiated between the readiness groups uniquely, indicating that children who had more difficulty monitoring attention and controlling impulsivity on a boring, but demanding task at 54 months were also more likely to have difficulties adjusting to the behavioral demands of paying attention and controlling impulsivity in their first-grade classrooms. Next, the analysis was rerun on a smaller sample, controlling for earlier levels of teacher-rated problems at 54 months and including only the two CPT measures that were significant in the prior analysis ($\chi^2_{(5)}$ = 122.45, p<.001). CPT measures continued to predict low behavioral readiness, meaning that the CPT errors of omission (OR = 1.37, p<.001) and commission (OR = 1.17, p<.001) contributed information *distinct* from earlier ratings of problem behaviors.

Table 14.3

Logistic Regression Analyses Predicting Membership in Behavioral Readiness Groups: Demographic Variables, Child Characteristics, and Maternal Sensitivity and Depression

Variables	Model 1				Model 2				Model 3a				Model 4a			
	Wald χ²	b	SE	p	Wald χ²	B	SE	p	Wald χ²	b	SE	p	Wald χ²	b	SE	p
Demographic																
Maternal Education	9.55	-.12	.04	.002	4.19	-.09	.04	.041	9.63	-.11	.04	.002	7.87	-.11	.04	.005
Ethnicity	9.17	.56	.17	.002	2.16	.33	.23	.141	7.84	.53	.19	.005	5.09	.49	.22	.024
Income	.19	-.02	.04	.667												
Marital Status	10.88	.57	.17	.001												
Child Sex	.23	.07	.15	.632												
54-month Child Characteristics																
CPT Commission Errors					11.87	.14	.04	.001					21.6	.17	.04	.000
CPT Omission Errors					14.70	.29	.08	.000					18.2	.30	.07	.000
Delay of Gratification					.43	-.02	.03	.511								
Preschool Language					.082	.00	.00	.775								
Woodcock-Johnson																
Applied Problems					3.04	-.02	.01	.081								
Letter Word Identification					.00	.00	.01	.992								
Maternal Variables																
Sensitivity									4.91	-.16	.07	.027	.15	.03	.08	.699
Depressive Sx									6.62	.03	.01	.010	6.23	.03	.01	.013

Parental sensitivity and maternal depressive symptoms. Since maternal sensitivity and the HOME were correlated at .63, they were not examined simultaneously. We focused first on maternal sensitivity because it is a strong measure of relationship quality and because we had a parallel measure for fathers. Therefore, Model 3a addressed whether maternal depression and maternal sensitivity both predicted readiness group membership over and above maternal education and ethnicity ($\chi^2_{(4)}$ =68.66, p<001). Both measures were significant in the equation, with higher maternal depression and lower maternal sensitivity predicting the child's membership in the low behavioral readiness group.

The next analysis focused on fathers' participation in the study. The overall model was significant ($\chi^2_{(3)}$ =29.99, p<001); lower paternal sensitivity was also a unique predictor of lower behavioral readiness, over and above demographic variables. When both maternal and paternal sensitivity were included in the model, only paternal sensitivity remained significant over and above educational level.

With 54-month TRF scores controlled, maternal depressive symptoms, maternal sensitivity, and paternal sensitivity were no longer significant predictors of school readiness groups. This indicates that the effects of maternal depressive symptoms and parental sensitivity on children's readiness were confounded with the stability in problem behavior over time.

Model 4 examined the question of whether maternal sensitivity and depressive symptoms provided unique information over and above demographics and significant measures of children's regulatory skills (overall model ($\chi^2_{(6)}$ = 116.47, p<.001). With CPT errors of omission and commission in the regression equation, higher maternal depression scores, but not lower maternal sensitivity predicted membership in the low readiness group. When earlier teacher ratings were controlled, only child characteristics remained significant predictors.

HOME and maternal depressive symptoms. Finally, we examined whether the HOME added to the prediction of readiness groups over and above demographics and maternal depressive symptoms (Model 3b), and also whether the HOME added above and beyond child characteristics (Model 4b; see Table 14.4). Although the overall model was significant ($\chi^2_{(4)}$ =94.79, p<0001), once the HOME was included in the equation, all other variables (maternal education, ethnicity, and maternal depressive symptoms) became nonsignificant; only lower scores on the HOME uniquely predicted membership in the low readiness group. Even when earlier TRF scores were controlled ($\chi^2_{(5)}$ = 142.15, p<.001), however, the HOME remained a significant predictor of readiness group membership. The HOME continued to predict membership in the readiness groups with earlier CPT measures in the equation along with 54-month TRF scores ($\chi^2_{(7)}$ =144.23, p<001). These analyses underscore the fact that this measure of family context is especially robust, predicting behavioral readiness uniquely over and above maternal education and ethnicity, earlier teacher ratings, and laboratory measures of impulsivity and inattention.

Table 14.4

Logistic Regression Analyses Predicting Membership in Behavioral Readiness Groups: Demographic Characteristics, CPT, and HOME

Variables	Model 3b				Model 4b			
	Wald χ^2	B	SE	P	Wald χ^2	B	SE	P
Demographic								
Maternal Education	2.23	-.06	.04	.136	2.05	-.06	.04	.152
Ethnicity	2.50	.31	.20	.114	1.51	.27	.22	.219
54-month Child Characteristics								
CPT Commission Errors					18.67	.16	.04	.000
CPT Omission Errors					15.25	.27	.07	.000
Family/Parenting Variables								
Maternal Depressive Sx	2.92	.02	.01	.088	3.21	.02	.01	.073
HOME	26.35	-.10	.02	.000	6.26	-.06	.02	.012

Do family measures moderate the effects of impulsive responding or inattention in predicting readiness group membership? Six analyses were run to address this question. The 54-month CPT commission errors score, one index of impulsivity, was a robust predictor of readiness group membership. We examined whether three parenting/family measures (maternal depressive symptoms, maternal sensitivity, and HOME) interacted with impulsivity scores to predict readiness group. Our assumption was that less sensitive maternal behavior, higher maternal depressive symptoms, and a less stimulating and responsive home environment would exacerbate problems for children having difficulty with impulse control at 54 months, as operationalized by CPT commission errors. Only the interaction between HOME and CPT commission errors was significant (Wald $\chi^2_{(1)}$=5.36, p=.02). After conducting a median split on HOME scores and CPT commission error scores, we examined the proportion of children in the low and high readiness groups experiencing no risk (high HOME scores and low impulsivity scores), one risk (either low HOME or high impulsivity), or two risks (low HOME and high impulsivity). A chi-square test indicated that group distributions varied significantly ($\chi^2_{(3)}$=84.85, p<.001). Whereas only 8.5% of the children experiencing neither risk were in the low readiness group, 41.1% of those experiencing low stimulation and responsiveness across early childhood and also showing high levels of impulsivity at 54 months were in the low readiness group. Children experiencing just one of these earlier risks (either just a low HOME score or just a high impulsivity score) were in between, with 21.8% and 22.3%, respectively, in the low readiness group. (See Figure 14.1.)

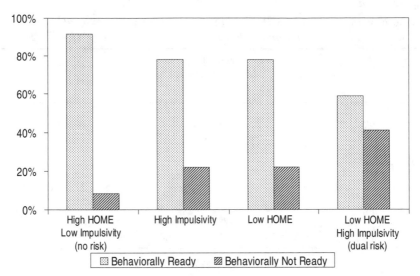

Figure 14.1. Interaction between child impulsivity at 54 months and HOME (6-54 months) as predictors of readiness groups.

A similar set of analyses was conducted on the interaction between CPT omission errors (lapses in attention) and family measures. Again, only the interaction between errors of omission and HOME was significant (Wald $\chi^2_{(1)}$=5.68, <.02). Follow-up tests conducted based on median splits showed a similar pattern ($\chi^2_{(3)}$=80.57, <.001). Children experiencing lower stimulation across early childhood and evidencing more omission errors on the CPT at 54 months were much more likely to be in the low behavioral readiness group in first grade (39.8%), in comparison to children showing neither risk (7.7%) or those with only lower HOME scores (23.7%) or only higher inattention scores (23.1%).

Discussion

These results confirm those of other studies, including findings discussed in companion chapters in this volume (Farkas & Hibel, this volume; Landry & Smith, this volume), indicating that school readiness is strongly associated with sociodemographic indicators and parenting. The data indicate that even in this relatively lower risk sample (i.e., that excluded very young mothers, substance abusing mothers, multiple births, and ill babies), children, especially minority children, living in single-parent households with mothers of a lower educational and income level were more likely to have difficulties adjusting to the behavioral demands and expectations of their first-grade classrooms. These difficulties were compounded when youngsters showed poorer cognitive and language skills and also poorer regulatory skills on laboratory measures of inhibitory and attentional control at 36 and 54 months. These data are important in delineating specific aspects of children's earlier development that predict behavioral control in other contexts, two to three years later. Indeed, children's ability to resist temptation, delay responding by selecting a larger reward over a smaller immediate reward, focus attention, and inhibit impulsive responding at the preschool-age were all linked to teacher ratings of behavioral readiness in first grade.

Errors of omission and commission on the CPT (inattention and impulsivity) were unique predictors of behavioral readiness group over and above demographic indicators, earlier behavior problems, and cognitive measures. This task requires children to self-monitor and focus attention on their own with minimal adult direction. It also requires that children withhold impulsive responses and process visual stimuli carefully and efficiently enough to recognize whether they are seeing a target or a non-target stimulus. Thus, this task may be a good proxy for some of the demands of the first-grade classroom. For example, when children are expected to work independently on worksheets, they are also required to sit still, not call out, monitor their own behavior without teacher intervention, and not respond carelessly because they are rushing through a task. Children who have mastered these self-regulatory skills by 54 months will be better prepared for first grade.

Children in the two behavioral readiness groups also came from very different families. Above and beyond demographic or "social address" indicators (Bronfenbrenner, 1986) of family context, more process-oriented measures of family functioning were important. Mothers whose children were more behaviorally ready for school reported fewer symptoms of depression over the 6- to 54-month period. Lower depression is related to more and better language input (Breznitz & Sherman, 1987; Pan, Rowe, Singer, & Snow, 2005), greater engagement, and better scaffolding of the skills needed for school success (NICHD ECCRN, 1999). In addition, depressive symptoms are associated with both more negative and fewer positive aspects of parenting behavior, and parenting is presumably one mechanism through which maternal depression has an effect on children's cognitive functioning and social-emotional adjustment (Cummings, Davies, & Campbell, 2000; McLoyd, 1998; NICHD ECCRN, 1999). Both maternal depression and maternal sensitivity emerged as significant predictors in some analyses, but not others.

It is also noteworthy that readiness groups differed on 36-month attachment security, with a higher proportion of children in the low behavioral readiness group classified as insecurely attached three years earlier. Several theorists have considered attachment security to be an early and important indicator of young children's ability to regulate their own behavior or to seek support from an attachment figure when their own capacities of self-regulation are being taxed (e.g., Carlson & Sroufe, 1995; Thompson, 1998). One possibility, albeit one beyond the scope of this report, is that children who were insecure, especially those who were disorganized or resistant at 36 months, were also showing poor regulatory skills in other contexts, and having difficulty appropriately utilizing their mothers for support in stressful situations when they required scaffolding, direction, and limit-setting. This may reflect maternal difficulties in providing appropriate guidance, support, and structure (e.g., Kochanska, 1997) as well as children's difficulties in communicating their needs or making use of support when it is offered. Unlike the infancy measure, at 36 months some of the indicators of insecure attachment may reflect coercive and manipulative child behavior (Cassidy, Marvin, & the MacArthur Working Group on Attachment, 1992; Greenberg, Speltz, & DeKlyen, 1993). Further analyses with this data set may allow us to disentangle some of these questions about the role of 36-month attachment security/insecurity in predicting behavioral readiness for school.

Another important finding was that maternal sensitivity differed across readiness groups. First, maternal sensitivity is strongly related to both attachment security and maternal depression, both in the current sample (Campbell et al., 2004; NICHD ECCRN, 1999, 2003) and in other samples (e.g., Cicchetti et al., 1998; DeMulder & Radke-Yarrow, 1991). Second, sensitivity and responsiveness as measured in this and other studies reflect not only warmth, but also support for autonomy and the ability to provide guidance when needed—important hallmarks of relationship quality (Kochanska, 1997). Thus, it is not surprising that maternal sensitivity was a significant predictor of readiness group membership. However, it is also important to consider the possibility of child effects, as analyses indicate that once stability in child behavior problems from 54 months to first grade was considered, maternal sensitivity was no longer a significant predictor of readiness group. Space precluded examining concomitant changes in child behavior problems and maternal sensitivity longitudinally, which might disentangle dynamic and bidirectional relationships between inattentive and noncompliant child behavior and maternal warmth and support for autonomy.

These data also underscore the importance of paternal engagement and sensitivity in predicting children's school readiness. When the quality of father-child interaction was examined as a predictor of readiness group, not only was it significant, but it was also significant over and above maternal sensitivity, indicating that fathers make a unique contribution to the development of regulatory skills in young children (Marsiglio, Amato, Day, & Lamb, 2000; NICHD ECCRN, 2004; Parke & Buriel, 1998). For example, it has been suggested that fathers challenge their children in ways that especially facilitate adaptation beyond the family circle and thus contribute to adjustment to school (NICHD ECCRN, submitted), possibly via effects on peer competence and independence. This is especially noteworthy given the somewhat skewed sample with participating fathers in these analyses.

Overall, the most robust predictor of readiness group membership was the HOME, in predicting over and above child characteristics, including earlier behavior problems. Although the HOME and maternal sensitivity were quite highly correlated, the HOME assesses aspects of relationship quality and maternal warmth, as well as limit-setting and important features of the environment associated with learning and cognitive functioning. This more comprehensive measure of the family environment, then, provided information that went beyond warmth and sensitivity and was an important predictor of aspects of behavioral control that ultimately are necessary for children's school success. In particular, the inclusion of items assessing the literacy environment of the home, support for learning, stimulation of cognitive development, and proactive controls may account for the robustness of this measure and its superiority over a measure focused more specifically on relationship quality. Moreover, the HOME may have fewer demand characteristics than the semi-structured play interaction utilized in this study, which was highly predictive of most outcomes, but still was unlikely to elicit much in the way of harshness or negativity, which were evident to some degree on the HOME.

The interactions between CPT measures and HOME scores highlight the fact that child characteristics, including the ability to monitor and focus attention and the ability to inhibit impulsive responses, can be enhanced by positive, engaged, supportive parenting or undermined when parenting is less engaged and stimulating, and possibly more impatient and negative. Thus, children who experienced both supportive parenting and were able to regulate their own behavior at 54 months were almost uniformly also behaviorally ready for first grade; in contrast with those children who had difficulty regulating their behavior at 54 months and also grew up in less stimulating homes—the latter group was much more likely to be in the low readiness group. However, children appeared to be somewhat protected by more stimulating and proactive parenting in the context of poor regulatory skills; children with good regulatory skills were also somewhat protected from the negative effects of less engaged and stimulating parenting in early childhood.

These data have implications for the early identification of children at risk for difficulties in first grade. Clearly when children are rated high in inattention and externalizing problems, perform poorly on language and cognitive readiness skills, and have difficulty with tasks tapping self-regulation at 54 months, they are at high risk of continuing to experience difficulties at school entry and beyond, as my prior research with hard-to-manage preschool children has clearly demonstrated (Campbell et al., 1994; Campbell et al., 1996; Pierce, Ewing, & Campbell, 1999). The likelihood of emerging school difficulties is also exacerbated when such children live in families lacking the psychological resources to provide adequate support and stimulation for readiness skills and when parenting is either harsh or disengaged. Although programs such as Head Start target many children who will not be ready for school, many other children who live above the poverty level (especially the working poor, but also families with a depressed parent or with other risk factors for children's problems) could also benefit from early interventions aimed at helping them to regulate their behavior and function cooperatively with peers in a school-like setting.

However, just placing children in large groups of similar peers may further exacerbate problems (Hanish et al., 2005); crucial to such prevention and intervention programs will be adequately trained staff, appropriate adult:child ratios, and the inclusion of a component that provides parental guidance and support. Clearly too, as results from several programs suggest, parental motivation and engagement may be one key to whether or not the program will succeed (Brotman et al., 2003; Conduct Problems Prevention Research Group, 1999; Reynolds & Temple, 1998; Webster-Stratton, 1998; Webster-Stratton, Reid, & Hammond, 2001). Teaching parents to be aware of their young children's attention (Landry & Smith, this volume) and problem-solving strategies, as well as providing direction that supports and respects children's autonomy, may also facilitate the emergence of better regulation.

Paternal involvement should be encouraged to the degree that a father is present in the home or is available to participate; the involvement of fathers in early prevention and intervention programs is relatively rare, but when fathers are interested and engaged in their children's early development they appear to scaffold and support children's academic and social competence in ways that differ from the role of mothers (NICHD ECCRN, 2004, submitted).

In addition, attention to maternal depression is important, as both father involvement and more positive parenting from both parents are likely to be associated with the level of maternal depressive symptoms. Although some evidence suggests that changing maternal feelings of competence in the parenting role also affects maternal mood (Patterson, DeGarmo, & Forgatch, 2004), other studies suggest that maternal depression may set other disruptive family processes in motion (Hammen, 2002). Given a systems perspective on parenting and children's school functioning, interventions at multiple levels will be more likely to lead to positive and lasting change than short-term approaches to isolated problems (Conduct Problems Prevention Research Group, 1999; Reynolds & Temple, 1998).

Taken together, behavioral readiness for school is multi-determined. The goal of making all children ready for school will require as much attention to behavioral readiness as it will to academic readiness. Prevention and intervention programs must cast a wider net in selecting children for participation, provide supportive environments that enhance children's regulatory strategies and prosocial skills, as well as their readiness for academics, and to the degree possible help parents help their children make the transition to school.

Acknowledgments

The data reported in this chapter were collected under the auspices of the multi-site NICHD Study of Early Child Care. We acknowledge the generous support of the National Institute of Child Health and Human Development (Grant No. U10-HD25420) to the Pittsburgh site (Susan B. Campbell, PI). We would like to thank the many investigators who designed the larger study, the site coordinators and research assistants who collected the data, and the children and families who continue to participate in this longitudinal study.

References

Achenbach, T. M. (1991). *Manual for the Teacher Report Form and profile.* Burlington: University of Vermont, Department of Psychiatry.

Ainsworth, M. D. S., Blehar, M., Waters, E., & Wall, S. (1978). *Patterns of attachment.* Hillsdale, NJ: Erlbaum.

Alexander, K. L. & Entwisle, D. R. (1988) Achievement in the first two years of school. *Monographs of the Society for Research in Child Development, 53* (Serial No. 218, Whole No. 2).

Barbarin, O. A. (1999). Social risks and psychological adjustment: A comparison of African American and South African children. *Child Development, 70,* 1348–1359.

Bates, J., Pettit, G., Dodge, K. A., & Ridge, B. (1998). Interaction of temperamental resistance to control and restrictive parenting in the development of externalizing behavior. *Developmental Psychology, 34,* 982–995.

Belsky, J., Hsieh, K. H., & Crnic, K. (1998). Mothering, fathering, and infant negativity as antecedents of boys' externalizing problems and inhibition at age 3 years: Differential susceptibility to rearing experience? *Development and Psychopathology, 10,* 301–319.

Bracken, B. A. (1984). *Bracken Basic Concept Scale-Revised.* San Antonio, TX: The Psychological Corporation, Harcourt Brace and Company.

Bretherton, I. (1985). Attachment theory: retrospect and prospect. In I. Bretherton & E.Waters (Eds.), *Growing points in attachment theory and research.* Monographs of the Society for Research in Child Development, *50* (Serial No. 209), 3–35.

Bretherton, I. (1990). Open communication and internal working models: Their role in the development of attachment relationships. In R. Thompson (Ed.), *Nebraska symposium on motivation: Vol. 36* (pp. 59–113). Lincoln: University of Nebraska Press.

Bretherton, I. (1991). Intentional communication and the development of an understanding of mind. In D. Frye & C. Moore (Eds.), *Children's theories of mind: Mental states and social understanding* (pp. 49–75). Hillsdale, NJ: Erlbaum.

Breznitz, Z., & Sherman, T. (1987). Speech patterning of natural discourse of well and depressed mothers and their young children. *Child Development, 58,* 395–400.

Bronfenbrenner U. (1986). The ecology of the family as a context for human development: A research perspective. *Developmental Psychology, 22,* 723–742.

Brotman, L. M., Klein, R. G., Kamboukos, D., Brown, E., Coard, S. I., & Sosinsky, L. S. (2003). Preventive intervention for low-income preschoolers at familial risk for conduct problems. *Journal of Clinical Child and Adolescent Psychology, 32,* 246–257.

Brown, J. R., & Dunn, J. (1996). Continuities in emotion understanding from three to six years. *Child Development, 67,* 789–803.

Caldwell, B. M., & Bradley, R. H. (1984). *Home observation for measurement of the environment.* Little Rock: University of Arkansas.

Campbell, S. B. (2002). *Behavior problems in preschool children: Clinical and developmental issues* (2nd Ed.). New York: Guilford Press.

Campbell, S. B., Brownell, C. A., Hungerford, A., Spieker, S., Mohan, R., & Blessing, J. (2004). The course of maternal depressive symptoms and maternal sensitivity as predictors of attachment security at 36 months. *Development and Psychopathology, 16,* 231–252.

Campbell, S. B., Cohn, J. F., & Meyers, T. (1995). Depression in first-time mothers: Mother-infant interaction and depression chronicity. *Developmental Psychology, 31*, 349–357.

Campbell, S. B., , Matestic, P., von Stauffenberg, C., Mohan, R., & Kirchener, T. (submitted). Trajectories of maternal depressive symptoms, maternal sensitivity and children's functioning at school entry.

Campbell, S. B., Pierce, E. W., March, C. L., Ewing, L. J., & Szumowski, E. K. (1994). Hard-to-manage preschool boys: Symptomatic behavior across contexts and time. *Child Development, 65,* 836–851.

Campbell, S. B., Pierce, E. W., Moore, G., Marakovitz, S., & Newby, K. (1996). Boys' externalizing problems at elementary school: Pathways from early behavior problems, maternal control, and family stress. *Development and Psychopathology, 8,* 701–720.

Carlson, E. A., & Sroufe, L. A. (1995). The contribution of attachment theory to developmental psychopathology. In D. Cicchetti & D. Cohen (Eds.), *Developmental processes and psychopathology: Vol. I. Theoretical perspectives and methodological approaches* (pp. 581–617). New York: Cambridge University Press.

Cassidy, J., Marvin, R. S., & the MacArthur Working Group on Attachment. (1992). *Attachment organization in preschool children: Procedures and coding manual.* Unpublished coding manual, The Pennsylvania State University.

Chase-Lansdale, P. L., & Gordon, R. L. (1996). Economic hardship and the development of 5- and 6-year-olds: Neighborhood and regional perspectives. *Child Development, 67,* 3338–3367.

Cicchetti, D., Rogosch, F. A., & Toth, S. L. 1998. Maternal depressive disorder and contextual risk: Contributions to the development of attachment insecurity and behavior problems in toddlerhood. *Development and Psychopathology, 10,* 283–300.

Clark, K. E., & Ladd, G. W. (2000). Connectedness and autonomy support in parent-child relationships: Links to children's socioemotional orientation and peer relationships. *Developmental Psychology, 4,* 485–498.

Cohen, N. J., Davine, M., & Meloche-Kelly, M. (1989). Prevalence of unsuspected language disorders in a child psychiatric population. *Journal of the American Academy of Child and Adolescent Psychiatry, 28,* 107–111.

Cole, P. M., Teti, L. O., & Zahn-Waxler, C. (2003). Mutual emotion regulation and the stability of conduct problems between preschool and early school age. *Development and Psychopathology, 15,* 1–18.

Conduct Problems Prevention Research Group. (1992). A developmental and clinical model for the prevention of Conduct Disorder: The FAST Track Program. *Development and Psychopathology, 4,* 509–527.

Conduct Problems Prevention Research Group. (1999). Initial impact of the Fast Track Prevention trial for conduct problems: I. The high-risk sample. *Journal of Consulting and Clinical Psychology, 67,* 631–647.

Crockenberg, S., & Litman, C. (1990). Autonomy as competence in 2-year olds: Maternal correlates of child defiance, compliance and self-assertion. *Developmental Psychology, 26,* 961–971.

Cummings, E. M., & Davies, P. T. (1994). Maternal depression and child development. *Journal of Child Psychology and Psychiatry, 35,* 73–112.

Cummings, E. M., Davies, P. T., & Campbell, S. B. (2000). *Developmental psychopathology and family process: Theory, research, and clinical implications.* New York: Guilford Press.

Deater-Deckard, K., Dodge, K. A., Bates, J. E., & Pettit, G. S. (1998). Multiple risk factors in the development of externalizing behavior problems: Group and individual differences. *Development and Psychopathology, 10,* 469–493.

DeMulder, E. K., & Radke-Yarrow, M. (1991). Attachment with affectively ill and well mothers: Concurrent behavioral correlates. *Development and Psychopathology, 3,* 227–242.

Denham, S. A., Workman, E., Cole, P.M., Weissbrod, C., Kendziora, K.T., & Zahn-Waxler, C. (2000). Prediction of behavior problems from early to middle childhood: The role of parental socialization and emotion expression. *Development and Psychopathology, 12,* 23–45.

DeWolff, M., & van IJzendoorn, M. (1997). Sensitivity and attachment: A meta-analysis on parental antecedents of infant attachment. *Child Development, 68,* 571-591.

Dorn, S. (1998). The political legacy of school accountability systems. *Education Policy Analysis Archives, 6,* 1–34.

Downey, G., & Coyne, J. C. (1990). Children of depressed parents: An integrative review. *Psychological Bulletin, 108,* 50–76.

Duncan, G. J., Brooks-Gunn, J., & Klebanov, P. K. (1994). Economic deprivation and early childhood development. *Child Development, 65,* 296–319.

Eisenberg, N., & Fabes, R. A. (1998). Prosocial development. In N. Eisenberg (Vol. Ed.), *Handbook of child psychology: Social, emotional, and personality development, Vol. 2* (pp. 701778). New York: Wiley.

Eisenberg, N., Fabes, R. A., Guthrie, I. K., Murphy, B. C., Maszk, P., Holmgren, R., & Suh, K. (1996). The relations of regulation and emotionality to problem behavior in elementary school children. *Development and Psychopathology, 8,* 141–162.

Gadow, K. D., Sprafkin, J., & Nolan, E .E. (2001). DSM-IV symptoms in community and clinic preschool children. *Journal of the American Academy of Child and Adolescent Psychiatry, 40,* 1383–1392

Gardner, F. E. (1987). Positive interaction between mothers and conduct-problem children: Is there training for harmony as well as fighting? *Journal of Abnormal Child Psychology, 15,* 283–293.

Greenberg, M. T., Speltz, M. L., & DeKlyen, M. (1993). The role of attachment in the early development of disruptive behavior problems. *Development and Psychopathology, 5,* 191–213.

Hammen, C. (2002). Context of stress in families of children with depressed parents. In S. H. Goodman & I. H. Gotlib (Eds.), *Children of depressed parents: Mechanisms of risk and implications for treatment* (pp. 175–199). Washington, DC: American Psychological Association.

Hanish, L. D., Martin, C. L., Fabes, R. A., Leonard. S., & Herzog, M. (2005). Exposure to externalizing peers in early childhood: Homophily and peer contagion processes. *Journal of Abnormal Child Psychology, 33,* 267–281.

Harrist, A, W., Pettit, G. S., Dodge, F, A. & Bates, J. E. (1994). Dyadic synchrony in mother-child interaction: Relation with children's subsequent kindergarten adjustment. *Family Relations, 43,* 417–424.

Hinshaw, S. (1992). Externalizing behavior problems and academic underachievement in childhood and adolescence: Causal relationships and underlying mechanisms. *Psychological Bulletin, 111,* 127155.

Kagan, S., Moore, E., & Bredekamp, S. (1995). *Reconsidering children's early development and learning: Toward common views and vocabulary.* Washington, DC: National Education Goals Panel.

Kochanska, G. (1997). Mutually responsive orientation between mothers and their young children: Implications for early socialization. *Child Development, 68,* 94–112.

Kochanska, G., & Aksan, N. (2004). Development of mutual responsiveness between parents and their young children. *Child Development, 75,* 1657–1676.

Kochanska, G., Aksan, N., Knaack, A., & Rhines, H. M. (2004). Maternal parenting and children's conscience: Early security as moderator. *Child Development, 75,* 1229–1242.

Kochanska, G., Aksan, N., & Nichols, K. E. (2003). Maternal power assertion in discipline and moral discourse contexts: Commonalities, differences, and implications for children's moral conduct and cognition. *Developmental Psychology, 39,* 949–963.

Kochanska, G., & Knaack, A. (2003). Effortful control as a personality characteristic of young children: Antecedents, correlates, and consequences. *Journal of Personality, 71,* 1087–1112.

Kochanska, G., Murray, K.T., & Harlan, E. (2000). Effortful control in early childhood: Continuity and change, antecedents, and implications for social development. *Developmental Psychology, 36,* 220–232.

Kohen, D., Brooks-Gunn, J., Leventhal, T., & Hertzman, C. (2002). Neighborhood income and physical and social disorder in Canada: Associations with young children's competencies. *Child Development, 73,* 1844–1860.

Kopp, C. (1989). Regulation of distress and negative emotions: A developmental view. *Developmental Psychology, 25,* 343–354.

Ladd, G. W. -(1990). Having friends, keeping friends, making friends, and being liked by peers in the classroom: predictors of children's early school adjustment? *Child Development, 61,* 1081–1100.

Ladd, G. W., Birch, S. H., & Buhs, E. (1999). Children's social and scholastic lives in kindergarten: Related spheres of influence? *Child Development, 70,* 1373–1400.

Ladd, G. W., Kochenderfer, B. J., & Coleman, C. C. (1996). Friendship quality as a predictor of young children's early school adjustment. *Child Development, 67,* 1103–1118.

Ladd, G. W., Kochenderfer, B. J., & Coleman, C. C. (1997). Classroom peer acceptance, friendship, and victimization: Distinct relational systems that contribute uniquely to children's school adjustment? *Child Development, 68,* 1181–1197.

Laible, D., & Thompson, R. (2000). Mother-child discourse, attachment security, shared positive affect, and early conscience development. *Child Development, 71,* 1424–1440.

Lin, H. L., Lawrence, F. R., & Gorrell, J. (2003). Kindergarten teachers' views of school readiness. *Early Childhood Research Quarterly, 18,* 225–237.

Maccoby, E. E., & Martin, J. A. (1983). Socialization in the context of the family: Parent-child interaction. In E. M. Hetherington (Ed.), *Handbook of child psychology, Vol. IV. Socialization, personality, and social development* (pp. 1–101). New York: Wiley.

Marsiglio, W., Amato, P., Day, R., & Lamb, M. E. (2000). Scholarship on fatherhood in the 1990s and beyond: Past impressions, future prospects. *Journal of Marriage and the Family, 62,* 1173–1191.

McClelland, M., & Morrison, F. J. (2003). The emergence of learning-related social skills in preschool children. *Early Childhood Research Quarterly, 18,* 206–224.

McLoyd, V. C. (1990). The impact of economic hardship on Black families and children: psychological distress, parenting, and socio-emotional development. *Child Development, 61,* 311–346.

McLoyd, V. C. (1998). Socioeconomic disadvantage and child development. *American Psychologist, 53,* 185–204.

NICHD Early Child Care Research Network (1999) Chronicity of maternal depressive symptoms, maternal sensitivity, and child functioning at 36 months. *Developmental Psychology, 35,* 1297–1310.

NICHD Early Child Care Research Network. (2001). Child care and family predictors of MacArthur preschool attachment and stability from infancy. *Developmental Psychology, 37,* 847–862.

NICHD Early Child Care Research Network. (2003a). Do children's attention processes mediate the link between family predictors and school readiness? *Developmental Psychology, 39,* 581–593.

NICHD Early Child Care Research Network. (2003b).Social functioning in first grade: Associations with earlier home and child care predictors and with current classroom experiences. *Child Development, 74,* 1639–1662.

NICHD Early Child Care Research Network. (2004). Father's and mother's parenting behavior and beliefs as predictors of child social adjustment in the transition to school. *Journal of Family Psychology, 18,* 628–638.

NICHD Early Child Care Research Network. (2005). Predicting individual differences in attention, memory, and planning in first graders from experiences at home, child care, and school. *Developmental Psychology, 41,* 99–114.

NICHD Early Child Care Research Network. (submitted). *The impact of fathers' support for child autonomy on early achievement in school.*

Pan, B. A., Rowe, M. L., Singer, J. D., & Snow, C.E . (2005). Maternal correlates of growth in toddler vocabulary production in low-income families. *Child Development, 76,* 763–782.

Parke, R. D., & Buriel, R. (1998). Socialization in the family: Ethnic and ecological perspectives. In N. Eisenberg (Ed.), *Handbook of child psychology: Vol. 3. Social, emotional, and personality development* (5th ed., pp. 463–552). New York: Wiley.

Patterson, G. R., DeGarmo, D., & Forgatch, M. S. (2004). Systematic changes in families following prevention trials. *Journal of Abnormal Child Psychology, 32,* 621–634.

Patterson, G. R., Reid, J. B., & Dishion, T. J. (1992). *Antisocial boys.* Eugene, OR: Castalia.

Pianta, R. (1999). *Enhancing relationships between children and teachers.* Washington, DC: American Psychological Association.

Pianta, R., & McCoy, S. (1997). The first day of school: The predictive validity of early school screening. *Journal of Applied Developmental Psychology, 18,* 1–22.

Pianta, R., Steinberg, M., & Rollins, K. (1995). The first two years of school: Teacher-child relationships and deflections in children's social adjustment. *Development and Psychopathology, 7,* 295–312.

Pierce, E. W., Ewing, L. J., & Campbell, S. B. (1999). Diagnostic status and symptomatic behavior of hard-to-manage preschool children in middle childhood and early adolescence. *Journal of Clinical Child Psychology, 28,* 48–57.

Radloff, L. S. (1977). A CES-D Scale: A self-report depression scale for research in the general population. *Applied Psychological Measurement, 1*, 385–401.

Reynell, J. (1991). *Reynell Developmental Language Scales* (U.S. Ed.). Los Angeles: Western Psychological Service.

Reynolds, A., & Temple, J. (1998). Extended early childhood intervention and school achievement: Age 13 findings from the Chicago Longitudinal Study. *Child Development, 69*, 231–246.

Rimm-Kaufmann, S. E., Pianta, R. C., & Cox, M. J. (2000). Teacher's judgments of problems in the transition to kindergarten. *Early Childhood Research Quarterly, 15*, 147–166.

Rosvold, H. E., Mirsky, A. E, Sarason, I., Bransome, E. D. J., & Beck, L. H. (1956). A Continuous Performance Test of brain damage. *Journal of Consulting Psychology, 20*, 343–350.

Rothbart, M. K., & Bates, J. E. (1998). Temperament. In N. Eisenberg (Vol. Ed.), *Handbook of child psychology: Vol. 3. Social, emotional, and personality development* (5th ed., pp. 105–176). New York: Wiley.

Rothbart, M. K., Posner, M. L., & Hershey, K. (1995). Temperament, attention, and developmental psychopathology. In D. Cicchetti & D. J. Cohen (Eds.), *Developmental psychopathology. Vol. I. Theoretical perspectives and methodological approaches* (pp. 315–340). New York: Wiley.

Rubin, K. H., Burgess, K. B., Dwyer, K. M., & Hastings, P. D. (2003). Predicting preschoolers' externalizing behaviors from toddler temperament, conflict, and maternal negativity. *Developmental Psychology, 39*, 164–176.

Ruff, H. A., & Rothbart, M. K. (1996). *Attention in early development: Themes and variations.* Oxford, UK: Oxford University Press.

Sameroff, A. J., & Chandler, M. J. (1975). Reproductive risk and the continuum of caretaking casualty. In F. D. Horowitz (Ed.), *Review of child development research* (Vol. 4., pp. 187–241). Chicago: University of Chicago Press.

Spira, E., & Fischel, J. E. (2005). The impact of preschool inattention, hyperactivity, and impulsivity on social and academic development: A review. *Journal of Child Psychology and Psychiatry, 46*, 755–773.

Sroufe, L. A. (1983). Infant-caregiver attachment and patterns of adaptation in preschool: The roots of maladaptation and competence In M. Perlmutter (Ed.), *The Minnesota Symposium on child psychology: Vol.16. Development and policy concerning children with special needs* (pp. 41–83). Hillsdale, NJ: Erlbaum.

Sroufe, L. A., & Fleeson, J. (1986). Attachment and the construction of relationships. In W. Hartup & Z. Rubin (Eds.), *Relationships and development* (pp. 51–71). Hillsdale, NJ: Erlbaum.

Shonkoff, J. P., & Phillips, D. A. (2000). *From neurons to neighborhoods: The science of early childhood development.* Washington, DC: National Academy Press.

Thomas, A., Chess, S., & Birch, H. G. (1968). *Temperament and behavior disorders in children.* New York: New York University Press.

Thompson, R. A. (1998). Early sociopersonality development. In N. Eisenberg (Vol. Ed.), *Handbook of child psychology: Vol. 3 Social, emotional, and personality development* (5th ed., pp. 25–104). New York: Wiley.

Webster-Stratton, C. (1998). Preventing conduct problems in Head Start children: Strengthening parent competencies. *Journal of Consulting and Clinical Psychology, 66*, 715–730.

Webster-Stratton, C., Reid, M. J., & Hammond, M. (2001). Preventing conduct problems, promoting social competence: A parent and teacher training partnership in Head Start. *Journal of Clinical Child Psychology, 30,* 283–302.

Wesley, P. W., & Buysse, V. (2003). Making meaning of school readiness in schools and communities. *Early Childhood Research Quarterly, 18,* 351–375.

Woodcock, R. W., & Johnson, M. B. (1989). *Woodcock-Johnson Psycho-Educational Battery—Revised.* Chicago: Riverside.

Woodcock, R. W., & Johnson, M. G. (1990). *Woodcock- Johnson Psycho-Educational Battery-Revised.* Allen, TX: DLM Teaching Resources.

Yeung, J., Linver, M., & Brooks-Gunn, J. (2002). How money matters for young children's development: Parental investment and family processes. *Child Development, 73,* 1861–1879.

Zahn-Waxler, C., Iannotti, R. J., Cummings, E. M., & Denham, S. (1990). Antecedents of problem behaviors in children of depressed mothers. *Development and Psychopathology, 2,* 271–291.

Zahn-Waxler, C., Radke-Yarrow, M., & King, R. K. (1979). Childrearing and children's prosocial initiations toward victims of distress. *Child Development, 50,* 319–330.

Zahn-Waxler, C., Schmitz, S., Fulker, D. W., Robinson, J., & Emde, R. (1996). Behavior problems in 5-year-old monozygotic and dizygotic twins: Genetic and environmental influences, patterns of regulation and internalization of control. *Development and Psychopathology, 8,* 103–122.

Zimmerman, I., Steiner, V., & Pond, R. (1979). *Preschool language scale.* Columbus, OH: Merrill.

15

USING DEVELOPMENTAL EVIDENCE ON BEHAVIORAL SCHOOL READINESS TO INFORM PREVENTION AND POLICY

Hirokazu Yoshikawa
Harvard University

Erin Brooke Godfrey
New York University

In their chapter, Campbell and von Stauffenberg (this volume) presented a detailed and sophisticated analysis of the relationship between family processes in early childhood and behavioral school readiness in the first grade. Using rich data from the NICHD Early Child Care and Youth Development study, the authors examined how early child emotional and behavioral functioning, parent human capital, socioeconomic status, and parenting practices influence children's externalizing (acting-out) behaviors and attention problems in the transition to first grade.

Campbell and von Stauffenberg's chapter is of particular theoretical and methodological relevance to developmentalists who study school readiness. First, the authors provided a comprehensive review of the behavioral challenges inherent in the transition to school, as well as a strong theoretical framework linking child and family characteristics to behavioral school readiness. Second, the authors addressed both children's early self-regulation (as measured through resistance to temptation, inattention, and impulsivity) and behavior problems. The interplay of these two aspects of socioemotional development is of considerable theoretical interest. Third, the analysis included data on father sensitivity. The inclusion of father data allowed the authors to examine the relative influence of paternal versus maternal sensitivity on child behavior problems.

From a methodological standpoint, the chapter is innovative in its presentation of data from multiple sources and multiple time points across the first five years of life. The combination of parent- and teacher-reported data, videotaped observation, and direct child assessments provides a comprehensive look at the predictors of children's classroom behavior in the first grade. In addition, the authors employed residualized-change models to address the possibility of selection bias, and directly compare models that control for earlier child outcomes with those that do not. Given the longitudinal structure of the data set, this technique is an effective way to guard against selection or omitted-variables bias, strengthening the causal inference that can be made (e.g., NICHD Early Child Care Research Network & Duncan, 2003).

The results of this analysis suggest that both early child behaviors and family process variables are important contributors to first-grade behavior. As predicted, the authors found links between self-regulatory ability (i.e., resistance to temptation), receptive and expressive language, and insecure attachment at 36 months, delay of gratification, impulsivity and inattention, language development, and Woodcock-Johnson tests of pre-academic skills at 54 months, and teacher-reported behavior problems in the first grade. The authors also found that impulsivity and inattention at 54 months contributed over and above 54-month teacher-reported child behavior in the prediction of first-grade readiness groups. This is powerful evidence of the role of early self-regulation in predicting later classroom behavior. In addition, family variables such as maternal depression, maternal sensitivity and paternal sensitivity were found to predict membership in teacher-reported school readiness groups, in expected directions. Interestingly, when paternal sensitivity was included in the same model with maternal depression and sensitivity, only paternal sensitivity remained a significant predictor of behavioral school readiness. This finding is similar to work on the Early Head Start data set, where father sensitivity was found to predict cognitive school readiness over and above mother sensitivity (Tamis-LeMonda, Shannon, Cabrera, & Lamb, 2004).

Testing Alternative Developmental Hypotheses in the Relation between Family Processes and Behavioral School Readiness

The findings presented in this chapter are quite provocative and raise fundamental questions about the development of behavioral school readiness. Children's behavior arises through a complex interplay between child characteristics, family processes, and other environmental factors over time (Gottlieb, 2002). In the NICHD, data on many important family-process constructs, including income-to-needs ratios, mother's marital status, maternal depression, maternal sensitivity, and the HOME assessment, as well as indicators of children's emotion regulation and behavior problems, were collected at multiple time points in the first five years of life. The data thus provide the opportunity to test a variety of reciprocal and unidirectional hypotheses about the causal influence of family processes and developing child behaviors in the first years of life. In the Campbell and von Stauffenberg study, when family process variables were used to model behavioral school readiness in the first grade, they were entered as averages across multiple assessment points. This approach, although powerful in suggesting composite, stable effects of family processes on behavioral school readiness, leaves some key questions about the dynamic interplay between family and child characteristics in the development of behavioral school readiness unexplored.

For example, one of the most noteworthy findings was that once teacher-reported behavior at 54 months was controlled, maternal depression, maternal sensitivity and paternal sensitivity were no longer significant predictors of school readiness groups. This residualized change analysis suggests that the causal relation between parental sensitivity and behavioral school readiness may occur *earlier* than 54 months. Causal influences of parental sensitivity on behavior may occur at several possible points in time. One possibility is that parental sensitivity causally influences child socioemotional indicators across infancy and early childhood, with little influence in the reverse direction (we might call this a cross-period, unidirectional model of causation; depicted in Figure 15.1). A second possibility is that parental sensitivity exerts its influence on socioemotional indicators very early in development, with those indicators remaining essentially stable (though likely changing in form) later in the early childhood years. We might call this an early, unidirectional causal model (depicted in Figure 15.2). Finally, a third possibility is that reciprocal influence between parent sensitivity and socio-emotional indicators occurs across the first five years of life. We term this a reciprocal causal model (depicted in Figure 15.3).

Modeling path analyses with unidirectional and reciprocal relationships between parental sensitivity and children's early behavior would be an effective way to distinguish between these alternative developmental possibilities. As illustrated in Figures 15.1–15.3, models with alternate pathways between sensitivity and behavior at three time points could be tested against each other as nested models. Models similar to these were recently tested on an adolescent sample in Eisenberg et al. (2005).

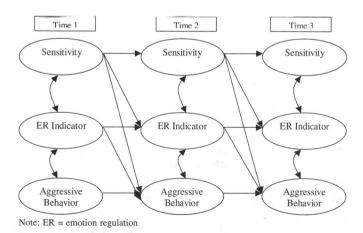

Note: ER = emotion regulation

Figure 15.1. Cross-period unidirectional causal model.

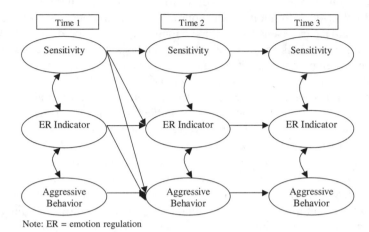

Figure 15.2. Early unidirectional causal model.

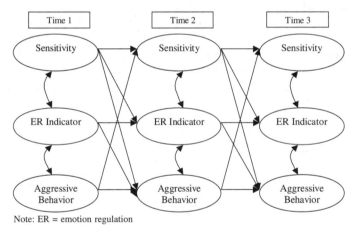

Figure 15.3. Reciprocal causal model.

The most robust family process finding presented by Campbell and von Stauffenberg involved the HOME assessment, a composite measure of home environment. Of all the parent and family variables, only the HOME remained a significant predictor of behavioral school readiness groups after controlling for teacher-reported behavior at 54 months. This may be surprising; however, as the authors pointed out; the HOME incorporates a wide variety of constructs related to parenting and the home environment, and is coded from observations that may be somewhat more naturalistic than videotaped interactions. The HOME variable used in the models was also an average of assessments made at 6, 15, 36, and 54 months. We therefore cannot determine the developmental time at which the constructs assessed by the HOME exert their greatest influence. Future work could model change in the HOME between particular time points (6–15 months; 15–36 months; 36–54 months, for example) to more finely pinpoint developmental mechanisms. In addition, synergistic risk interactions were found between the HOME and both impulsivity and inattention in predicting behavioral school readiness. These interactions might indicate that children who are high on impulsivity and/or inattention and have a less stimulating and stable home environment are at the greatest risk for being behaviorally unready for school. However, the interactions are somewhat hard to interpret because the HOME was averaged across 6 to 54 months whereas impulsivity and inattention were measured only at 54 months. This approach ignores the possibility that aspects of the home environment might have had an effect on impulsivity and inattention at 54 months.

In addition to elucidating the interplay between family context and early child characteristics, modeling path analyses would also highlight important developmental trajectories in behavioral school readiness itself. If the trajectory of behavioral school readiness is set by 54 months, it may be less amenable to influences. One indicator of this would be the stability of teacher-reported child behavior (CBCL) between 54 months and the first grade. The models presented in Figures 15.1–15.3 would test for the stability of aggressive and inattentive behavior between these two developmental periods. Finally, the role of parental sensitivity in first-grade behavior could be more fully explored by asking: Does *change* in parental sensitivity relate to *change* in CBCL between 54 months and first grade? Modeling change in predictors as well as outcomes can be particularly useful in identifying developmental processes.

As developmentalists have begun to focus attention on the role of reciprocal influences and change processes in development, they have also become increasingly concerned with delineating the specific aspects of the family context, as well as other contexts, that might affect child development. Attention to these aspects is important not only for understanding basic developmental processes, but for identifying key targets for intervention. Unfortunately, we do not know which aspects of the home environment tapped by the HOME were actually responsible for the association between the assessment and behavioral school readiness. Was cognitive stimulation the key factor? Or was it parental warmth? What role might limit setting or family activities play? Prior work (including studies conducted by the first author of this study) suggests that some aspects of the home environment may be more central to behavioral school readiness than others (Campbell, 2002).

One of the most intriguing findings of this chapter was the large difference found between behavioral school readiness groups in the percentage of mothers classified as "not stably married". In the "ready-for-school" group, 28% of children had mothers who were not stably married, whereas this percentage jumped to 51% among children in the "less-ready-for-school" group. Even in multivariate models with other demographics entered, marital status was still a *highly* significant predictor (see Model I in Table 14.3) of readiness-group membership. Thus, there is some compelling evidence that family structure plays an important role in behavioral school readiness.

The particular family structure pattern that contributes most to developmental differences in behavioral school readiness could be clarified. According to the authors' definition, mothers who endorsed being single, divorced, widowed, or living with a domestic partner at any time during the study period were all labeled as "not stably married." Thus, any mother cohabiting with a partner, even for the entire span of the child's life, would be considered "not stably married," as would a mother who experienced divorce or the death of her spouse. It would be interesting to distinguish between these family structure patterns as well as explore the dynamics of these relationships. In addition, how do parenting and the quality of the home environment mediate the association between family structure and children's behavioral adjustment? Given that mother's relationship and marital status were assessed at multiple points in children's early development, analyses could examine relationship trajectories and marital instability.

Future work could also consider certain dimensions of parenting that are particularly important for children's emotional development. Emotional expressivity and emotion labeling, for example, are important parent and family environment factors that influence children's early emotional development (Raver, 2002). How would these constructs fare in this model, if they were added?

Building Implications for Prevention and Policy from Information on Developmental Mechanisms

As many have noted, "basic" developmental research can have a productive and reciprocal relationship with the development of prevention and policy approaches (Shonkoff, 2000; Stokes, 1997; Yoshikawa & Hsueh, 2001). The oft-cited dichotomy between "basic" and "applied" developmental science is at best a heuristic and at worst a barrier to considering the ways in which different forms of science can contribute to facilitating the well-being of children. However, "basic," or non-intervention-based, developmental research can be more or less useful in implying specific approaches to the setting, timing, intensity, and content of preventive intervention.

The current study has potentially strong implications for how parent-focused programs in early childhood could be strengthened to increase their preventive impact on subsequent behavior problems. In the discussion of their findings, the authors suggested developing child-focused interventions to promote self-regulation and social competence with peers. For example, they recommended teaching parents, caregivers and/or teachers to be aware of their young children's attention and problem-solving strategies. These are important suggestions. However, clearer lessons may be be drawn from this study about when and how to intervene.

Timing of Interventions

As discussed above, the fact that controlling for 54-month teacher reported behavior (CBCL scores) eliminates the association between parental sensitivity and first-grade CBCL scores does not mean that parental sensitivity does not exert a causal influence on child behavior prior to 54 months. Using this data set, researchers can model the differential effects of changes in maternal sensitivity at particular time periods during the first five years of life. Information of this kind could be very revealing about how early parent-focused interventions should be implemented for this population.

The three competing causal models presented in Figures 15.1–15.3 are not only important from a developmental point of view; they have very different implications for prevention programs focused on family processes. For example, if the early unidirectional causal model holds, parent-focused interventions to increase sensitivity would be most powerful very early in development, and less powerful later on. If either of the other two models hold, there is a rationale for such intervention across the first years of life. Modeling these alternative developmental hypotheses would provide powerful guidance for targeting particular points in infancy and early childhood for parent-focused programs.

Content of Interventions

The composite measure of home environment, the HOME, appears to be powerful in influencing first-grade externalizing behavior. However, we have noted that the particular aspects of the home environment that are most influential on first-grade behavior are not clear. For this reason, the focus and content of an intervention program stemming from these data are also unclear. Statistical models like the ones suggested above would help tease apart the particular family processes to be targeted via intervention. If components of the HOME tapping sensitivity, for example, are particularly powerful in predicting first-grade behavioral school readiness, interventions such as the PALS program (Landry & Smith, this volume) could be targeted to the ages and populations suggested by the NICHD data set analyses. If, on the other hand, indicators of resources in the home also show a strong influence, efforts to increase resources and the amount of cognitively stimulating materials in the home could also be tested in addition to interventions that target sensitivity and responsiveness. Policies that increase income for parents in poverty, for example, could be combined with the PALS approach for a potentially larger preventive effect (Huston et al., 2001).

Information on how contexts outside the home determine or moderate the associations presented in this study could also help inform interventions to prevent behavior problems in young children. The current study could be expanded, for example, to include information on childcare, preschool, and first-grade classroom environments. Given the rich data available in the NICHD concerning the process and structural characteristics of each of these contexts, future analyses could incorporate these constructs. For example, does the quality of these early school experiences add to the predictions one can make from earlier child behavior and family processes? Is the impact of family processes on child behavior enhanced or mitigated by early school environments? These mesosystem-level analyses would provide valuable specifics on how interventions focused on care environments of young children could be combined with specific parent-focused intervention to prevent the development of serious behavioral difficulties in children.

Targeting of Interventions

Given limited resources, which populations of children/families should be targeted for family-focused, preventive intervention? Campbell and von Stauffenberg's results suggest that children high in impulsivity and inattention in the preschool years may be particularly at risk for the negative influence of poorer home environments. Thus, parenting interventions that target children with high levels of impulsivity and inattention might be particularly effective. The authors are correct in stating that non-poor children like those in the majority of the NICHD study have been nearly totally neglected in the field of early childhood intervention. These findings suggest an important subgroup of the larger population that would benefit from intervention.

Targeting of populations must consider not just sets of individuals, but service systems within which populations are accessible. Pre-kindergarten programs are increasing their coverage across the country. In some locations, these programs are designed for a universal population with characteristics more similar to the sample in the NICHD than the children targeted for Head Start. These pre-kindergarten programs, then, are an appropriate set of service systems within which to implement universally targeted interventions designed to prevent behavioral school readiness problems. The integration of high-quality prevention efforts in large-scale service systems shows promise not only in promoting positive development in young children, but in improving the quality of programs at the state and local levels (Yoshikawa & Knitzer, 1997).

References

Campbell, S. B. (2002). *Behavior problems in preschool children: Clinical and developmental issues—Second edition.* New York: Guilford Press.

Duncan, G. J., Dowsett, C., Brooks-Gunn, J., Claessens, A., Duckworth, K., Engel, M., Feinstein, L., Japel, C., Huston, A. C., Klebanov, P., Magnuson, K. A., Pagani, L., & Sexton, H. (2005). *School readiness and later achievement.* Manuscript under review.

Eisenberg, N., Zhou, Q., Spinrad, T. L., Valiente, C., Fabes, R.A., & Liew, J. (2005). Relations among positive parenting, children's effortful control, and externalizing problems: A three-wave longitudinal study. *Child Development, 76,* 1055–1071.

Gottlieb, G. (2002). *Individual development and evolution: The genesis of novel behavior.* Mahwah, NJ: Erlbaum.

Huston, A. C., Duncan, G. J., Granger, R., Bos, H., McLoyd, V. C., Mistry, R., et al. (2001). Work-based antipoverty programs for parent can enhance the school performance and social behavior of children. *Child Development, 72,* 318–336.

NICHD Early Child Care Research Network & Duncan, G. J. (2003). Modeling the impacts of child care quality on children's preschool cognitive development. *Child Development, 74,* 1454–1475.

Raver, C. C. (2002). Emotions matter: Making the case for the role of young children's emotional development in school readiness. *Social Policy Reports, 6,* 1–18.

Shonkoff, J. (2000). Science, policy, and practice: Three cultures in search of a shared mission. *Child Development, 71,* 181–187.

Stokes, D. E. (1997). *Pasteur's quadrant: Basic science and technological innovation.* Washington, DC: Brookings Institution.

Tamis-LeMonda, C. S., Shannon, J. D., Cabrera, N., & Lamb, M. (2004). Fathers and mothers at play with their 2- and 3- year olds: contributions to language and cognitive development. *Child Development, 75,* 1806–1820.

Yoshikawa, H., & Hsueh, J. (2001). Child development and public policy: Towards a dynamic systems perspective. *Child Development, 72,* 1887–1903.

Yoshikawa, H., & Knitzer, J. (1997). *Lessons from the field: Head Start mental health strategies to meet changing needs.* New York: National Center for Children in Poverty and American Orthopsychiatric Association.

16
BEHAVIORAL UNREADINESS FOR SCHOOL: ISSUES AND INTERVENTIONS

Ray DeV. Peters
Diana Ridgeway
Queen's University
Kingston, Ontario, Canada

Three major questions concerning school readiness are discussed in this chapter.

1. How do child risk characteristics and family processes combine to undermine the development of children's behavioral control in ways that jeopardize their ability to adapt well to school?
2. What challenges are faced by program development specialists in this area?
3. What are some creative solutions to those challenges?

Child and Family Correlates of School Unreadiness

In their study designed to provide some answers to the first question, Campbell and von Stauffenberg (this volume) present an analysis of child and family characteristics that predict unsuccessful behavioral outcomes in children at primary school entry. The data were drawn from the NICHD Longitudinal Study of Early Child Care, and include measures of child and family characteristics collected from children and their parents when the children were 1, 6, 15, 24, 36 and 54 months, and again in the first grade. The major parent/family measures included standard demographic characteristics of maternal education, family income, ethnicity and marital status/stability. Additional, more proximal measures of parent characteristics included maternal depression and sensitivity, and the HOME scale, all collected when children were 6, 15, 24, 36 and 54 months. Paternal sensitivity was also collected at 54 months. For child characteristics, the results from a battery of individually administered tests at 36 months were analyzed (including resistance to temptation, language skills, general school readiness, and attachment states), and another battery at 54 months (including the Continuous Performance Test [CPT], language skills, and delay of gratification).

The outcome measure for behavioral readiness or, more accurately, "behavioral unreadiness" was the combination of scores from the "externalizing scale" and the "attention problems scale" (Chapter 14, p. 237), from Achenbach's (1991) Teacher Report Form (TRF). Children scoring higher than one SD above the mean on "Attention and/or Externalizing Problems" were considered to be behaviorally unready for the first grade based on these teacher ratings. Since most of the school readiness research literature has employed cognitive/linguistics indices of school readiness, the current research expands the notion of readiness to include behavioral readiness and is an important contribution to this field.

An issue that arises immediately from this research is the definition of behavioral readiness and where this concept fits in the larger context of school readiness. Since the publication of a report from the U.S. Task Force for Goals in Education (Kagan, 1992), the term *school readiness* has become commonplace in development and social policy research. As defined by Kagan, school readiness covers five domains of children's development. These five domains have been incorporated into a kindergarten teacher-completed scale of school readiness by Janus and Offord (2000). This scale, called the Early Development Instrument (EDI), is comprised of five domains of children's functioning (Table 16.1). Another school readiness measure, presented in Farkas and Hibel (this volume), is based on work from the Early Childhood Longitudinal Study of Kindergarten children (ECLS-K; Table 16.2).

Table 16.1
School Readiness Early Development Instrument (Janus & Offord, 2000)

Domains
1. Physical Health and Well-being
2. Social Competence
3. Emotional Maturity
4. Language and Cognitive Development
5. Communication Skills and General Knowledge

Table 16.2
ECLS-K School Readiness Measure (Farkas & Hibel, chapter 5)

Cognitive Domain	Social Behavioral Domain
Reading	Approaches to Learning
Mathematics	Self Control
General Knowledge	Interpersonal Skills
	Externalizing Problem Behaviors

Both of these approaches to assessing school readiness are broad-based, including many different aspects of children's development considered important for school readiness. However, neither the EDI nor the ECLS-K includes the specific measures of behavioral (un)readiness employed in the study by Campbell and von Stauffenberg (this volume). As noted above, their index of behavioral unreadiness consists of high scores on *either* the Attention Problems Scale *or* the Externalizing Scale from the TRF. Examples of items from these TRF scales are presented in Table 16.3.

Table 16.3

Behavioral Unreadiness (Campbell & von Stauffenberg, chapter 14)

Attention Problems	Externalizing Problems
e.g. Can't concentrate Impulsive Poor school work Fails to finish Fidgets Inattentive Underachieving	Aggressive Behavior e.g. Argues Mean Disobedient Fights Defiant Delinquent Behavior e.g. Lies Steals at home Swearing Lacks guilt Tardy

As outlined in Table 16.3, the Behavioral Readiness measure employed by Campbell and von Stauffenberg is quite complex, actually consisting of three of Achenbach's TRF subscales: Attention Problems, Aggressive Behavior, and Delinquent Behavior (the last two being subscales of the broad-based "Externalizing" factor). A first-grade child is considered behaviorally unready if rated by his/her teacher as high on one and/or the other of these scales. It would be interesting and informative to know how many of the 257 children identified by Campbell and von Stauffenberg as behaviorally unready for school had only attention problems, only externalizing problems (aggressive or delinquency behaviors), or both. If the analyses were done on these distinct subgroups of behaviorally unready first graders, the family and / or child predictors might be different.

The main results of Campbell and von Stauffenberg's logistic regression analyses, presented in their Tables 14.3 and 14.4 (see Chapter 14, pp. 243 – 245), are that the only significant *independent* child predictor of Grade 1 behavioral unreadiness was CPT errors at 54 months. For parent/family characteristics, the only independent predictor was the composite of HOME ratings collected five times between 6 and 54 months of age. Their overall findings, then, might be summarized in a form similar to that presented in Figure 16.1.

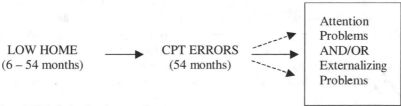

Figure 16.1. Behavioral unreadiness.

Several points of clarification concerning the analyses would help us to understand the results. First, it is not clear why Marital Status (actually marital stability) was not employed as a covariate in the logistic regressions presented in Tables 14.3 and 14.4. In Model 1, Marital Status had the most significant association with behavioral readiness scores, but only Maternal Education and Ethnicity were employed in subsequent model analyses. Also, it is not clear why Parental Sensitivity scores were not included in any of the logistic regression analyses. Surprisingly, none of the child characteristic measures collected at 36 months appear in any of the logistic regression models presented in Tables 14.3 or 14.4 despite significant differences between readiness groups on all five child measures collected at 36 months presented in their Table 14.2 (p. 240). It is possible that some of these 36-month differences may have mediated subsequent child outcomes at 54 months and Grade 1. Identifying such pathways would be extremely interesting and have valuable implications for interventions.

Many of the maternal/family characteristic measures were composite scores, based on repeated observation from 6 to 54 months. There is no indication in the results reported that Campbell and von Stauffenberg attempted to determine whether, for example, early HOME scores, say at 6 and 15 months, had greater or less predictive power than those collected at 24, 36 or 54 months. One also wonders about time course effects for other measures such as Marital Stability or Maternal Depression, indicating, for example, that early maternal depression may be more (or less) strongly related to behavioral readiness than later depression. Was there any indication from other early child measures (e.g., temperament) of these child characteristics creating pathways or trajectories to poor behavioral readiness at 54 months or Grade 1? Finally, to repeat a point made earlier, the complex measure of behavioral unreadiness employed in this study deserves further attention to ascertain whether the more specific types of behavioral difficulties at school entry (aggression vs. attention problems) have distinct child and family precursors.

Challenges to Program Development Specialists: The Risky Business of Risk in Early Childhood Programs

Virtually all of the well-researched early childhood development programs designed to impact school readiness and primary school performance have adopted a targeted or high-risk approach. A major challenge facing such programs is the relative strength and prevalence of the risk variables selected. Of interest here is the epidemiological concept of *population-attributable risk*. The calculation of population attributable risk combines measures of relative risk and prevalence to indicate the maximum reduction in the incidence of a disease or disorder that could be expected if the effects of the causal risk factor could be eliminated (Tu, 2003). For example, Offord, Boyle, and Racine (1989) identified five family risk factors for children's mental health problems and, based on an analysis of attributable risk, concluded that even if it were possible to eliminate these risk factors, the reduction in the overall prevalence of children's mental health problems would be only from 18% to 14%.

Also, Willms (2002) recently reported attributable risk analyses of the Canadian National Longitudinal Survey of Children and Youth (NLSCY). The NLSCY is a longitudinal study of a nationally representative sample of over 30,000 Canadian children and their families that began in 1994 to track children from birth to their early 20s. Willms found that the five most important family risk factors associated with children's cognitive, emotional, and behavioral problems during primary school were low maternal education, teenage motherhood, low family income, single parenthood, and low paternal occupational status. However, the total cumulative attributable risk for these five risk factors was 19.2%. According to Willms (2002), this finding "...indicates that even if we could eliminate all the risk factors associated with family background, we would reduce childhood vulnerability by less than twenty percent" (p. 90).

These findings suggest that the major risk factors that have been identified for compromised early childhood development (e.g., family dysfunction, low income, lone-parenthood) appear to have a low population attributable risk, presenting serious challenges to targeted, high-risk prevention interventions. Even if it were possible to eliminate these risk factors from society, the overall reduction in children's vulnerability would not be great. These results also indicate that 80% of young children manifesting serious cognitive, emotional, and behavioral problems do not come from "high-risk" families, but rather from two-parent families with adequate income and parental education. Thus, targeted programs for high-risk children or families only, even if highly effective, may have little impact on the community rates for early childhood difficulties.

It is possible, of course, that the population attributable risk of these and other family risk factors may be greater for U.S. children than for those in Canada. Minority status, coupled as it so often is with poverty, may be more prevalent in the U.S. and may have stronger relationships with child problems due to the lack of certain universal protective programs available to all children in Canada as described later in this chapter. A determination of whether these speculations are true requires research on U.S. samples employing measures of population-attributable risk— research that is lacking at present.

Given the limitations of high-risk, targeted programs for early childhood development, there is an increased interest in universal programs for young children and their families (McCain & Mustard, 2002; Offord, 1996; Offord et al., 1998; Peters, Petrunka, & Arnold, 2003; Willms, 2002). From a universal perspective, all children are considered to be at risk or potentially vulnerable for developmental problems and therefore should be eligible to participate in programs designed to prevent them. This is similar to the public health approach to preventing many diseases in young children, such as polio and rubella, where vaccinations are considered important for all children, not just those considered to be at "high risk" for contracting the diseases.

What are Some Creative Solutions to These Challenges?

Rouse, Brooks-Gunn, and McLanahan (2005) recently summarized current research on early childhood development programs in the U.S. that might be effective in reducing racial and ethnic gaps in school readiness. They argued that "by far the most promising strategy is to increase access to high quality center-based early childhood education programs for all low-income three- and four-year-olds" (p. 12). It is interesting to note that the studies on which these conclusions are based were initiated more than 30 years ago and were targeted to high-risk poor, predominantly black children and their families in the U.S., namely Perry Preschool Program (Schweinhart et al., 1993), the Abecedarian program (Ramey & Campbell, 1984), and the Chicago Child-Parent Centers program (Reynolds, Temple, Robertson, & Mann, 2001).

Rouse et al. (2005) outlined the characteristics of these successful programs as follows:
- *High-quality Learning Environment*: The education component must be high quality, with small class sizes, a low teacher-pupil ratio, and teachers with bachelor degrees and training in early childhood education, using a curriculum that is cognitively stimulating.
- *Teacher Training:* Teachers should be trained to identify children with moderate to severe behavioral problems and to work with these children to improve their emotional and social skills.
- *Parent Training:* Parent training reinforces what teachers are doing in school to enhance children's development. Examples include encouraging parents to read to children on a daily basis and teaching parents how to deal with behavior problems. Improving parental skills would have important multiplier effects on what teachers were doing in the classroom.
- *Home Visits:* Staff should be available to identify health problems in children and to help parents get ongoing health care for their children. Including optional home visits would allow staff to further screen for serious mental health problems among parents or other behaviors that are not conducive to good child development.
- *Integration:* Finally, new programs should be well aligned with the kindergarten programs that their children will eventually attend so that the transition from preschool to kindergarten is successful for children, parents, and teachers.

High-quality early childhood programs with these characteristics do exist, but as Rouse et al. (2005) pointed out, they reach only a very small proportion of poor children. It is interesting to note that many non-poor children also do not have access to high-quality preschool either (Barnett, Hustedt, Rubin, & Schulman, 2004). In their review of early childhood education programs, Magnuson and Waldfogel (2005) estimated that if all poor children had equal access to center-based care, up to 26% of the school readiness gap between black and white children in the U.S. would be closed. Haskins and Rouse (2005) estimated that such a high-quality preschool would cost approximately $8,000 per child annually, a figure comparable to the average annual cost of primary education. In general terms, then, if providing two years (ages 3 and 4) of high-quality preschool for all low-income children would reduce the black-white school readiness gap by 26%, 74% of the gap would remain. Although making two years of high-quality preschool available to all low-income children would be a tremendous benefit for many children and families, it is clearly not enough to assure that no child will be left behind.

The estimate from Magnuson and Waldfogel (2005) that two years of high-quality preschool made available to all low-income children would only reduce the black-white school readiness gap by 26% indicates that more is required if the U.S. is serious in ensuring that all children enter kindergarten on an equal basis.

In recent years, there has been increasing interest within early childhood social policy in the concept of a comprehensive universal system for early childhood development from the prenatal period to primary school entrance (Halfon, 2004; Peters, 2003). The U.S. and other developed countries have had a universal, comprehensive primary and secondary educational system in place for a century. If early childhood development (i.e., the time between conception and primary school entry) is as important to subsequent successful adaptation and development of children as current research indicates (e.g., McCain & Mustard, 2002; Shonkoff & Phillips, 2000; Young, 2002), then our society needs to invest *at least* as many resources in providing optimizing experiences for all children from 0–5 years of age as in good quality primary, secondary, and post-secondary education and training. In fact, recent economic analyses of the long-term benefits of investing in early childhood programs in the U.S. indicate a larger long-term return on investment during this period than at any other time in an individual's life, including primary, secondary, and post-secondary program investments (see especially Heckman, 2004; Heckman & Krueger, 2004).

In the U.S., work on comprehensive systems of early childhood development is being carried out through the Build Initiative (www.buildinitiative.org). The focus of the Build Initiative is on the first five years of life, with a broad conception of systems building that includes health, family support, early intervention and early education and care. The Build Initiative began in 2002 in four states: Illinois, Minnesota, New Jersey, and Ohio. Pennsylvania was added in 2003, as were four learning partner states—Hawaii, Michigan, Oklahoma, and Washington. The Build Initiative in these states is attempting to establish a universal, comprehensive early learning system for all children aged 0–5 years and their families. This initiative receives technical support from the State Early Childhood Policy Technical Assistance Network (SECPTAN; www.finebynine.org). SECPTAN provides current information about early education policy and school readiness initiatives to state policy makers and assists them in assessing the best available evidence and information about effective policies and practices in early childhood development. The universal, comprehensive ECD systems being promoted by the Build Initiative include but go far beyond the two years of high-quality preschool programs for 3- and 4-year-olds promoted by Rouse et al. (2005), with programs and supports for all children and their families from the prenatal period to school entry (Bruner, Wright, Gebhard, & Hibbard, 2004). Such a comprehensive system, if developed and supported with resources at the level of $8,000 per child per year as proposed by Haskins and Rouse (2005), would likely decrease the gap between blacks and whites, poor and non-poor, by substantially more than the 26% estimated from two years of high-quality preschool. Perhaps such a system should be the foundation for a U.S. national policy that would, in fact, assure that no child is left behind and all enter kindergarten ready to learn.

An International Perspective

In Canada, England, and Australia, as in the U.S., there is substantial interest in designing and implementing universal, comprehensive ECD systems (Halfon, 2004; Mustard, 2004; Peters, 2003, Santos, 2004). Early childhood development is currently supported in Canada by a Universal Health Care System and a National Parental Leave Policy, through which parents receive 52 weeks of paid leave for the first year of an infant's life. Home visits are offered to all families with new babies in most Canadian provinces through initiatives such as Healthy Babies, Healthy Children Ontario, providing parenting information, support, and referrals to other services. Junior kindergarten (or pre-kindergarten) programs provide free, half-day education for all 4-year-olds in several Canadian provinces. In Ontario, a new "Best Start" program will offer all 4- and 5-year-olds a half day of junior and senior kindergarten as well as a half day of high-quality early childhood education in or very near the school. Parent programs will also be offered through Best Start. In England, the Sure Start program (www.surestart.gov.uk/) offers free, part-time education to 3- and 4-year-olds, and a range of early learning, health and family services in disadvantaged neighborhoods. In the next section, we describe a "universal" early childhood development project being carried out in Ontario, Canada, in eight disadvantaged neighborhoods.

Better Beginnings, Better Futures: A Comprehensive Community-based Early Childhood Development Project

The Better Beginnings, Better Futures Project is one of the most ambitious research projects on the long-term impacts of early childhood development programming ever initiated in Canada. The Better Beginnings model has been implemented in eight socioeconomically disadvantaged communities in Ontario since 1991 to improve the well-being of all children living in those neighborhoods.

The Model

The following aspects are incorporated into a single program model:
- *ecological view*, which requires program strategies focusing on individual children, their families, and their neighborhoods, including childcare and school programs.
- *holistic view* of children, including social, emotional, behavioral, and cognitive development.
- *universally available programs* for all 0- to 4-year-old children and their families in the five *younger child sites* and for all 4- to 8-year-old children and their families in the three *older child sites*.
- *resident involvement* in all aspects of the organization, management, and delivery of programs.
- *partnerships* with local social service, health, and educational organizations.

Goals

- *prevention*—to reduce emotional and behavioral problems in children.
- *promotion*—to foster the optimal emotional, behavioral, social, physical and cognitive development in children.
- *community development*—to strengthen the ability of communities to respond effectively to the social and economic needs of children and their families.

Programs

- *required*—*younger child sites* were required to provide paraprofessional home visiting programs and enhancements to childcare; *older child sites* were required to provide enhancements to childcare and in-class or in-school programs.
- *additional programs* determined by local needs. On average, 20 programs were offered per site (e.g., before/after school programs, breakfast, parent training, leadership training).

Research Design

Major research objectives:
- · *describe* the local project organization and management.
- · determine *effect sizes* of child, family and neighbourhood outcomes.
- · investigate the *cost* of the project and carry out an economic analysis.

Longitudinal research groups of children and their families who experienced four years of Better Beginnings prevention programming in eight communities are being studied along with groups of children and their families in three demographically matched communities that did not receive Better Beginnings funding. From 1993–2003, data were collected from over 1,500 children and their families and teachers in these sites. In the younger child sites (approximately 800 children), data collection occurred when the children were 3-, 18-, 33-, and 48-months-old, and in Grades 1 and 3. In the older child sites (approximately 700 children), data collection occurred when the children were in junior kindergarten, senior kindergarten, and Grades 1, 2, 3, 6, and 9.

More than 100 outcome measures have been gathered at each data collection point, covering a wide range of areas such as children's social, emotional behavioral and academic functioning, child and parent health promotion and health risk behaviors, parent social and emotional functioning, family functioning, community involvement, and neighborhood quality. The diversity of the participating communities (e.g., Aboriginal, Francophone, inner-city, multi-cultural) increases the generalizability of research findings to disadvantaged communities across Canada.

Key Short-Term Outcomes Immediately Following the 4-Year Prevention Program (1998)

Children residing in several of the Better Beginnings communities showed decreased anxiety and depression and improved social skills. Children in the Better Beginnings communities generally benefited from reduced smoking in the home and improved dietary intake. In the younger child sites, children had more timely immunizations at 18 months and parents felt they had better access to professionals, such as doctors and social workers, for their children. In the older child sites, parent ratings of the children's health improved. The percentage of students receiving special education services decreased in two older child sites, while schools in comparison sites showed increases. Parents in all sites reported an improved quality-of-life in the Better Beginnings communities (e.g., feeling safer or more satisfied with their neighborhood). The average cost of the Better Beginnings, Better Futures project is approximately $1,000/child/year, which is modest in comparison to the costs of the model U.S. prevention projects highlighted by Rouse et al. (2005), which cost $4,300–$16,000/child/year.

Key Medium-Term Findings in the Older Child Sites in Grade 6 (2001)

Data collected in the older child sites three years after the program ended have yielded a picture of generally positive impacts of the Better Beginnings project on children and their families. Better outcomes occurred in the areas of school functioning, health promotion and health risk prevention for the Grade 6 children, as well as greater feelings of social, emotional and neighborhood support by the children and their parents.

The Better Beginnings Project has demonstrated that effective early childhood projects can be successfully developed and implemented in disadvantaged neighborhoods by local residents working in partnership with service providers. For the modest investment of $1,000 per child/family annually, an effective infrastructure or platform for delivering a wide range of supports and services for young children and their families has been established. If and when additional resources are invested in these neighborhoods for more intensive early childhood development and parent support programs, up to the recommended level of $8,000/ year, the local Better Beginnings organizations will be in an excellent position to support their implementation and dissemination. It is this model that also forms the basis for the Sure Start birth-to-five programs in England, and may characterize the comprehensive statewide early learning system developed through the Build Initiative in the United States.

Creative Solutions to Informing and Influencing Early Child Development Policy and Practice

A major challenge to the field of child development is to connect research, policy, and practice. This is an important goal of SECPTAN in the U.S., as noted earlier. In Canada, the Centre of Excellence for Early Childhood Development (CEECD) recently was created to synthesize and disseminate the most current scientific knowledge on the social and emotional development of young children. One of the products available on the CEECD web site (www.excellence-earlychildhood.ca) is the *Encyclopedia on Early Childhood Development* (Tremblay, Barr, & Peters, 2005). This online encyclopedia has been developed primarily for policy makers, planners and service providers. Based on a compilation of papers from leading international researchers, the encyclopedia covers 33 topics related to the social and emotional development of young children, from conception to age 5, and addresses three perspectives: determinants of development, effective services, and effective policies. The CEECD encyclopedia presents a user-friendly synthesis of the best and most current scientific work in the field of early childhood development.

Finally, a creative solution to providing a web-based training program on early childhood development has recently been developed in Canada, entitled "The Science of Early Child Development: A Multi-Media Resource" (www.scienceofecd.com). This education and training program incorporates a pedagogical approach based on adult education principles, is highly interactive, uses multiple audio-visual resources, and emphasizes problem-based learning. The curriculum consists of five modules: Developmental Health, Brain Development, Genetics and Experience, Coping and Competence, and Communication and Learning. The course is designed for instructional use with students in early childhood education, child development, primary education, and social services. It is also an excellent resource for service providers and policy makers involved with young children.

Summary and Conclusion

Inequality in children's school readiness among socioeconomic and racial/ethnic groups in the U.S. and other western countries remains a persistent social problem. Despite the tremendous efforts in the U.S. beginning with the War on Poverty on the 1960s and the expansion of Head Start programs through the 1980s and 1990s, many children enter the primary school system with serious social, cognitive, and language problems that have long-lasting consequences on their subsequent school performance.

The research presented in this volume contributes to a much fuller understanding of the myriad child, family, and community factors associated with "school unreadiness." Unfortunately, social policy has not been effective in translating this knowledge into child development and support programs that address these factors in a way that has had a significant impact on school readiness problems.

A major thesis of the research presented in this chapter is that one or two years of high quality preschool education for poor children, although important, will not be adequate to resolve the income and racial disparities in school readiness that persist. Rather, it is argued that what is required is a comprehensive, universal, well-financed system of early childhood and family support programs for all children from prenatal to school entry (0–5) and their families. Research consistently indicates that societal investments in high-quality early childhood programs return excellent long-term societal and personal benefits. It is time to translate these research findings into national social policy and resource allocation that will allow for the development of high-quality universal early learning systems. Initiatives in several U.S. states as well as in Canada and England that are moving in the direction of establishing an early child development learning system are briefly discussed in this chapter, and links to these initiatives are provided. Such early learning systems will require resources equal to or in excess of the average annual costs of financing the universal primary education system. Assuring optimal early childhood development for all children must be given at least as much national priority as assuring good quality primary, secondary, and post-secondary education and training. Developing high-quality early learning and family support systems will go a long way toward finally reaching the national goals of assuring that all children will enter primary school ready to learn and that no child will in fact be left behind.

References

Achenbach, T. M. (1991). *Integrative guide for the 1991 CBCL/4-18, YSR, and TRF Profiles.* Burlington, VT: University of Vermont Department of Psychiatry.

Barnett, W. S., Hustedt, J. T., Robin, K. B., & Schulman, K. L. (2004). *The state of preschool: 2004 state preschool yearbook.* New Brunswick, NJ: National Institute for Early Education Research. Available at http://nieer.org/yearbook.

Bruner, C., Wright, M. S., Gebhard, B., & Hibbard, S. (2004). *Building on an early learning system: The ABCs of planning and governance structures.* Retrieved November 14, 2005 from http://www.finebynine.org/pub.html.

Halfon, N. (2004). *Building early childhood systems to support optimal development.* Presented at Conference on Building a Comprehensive Early Childhood Development System, Quebec City, Quebec. Available at: http://www.excellence-earlychildhood.ca/documents/Neal%20Halfon_ANG.pdf.

Haskins, R., & Rouse, C. (2005). Policy brief: Closing achievement gaps. Companion document to *The Future of Children, 15*(1).

Heckman, J. J. (2004). Invest in the very young. In R. E. Tremblay, R. G. Barr, & R. DeV. Peters (Eds.), *Encyclopedia on early childhood development* [online]. Montreal, Quebec: Centre of Excellence for Early Childhood Development, 1-2. Available at: http://www.excellence-earlychildhood.ca/documents/HeckmanANG.pdf. Accessed November 14, 2005.

Heckman, J. J., & Krueger, A. B. (2004). *Inequality in America.* Cambridge, MA: MIT Press.

Janus, M., & Offord, D. R. (2000). Reporting on readiness to learn at school in Canada. *ISUMA: Canadian Journal of Policy Research, 1*, 71–75.

Kagan, S. L. (1992). The strategic importance of linkages and the transition between early childhood programs and early elementary school. In *Sticking together: Strengthening linkages and the transition between early childhood education and early elementary school* (Summary of a National Policy Forum). Washington, DC: U.S. Department of Education.

Magnuson, K. A., & Waldfogel, J. (2005). Early childhood care and education: Effects on ethnic and racial gaps in school readiness. *The Future of Children, 15*, 169–196.

McCain, M. N., & Mustard, J. F. (2002). *The early years study three years later: From early development to human development: Enabling communities.* Retrieved November 14, 2005 from http://www.founders.net.

Mustard, J. F. (2004). *Experience-based brain development.* Presented at Conference on Building a Comprehensive Early Childhood Development System, Quebec City, Quebec. Available at: http://www.excellence-earlychildhood.ca/documents/Fraser%20Mustard_ANG_May04.pdf.

Offord, D. R. (1996). The state of prevention and early intervention. In R. DeV. Peters & R. J. McMahon (Eds.), *Preventing childhood disorders, substance abuse and delinquency* (pp. 329–344). Thousand Oaks, CA: Sage Publications.

Offord, D. R., Boyle, M. H., & Racine, Y. (1989). Ontario Child Health Study: Correlates of disorder. *Journal of the American Academy of Child and Adolescent Psychiatry, 28,* 856–860.

Offord, D. R., Kramer, H. C., Kazdin, A. E., Jensen, P. S., & Harrington, R. (1998). Lowering the burden of suffering from child psychiatric disorder: Trade-offs among clinical, targeted and universal interventions. *Journal of the American Academy of Child and Adolescent Psychiatry, 37,* 686–694.

Peters, R. Dev. (2003). *Comprehensive, community-based projects for early childhood development.* Presented at the 35th Annual Banff International Conference on Behavioral Science, Banff, Alberta. Available at: http://www.excellence-earlychildhood.ca/documents/Ray%20Peters_Address_ANG.pdf.

Peters, R. DeV., Petrunka, K., & Arnold, R. (2003). The Better Beginnings, Better Futures Project: A universal, comprehensive, community-based prevention approach for primary school children and their families. *Journal of Clinical Child and Adolescent Psychology, 32,* 215–217.

Ramey, C. T., & Campbell, F. A. (1984). Preventive education for high-risk children: Cognitive consequences of the Carolina Abecedarian Project. *American Journal on Mental Deficiency, 88,* 515–523.

Reynolds, A. J., Temple, J. A., Robertson, D. L., & Mann, E. A. (2001). Long-term effects of an early childhood intervention on educational achievement and juvenile arrest: A 15-year follow-up of low-income children in public schools. *Journal of American Medical Association, 285,* 2339–2346.

Rouse, C., Brooks-Gunn, J., & McLanahan, S. (2005). Introducing the special issue of school readiness: Closing racial and ethnic Gaps. *The Future of Children, 15,* 5–15.

Santos, R. (2004). *Building a comprehensive early childhood development system: What we've learned in Quebec and Manitoba.* Presented at Conference on Building a Comprehensive Early Childhood Development System, Quebec City, Quebec. Available at: http://www.excellence-earlychildhood.ca/documents/Rob%20Santos_ANG.pdf.

Schweinhart, L. J., Barnes, H. V., Weikart, D. P., Barnett, W. S., & Epstein, A. S. (1993). *Significant benefits: The High/Scope Perry Preschool Study through age 27.* Monographs of the High/Scope Educational Research Foundation, 10. Ypsilanti, MI: High/Scope Educational Research Foundation.

Shonkoff, J. P., & Phillips, D. A. (Eds.). (2000). *From neurons to neighborhoods: The science of early childhood development.* Washington, DC: National Academy Press.

Tremblay, R. E., Barr, R. G., & Peters, R. DeV. (Eds.). (2005). *Encyclopedia on early childhood development* [online]. Montreal, Quebec: Centre of Excellence for Early Childhood Development. (http://www.excellence-earlychildhood.ca)

Tu, S. (2003). Developmental epidemiology: A review of three key measures of effect. *Journal of Clinical Child and Adolescent Psychology, 32,* 187–192.

Willms, J. D. (2002). Socioeconomic gradients for childhood vulnerability. In J. D. Willms (Ed.), *Vulnerable children* (pp. 71–102). Edmonton, Canada: The University of Alberta Press.

Young, M. E. (2002). *From early child development to human development: Investing in our children's future.* Washington, DC: World Bank.

17

USING FAMILY-FOCUSED INTERVENTIONS TO PROMOTE CHILD BEHAVIORAL READINESS FOR SCHOOL

Karen L. Bierman
Robert L. Nix
Kerry N. Makin-Byrd
Pennsylvania State University

The Importance of Focusing on Behavioral Readiness

No Child Left Behind has increased recent efforts to understand and promote academic achievement and to reduce socioeconomic and ethnic/cultural disparities in school performance. Academic school readiness—the child's language, pre-literacy skills, and number concepts at school entry—has emerged as a critical predictor of later academic achievement. This has spurred renewed efforts to develop and evaluate effective early intervention strategies that can promote these critical child competencies. We argue that behavioral readiness for school (a child's ability to appropriately manage attention, emotions and behavior within the school setting) is equally important, both as a predictor of child school adjustment, and also as a critical domain of socialization that, along with academic attainment, represents a central goal of the educational system.

Predictive Significance of Disruptive Behaviors at School Entry

Campbell and von Stauffenberg (this volume) emphasize the important role played by child regulatory skills in promoting children's behavioral adjustment to school demands. Children must be able to control attention, inhibit impulsive reactions, delay gratification, cooperate with others, and engage in goal-oriented behavior. If children fail to develop these skills during the preschool years and enter kindergarten exhibiting high rates of disruptive behavior problems, they are at risk for ongoing behavioral maladjustment, mental health problems, antisocial behavior, and substance use (Coie & Dodge, 1998; Dishion, French, & Patterson, 1997). Once in school, disruptive children are likely to elicit negative reactions from teachers and peers (Coie & Dodge, 1998; Miller-Johnson et al., 2002). Exclusion from positive peer networks and exposure to high rates of problem behaviors among classmates fuel the continuity of problem behaviors in school settings; these contribute to school disengagement, special education placement, and eventual drop-out (CPPRG, 1992; Thornberry, Lizotte, Krohn, Farnworth, & Jang, 1994).

Disruptive behavior problems, which include various forms of oppositional, aggressive, and hyperactive-inattentive behaviors, represent the most prevalent form of mental health problems in childhood (Anderson, Williams, McGee, & Silva, 1987). One review concluded that about 10–15% of all preschool children exhibit mild to moderate behavior problems (Campbell, 1995); some studies have estimated prevalence rates as high as 20–30% among children from socioeconomically disadvantaged families (Hawkins et al. 1999; Lavigne et al., 1996; Qi & Kaiser, 2003). For example, Kaiser et al. (2000) found that 17–21% of the socioeconomically disadvantaged children they studied had behavior problems severe enough to warrant mental health referrals. This was almost four times the rate expected in a representative sample of children. In addition, over 40% of the children in that study demonstrated social skills and language skills that were well below the normal range. Children who live in poverty not only are more likely to have high levels of externalizing problems in preschool, but they also are more likely to experience greater increases in externalizing problems during the first two years of elementary school (Macmillan, McMorris, & Kruttschnitt, 2004). Despite their prevalence and severity, the mental health needs of disadvantaged preschoolers often go undetected and untreated (Fantuzzo et al., 2003).

Reflecting the stability of these problems over time, teacher ratings of disruptive behavior in kindergarten can be used effectively to identify children who will need special education, mental health, and juvenile justice services later in elementary school (Jones et al., 2002). By the end of first grade, teacher ratings of disruptive behavior problems detect future conduct disorder and oppositional defiant disorder psychiatric diagnoses with sensitivity rates above .50 and specificity rates above .90 (Hill et al. 2004).

Disruptive Behaviors and Academic Difficulties

Not only are children with disruptive behaviors at risk for continuing problems, but they also show academic underachievement with specific delays in language and reading skills (Campbell et al., 1991; Pianta & Castaldi, 1989; Vaughn et al., 1992). In one prospective study, children with conduct disorder were more likely than their nonproblematic peers to have educational difficulties, even after controlling for their intellectual ability and concurrent attention-deficit/hyperactivity disorder symptoms (Kim-Cohen et al., 2005). Specifically, 65% of the children with conduct disorders at school entry had one or more serious academic problems in school two years later (Kim-Cohen et al., 2005). Not surprisingly, when children experience the dual risks of low levels of social competence and high rates of behavior problems, they are more likely to have to repeat a grade early in elementary school (Beebe-Frankenberger, Bocian, MacMillan, & Gresham, 2004). These children also require more school resources, representing a large percentage of children receiving special education services (National Center for Health Statistics, 2005; Wagner & Blackorby, 2002) and a significant proportion of school districts' high-expenditure pupils (Chambers, Kidron, & Spain, 2004).

To some extent, the frequent co-occurrence of disruptive behavior problems and academic difficulties may reflect the developmental interplay between language and self-regulation skills (Blair, 2002; Greenberg, Kusche, & Speltz, 1991). Normatively, aggressive behaviors appear early in the social repertoire of young children, peaking when children are about two or three years old. The frequency of these behaviors decreases sharply during the preschool years, however, as children develop the verbal, emotional, and social skills that allow them to inhibit their first impulses, comply with social protocol, and "use their words" to voice dissatisfaction and resolve disagreements (Greenberg, Kusche, & Speltz, 1991). Language plays a key role in promoting self and social regulation. Once children are able to use language to describe internal affective states, they can share their feelings verbally with others. This, in turn, fosters new avenues for understanding themselves and others, for coping with frustrations, and for managing conflicts. In addition, the ability to label unpleasant arousal with specific words empowers children to identify cause-effect sequences associated with those feelings, promoting anticipatory problem solving (Cole, Michel, & Teti, 1994). Conversely, low levels of emotional understanding increase the likelihood that children will misinterpret in a negative way the actions of others, thus fueling interpersonal conflicts (Dodge, 1986).

Child attention problems also may be responsible for some of the overlap between academic difficulties and disruptive behavior. For example, child attention problems predict lower language outcomes in first grade (NICHD Early Child Care Research Network, 2003), academic problems (Spira & Fischel, 2005), and delayed emergent literacy skills in both middle- and low-income families (Lonigan et al., 1999). Attention problems are associated with slower gains in reading through first grade and, more important still, reduce by half the impact of individualized tutoring (Rabiner, Coie, & CPPRG, 2000). Attention problems also are associated with increased risk for behavioral and social adjustment problems in school (Pope & Bierman, 1999). Moreover, severe attention problems appear to co-occur with a wide range of psychiatric diagnoses (Biederman, Newcorn, & Sprich, 1991).

Common Parenting Influences

Given the intertwined development of language skills, emotion regulation, and behavioral control, it is not surprising that some similar family processes are associated with adaptive development across these domains. For example, positive parent-child relationships foster secure attachment, child compliance, the development of joint attention, and positive language learning (Campbell & von Stauffenberg, this volume; Dickinson & Smith, 1994). Similarly, warm involvement and sensitive responding play central roles in promoting the kinds of caregiver-child interactions that promote child language skills. These interactions involve caregiver utterances that expand upon children's comments and provide grammatical input that builds vocabulary and syntax skills (Landry, Smith, Swank,

& Miller-Loncar, 2000; Nelson et al., 2001). The child temperament factors associated with low levels of behavioral readiness for school—including negative affect and reactivity, difficulty focusing and maintaining attention, and poor impulse control––may all decrease the child's capacity to engage positively in conversations with parents. Similarly, sociodemographic and family process risks associated with low levels of behavioral readiness at school entry—including low levels of maternal education, maternal depression, maternal and paternal insensitivity, and a less stimulating home environment—are also factors likely to impair child cognitive and language development.

Implications for Family-focused Interventions to Promote School Readiness

These developmental findings provide a basis for the design of family-focused preventive interventions by identifying protective factors that may promote the child skills associated with school readiness and counteract the risks associated with socioeconomic disadvantage (Coie et al., 1993). As summarized in the Campbell and von Stauffenberg chapter (this volume), sociodemographic risks associated with low levels of behavioral readiness at school entry include low levels of maternal education, single parent status, minority status, and maternal depression. Child characteristics that constitute risks to behavioral readiness include delays in language and cognitive skill development, poor regulation of negative affect, difficulty focusing and maintaining attention, and poor impulse control. Several key family process such as maternal and paternal sensitivity and warm involvement, a stimulating home environment, and appropriate limit-setting could be targeted in early interventions, and could protect children against the risks associated with socioeconomic disadvantage. Interventions targeting these parenting skills might have particularly strong effects on child school readiness if they were designed with a dual focus on the promotion of academic readiness (language and cognitive skills) and the promotion of behavioral readiness (attentional, emotional, and behavioral regulatory control).

To date, family-focused interventions have tended to target either the domain of academic or behavioral school readiness, rather than addressing both skill domains. In the following sections, we illustrate three approaches to family-focused intervention addressing school readiness. Then, we discuss the need to develop a more comprehensive model to guide family-focused interventions that addresses the concurrent cognitive and behavioral needs of children who show delays in behavioral readiness.

Home Visiting Programs to Promote Language and Cognitive Development

A number of home visiting programs have been designed primarily to enrich the home environment to promote child language and cognitive development. For example, the Infant Health and Development Program focused on increasing parental nurturance and sensitive responding as a strategy to protect very young children from the risks associated with preterm birth and corresponding cognitive and social-emotional delays (Landry et al., 2000). In general, home visiting programs have demonstrated capacity to improve maternal sensitive responding; in their review, Brooks-Gunn, Berlin and Fuligni (2000) found that 11 of 13 home-visiting evaluations that observed mother-child interactions found increases in parental sensitivity. Correspondingly, a recent meta-analysis demonstrated that, on average, home visiting programs produced a statistically significant improvement in children's cognitive development and social-emotional functioning, with effect sizes of .18 and .10, respectively (Sweet & Appelbaum, 2004). Three popular home visiting programs have focused specifically on promoting school readiness among low-income children: the Mother-Child Home Program/Parent-Child Home Program; the Nurse-Family Partnership Program, and the Home Instruction Program for Preschool Youngsters (HIPPY).

The Parent-Child Home Program (originally called the Mother-Child Home Program) provides biweekly home visits by paraprofessionals, spread over seven months, for each of two years, usually when children are two and three years old. Altogether, families are expected to receive 92 home visits. The paraprofessionals who conduct these home visits present the parent with a new toy or book at each home visit and show them how they can use the learning material in ways that motivate verbal interactions and improve children's language development.

Quasi-experimental evaluations of the Parent-Child Home Program have been quite promising. Children who participated in the Parent-Child Home Program were much more likely than other poor children in the state of South Carolina to pass a broad assessment battery of cognitive skills (Levenstein, Levenstein, & Oliver, 2002). In fact, participation in the Parent-Child Home Program erased many of the school readiness deficits that low-income children often display in school, making these children comparable to their non-poor classmates (Levenstein, Levenstein, & Oliver, 2002). In another quasi-experimental evaluation, the home visiting program resulted in higher IQ scores as children entered kindergarten and when they were in third grade (Madden, Levenstein, & Levenstein, 1976). Moreover, the effects of the program appeared to be sustained: There is some evidence that the Parent-Child Home Program may have increased the likelihood that children graduated from high school (Levenstein, Levenstein, Shiminski, & Stolzberg, 1998).

Randomized control trials of the Parent-Child Home Program, however, have not been as favorable. Two large-scale trials have failed to demonstrate statistically significant differences in IQ between children who did and did not receive the program (Madden, O'Hara, & Levenstein, 1984; Scarr & McCartney, 1988). The lack of findings in these trials might highlight problems in the comparison samples of the quasi-experimental evaluations. They also might reflect socioeconomic and cultural differences in the populations studied or the more common use of child care, which may have washed out the effects of improved parental involvement.

Focusing on older children who are preparing to make the transition into school, the Home Instruction Program for Preschool Youngsters (HIPPY) is a two-year program that enrolls 4-year-old children and their parents and spans the transition into kindergarten. Paraprofessionals conduct bimonthly home visits, providing books and activities designed to enhance children's language skills, sensory and perceptual discrimination skills, motor skills and problem-solving skills.

In one quasi-experimental evaluation, a statewide comparison suggested that family participation in this home visiting program enhanced child academic performance in grade-school, promoting higher grades, improved achievement scores, more favorable teacher ratings of social adjustment (Bradley & Gilkey, 2002). A randomized control trial of the HIPPY program, however, revealed meaningful effects for children in one cohort at the end of kindergarten and at the end of first grade, but no effects for children in a second cohort (Baker, Piotrkowski, & Brooks-Gunn, 1998).

Another home visiting program that targets mothers and infants is the Nurse-Family Partnership program. In this program, first-time mothers receive weekly, biweekly, or monthly home visits by registered nurses during pregnancy and the first two years of their child's life, for a total of about 30 home visits. In contrast to the Parent-Child Home Program or HIPPY, the focus of the home visits in the Nurse-Family Partnership does not focus intensively on enhancing parent-child verbal interactions and cognitive stimulation, but takes a broader approach. In this program, nurses strive to improve mothers' and children's physical health, family life issues—such as economic stability and maternal depression—along with increasing positive parenting practices.

In one experimental evaluation, this program appeared most effective for mothers with the highest level of need, in terms of being young, single, and with limited social support or psychological resources (Olds, Robinson et al., 2004). Among this subgroup of mothers, the program promoted more stimulating home environments for children, and these children had statistically significantly higher scores on tests of language development and executive functioning at age four (Olds, Robinson et al., 2004). The children also displayed better behavioral adaptation during testing sessions, suggesting improved behavioral school readiness. According to mothers' reports, however, these children were not displaying fewer behavior problems at home.

Another experimental trial of the Nurse Family Partnership program produced statistically significant differences in children's intellectual functioning, mathematical achievement, and receptive vocabulary—but not reading achievement —just after children entered school, when they were about six years old (Olds,

Kitzman et al., 2004). Although mothers in this trial were less likely to report clinically significant behavior problems at home and children exhibited fewer aggressive social-cognitive biases, teachers' reports of behavior problems at school did not show intervention effects.

Because about 90% of home visiting programs focus on children younger than three years old (Sweet & Appelbaum, 2004) and most programs do not focus specifically on school readiness, the effects of these programs on children's language development, academic skills, and behavioral regulation at school entry remain unclear. The results of quasi-experimental and experimental evaluations of the home visiting programs that are most relevant to school readiness and that examine outcomes appropriate to this domain are mixed. However, qualitative and quantitative reviews (Brooks-Gunn et al., 2000; Sweet & Appelbaum, 2004) support the hypothesis that parental sensitivity and home stimulation can be increased through home visiting programs, and they suggest that changes in these parenting factors promote child skill development. Hence, the approach warrants further examination and refinement as one potential strategy to enhance parenting in ways that reduce the negative effects of socioeconomic disadvantage on child school readiness.

Interventions Focused on Parent-Child Reading

Another approach to parent interventions targeting child school readiness involves teaching parents to use interactive reading techniques at home with their children. Theoretically, interactive book-reading provides an ideal setting for the types of conversational exchanges that appear most central to supporting child oral language skill development. Furthermore, interventions in preschool classrooms demonstrate positive effects on child vocabulary acquisition, story comprehension, and child oral language skills when teachers use interactive reading techniques (e.g., Wasik & Bond, 2001; Whitehurst, Arnold et al., 1994; Whitehurst, Epstein et al., 1994).

In the reading program developed by Whitehurst and his colleagues (Whitehurst, Arnold et al., 1994; Whitehurst, Epstein et al., 1994), parents are taught to encourage their child to tell the story they are hearing in their own words. Parents are taught to be active listeners, to praise their child's ideas, to ask probing questions about the story, and to expand on their child's comments as a means of modeling more sophisticated languague use (Lonigan & Whitehurst, 1998). The goal of this intervention is to enhance preschoolers' vocabulary, comprehension, and narrative skills in preparation for future literacy.

Direct parent training consists of a group of six to twelve parents and one trainer. During two one-hour training sessions (an initial training session and a later "booster" session), the trainer teaches dialogic reading techniques by showing a video that models dialogic reading skills and role-playing these skills with group members. Video self-instruction alone has also been explored as a parent-training technique, but is significantly less effective in increasing parent dialogic reading behaviors and decreasing other parent reading behaviors (Huebner & Meltzoff, 2005). Parents are then expected to read to their child 10–15 minutes a day, three to five times a week. Home interventions vary in length from four to eight weeks, while school and home combination interventions may last up to 30 weeks.

Whitehurst's dialogic reading program has been shown to significantly improve language skills in typical preschoolers from both middle- and low-income backgrounds (Whitehurst et al., 1988; Whitehurst, Arnold et al., 1994). In addition, this intervention has increased pre-literacy skills in preschoolers who performed significantly below average on tests of expressive and receptive vocabulary (Lonigan & Whitehurst, 1998). More recent work has assessed the efficacy of a combination intervention consisting of Whitehurst's dialogic reading program implemented at home and at school in addition to the phonemic awareness program, Sound Foundations, implemented within the school setting (Whitehurst et al, 1999; Zevenbergen, Whitehurst, & Zevenbergen, 2003). Although this intervention appeared to improve emergent literacy skills immediately following treatment, there were no sustained intervention effects in first and second grade (Whitehurst et al, 1999; Zevenbergen, Whitehurst, & Zevenbergen, 2003).

In sum, interactive book-reading was designed to target very specific parenting behaviors that enhance child language and pre-literacy skills. As such, this intervention appears to improve children's academic school readiness. Additional studies are needed to determine how intervention effects can be sustained in a way that makes a meaningful difference for children's academic success. In addition, studies have not examined potential cross-over effects of children's academic school readiness on their behavioral school readiness. One might anticipate that cross-over effects could emerge, as improved language skills and reduced frustration with learning tasks at school might promote behavioral regulation.

Parenting Interventions to Reduce Child Disruptive Behaviors

In contrast to those home visiting and dialogic reading programs that target children's academic school readiness, parent training programs target factors related to children's behavioral school readiness. Originally designed as clinical interventions for parents of children with conduct problems, these programs attempt to teach positive interactions and consistent limit-setting. They focus on increasing praise and positive rewards, minimizing criticism, and reducing or eliminating spanking and harsh punishment (Brestan & Eyeberg, 1998; McMahon, 1999). Research with clinical samples suggests that parent training programs are one of the most effective ways to reduce children's conduct problems at home (Kazdin & Weisz, 1998).

It is less clear, however, whether changes in parenting and conduct problems at home translate to improvements in children's behavioral school readiness. To examine this possibility, the Incredible Years Parent Training Program has been tested as a prevention strategy in two randomized trials with Head Start families

(Webster-Stratton, 1998; Webster-Stratton, Reid, & Hammond, 2001). The program teaches parents to use child-directed play skills, positive and consistent discipline strategies, strategies for coping with stress, and ways to strengthen children's social skills. Parents meet with a certified trainer in small groups that are held weekly for about two or three months, with each session lasting about two hours. To promote consistency across the home and school contexts, Head Start teachers also participate in extensive training in which they learn many of the same behavior management strategies as the parents.

In one trial (Webster-Statton, 1998), the Incredible Years Parent Training Program improved parenting practices at home. Although there were no treatment effects on parents' reports of children's behavior at home, there were treatment effects on children's observed behaviors at home. Moreover, there were treatment effects on Head Start teachers' reports of children's social competence, but not externalizing problems, at school. One year later, those same treatment effects were still apparent, except the impact on children's social competence at school had disappeared. In another trial (Webster-Stratton, Reid, & Hammond, 2001), participating in the Incredible Years Parent Training Program resulted in increases in positive parenting practices, decreases in negative parenting practices, and reductions in children's conduct problems at home and at Head Start.

It appears that parent training programs, like the Incredible Years, are effective in teaching the kinds of sensitive and responsive parenting practices that should be related to children's school readiness. When implemented with integrity, these programs reliably reduce children's conduct problems at home. It is difficult to determine whether the parent training or teacher training component of this program is responsible for the changes in children's behavior at Head Start. However, in another trial of the Incredible Years for the middle-income families of older children with oppositional defiant disorder, parent training alone resulted in improvements in children's behavior at school (Webster-Stratton, Reid, and Hammond, 2004). Like the home visiting programs and the dialogic reading programs, there is some initial reason to believe that parent training might be able to improve children's school readiness.

Implications for Preventive Intervention Design

Developmental research has confirmed the critical importance of children's behavioral as well as academic school readiness. High rates of disruptive behavior at school entry often are associated with maladjustment and poor academic and social outcomes (Campbell & von Stauffenberg, this volume). To date, most family interventions seeking to reduce disparities among children living in poverty have focused on academic school readiness. In general, they have sought to increase responsive and appropriately stimulating parenting as a means of facilitating children's cognitive development. Relatively fewer family interventions have focused on the developmental pathways associated with low levels of behavioral school readiness in a comprehensive way. Because so many of the children who lag in the acquisition of language skills and executive functioning skills also have problems with emotional and behavioral regulation, it is critical to consider academic and behavioral school readiness in tandem (Blair, 2002). Effective preventive intervention programs may need to address the multiple developmental needs of children, rather than focusing on cognitive-linguistic or behavioral domains of adjustment in isolation.

More comprehensive interventions could involve multi-component treatment packages, such as those being used in elementary school prevention programs for children with significant conduct problems (e.g., CPPRG, 1992; Dumas, Prinz, Phillips, & Laughlin, 1999; Tremblay et al., 1995). Separate but coordinated efforts could provide academic tutoring, social-emotional skill training, and parent training. Alternatively, given that a core of common parenting practices appear to be associated with children's language development and self-regulation abilities, it might be possible to create an integrated parent training intervention that targets parenting skills associated with both child academic and behavioral readiness for school. Yet a third preventive intervention design option would be the use of an adaptive design (Collins, Murphy & Bierman, 2004), in which parents are offered specific components of treatment based on an individualized assessment of child and family need.

Designing Prevention Trials to Explore Developmental Mechanisms

More prevention trials are clearly needed to identify the optimal strategies for addressing the multiple needs of children with delays in academic and behavioral readiness for school. These trials are likely to be most useful if they are designed to test developmental mechanisms of change, as well as to assess the impact on child outcomes. Our best interventions articulate in advance the mechanisms by which they expect to influence identified risk and protective factors to promote child adaptation (Coie et al., 1993). When trials are designed in this way, they simultaneously test the efficacy of interventions and contribute to the developmental understanding of the phenomena.

In the area of school readiness, we need to understand better how academic functioning and child behavior are related. In particular, we need to understand how inattention might underlie problems in both areas and might moderate treatment effects. Equally important, we need to understand how common family characteristics, such as sensitive responding, affect both domains of development. By creating and testing more integrated preventive intervention programs, we are most likely to make progress in ameliorating the disadvantages so often experienced at school entry by children living in poverty.

References

Anderson, J. C., Williams, S. M., McGee, R., & Silva, P. A. (1987). DSM – III disorders in preadolescent children: Prevalence in a large sample from the general population. *Archives of General Psychiatry*, *44*, 69–76.

Baker, A. J. L., Piotrkowski, C. S., & Brooks-Gunn, J. (1998). The effects of the Home Instruction Program for Preschool Youngsters (HIPPY) on children's school performance at the end of the program and one year later. *Early Childhood Research Quarterly*, *13*, 571–588.

Beebe-Frankenberger, M., Bocian, K. M., MacMillan, D. L., & Gresham, F. M. (2004). Sorting second-grade students: Differentiating those retained from those promoted. *Journal of Educational Psychology*, *96*, 204–215.

Biederman, J., Newcorn, J., & Sprich, S. (1991). Comorbidity of attention deficit hyperactivity disorder with conduct, depressive, anxiety, and other disorders. *American Journal of Psychiatry*, *148*, 564–577.

Blair, C. (2002). School readiness: Integrating cognition and emotion in a neurobiological conceptualization of children's functioning at school entry. *American Psychologist*, *57*, 111–127.

Bradley, R. H., & Gilkey, B. (2002). The impact of the Home Instructional Program for Preschool Youngsters (HIPPY) on school performance in 3rd and 6th grades. *Early Education and Development*, *13*, 301–311.

Brestan, E. V. & Eyberg, S. M. (1998). Effective psychosocial treatments of conduct-disordered children and adolescents: 29 years, 82 studies, and 5,272 kids. *Journal of Clinical Child Psychology, 27*, 180–189.

Brooks-Gunn, J., Berlin, L. J., & Fuligni, A. S. (2000). Early childhood intervention programs: What about the family? In J. P. Shankoff & S. J. Meisels (Eds.), *Handbook of early childhood intervention* (2nd ed.) (pp. 549–588). Cambridge, UK: Cambridge University Press.

Campbell, S. B. (1995). Behavior problems in preschool children: A review of recent research. *Journal of Child Psychology and Psychiatry*, *36*, 113–149.

Campbell, S. B., March, C. L., Pierce, E., Ewing, L. J., & Szumowski, E. K. (1991). Hard-to-manage preschool boys: Family context and the stability of externalizing behavior. *Journal of Abnormal Child Psychology, 19,* 301–310.

Chambers, J. G., Kidron, Y., & Spain, A. K. (2004). *Characteristics of high-expenditure students with disabilities, 1999–2000*. Washington, DC: American Institutes for Research.

Coie, J. D., & Dodge, K. A. (1998). Aggression and antisocial behavior. In W. Damon (Ed.), *Handbook of child psychology, fifth edition. Vol. 3: Social, emotional, and personality development* (pp. 779–862), (N. Eisenberg, Vol. Ed.). New York: Wiley.

Coie, J. D., Watt, N. F., West, S. G., Hawkins, J. D., Asarnow, J. R., Markman, H. J., Ramey, S. L., Shure, M. B., & Long, B. (1993). The science of prevention: A conceptual framework and some directions for a national research program. *American Psychologist*, *48*, 1013–1022.

Cole, P. M., Michel, M. K., & Teti, L. O. (1994). The development of emotion regulation and dysregulation: A clinical perspective. *Monographs of the Society for Research in Child Development, 59,* 53–72.

Collins, L. M., Murphy, S. A., & Bierman, K. L. (2004). A conceptual framework for adaptive preventive interventions. *Prevention Science*, *5*, 185–196.

Conduct Problems Prevention Research Group (CPPRG). (1992). A developmental and clinical model for the prevention of conduct disorder: The Fast Track Program. *Development and Psychopathology, 4,* 509–527.

Dickinson, D. K., & Smith, M. W. (1994). Long-term effects of preschool teachers' book readings on low-income children's vocabulary and story comprehension. *Reading Research Quarterly, 29*, 105–102.

Dishion, T. J., French, D. C., & Patterson, G. R. (1995). The development and ecology of antisocial behavior. In D. Cicchetti & D. J. Cohen (Eds.), *Developmental psychopathology, Vol. 2: Risk, disorder, and adaptation* (pp. 421–471). Oxford, England: John Wiley & Sons.

Dodge, K. A. (1986). A social information processing model of social competence in children. In M. Perlmutter (Ed.), *Minnesota symposium on child psychology* (pp. 77–125). Hillsdale, NJ: Erlbaum.

Dumas, J. E., Prinz, R. S., Phillips, E., & Laughlin, J. (1999). The Early Alliance prevention trial: An integrated set of interventions to promote competence and reduce risk for conduct disorder, substance use, and school failure. *Clinical Child and Family Psychology Review*, *2*, 37–53.

Fantuzzo, J., Bulotsky, R., McDermott, P., Mosca, S., & Lutz, M. N. (2003). A multivariate analysis of emotional and behavioral adjustment and preschool educational outcomes. *School Psychology Review*, *32*, 185–203.

Greenberg, M. T., Kusche, C. A., & Speltz, M. (1991). Emotional regulation, self control, and psychopathology: The role of relationships in early childhood. In D. Cicchetti & S. L. Toth (Eds.), *Internalizing and externalizing expressions of dysfunction: Rochester symposium on developmental psychopathology* (Vol. 2, pp. 21–66). Hillsdale, NJ: Erlbaum.

Hawkins, J. D., Catalano, R. F., Kosterman, R., Abbott, R., & Hill, K. G. (1999). Preventing adolescent health-risk behaviors by strengthening protection during childhood. *Archives of Pediatrics and Adolescent Medicine*, *153*, 226–234.

Hill, L. G., Lochman, J. E., Coie, J. D., Greenberg, M. T., & the Conduct Problems Prevention Research Group. (2004). Effectiveness of early screening for externalizing problems: Issues of screening accuracy and utility. *Journal of Consulting and Clinical Psychology*, *72*, 809–820.

Huebner, C., & Meltzoff, A. (2005). Intervention to change parent-child reading style: A comparison of instructional methods. *Applied Developmental Psychology, 26*, 96–313.

Jones, D. E., Dodge, K. A., Foster, E. M., Nix, R., & the Conduct Problems Prevention Research Group. (2002). Early identification of children at risk for costly mental health service use. *Prevention Science*, *3*, 247–256.

Kaiser, A. P., Hancock, T. B., Cai, X., Foster, E. M., & Hester, P. P. (2000). Parent-reported behavioral problems and language delays in boys and girls enrolled in Head Start classrooms. *Behavioral Disorders*, *26*, 26–41.

Kazdin, A. E., & Weisz, J. R. (1998). Identifying and developing empirically supported child and adolescent treatments. *Journal of Consulting and Clinical Psychology*, *66*, 19–36.

Kim-Cohen, J., Arseneault, L., Caspi, A., Tomas, M. P., Taylor, A., & Moffitt, T. E. (2005). Validity of DSM-IV conduct disorder in 4 ½-5-year-old children: A longitudinal epidemiological study. *American Journal of Psychiatry, 162*, 1108–1117.

Landry, S. H., Smith, K. E., Swank, P. R., & Miller-Loncar, C. L. (2000) Early maternal and child influences on children's later independent cognitive and social functioning. *Child Development, 71*, 358–375.

Lavigne, J. V., Gibbons, R. D., Christoffel, K., Arend, R., Rosenbaum, D., Binns, H., Dawson, N., Sobel, H., & Isaacs, C. (1996). Prevalence rates and correlates of psychiatric disorders among preschool children. *Journal of the American Academy of Child and Adolescent Psychiatry, 35*, 204–214.

Levenstein, P., Levenstein, S., & Oliver, D. (2002). First grade school readiness of former child participants in a South Carolina replication of the Parent-Child Home Program. *Applied Developmental Psychology, 23*, 331–353.

Levenstein, P., Levenstein, S., Shiminski, J. A., & Stolzberg, J. E. (1998). Long-term impact of a verbal interaction program for at-risk toddlers: An exploratory study of high school outcomes in a replication of the Mother-Child Home Program. *Journal of Applied Developmental Psychology, 19*, 267–285.

Lonigan, C., Bloomfield, B., Anthony, J., Bacon, K., Phillips, B., & Samwel, C. (1999). Relations among emergent literacy skills, behavior problems, and social competencies in preschool children from low- and middle-income backgrounds. *Topics in Early Childhood Special Education, 19*, 40–54.

Lonigan, C., & Whitehurst, G. (1998) Relative efficacy of a parent and teacher involvement in a shared-reading intervention for preschool children from low-income backgrounds. *Early Childhood Research Quarterly, 13*, 263–290.

Macmillan, R., McMorris, B. J., & Kruttschnitt, C. (2004). Linked lives: Stability and change in maternal circumstances trajectories of antisocial behavior in children. *Child Development, 75*, 205–220.

Madden, J., Levenstein, P., & Levenstein, S. (1976). Longitudinal IQ outcomes of the Mother-Child Home Program. *Child Development, 47*, 1015–1025.

Madden, J., O'Hara, J., & Levenstein, P. (1984). Home again: Effects of the Mother-Child Home Program on mother and child. *Child Development, 55*, 636–647.

McMahon, R. J. (1999). Parent training. In S. W. Russ & T. H. Ollendick (Eds.), *Handbook of psychotherapies with children and families: Issues in clinical psychology* (pp. 153–180). Dordrecht, Netherlands: Kluwer Academic Publishers.

Miller-Johnson, S., Coie, J. D., Maumary-Gemaud, A., Bierman, K., & the Conduct Problems Prevention Research Group. (2002). Peer rejection and aggression and early starter models of conduct disorder. *Journal of Abnormal Child Psychology, 30*, 217–230.

National Center for Health Statistics. (2005). *NCHS data about special education.* Atlanta, GA: Centers for Disease Control.

Nelson, K. E., Welsh, J., Camarata, S., Heimann, & Tjus, T. (2001). A rare event transactional dynamic model of tricky mix conditions contributing to language acquisition and varied communicative delays. In K. E. Nelson, A. Koc, & C. Johnson (Eds.), *Children's language, Vol. 11*. Hillsdale, NJ: Erlbaum.

NICHD Early Child Care Research Network. (2003). Do children's attention processes mediate the link between family predictors and school readiness? *Developmental Psychology, 39*, 581–593.

Olds, D. L., Kitzman, H., Cole, R., Robinson, J., Sidora, K., Luckey, D. W., Henderson, C. R., Hanks, C., Bondy, J., & Holmberg, J. (2004). Effects of nurse home visiting on maternal life course and child development: Age 6 follow-up results of a randomized trial. *Pediatrics, 114,* 1550–1559.

Olds, D. L., Robinson, J., Pettitt, L., Luckey, D. W., Holmberg, J., Ng, R. K., Isacks, K., Sheff, K., & Henderson, C. R. (2004). Effects of home visits by paraprofessionals and by nurses: Age 4 follow-up results of a randomized trial. *Pediatrics, 114,* 1560–1568.

Pianta, R. C., & Castaldi, J. (1989). Stability of internalizing symptoms from kindergarten to first grade and factors related to instability. *Development and Psychopathology, 1,* 305–316.

Pope, A. W. & Bierman, K. L. (1999). Predicting adolescent peer problems and antisocial activities: The relative roles of aggression and dysregulation. *Developmental Psychology, 35,* 335–346.

Qi, C. H., & Kaiser, A. P. (2003). Behavior problems of preschool children from low-income families. *Topics in Early Childhood Special Education, 23,* 188–216.

Rabiner, D., Coie, J., & the Conduct Problems Prevention Research Group. (2000). Early attention problems and children's reading achievement: a longitudinal investigation. *Journal of the American Academy of Child and Adolescent Psychiatry, 39,* 859–867.

Scarr, S., & McCartney, K. (1988). Far from home: An experimental evaluation of the Mother-Child Home Program in Bermuda. *Child Development, 59,* 531–543.

Sweet, M. A., & Appelbaum, M. I. (2004). Is home visiting an effective strategy? A meta-analytic review of home visiting programs for families with young children. *Child Development, 75,* 1435–1456.

Spria, E. G., & Fischel, J. (2005). The impact of preschool inattention, hyperactivity, and impulsivity on social and academic development: A review. *Journal of Child Psychology and Psychiatry, 46,* 755–773.

Thornberry, T. P., Lizotte, A. J., Krohn, M. D., Farnworth, M., & Jang, J. J. (1994). Delinquency of peers, beliefs, and delinquent behavior: A longitudinal test of interactional theory. *Criminology, 32,* 47–83.

Tremblay, R. E., Pagani-Kurtz, L., Masse, L. C., Vitaro, F., & Pihl, R. O. (1995). A bimodal preventive intervention for disruptive kindergarten boys: Its impact through mid-adolescence. *Journal of Consulting and Clinical Psychology, 63,* 560–568.

Vaughn, S., Hogan, S., Lancelotta, G., Shapiro, S., & Walker, J. (1992). Subgroups of children with severe and mild behavior problems: Social competence and reading achievement. *Journal of Child Clinical Psychology, 21,* 98–106.

Wagner, M., & Blackorby, J. (2002). *Disability profiles of elementary and middle school students with disabilities.* Washington, DC: Office of Special Education Programs, U.S. Department of Education.

Wasik, B. A., & Bond, M. A. (2001). Beyond the pages of a book: Interactive book reading and language development in preschool classrooms. *Journal of Educational Psychology, 93,* 243–250.

Webster-Stratton, C. (1998). Preventing conduct problems in Head Start children: Strengthening parenting competencies. *Journal of Consulting and Clinical Psychology, 66,* 715–730.

Webster-Stratton, C., Reid, M. J., & Hammond, M. (2001). Preventing conduct problems, promoting social competence: A parent and teacher training partnership in Head Start. *Journal of Clinical Child Psychology, 30,* 283–302.

Webster-Stratton, C., Reid, M. J., & Hammond, M. (2004). Treating children with early-onset conduct problems: Intervention outcomes for parent, child, and teacher training. *Journal of Clinical Child and Adolescent Psychology, 33,* 105–124.

Whitehurst, G., Arnold, D., Epstein, J., Angell, A., Smith, M., & Fischel, J. (1994). A picture book reading intervention in day care and home for children from low-income families. *Developmental Psychology, 30,* 679–689.

Whitehurst, G. J., Epstein, J. N., Angell, A. L., Payne, A. C., Crone, D. A., & Fischel, J. E. (1994). Outcomes of an emergent literacy intervention in Head Start. *Journal of Educational Psychology, 86,* 542–555.

Whitehurst, G., Falco, F., Lonigan, C., Fischel, J., DeBaryshe, B., Valdez-Menchaca, M., & Caulfield, M. (1988). Accelerating language development through picture book reading. *Developmental Psychology, 24,* 552–559.

Whitehurst, G., Zevenbergen, A., Crone, D., Schultz, M., Velting, O., & Fischel, J. (1999). Outcomes of an emergent literacy intervention from head start through second grade. *Journal of Educational Psychology, 91,* 261–272.

Zevenbergen, A., Whitehurst, G., & Zevenbergen, J. (2003). Effects of a shared reading intervention on the inclusion of evaluative devices in narratives of children from low-income families. *Applied Developmental Psychology, 24,* 1–15.

18
PROCESSES AND FACTORS INFLUENCING FAMILY CONTRIBUTIONS TO SCHOOL READINESS

Rebecca M. Sanford DeRousie
Rachel E. Durham
The Pennsylvania State University

Introduction

In recent years, public policy has become increasingly concerned with educational equality. Past research has emphasized the importance of the transition to formal schooling and the requisite set of skills that accompany this event. While much of the educational literature has explored literacy-related readiness behaviors, psychological and social researchers have also emphasized the importance of socioemotional behaviors as complements to literacy readiness. Indeed, children beginning formal schooling are entering an entirely new realm, one in which they must be attentive for long periods of time, follow instructions, display positive social behaviors (sharing, non-aggressiveness, peer relationship formation, etc.), work independently, and demonstrate self-regulatory skills, in addition to having the necessary cognitive skills fundamental to understanding the material being presented. These skill expectations may stand in stark contrast to either their home experiences or those encountered in the preschool setting.

The concept of school readiness catapulted into the nation's consciousness in fall 1989 when President George Herbert Bush met with the governors of all 50 states to declare the federal commitment to education. This National Education Summit, organized to provide a national framework for education reform and to promote systemic changes needed to ensure equitable educational opportunities and high levels of achievement for all students, introduced the National Educational Goals, a series of eight goals designed to improve learning and teaching in the nation's education system by the year 2000 (NEGP, 1991). First among the goals was the following: "By the year 2000, all children will start school ready to learn." This goal was developed to stimulate a renewed interest in how best to promote school readiness. Now, with the year 2000 come and gone, and the goal of having all children enter school ready to learn not met, school readiness remains a major concern for educators, policy makers, and researchers concerned with child development.

The authors contributing to this volume, while presenting school readiness under various conceptualizations, invoke five questions that warrant further discussion. First, how do we conceptualize "school readiness," and what is the utility of this concept? Second, what can be learned by examining distal and proximal influences? Third, where does culture come into play? Fourth, does the research direct us to certain intervention approaches? Finally, what are the methodological strengths and weaknesses of the current approaches to understanding school readiness? We address each of these questions in turn, and begin by highlighting the divergent approaches to studying school readiness presented in this volume.

Defining School Readiness

What is school readiness? Is it a disposition? Is it a set of achieved behaviors or cognitive abilities? Interestingly, although the chapters in this volume present different ideas of what school readiness entails, this is not necessarily a weakness. In fact, multiple conceptions of school readiness serve to fuel a broader and more complete research agenda within the educational and sociological literature. Further, the different dimensions of school readiness discussed by the authors in this volume, when combined with diverging conceptualizations of readiness, suggest a rich research agenda.

The NEGP defined school readiness as consisting of five domains: *physical well being and motor development*, which includes such elements as health factors and gross and fine motor abilities; *social and emotional development*, with components such as social skills, self confidence, and the ability to establish stable, caring relationships; *approaches toward learning*, which refers to such characteristics as curiosity, independence, cooperativeness and task persistence; *language usage*, which includes the ability to communicate with both peers and adults; and finally, *cognition and general knowledge*, which refers primarily to general information and problem-solving skills (NEGP, 1995).

Although researchers and policy makers alike applaud this comprehensive definition of school readiness for expanding the construct from a narrow, academic skill-centered view to a broader approach focused on the healthy development of the whole child, this holistic approach is difficult to operationalize. Few measures have been developed that fully assess all five domains of readiness described by the NEGP, though there have been some attempts. Peters and Ridgeway (this volume) describe the Early Development Instrument (Janus & Offord, 2000), a measure developed in Canada, with domains similar to those of the NEGP: physical well-being, social competence, emotional maturity, language and cognitive development and communication skills and general knowledge.

Typically, even when data from multiple domains are available, researchers have chosen to limit studies to one or two domains in order to simplify the analyses, with cognitive and behavioral measures most often used. Despite the tendency to limit analyses to one or two domains, the authors in this volume acknowledge the importance of viewing readiness from a holistic perspective. All domains of readiness are intertwined and should not be studied in isolation because, quite frequently, deficits in one domain are associated with deficits in another. Efforts to improve readiness should focus on the whole child rather than on one limited domain.

Landry and Smith (this volume) suggest that school readiness is driven by behavioral regulation and can be encouraged and supported through responsive parenting, which includes contingent responding, affective support, interest scaffolding, and rich language stimulation. Thus, we can infer that the Landry and Smith definition of school readiness is the cognitive and socioemotional end-result of warm, attentive, and purposeful parenting during the early years of life. Campbell and Von Stauffenberg (this volume) also focus on behavioral readiness but use teacher reports of externalizing or attention problems to capture readiness.

Farkas and Hibel (this volume) use cognitive (as measured through reading, math and general knowledge tests) and behavioral outcomes (teacher-rated approaches to learning) assessed at entry to kindergarten, a strategy that implies readiness is a cognitive and behavioral status achieved by the time of entry into kindergarten. Perspectives also support moving definitions of readiness beyond a focus on child characteristics possessed by the child when entering school. Vernon-Feagans, Odom, Pancsofar and Kainz (this volume) suggest understanding readiness as the process through which children learn to navigate the world of formal education. They recommend using growth curve modeling to assess readiness over the course of the kindergarten year rather than using a static measurement upon entrance to school. Their suggestion that readiness should be considered an ongoing, time-sensitive construct is unusual because, by definition, readiness implies a state of preparedness for a given event, rather than a course or path through the event. In support of the idea that readiness is achieved by the time of school entry, Campbell and Stauffenberg's findings (this volume) suggest that a child's self-regulatory skills (i.e., behavioral readiness) are stable by 54 months of age.

Others have suggested that readiness is also the responsibility of the school, with recommendations towards ensuring that the school is "ready" for children of varying skill levels (Pianta & Cox, 1999). Including the community in the definition of readiness along with the child suggests that specific definitions of school readiness may vary depending on the expectations of the local community (Graue, 1993). But regardless of whether readiness is conceptualized as a static or transactional construct, its salience for later performance is indisputable. As the literature accumulates, researchers continue to find that the best predictor of later performance is early performance, in both cognitive ability (Alexander, Entwisle, &

Horsey 1997; Lonigan et al., 2000; Whitehurst & Lonigan, 2001) and behavioral regulation (Bradley et al., 2001;). Given school readiness's strong relation to later educational outcomes, researchers should endeavor to encourage better transitions to formal schooling by determining *what* predicts school readiness.

The Ecology of Child Development

Though trained and versed in different disciplines, many researchers in this volume build upon the ecological framework suggested by Urie Bronfenbrenner (1979) to explain the influence of contexts and processes on children's psychological and social development. Ecological models invoke an image of the child at the center of multiple influences in which micro- and macro-level environments interact to create a unique context for the developing child. Macro-systems are imposed on individuals through more proximal institutional (micro) contexts, such as the family or school. The Social Structure and Personality (SSP) paradigm is similarly concerned with macro structural influences on the individual and how psychological perceptions shape how one interacts with the environment (see McLeod, this volume). Emphasizing the critical need for time-sensitive analyses, Snow (this volume) advocates the Person-Process-Context-Time model, which suggests that in addition to individuals' central place within both social contexts and related processes, they are also situated within time-varying forces that alter development (Williams & Ceci, 1997).

An important facet of the ecological model is consideration of how learning occurs within a social context. The ecological framework places the child at the center of multiple contexts. It conceptualizes the child as being on the receiving end of various influences, processing these influences from his/her own changing perspectives and acting on the environment as well. The ecological perspective of child development could be strengthened by a systemic understanding of processes at different levels of the social environment. Individuals at different locations in the social hierarchy interact among disparate and overlapping spheres, and have differing perceptions of these relationships; further, their perceptions are likely to change with time.

Proximal Processes

The ecological framework suggests that the most important influence on children's development, and thus their early preparation for schooling, is the proximal family and childcare processes that translate background characteristics into dynamic social contexts for learning. The chapters by Landry and Smith (this volume) and Campbell and Von Stauffenberg (this volume) both contain an explicit proposal to examine how interactions between parent and child directly bear on the child's cognitive ability and behavioral dispositions. Similarly, but more implicitly, Farkas and Hibel (this volume) suggest that the quality of parent-child activities influences children's readiness for formal instruction in kindergarten. Finally, Lareau and Weininger (this volume) directly assess children's most proximal environment by conducting observations of children's homes and family activities as well as intensive interviews with family members.

We concur that research should first focus on the proximal processes involved in the development of the skills and behaviors that compose readiness, since the ongoing interactions among the child, caregivers, and the environment act as the "primary mechanisms producing human development" (Bronfenbrenner & Morris, 1998, p. 994). While distal factors are often important correlates of school readiness, it is through proximal processes that child development is impacted daily; thus, it is critical to understand what such processes look like (Snow, this volume). Within the life of a young child, parents typically play the headlining role; this necessitates a focus on parenting practices as the premier example of proximal processes impacting school readiness.

Theoretical Grounding

The theoretical background on the importance of parenting on child outcomes comes from two perspectives—attachment theory and socio-cultural theory—as described by Landry and Smith (this volume). Attachment theory argues that from birth on, through ongoing interactions with the parent, the child develops an understanding of relationships, and this evolving model provides a base from which the child can learn about the world. Sociocultural theory, as put forth by developmental theorists such as Vygotsky and Piaget, argues that it is through interactions with adults that children are able to practice advanced developmental skills that they eventually learn to master. These two perspectives, with their emphasis on the parent-child relationship, provide a theortical basis, along with the ecological model's stress on interactions (Bronfenbrenner &Morris, 1997), for the notion that that it is through proximal processes, especially parent-child interactions, that the early development of a child is shaped.

Parenting as Proximal Processes

To consider parent-child interactions as proximal processes influencing school readiness, we need to understand the important components of parent behavior during these interactions. The literature highlights the following parenting behaviors as influencing early development: sensitivity (e.g., Beckwith, Rozga, & Sigman, 2002; NICHD, 2003), restrictiveness (e.g., Landry, Smith, Swank, & Miller-Loncar, 2000; Linver, Brooks-Gunn, & Kohen, 2002), warmth (e.g., Ispa, Fine et al., 2004) and directiveness (e.g., Marfo, 1990). Campbell and von Stauffenberg, (this volume) focus on specific parent behaviors such as warmth, sensitivity, proactive limit setting, mutuality and affective engagement as keys to stimulating school readiness in children. Others have preferred to focus on the concept of parent responsiveness. Landry and Smith (this volume) argue that responsiveness is composed of four separate parenting behaviors: contingent responding, emotional/ affective support, joint attention and rich language input. Many of these parenting behaviors vary according to the characteristics of the parent, such as socioeconomic status, which may help explain group differences in school readiness described in Farkas and Hibel (this volume).

While the majority of parenting research involves mothers, it is likely that fathers also play a critical role in a child's development (Marsiglio, Amato, Day, & Lamb, 2000; Yoshikawa, this volume). Campbell and von Stauffenberg (this volume) make an important contribution to the literature by including fathers in their analyses. Indeed, they find that the quality of the father-child interactions accounts for significant variation in children's school readiness, over and above maternal sensitivity, providing evidence that fathers make a unique contribution to their children's development.

Parents also play specific roles during their interactions with their children, such as cognitive agent (Landry & Smith, this volume). Through specific behaviors, parents have the capacity to influence their child's cognitive development. Language use is of particular concern in early childhood. Parents who speak often, read to their children, and use a broad range of vocabulary have children with greater language skills when they enter school (Dickinson & Tabors, 2001).

The parent may also indirectly promote positive development through facilitation of experiences outside of the family, whether through the choice of preschool/day care or enrolling their children in other organized, educational activities. Through the interactions experienced in these non-parental activities, and through parent-child discussions about the activities, these organized activities can stimulate development of competence in multiple domains (Laureau & Weininger, this volume; Mahoney & Eccles, this volume). This may vary by social class. Lareau and Weininger for example, note that middle-class parents more frequently take advantage of teachable moments by asking questions about children's activities as compared to lower-class parents.

Authors in this volume also call for mapping the specific aspects of parenting behavior that are related to specific outcomes (Blair, this volume; Snow, this volume). Yoshikawa (this volume) is especially interested in trying to document causal linkages between aspects of parenting behavior as measured at specific timepoints in early childhood and later outcomes. Blair cites examples from non-human animal studies to propose that parenting behavior may affect child outcomes by actually altering the biological substrate underlying child behaviors. Of the four behaviors considered under the comprehensive term of responsiveness, contingent responding and emotional support are commonly linked with social and emotional outcomes, while joint attention and rich stimulation are typically associated with the development of cognitive skills (Landry & Smith, this volume). Changes in the frequency of these behaviors are then related to early child outcomes. However, because readiness is a multi-dimensional construct, it is likely that multiple parenting behaviors must be employed to support school readiness (Snow, this volume).

Moderators of Proximal Processes

Although a wealth of research documents the effect of parenting behavior on child school readiness outcomes (for examples, see Campbell & von Stauffenberg, this volume; Landry &Smith, this volume), additional factors may moderate the associations between parent and child behaviors. Child characteristics, such as genetic makeup, health and physical attributes, temperament, attention, and gender, may influence the effects of parenting behaviors. Guo (this volume) underscores the need to study the genetic determinants of readiness-related behaviors such as reading disability. Snow (this volume) suggests that aspects of a child's temperament, such as uninhibited versus inhibited, may influence the effects of certain parenting behaviors. Kochanska (1997) found that for children who tend to be shy and withdrawn, high levels of parental warmth and gentle discipline are more strongly related to the development of positive social orientations as compared to parenting styles marked by stricter discipline.

Biological risk level of the infant is another child characteristic that may moderate the effect of parenting behaviors. Farkas and Hibel (this volume) includes low birthweight as a potential predictor of cognitive and behavioral readiness, and Landry and Smith (this volume) describe findings in which children with high levels of biological risk incur the worst developmental outcomes when experiencing high levels of parent restrictiveness. Hammond, Landry, Swank and Smith (2000) found that having an infant with high biological risk can stimulate a mother with a family history of hostile parenting practices to break the cycle and behave as a highly responsive and sensitive parent.

Parent characteristics can also influence the proximal processes between parent and child. Single-parent status, education level, employment, and income have all been linked to aspects of readiness as described earlier (see Farkas & Hibel, this volume). These may contribute to proximal processes of readiness (i.e., parenting behavior) by affecting the stress level and the psychological well-being of the parent. Numerous studies have documented the negative effects of maternal depression on parenting practices (Cummings & Davies, 1994; Lovejoy et al., 2000; NICHD ECCRN, 1999) and maternal depression has been linked to various demographic risk factors (NICHD ECCRN, 1999). In addition, adults' views of their own developmental history, as well as their conceptions of their own role in their children's development, are identified as influential factors (Landry & Smith, this volume).

The timing of parental behaviors may also contribute to the effects of proximal processes on school readiness. Snow (this volume), along with others, asks whether there is a critical period during which parent responsiveness is crucial. The attachment literature suggests that interactions during the first year of life set the stage for the quality of the parent-child relationship later. Findings from research on the PALS project (Landry & Smith, this volume) suggest that optimal outcomes are achieved when parents maintain high levels of responsiveness across the whole period of early development (0–5 years) rather than focusing on either infancy/toddlerhood or the preschool period. In addition, research from the early childhood intervention literature suggests that the earlier an intervention starts, and the longer it lasts, the more likely it is to be effective (Gorey, 2001; Ramey & Landesman-Ramey, 1998).

Distal Factors

The chapters in this volume continually distinguish between processes that are "distal" and those that are "proximal." The findings from the Farkas and Hibel study highlight the importance of more distal characteristics in the early years, as well as mediating factors (loosely referred to as "parenting resources"). They test a rather exhaustive list of factors hypothesized to relate to readiness, including parents' education, family income and poverty status, ethnicity, gender, family structure, mother's age at child's birth, number of siblings, census region, home educational resources and activities, preschool program and supplemental program participation (i.e., WIC, TANF, food stamps). As such, the Farkas and Hibel analysis is relatively exploratory. They find that almost all factors generated risk for being unready for schooling, while low parental education (particularly being a high school dropout), and being from a poor family had the strongest associations with cognitive unreadiness. For behavioral unreadiness, low parental education and income, having a computer, higher levels of parental involvement, and the child's participation in sports activities were important. While its comprehensive scope is a strength of their chapter, the reader may be left speculating about *how* these many risk factors result in school unreadiness.

All of the authors in this volume have demonstrated that a number of distal risk factors seem to be consistently related to school unreadiness. Farkas and Hibel demonstrate the salience of low maternal education, ethnicity, single parenthood, and poverty status for cognitive performance in kindergarten, while Landry and Smith and Campbell and Stauffenberg show that these same risk factors are strongly associated with behavioral skills such as self-regulation, attachment, and attention maintenance. We also know that these risk factors are intercorrelated (see Lopez and Barrueco, this volume, for further discussion). Members of ethnic minority groups are more likely to be poor and have lower educational levels, parents with lower educational levels are more likely to be poor, and parents with lower educational levels who are poor are also more likely to be single. Intercorrelations not only complicate social scientists' analyses of the relationship between background characteristics and outcomes, but raise the question of why certain risk factors seem to cluster together.

Researchers continue to struggle with how socioeconomic status affects parenting. A problem in many analyses is the lack of sufficient data to capture specific behaviors or events that directly predict an outcome. Instead, researchers often employ "proxies" for certain behaviors. For example, Farkas and Hibel acknowledge the importance of verbal interaction, but do not have access to the nature and frequency of verbal interactions between parent and child in the Early Childhood Longitudinal Study. Instead, they use mother's education as a proxy for the quality of oral language to which the child is likely exposed. Undoubtedly, mother's education underlies many maternal behaviors related to child development. As such, it can explain much of the variation in school readiness outcomes by capturing the relationship among the distal characteristic, education, and more proximal processes such as the mother's speech with her child. However, the use of this variable does not identify specific behaviors that predict child's verbal ability; we only know that they are related. Further, the use of distal variables cannot capture the beliefs or perceptions that determine their relationship to substantive outcomes.

The Role of Culture

In order to understand how background factors are related to a given outcome, researchers must include a consideration of culture. Cultural orientations may determine actors' understanding about the appropriate use of social or economic resources to achieve an end, such as preparedness for schooling, or even determine parents' beliefs about whether explicit preparation for formal schooling is necessary.

Defining Culture

Pierre Bourdieu, one of the most prolific writers on culture, suggests that culture is a set of long-lasting dispositions embodied in the mind (1973). This means that parents may use the resources they possess in a manner different from that of other parents, due solely to their own beliefs, experiences, habits, and knowledge. Landry and Smith (this volume) demonstrate the importance of maternal responsiveness and sensitivity. However, the question remains: what determines whether a mother will display appropriate responsive and sensitive behaviors, besides distal characteristics such as education or income? We may presume that this is determined by a cultural disposition, or more specifically, her *habitus*, which is defined by Bourdieu (1986) as the unconsciously acquired set of habits and dispositions (also known as cultural capital).

Ann Swidler (1986, p. 273) defined acquired culture as a "tool kit" of habits, skills, and styles from which people construct "strategies of action." This definition aptly relates to a question: why might one parent encourage literate behaviors in their child while another parent might not? One parent may be an avid reader and consequently may anticipate and encourage such behavior in their child. Another parent may have been raised in a household with little reading material and would not consider it, therefore, to be an essential skill that should be encouraged at an early age. Bourdieu also explained that cultural *capital* represents knowledge about how to interact within given fields, like the institution of school. Some parents may actively cultivate relationships with their child's school officials — actions that could lead teachers to anticipate behaviors from the child that they would not from children of parents who do not directly interact with the school.

Culture in Daily Life

The complexities and realities of individuals' daily lives and their own parents' childrearing strategies produce unique viewpoints and beliefs about behaviors that influence how they will ultimately prepare their child for the first day of school. Importantly, Lareau and Weininger (this volume) find more differences between social classes than racial groups. They suggest that the financial and occupational realities of middle-class versus working-class life shape how parents spend time with children, how they prepare them for interactions at school, and how they intervene at their children's school. These realities and daily exigencies subtly characterize everyday life in ways that differentially prepare children for formal schooling, and ultimately translate distal characteristics into proximal processes. For example, because middle-class parents may not have the financial insecurity that lower-class parents experience, they have more expendable income to use for beneficial organized activities.

Many middle-class parents also have more autonomy in the workplace, which allows them to organize their work hours around children's activities. Lower- and working-class parents may not have such freedom; thus, their time use is more constrained. Therefore, the fact that working-class parents do not enroll their children in as many, if any, extracurricular activities may not reflect an underlying lack of appreciation for such activities but rather may point to constraints on financial resources or schedule inflexibility (see Hughes; Mahoney & Eccles, this volume). On the other hand, it may be that some working-class parents eschew over-scheduling of their children's lives. What predicts these differing philosophies?

Research has shown that culture drives beliefs about the appropriateness of certain practices. Shirley Bryce Heath (1983) found differences between the parenting beliefs of middle- and lower-class parents in an ethnographic study of two rural communities. Specifically, she found that middle-class parents engaged their children in more conversations, used activities to prepare children for learning in school, and provided more literacy-related materials at home. In contrast, the working- and lower-class children had not had these experiences, nor had they experienced the settings and expectations that would make school a familiar environment. The parents in Heath's communities naturally structured their children's lives in ways that reflected their own childhood experiences. This tendency echoes Bourdieu's concept of habitus, where behaviors are more often the result of unconscious habits rather than deliberate decisions.

Understanding how parents' cultural dispositions determine beliefs and, further, how cultural orientations are shaped by everyday realities would be an important contribution to research on the relationships among demographic characteristics, parenting practices, and school readiness outcomes (see Hughes, this volume). This would also help to explain why some people engage in behaviors that lead to poor outcomes. For instance, some parents do not necessarily believe their child needs to know the letters of the alphabet before school begins. On the other hand, Farkas and Hibel (this volume) find evidence that some parents delay their sons' entrance to kindergarten for a year to deliberately increase their cognitive maturity. What determines the different beliefs behind these behaviors, and what determines how parents relay their beliefs into practice? Further, how does culture affect perceptions of the larger social structure? The answers to these questions are elusive, especially considering the complex processes that determine how such beliefs are acquired.

Interventions

Given the wealth of information on family contributions to school readiness through broader level factors and specific proximal processes, such knowledge can be applied in the design of interventions that ensure that all children enter school ready to learn. Successful interventions already target the proximal processes of parenting behaviors discussed above. Landry and Smith (this volume) describe the PALS program in which mothers receive in-home coaching on how to increase their responsiveness in order to improve child outcomes. Results show greater gains for children's social and cognitive development when mothers receive PALS as compared to the control families. Bierman, Nix, and Makin-Byrd (this volume) describe several successful family-based interventions, including the Nurse-Family Partnership (Olds, Robinson et al., 2004), HIPPY (Baker, Potrkowski, & Brooks-Gunn, 1998) and Dialogic Reading (Whitehurst et al., 1994). Knowledge from both basic research studies as well as those in the field of prevention science can help us answer the many questions associated with designing an effective family-focused intervention aimed at improving children's school readiness, including whom to target, when to intervene, and what the intervention will include.

Intervention Participants

The question of whom to include in an intervention concerns two components: the ecological level to be targeted and who specifically will receive the program. In regard to the former concern, there are many levels on which to intervene: the child, the parent, or other targets such as daycare. Others might even suggest tackling broader ecological levels such as societal poverty or discrimination (see Hofferth, this volume; Vernon-Feagans et al., this volume). All have been targets in previous prevention efforts, and have experienced varying degrees of success.

In deciding whom to target for optimal school readiness outcomes, it is best to recall Bronfenbrenner's emphasis on proximal processes and the focus on parenting behaviors. The most effective interventions will directly or indirectly affect the quality of parenting, which in turn will influence child outcomes.

Once the ecological-level target has been chosen, the next question is, to whom will the intervention be offered? The field of prevention science continually debates the merits of a universal versus a targeted approach (Institute of Medicine, 1994; Offord, 2000). For interventions targeting school readiness, a universal approach would include all parents of young children, while a targeted approach would mean concentrating on families with one or more known risk factors for low rates of school readiness, such as low-income. Research on risk factors associated with low rates of school readiness (e.g., Farkas and Hibel, this volume) suggests that it would be possible to identify several risk factors and to use the presence of those factors as criteria for selecting a sample of intervention participants. This approach is quite common in early childhood interventions (e.g., Carolina Abecedarian Project: Campbell & Ramey, 1994; Chicago Child-Parent Centers: Conyers et al., 2003; High Scope/Perry Preschool: Weikart & Schweinhart, 1997), with low-income children usually the target. Often, interventions are most effective for the individuals with the highest levels of risk.

It is important to note, however, that targeting a selected at-risk population may not significantly reduce the rates of the problem (i.e., low levels of school readiness). While a high-risk group may be expected to have a greater proportion of individuals who develop the condition of interest, the vast majority of cases will still come from the low-risk group (Offord, 2000). Using the concept of population attributable risk, Peters and Ridgeway (this volume) suggest that even if we were able to eliminate risk factors for poor school readiness (e.g., family dysfunction, poverty, single parenthood), we would only reduce the incidence of unreadiness by less than 20%. This invokes the notion of the moving target (see McLeod, this volume) where the successful elimination of one risk factor for unreadiness would simply mean that another risk factor would emerge as a stronger predictor.

Thus, with Peters and Ridgeway's (this volume) suggestion that even complete elimination of up to five known risk factors will reduce the incidence of school readiness problems by only 20%, a universal approach may actually be most beneficial. Indeed, recent efforts to develop universal state-funded preschool programs reflect such reasoning (Reynolds, Wang, &Walberg, 2003). Inevitably, the answer to the question of who should be offered the intervention may simply come down to the amount of funding available.

Intervention Components

Knowing that we should be using a universal approach to target the parent-child interaction in order to improve school readiness outcomes, the next concern is the components to include in an effective family-based intervention. Home visiting is not only an especially effective way to reach families with young children, but it eliminates the need for the participating families to have transportation, a common obstacle for those living in poverty, especially with young children. Other components may include coaching in responsive parenting techniques, modeling emotion-coaching strategies, instruction in dialogic reading, as well as providing support to increase parent well-being such as basic social support or encouragement and support vis-a-vis educational or employment goals. Components of effective family interventions may vary as a function of community or cultural group. Different groups may not share the same expectations for what constitutes appropriate parent-child interaction, which may make intervention difficult. This should not be overlooked since opinions about effective parent-child interactions, even those based on research, have not always been the same historically (see McLeod, this volume).

Intervention Timing

We can also consider when the intervention should take place based on our earlier consideration of sensitive periods. Previous research suggests that the most effective interventions take place early and often (Gorey, 2001; Ramey & Landesman-Ramey, 1998). Thus, targeting parents of newborns is probably not too early. At the very least, programs targeting school readiness outcomes should consider beginning during infancy, and should continue throughout the early childhood period in order to be most effective. After all, the pattern of proximal processes develops over time and has the most lasting effects on child development. Thus, an extended period of intervention will help facilitate the development of those behaviors that contribute to the assessment of whether a child is "ready" when she or he enters school.

Methodological Issues

The authors in this volume have conducted their research using a variety of methods. Farkas and Hibel (this volume) solely rely on secondary data analysis of a large nationally representative data set, while Landry and Smith and Campbell and Von Stauffenberg use data collected within the context of parenting interventions. Lareau and Weininger use ethnographic techniques with a small sample of families. However, even with the wide scope of data and data collection techniques presented in this volume, the reader may struggle to gain an accurate picture of how all factors relate and how the process of school preparation takes place. Difficulties in the identification of specific processes are sometimes artificially created by social scientists' methods. Secondary data analysis, while useful in the estimation of average relationships between indicators and outcomes, may be less useful when attempting to delve into the texture of a child's life or the quality of interactions or interventions. For this kind of question, more purposeful data collection or ethnographic research becomes necessary. Lareau and Weininger provide detailed data from their observations of children's home lives and daily activities. However, the comprehensive data collected for each child precludes data collection on a large sample. In the future, it would be useful for researchers to use mixed methods, where detailed, nuanced ethnographic data complement findings from larger data sets that can be generalized to the population.

An advantage of using large nationally representative data sets is the potential for identifying processes at multiple levels. Data collection on siblings, neighborhoods, schools, and larger regions presents the opportunity to analyze differences in individuals' beliefs and actions within different contexts. Statistical methods have just become able to exploit this opportunity. One such technique, hierarchical linear modeling (HLM), enables unbiased estimates by accounting for the correlated residuals of subjects clustered at higher levels of aggregation.

In order to understand what factors and processes drive preparation for school, researchers must move towards the use of multi-level data that can relate individuals' experiences to the influences of different environments and contextualized situations. Also, the examination of time-varying processes necessitates the use of time-sensitive data and measures. Campbell and Von Stauffenberg demonstrate the value of over-time measures by showing that parenting behaviors can mediate the relationship between early self-regulatory skills and later school readiness. Similarly, Landry and Smith employ time-varying measures of children's cognitive and social skills and show that early childhood is a particularly sensitive and critical period for development. More refined ecological models, such as those dictated by a person-process-context-time model, will require the collection of data at multiple levels and at multiple time points. Simple cross-sectional analyses capture only associations and cannot provide evidence for causal processes (moreover, causation can only be determined when treatment is randomly assigned). Further, researchers must employ methods that can fully exploit time-varying data. Again, HLM has proved to be a superior technique in growth modeling by enabling the decomposition of variance by parsing it to within-person variance (i.e., repeated measures) and between-person variance.

Recommendations for Future Research

The selection of chapters included in this volume demonstrates the breadth and diversity of approaches to studying issues concerning family contributions to school readiness. Many research studies can be imagined that build upon the ideas encompassed in the previous chapters. We suggest several areas that we feel are particularly important.

One issue regarding school readiness that was not fully discussed within this volume is the interplay of parenting *and* early childhood educational experiences in facilitating the development of school readiness. Within the framework of the ecological model, the family and the non-parental care experiences represent the two main settings for proximal interactions with young children and overlap in their effects on child development. Consideration of the effects of non-parental educational experiences is necessary when children under age 6 spend an average of 30 hours per week in non-parental care (NCES, 2005). While the issues involved in early childhood education (including topics such as availability, quality and accessibility) could fill a volume on their own (see Bowman, Donovan, & Burns, 2001; Cryer & Clifford, 2003; Pianta & Cox, 1999), they are also intricately linked to family. The parent is likely the main facilitator of a child's early education either indirectly by choosing the preschool or daycare setting or directly by accompanying the child on family trips to museums, and libraries, or to art performances. Both Lareau and Weininger (this volume) and Hughes (this volume) discuss how parent beliefs shape the style of interaction with children; these same beliefs may also contribute to the kinds of early education and care experiences parents choose for their children. Thus, it is the totality of both non-parental care and parenting that constitutes important influences on the development of school readiness. Though the relative strength of the contributions of early educational experiences continues to be debated (see Farkas & Hibel, this volume; Mahoney & Eccles, this volume), these experiences should be considered in tandem with family experiences in school readiness research (Lopez & Barrueco, this volume). Thus, future research should strive to better understand how the interaction of the two domains contributes to the development of school readiness.

Research should also try to embrace school readiness as a multi-dimensional construct, rather than limiting analyses to one or two domains. Elementary school teachers have to deal with children as a whole and thus have expectations across domains. Future research should try to incorporate measures that document school readiness levels across domains, whether through a combination of measures targeting different domains or through comprehensive measures such as the Early Development Instrument (Janus & Offord, 2000) mentioned by Peters and Ridgeway (this volume).

A third suggestion for future research is to continue to investigate the optimal method through which to intervene to promote school readiness. The most effective interventions may be those that target multiple levels of a child's environment. Such interventions may target proximal processes (i.e., parenting, as discussed extensively by Landry & Smith, this volume), family activities (see Lareau & Weininger, this volume; Mahoney & Eccles, this volume), childcare experiences (Lopez & Barrueco, this volume; Yoshikawa, this volume), and/or society-level factors such as neighborhood violence or community discrimination (Vernon-Feagans et al., this volume). Previous research on school readiness has certainly emphasized the multiple factors that contribute to whether a child is ready for school; thus, interventions targeting the promotion of school readiness may be most effective when they are able to include components at multiple levels. However, successful examples of such multi-level interventions in the literature are scant. Clearly, then, more research is needed on multi-level interventions for the promotion of school readiness.

Conclusion

We conclude with three main points that we hope will guide future discussions of school readiness. First, the criteria used to determine readiness should be predictive of future school outcomes because this is what we really mean when we use the phrase "ready for school." While this is implicitly understood by most individuals interested in school readiness, it is important to document how exactly the skills and characteristics measured at the entrance to kindergarten are related to future school performance.

Second, school readiness is a multi-dimensional construct that includes aspects of development from multiple domains. Research or policy initiatives that utilize a definition of school readiness consisting of only one or two dimensions (such as only knowing ABCs) fail to capture the complexity of skills that a child draws on in order to be successful in school.

Third, because school readiness is built through the experiences of a child prior to entry into kindergarten, the family is of utmost importance in shaping those experiences. This volume's focus on the effects of family processes on school readiness speaks to the importance of the family in understanding how children become ready for school.

Although not all parents are sufficiently able to prepare their children for school, whether through parenting practices, lack of education or limited social and economic resources, all parents do have the capacity to provide for their children the experiences needed to get them ready for school. Through culturally sensitive, evidence-based, multi-level interventions, we have the means for closing the gap between "ready" and "unready" children. Knowing the negative outcomes that can accrue as a result of school failure, it is our responsibility as researchers concerned with child well-being to further our understanding of the factors that contribute to school readiness so that we can finally realize the first National Education Goal of having all children enter school "ready to learn."

References

Alexander, K., Entwisle, D., & Horsey, C. (1997). From first grade forward: Early foundations of high school dropout. *Sociology of Education, 70*, 87–107.

Baker, A. J. L., Piotrkowski, C. S., & Brooks-Gunn, J. (1998). The effects of the Home Instruction Program for Preschool Youngsters (HIPPY) on children's school performance at the end of the program and one year later. *Early Childhood Research Quarterly, 13*, 571–588.

Beckwith, L., Rozga, A., & Sigman, M. (2002). Maternal sensitivity and attachment in atypical groups. In R. V. Kail (Ed.) (2002), *Advances in child development and behavior, Vol. 30*. (pp. 231–274). San Diego, CA: Academic Press.

Bourdieu, P. (1973). Cultural reproduction and social reproduction. In first initial Brown (Ed.), *Knowledge, education, and cultural change* (pp. 71–112). London: Tavistock.

Bourdieu, P. (1986). Forms of capital. In J. G. Richardson (Ed.), *Handbook of theory and research for the sociology of education* (pp. 241–258). New York: Greenwood Press.

Bowman, B. T., Donovan, M. S., & Burns, M. S. (Eds). (2001). *Eager to learn: Educating our preschoolers*. Washington, DC: National Academy Press.

Bradley, R. H., Corwyn, R. F., Burchinal, M., McAdoo, H. P., & Garcia Coll, C. (2001). The home environments of children in the United States part II: Relations with behavioral development through age thirteen. *Child Development, 72*, 1868–1886.

Bronfenbrenner, U. (1979). *The ecology of human development*. Cambridge, MA: Harvard University Press.

Bronfenbrenner, U., & Morris, P.A. (1998). The ecology of developmental processes. In W. Damon (Ed.), *Handbook of child psychology* (5th ed., pp. 993–1028). New York: Wiley.

Campbell, F. A., & Ramey, C. T. (1994). Effects of early intervention on intellectual and academic achievement: A follow-up study of children from low-income families. *Child Development, 65*, 684–698.

Conyers, L. M., Reynolds, A. J., & Ou, S. (2003). The effect of early childhood intervention on subsequent special education services: Findings from the Chicago Child-Parent Centers. *Educational Evaluation and Policy Analysis, 25*, 75–95.

Cryer, D., & Clifford, R. (2003). *Early childhood education and care in the USA*. Baltimore, MD: Brookes.

Cummings, E. M., & Davies, P. T. (1994). Maternal depression and child development. *Journal of Child Psychology and Psychiatry, 35*, 73–112.

Dickinson, D. K., & Tabors, P. O. (2001). *Beginning literacy with language: Young children learning at home and school*. Baltimore, MD: Brookes.

Gorey, K. M. (2001). Early childhood education: A meta-analytic affirmation of the short-and long term benefits of educational opportunity. *School Psychology Quarterly, 16*, 9–30.

Graue, M. E. (1993). *Ready for what?: Constructing meanings of readiness for kindergarten*. Albany, NY: State University of New York Press.

Hammond, M. V., Landry, S. H., Swank, P. R., & Smith, K. E. (2000). Relation of mothers' affective developmental history and parenting behavior: Effects on infant medical risk. *American Journal of Orthopsychiatry, 70*, 95–103.

Heath, S. B. (1983). *Ways with words: Language, life, and work in communities and classrooms.* New York: Cambridge University Press.

Institute of Medicine. (1994). *Reducing risks for mental disorders: Frontiers for preventive intervention research.* Washington, DC: National Academy Press.

Ispa, J. M., Fine, M. A., Halgunseth, L. C., Harper, S., Robinson, J., Boyce, L., Brooks-Gunn, J., & Brady-Smith, C. (2004). Maternal intrusiveness, maternal warmth, and mother-toddler relationship outcomes: Variations across low-income ethnic and acculturation groups. *Child Development, 75,* 1613–1631.

Janus, M., & Offord, D. R. (2000). Reporting on readiness to learn at school in Canada. *ISUMA: Canadian Journal of Policy Research, 1,* 71–75.

Kochanska, G. (1997). Multiple pathways to conscience for children with different temperaments: From toddlerhood to age 5. *Developmental Psychology, 33,* 228–240.

Landry, S. H., Smith, K. E., Swank, P. R., & Miller-Loncar, C. (2000). Early maternal and child influences on children's later independent cognitive and social functioning. *Child Development, 71,* 358–375.

Linver, M. R., Brooks-Gunn, J., & Kohen, D. E. (2002). Family processes as pathways from income to young children's development. *Developmental Psychology, 38,* 719–734.

Lonigan, C., Burgess, S. R., & Anthony, J. L. 2000. Development of emergent literacy and early reading skills in preschool children: Evidence from a latent-variable longitudinal study. *Developmental Psychology, 36,* 596–613.

Lovejoy, M. C., Graczyk, P. A., O'Hare, E., & Neuman, G. (2000). Maternal depression and parenting behavior: A meta-analytic review. *Clinical Psychology Review, 20,* 561–592.

Marfo, K. (1990). Maternal directiveness in interactions with mentally handicapped children: An analytical commentary. *Journal of Child Psychology and Psychiatry, 4,* 531–549.

Marsiglio, W., Amato, P., Day, R., & Lamb, M. E. (2000). Scholarship on fatherhood in the 1990s and beyond: Past impressions, future prospects. *Journal of Marriage and the Family, 62,* 1173–1191.

National Center for Educational Statistics (NCES). (2005). *Child care and early education arrangements of infants, toddlers, and preschoolers: 2001 statistical analysis report.* Washington, DC: U.S. Department of Education, Institute of Education Sciences, #2006-039. Available online at http://nces.ed.gov/pubsearch/pubsinfo.asp?pubid=2006039

National Education Goals Panel (NEGP). (1991). *The national education goals report.* Washington, DC: Author.

National Education Goals Panel (NEGP). (1995). *Reconsidering children's early development and learning: toward common views and vocabulary.* Goal 1 Technical Planning Group. Washington, DC: Author.

NICHD Early Child Care Research Network. (1999). Chronicity of maternal depressive symptoms, maternal sensitivity, and child functioning at 36 months. *Developmental Psychology, 35,* 1297–1310.

NICHD Early Child Care Research Network. (2003). Social functioning in first grade: Associations with earlier home and child care predictors and with current classroom experiences. *Child Development, 74,* 1639–1662.

Offord, D. R. (2000). Selection of levels of prevention. *Addictive Behaviors, 25,* 833–842.

Olds, D. L., Robinson, J., Pettitt, L., Luckey, D. W., Holmberg, J., Ng, R. K., Isacks, K.,Sheff, K., & Henderson, C. R. (2004). Effects of home visits by paraprofessionals and by nurses: Age 4 follow-up results of a randomized trial. *Pediatrics, 114*, 1560–1568.

Pianta, R.C., & Cox, M. J. (Eds.). (1999). *The transition to kindergarten.* Baltimore, MD: Brookes.

Ramey, C. T., & Landesman-Ramey, S. (1998). Early intervention and early experience. *American Psychologist, 53*, 109–120.

Reynolds, A. J., Wang, M. C., & Walberg, H. J. (Eds.). (2003). *Early childhood programs for a new century* [University of Illinois at Chicago series on children and youth—Issues in children's and families' lives]. Washington, DC: Child Welfare League of America, Inc.

Schweinhart, L. J., & Weikart, D. P. (1997). Lasting differences: The high/scope preschool curriculum comparison study through age 23. *High/Scope Educational Research Foundation, Monograph 12.* Ypsilanti. MI.

Swidler, A. (1986). Culture in action: Symbols and strategies. *American Sociological Review, 51*, 273–286.

Whitehurst, G., Arnold, D., Epstein, J., Angell, A., Smith, M., & Fischel, J. (1994). A picture book reading intervention in day care and home for children from low-income families. *Developmental Psychology, 30*, 679–689.

Williams, W. M., & Ceci, S. J. (1997). A person-process-context-time approach to understanding intellectual development. *Review of General Psychology, 1*, 288–310.

Subject Index

Author Index

National Education Goals Panel, 299, 300
NICHD Early Child Care Research Network, 7, 21, 42, 201, 226, 229, 230, 231, 247, 248, 250, 285, 303, 305
NICHD Early Child Care Research Network & G. J. Duncan, 259
National Research Council, 201
National Research Council and Institute of Medicine, 207, 208, 209
Nelson, K. E., J. Welsh, S. Camarata, S. Heimann, & T. Tjus, 286
Neuman, S. B., 88, 97
Neuman, S. B., & D. Celano, 70
Noonan, D., 208
Nopola-Hemmi, J., M. Taipale, et al., 125, 127
Nordin, J., S. Rolnick, et al., 72
Norton, D. G., 97
Nothen, M. M., G. Schulte-Korne, et al., 125

O

O'Connor, T. G., M. Rutter, et al., 111
Offord, D. R., 273, 310
Offord, D. R., M. H. Boyle, et al., 42
Offord, D. R., M. H. Boyle, & Y. Racine, 272
Offord, D. R., H. C. Kramer, A. E. Kazdin, P. S. Jensen, & R. Harrington, 273
Ogbu, J., 62
Olds, D. L., J. Kitzman, et al., 292
Olds, D. L., J. Robinson, et al., 288, 309
Oliver, T., & M. Sharpiro, 174
Olson, R., B. Wise, F. Conners, J. Rack, & D. Fulker, 123
Opie, I., & P. Opie, 162
Osgood, D. W., J. K. Wilson, P. M. O'Malley, J. G. Bachman, & L. D. Johnston, 216

P

Pampel, F. C., 57
Pan, B. A., M. L. Rowe, J. D. Singer, & C. E. Snow, 247
Parke, R. D., & R. Buriel, 248
Parpal, M., & E. E. Maccoby, 88
Patterson, G. R., D. DeGarmo, & M. S. Forgatch, 232, 250
Patterson, G. R., J. B. Reid, & T. J. Dishion, 232, 250
Paulesu, E., J. F. Demonet, et al., 121
Payne, A. C., G. J. Whitehurst, & A. L. Angell, 88
Pennington, B. F., 123
Pennington, B. F., J. W. Gilger, et al., 123
Pennington, B. F., & D. L. Lefly, 123
Peters, R. DeV, 275, 276
Peters, R. DeV, K. Petrunka, & R. Arnold, 273
Petit, G. S., J. F. Bates, K. A. Dodge, & D. W. Meece, 191, 216
Phillips, M., J. Brooks-Gunn, et al., 6, 34
Pianta, R. C., 144, 226
Pianta, R. C., & J. Castaldi, 284
Pianta, R. C., & M. J. Cox, 63
Pianta, R. C., & K. L. Harbers, 144, 146
Pianta, R. C., & M. J. Cox, 301, 313
Pianta, R. C., & S. McCoy, 227
Pianta, R. C., S. Nimetz, & L. Bennett, 144
Pianta, R. C., S. Rimm-Kaufman, & M. Cox, 140
Pianta, R. C., M. Steinberg, & K. Rollins, 39, 226
Pierce, E. W., L. J. Ewing, & S. B. Campbell, 249
Pierce, K. M., J. V. Hamm, & D. L. Vandell, 218
Pope, A. W., & K. L. Bierman, 285
Powell, B., R. Weum, & L. Steelman, 56